SCHOOLS
ACROSS FRONTIERS

Schools Across Frontiers

The Story of the International
Baccalaureate and the United
World Colleges

Second Edition

A.D.C. Peterson

Foreword by His Royal Highness
the Prince of Wales

Open Court
Chicago and La Salle, Illinois

FOREWORD

The absorbing story told so admirably by Alec Peterson in this book, starts with a man who believed deeply in international education, Kurt Hahn: but Kurt Hahn had one other strong educational conviction which he used to describe by quoting a doctrine of Plato's that "He who wishes to serve his country must have not only the power to think, but the will to act."

The two educational projects so faithfully described here are closely linked and have similar origins in individual action. The author himself played a crucial pioneering role in each. The founding of Atlantic College, the first of the chain of United World Colleges, in 1962 was due to the action, under Hahn's inspiration, of a group of individuals, mainly from industry and the Services with a sprinkling of educators and politicians, based in Britain. The establishment of the International Baccalaureate Office in 1967 was due to the action of a group of teachers based in Geneva. In neither case was the initiative taken by governments or existing international organizations such as Unesco.

The challenge to which these two groups responded was the interdependence of human kind, North and South, Rich and Poor, Industrialised and Rural, in the aftermath of the Second World War. To the United World College group it called for the establishment of a new kind of school where young people of all nations and backgrounds could live and learn together at the most formative period of their adolescence and so form those ties of friendship and understanding that would last them through their lives.

For the Geneva group the schools already existed through the rapid expansion of international schools serving the new internationally mobile population. The challenge was to provide for students in these schools a common, internationally oriented course of study that would enable them to live and learn together, rather than in national groups. It was no empty symbol when last year, the Italian Minister of Public Instruction presented the ten thousandth International Baccalaureate Diploma to the son of a Finnish forestry expert who had been to school in Malaysia, Thailand, Finland, and Mozambique and completed his International Baccalaureate at Moshi in Tanzania.

No one understood better the value and the interdependence of the two projects than Lord Mountbatten. He it was who developed from the original model of Atlantic College in South Wales the still growing chain of six United World Colleges in four of the five continents; and it was he who in 1971 presented the first International Baccalaureate Diplomas in Geneva. In succeeding him as the second President of the United World Colleges, I have tried to build on his work and perhaps to relate the Colleges more directly to some of the common problems of our shrinking world.

How far can private initiatives of this limited kind affect education as a whole? I suppose it is a question of a slowly spreading 'climate'. One of Kurt Hahn's great insights was that the "will to act" needed education as much as the "power to think" and that this was best developed through shared, skilled, challenging, sometimes even dangerous, service to others in need. The IB includes a requirement for such social service in its diploma course and it is clear that in many parts of the world this sort of activity has been increasingly recognised as an essential part of the education of the adolescent. Not all of it, perhaps, has been as skilled as Hahn would have wished, but the impetus has been there. How great a part these two projects have played in the spread of that climate is not for me to judge.

Governments, as I have said, played little or no part in the launching of the two projects, but their contribution to future development has steadily grown and in Canada and Italy has meant massive support for their own United World Colleges. The story of the early days deserved to be told before the memories faded and Alec Peterson, the first Director-General of the International Baccalaureate Office and the second Chairman of the International Board of Directors of the United World Colleges, is surely uniquely qualified to tell it.

PREFACE TO THE SECOND EDITION

This book is an account of two international institutions that are changing the shape of education in many countries of the world: the United World Colleges and the International Baccalaureate Organization. The United World Colleges (UWC) are a chain of ten schools where young people, selected for scholarships by some 120 selection committees across the world, live, learn and undertake community service together while studying the International Baccalaureate (IB) Diploma Program (the College in Venezuela is an exception—the students are post-secondary and are trained in agricultural management techniques). The IB program is a two-year curriculum that prepares students for an entrance examination and diploma giving access to higher education; it can currently be taken in 110 countries and is recognized by colleges and other higher education institutions across the globe.

Many schools in places like the United States, where there is now intense concern about weak national educational performance, have adopted the IB Diploma Program or one of its offshoots— the Middle Years Program (MYP) and the Primary Years Program (PYP)—in order to improve the quality of education and to provide an international perspective. More than 1,300 schools in the US and around the world now offer these programs, with splendid results in academic performance. The programs have been more recently welcomed in countries such as China, Russia, and other parts of Central and Eastern Europe, where acceptance prior to the political changes at the end of the 1980s was more difficult.

The late Alec Peterson's engagingly personal account of the origins of the International Baccalaureate and the United World Colleges continues to be in demand. Since both institutions have seen important changes following the release of the first edition of this book in 1987 and the death of Alec Peterson the following year, Open Court decided that a new, expanded edition would be warranted, bringing the story right up to date.

The four new chapters highlight the main developments of the United World Colleges and the International Baccalaureate Organization since 1987. Like the rest of the book, these new more years mistakes were made. The men and women who made them were those same friends and myself. Yet the story must be told truthfully. I hope those to whom I dedicate this book in gratitude will forgive me if I do not gloss over our failings.

The breakthrough in the history of the IB, when it ceased to be a pipe-dream at the International School of Geneva and began to become a reality, came with a grant of $75,000 from the Twentieth Century Fund in 1965. The Fund commissioned Martin Mayer, whose book *The Schools* had caused quite a sensation in America, to produce a report (published by the Foundation under the title *Diploma* in 1968) on the feasibility of establishing a common curriculum and examination for international schools, which would be acceptable for entry to universities world-wide. *Diploma* still provides the only objective, though sometimes very critical, description of the early days of the IB. In the course of a rapid tour Martin visited the three leading schools concerned and consulted with the founder headmaster of Atlantic College, Desmond Hoare, the principal of UNIS (United Nations International School, New York), Desmond Cole, and the English headmaster of Ecolint (Geneva International School), Desmond Cole-Baker. When we first met in Geneva, Martin's opening words were: "How the hell did you get involved in this business if your name isn't Desmond?" So let me begin on a very personal note by answering his question.

ACKNOWLEDGEMENTS

It would be impossible to mention everyone who has contributed to building up this story over the years, but I would like to record my particular thanks to those who have so generously helped me with the compilation of this record of it:

Robert Blackburn, Ruth Bonner, John Goodban, Derek Goulden, Gilbert Nicol, Gérard Renaud, Roz Sievers, and Peter Stoyle in the IBO offices; Sir Ian Gourlay, Lord Hankey, Jack Matthews, Ted Lockwood, David Sutcliffe, and Michael Schweitzer in the United World Colleges; Blouke Carus, Harlan Hanson, and Seymour Eskow in the USA; Kay Pennock and Ken Rotenberg in Canada; Madame Roubinet and Madame Bardinet in Paris; Erik Mortensen for help with the bibliography; the teachers and administrators in the 13 schools described in the text; and Doris Crane and Odette Horrocks who typed from a sometimes scarcely legible manuscript.

GLOSSARY

ABITUR. In Germany, a nationally-recognized examination used to control entry to universities.

A-LEVEL. In the UK, Advanced Level of the GCE. A qualification for entry to university. Usually taken two or three years after Ordinary Level (O-level).

BACCALAURÉAT. In France, a national examination, controlling entry to universities.

BACCALAUREATE. In the European sense, a high school diploma controlling the transition from school to university by means of an examination.

CASS. Creative Aesthetic or Social Service activities, a mandatory component of the International Baccalaureate curriculum.

CEIC. Centre for the Study of Education in an International Context. Established at the University of Bath in 1992, this centre offers post-graduate courses and degrees in international education on a world-wide scale.

CLASSES TERMINALES. In French-speaking countries, similar to the British sixth form.

EC. See EEC.

ECIS. European Council of International Schools, established in 1965 with headquarters in the UK. The majority of its member schools across the world offer an IB program. It provides a number of services to international schools, such as school accreditation, teacher recruitment, head searches, annual conferences for teachers and administrators, fellowships in international education, and specialist publications.

ECOLINT. École Internationale de Genève, the International School of Geneva.

EEC. European Economic Community, or European Community, or Common Market. An association of nations, signatories of the Treaty of Rome. Each member nation is bound to follow certain commercial, legal, and regulatory requirements.

EUROPEAN BACCALAUREATE. The special baccalaureate administered by the EC for the use of European Community Schools.

EUROPEAN COMMUNITY SCHOOLS. Schools established and administered by the EC.

1
THE FOUNDING
OF ATLANTIC COLLEGE

In 1954, I returned from Malaya, where I had been summoned from my normal job, as headmaster of a Shropshire grammar school, to direct the Information Services under General Templer in "winning the hearts and minds of the people". One experience in Malaya had affected my ideas about education. Most of my job—much more than 'Fighting communism'—had consisted in trying to develop commitment to the idea of a single, unified Malayan nation in three culturally very separate communities: Chinese, Indian, and Malay. My only directly educational responsibility was the establishment, in an abandoned palace belonging to the Sultan of Negri Sembilan, of a training school for field officers who ran mobile film units for the rural communities. Going down to attend a passing out or graduation ceremony, I found that the students had written up slogans in Chinese, Malay, and Tamil over the gates. They were not, I hoped, mutually conflicting, but being unable to read any of the three scripts I asked a student what they meant. "We have written", he said, "each in our own language 'All Men are Brothers'."

At my new school, Dover College, influenced no doubt partly by the need to give the school some special character which would distinguish it from competitors, but mainly by the conviction that it was time education began to break down the barriers of national prejudice and prepare young people for life in an interdependent world, I started, in a very small way, an 'international sixth form'. In 1957 this led to my being invited to a conference on international education at Bruges, organized by NATO. At this conference I met, for the first time, Kurt Hahn. Hahn, a German of Jewish origin who subsequently became a naturalised Englishman, was one of the most remarkable educators of his time. He had worked for a negotiated peace towards the end of the First World War.

The school at Salem, of which he became headmaster in 1920, brought together children of former enemies, German and British, and when, in 1932, Hitler showed his true colours, Hahn took the courageous step of writing to all former pupils telling them that "if they were members of the SA or the SS they must break with Hitler or break with Salem".[1] It led to his arrest, and only the intervention of Ramsay Macdonald, the British Prime Minister, got him out into exile in Britain.

In Britain Hahn founded, or was instrumental in founding, Gordonstoun School, at which Prince Charles, now Prince of Wales and President of the United World Colleges, was educated; The Outward Bound movement, which has spread to many other countries; the Duke of Edinburgh's Award; and finally, the United World Colleges.

All of these were attempts to actualise the profound educational convictions which governed his life. In themselves they exemplify one of the profoundest of all these convictions—that if you believe in something, you must not just think or talk or write, but must act. All education that Hahn cared for was aimed at changing young people's attitudes in such a way as to lead them to change their actions. The attitudes he wanted to change were: national and racial prejudices and the causes of war; something which he used to call 'spectatoritis', the preference for watching other people do things rather than doing them oneself; and what he often described as the 'declines' which were affecting youth as a result of the exhausted, disenchanted, and increasingly cynical culture of post-war Europe and America: the decline in physical fitness, in enterprise, in memory and imagination, in skill and care, in self-discipline, and in compassion. Long before most educators, Hahn was shocked by the catchwords '*Ohne mich*' and 'I couldn't care less'. He would, I believe, be shocked today to find 'caring' transformed into a politician's catchword and 'compassion' into a cliché. As educational remedies for these attitudes, he saw the common involvement of young people of different nations and cultures in active, skillful, challenging (even physically dangerous) service to others, particularly the saving of life: in academic studies that taxed the memory and imagination; in teamwork which involved both exercising and accepting leadership; and in the pursuit by each individual of his 'grand passion'—whether that was playing the cello, building boats, entomology, or Renaissance architecture. It was the vision of an idealist and of a teacher, but Hahn was both a Platonist and a realist, a teacher who had a genius for translating his visions, and inspiring others to translate his visions, into action. In a later chapter I hope to show how much of Hahn's vision is embodied in that most prosaic of frameworks, syllabuses and examinations—in this case the syllabuses and examinations for the International Baccalaureate.

There seems little doubt that the stimulus which made Hahn seek to embody his vision in an international school was his friendship with the first commandant of the NATO Staff College, Air Marshal Sir Lawrance Darvall. He was deeply impressed by the way in which Darvall had succeeded in welding together former enemies—Germans, French, Americans, and British—in a college devoted to tackling common problems. Darvall was equally enthusiastic for Hahn's idea of replicating this experience in an international school or college.

It may seem strange that a movement which seeks to transcend all political and racial boundaries, which has over the years spent a lot of its limited time and money on trying to attract and finance students from the socialist bloc of Eastern Europe to mix with their peers in the West, should have been conceived in the womb of NATO. We tend nowadays to forget how desperately concerned internationally-minded people in the forties and early fifties were with the prevention of a fourth Franco-German war. Russia and 'the West' might have drifted far from the days of the alliance against Hitler, but it was hoped that this was temporary: in historical terms the enemies who needed first to be reconciled seemed close at hand within Western Europe. Moreover Hahn urged constantly that NATO should take the lead in restoring a civilised and humane code of the Laws of War, notably by renouncing the first use of nuclear weapons.[2]

Hahn had influential friends in England, and in the late fifties he and Darvall began to gather around them a group of people, drawn from industry, banking, politics, and education, who were determined to translate Hahn's vision into reality. This promotion committee, whose members were mainly British,[3] had close contacts in Germany and Scandinavia, and through Darvall, with the other countries of the Western alliance. It had three tasks: to find a site, to find the money to buy the site and develop it as a college, and to find a principal. It is typical, I think, of the way in which the UWC movement has worked that we tackled the last task first.

There is nothing more important in launching a new college

than the man or woman who is to be the first principal. It is not merely that the founding years of the new institution are crucial to its success: the quality of the person selected can be of the greatest importance in the choice of the site and in creating the confidence on which the raising of the necessary funds depends. It may be significant that the same pattern of choosing the principal first was subsequently followed in the founding of the Lester B. Pearson United World College of the Pacific on Vancouver Island and the Armand Hammer United World College of the American West in New Mexico.

The invitation made in 1958 to Rear-Admiral Desmond Hoare to join the group as 'founder headmaster', was a bold stroke. Many people might have said, and no doubt some did, that an Admiral, who had never been headmaster of a school or college, was a strange choice. Moreover, in the public eye, which was not, fortunately, much concerned at that time with the college, it may have reinforced the image of a college associated with NATO. But Desmond Hoare was no ordinary Admiral. His work in the navy (he was an Engineer Admiral) had involved him in training apprentices and his voluntary work had been with boys' clubs. Possibly as a result, he had a remarkable judgement about people and a remarkable capacity to relate to and understand individual students. A number of Hahn's principles were close to his heart: the importance to adolescents of shared commitment to a common task, the importance of serious training in the skills needed to carry out that task effectively, the importance of commitment to the service of those in need, and the importance of mutual understanding between young people from different cultures. Moreover, he had additional qualities which endeared him to his staff, to the first group of multinational students who came to the College, and to potential responders to the appeal for funds: a sense of humour, a burning commitment to the project, a readiness to listen to experts, and an engineer's sense of the practical.

Having found a headmaster, we began to look for a site and plan a college. An underlying assumption of the whole project was that the close ties of friendship which young people develop in their school and college days often last right through life. The role of the 'college room-mate', the *normalien*, or *enarch* who can pick up the telephone and *tutoyer* other *normaliens* throughout the French government service, or of the 'old boy net' in England has been well established. A new generation of such school friends, linked across national frontiers might, in their maturity, make some small contribution to better understanding and the prevention of war between nations. Of course we hoped that the college would act as a pilot project, influencing education in all countries, but the first thing was to get one college started. Who should go to it? Where should it be? How should it be financed? If the students were to become 'multipliers' in the sense indicated above—people who in their middle years might be expected to have influence in their own countries—they should clearly be drawn from those destined for higher education. This indicated the last two years of secondary education, an age range approximately between sixteen and nineteen. It is interesting that Hegel, when he was director of a gymnasium in Nuremberg, identified this as the best age for youths to meet with a culture other than their own, the age at which they are sufficiently rooted in their own culture not to risk becoming disoriented, and sufficiently open to learn quickly from the new experience. We sought not to produce a generation of rootless 'world citizens' but one of Americans, English, French, Germans, Mexicans, Russians, and others, who understood each other better, sought to co-operate with each other, and had friends across frontiers.

Wrongly, as it turned out, the College was conceived and started life as a single-sex boys' college. The decision to include girls was not taken until 1970, but is best treated here in relation to the founding of the college. From 1967 onwards a few 'day girls' were admitted, living in teachers' houses. Co-education was vehemently urged by Desmond Hoare and by his wife Naomi. The great majority of the teaching staff supported this as a result of the first five years of experience, but it was opposed, even to the point of resignation, by some members of the governing body. There were some governors, I think, who were affected by nostalgia for their own schoolboy experience and some who did not recognise the already changing position of women in society, but the main hesitation was concerned with the relationships likely to develop between boys and girls coming from very different cultural traditions. Would not a South American boy 'misread the signals' coming from a Scandinavian girl? I think the objectors underestimated the capacity of the young for reading each other's signals and establishing that understanding across cultures which is one of the objectives of the college. Part of the initiation week, when students, coming now from as many as 50 different nations arrive at the college, is a week's fairly tough camping in the Welsh mountains. Climbing a mountain path, an Arab boy once turned to the girl behind him and said:

"Will you carry my pack, please?"

"What?"

"In my country women always carry burdens for the men."

"Well you're in bloody Wales now and you can carry your own."

No one would now contemplate for a moment going back to a single-sex college. The funding of the first girls' bedrooms was due to a gift from an American, Sonny Maresi, the greatest individual benefactor of the college.

The acquisition of a site was also due to an individual benefactor, the Frenchman Antonin Besse, a member of the original promotion group, and still a member of the international boards of UWC and IB. Kurt Hahn believed, with a Wordsworthian conviction, in the importance of natural beauty for the kind of soul-building that he was seeking. If the graduates of the college were to be affected throughout life by the memory of their schooldays, these must be days passed in a physically and spiritually healthy environment, if possible with the addition of historical associations. This led initially to consideration of a castle on the Scottish sea coast, but that seemed too remote. Tony Besse's donation made possible the purchase of St Donat's Castle, on the coast of Wales, some 14 miles west of Cardiff and within easy reach of Heathrow Airport. St Donat's seemed ideal for the purpose. The castle and the terraced gardens running down to the sea are of outstanding natural beauty. Built in the fourteenth century, it had been bought by William Randolph Hearst, who had added to it other medieval buildings, re-erected stone by stone, from other parts of Britain. The story goes that when he brought Marion Davies there, the weather was bad and she was kept awake by the fog-horns of the passing ships. "Randolph," she is supposed to have said, "I can't stand this place. Build me a castle in California, where the sun shines." Whether the story is true or not, Hearst certainly transferred his interest from St Donat's to his other castle at San Simeon.

When I first went to see it in 1961 it had been empty for some time, but there were still some of Hearst's elaborate bathrooms in evidence, which I hated to see destroyed, while the additional buildings he had purchased provided a school hall and refectory. Above all, the large swimming pool was ideal for training in life-saving and the sea beyond the cliffs was, as Desmond Hoare never tired of pointing out, the Atlantic Ocean and not the Bristol Channel. It is a rough coast and the sea and cliff rescue services, which he introduced from the very start of the college, had been credited by 1981 with the saving of some 190 lives.[4] On this first occasion I took my three small children and I can still remember them playing under Hearst's billiard table and talking of the three grown-ups who had come down to see the castle: the Admiral, the General (General Hare, the first secretary of the promotion committee), and the 'Air Marvel'.

Desmond needed an experienced schoolmaster as his second-in-command and we were lucky to find Robert Blackburn, a historian, then teaching at Merchant Taylors School, an enthusiast for the kind of education we were planning. I had already met him during discussions about broadening the curriculum of English upper secondary education. But of that more hereafter. Today he is Deputy Director-General of the International Baccalaureate Office. Meanwhile the fact that we had got a headmaster and deputy headmaster who could work out between them the kind of education through which Hahn's vision might be implemented, and that we had an exciting site on which to provide that education, produced a dramatic change in the prospects for fund-raising. This was needed to equip the college, to finance scholarships for those whose parents could not afford to pay the fees that this kind of education inevitably cost, and to cover the operating deficit until the college built up its numbers. Fund-raising is never easy, but the 1960s were a relatively good time in which to seek funds for idealistic and international projects. Capital donations came mainly from British industry, particularly the steel companies in Wales, followed by some of the big foundations, above all the Dulverton Trust and the Bernard Sunley Foundation which has just given a further half million for new dormitories. The only governments contributing were the British and Federal German. The college had been named Atlantic College, which reflected Desmond Hoare's belief in the sea as an educator, partly because of the residual NATO connection, partly because the first intake of students came from countries bordering on the Atlantic, and partly because it was believed that the name would attract financial support from the USA. Apart from the generosity of Mr Maresi noted above, and a grant from the Ford Foundation, this hope proved illusory. Enough capital donations did come in, however, to enable the college to open in

1962 with an initial intake of 56 boys. They came mainly from Britain, Scandinavia, and the Federal Republic of Germany, with a sprinkling of other Europeans and North Americans. With such small numbers and the commitment to a scholarship policy sufficiently generous to ensure that no deserving candidate was turned away because his family could not afford the fees, the college was a long way from breaking even and often came near to foundering. I can remember one governors' meeting at which we were told that the only way to pay the teaching staff their next month's salary would be for the individual governors to make interest-free loans to the college. This precarious financial situation was not brought to an end until 1964 when Sir George Schuster, recently retired chairman of the Westminster Bank, joined the governing body. That stage in the College's history will be found in chapter five.

A principal, a castle, and enough money to open the doors were the objectives which had claimed the attention of most members of the promotion committee. But Atlantic College was to be a completely new type of school: it needed a new curriculum. I use this word in its widest sense, to cover all the experience, social, intellectual, aesthetic and moral, through which a school seeks to influence the attitudes and behaviour of its students. As a technical term, it tends to bemuse school governors or perhaps even school boards, who, in England at least, will often leave it to the principal as the expert. I remember, when I was a grammar school headmaster in Shropshire, a colleague who took unfair advantage of this. His governors, concerned, I suspect, mainly for economy, wanted to turn the boys' grammar school into a co-educational school. My friend approached the chairman, a large-scale farmer, with the following horror story:

"You do realise, chairman, that it doesn't just mean that boys and girls would be studying together. They'd be using the same curriculum."

"My God, if I'd known that", said the farmer, "I'd never have agreed to it."

And no girls entered the grammar school for a few years more. My own chairman at that time announced that the first girl would cross the threshold of the grammar school over his dead body—unaware that I already had girls from the local high school attending our sixth-form science classes.

The activity side of the curriculum was already determined in essence by Hahn's principles, which meant that, although Atlantic College inevitably incorporated much of English public school traditions, the place of team games—even of Rugby in Wales—was taken by the sea and cliff rescue services, beach patrols, camping, and mountain walking, with some individual sports. This was surely a wise decision. Team games would inevitably have led to national groupings.

But there was a more serious reason for the decision. Apart from the positive lessons to be learned from the new activities, the English tradition of team games, as an element in social and moral education, had already lost its original, nineteenth-century justification. At the beginning of this century a foreigner to England could observe an educational ethos in them, exemplified by such phrases as: 'Let the best man win', '*Le fair-play*', 'play for the team not yourself', 'The game's the thing'. Proust's Odette in *Time Regained* "never failed, relevant or not, to quote the expression 'fair play' (and to point out that in the eyes of the English the Germans were unfair players)".[5] By the 1960s things were very different. I found, as a headmaster, school games coaches teaching the opposite: 'Your job is to go in and win', 'A bit of rough stuff is all right, provided the referee is unsighted. Everyone does it.' Stardom and spectatoritis had invaded not only the reality, which is apparent as far back as *Tom Brown's Schooldays*, but even the rhetoric. Across the Atlantic, cheerleaders had become an institution. This change in attitudes towards team games is discussed further in chapter eight.

Robert Blackburn and I worked throughout the summer of 1962 on the academic curriculum. By this time I had left Dover College to become Director of the Department and Institute of Education at Oxford University, where I was already deeply involved in the movement to broaden the English sixth-form curriculum. My own range of disciplines was in the humanities. Sir John Cockroft, for the sciences, and I were therefore asked to advise on a programme of academic studies for the new college.

The problem was not an easy one. It was a cardinal principle of the founders that, though Atlantic College was to be an international school, promoting an international outlook, the students should normally return to their own countries for higher education. Entry to universities, except in North America, was then restricted, highly competitive, and dependent on performance in examinations—the *baccalauréat*, the GCE, the *Abitur*, the *matura*, and so forth. These examinations were based on differing curricula.[6] Clearly, Atlantic College students could not be separately prepared for the university entrance examinations of each of their own countries. Apart from the wide differences between these examinations and the cost of such private tuition, it would have destroyed the whole purpose of the college by dividing it up into separate national groups and rendering impossible the introduction of a common language of instruction. The only obvious solution was to base the Atlantic College academic curriculum on the Advanced Level of the British General Certificate of Education, and to adopt English as the language of instruction. In theory, such a proposal was not impracticable. Success in these examinations qualified the students to apply for admission to the university in the seventeen member-countries of the Council of Europe under the European Convention on the Equivalence of Diplomas of 1953.[7] Entry to American universities presented no problems since it depended on scholastic aptitude tests, taken much earlier in the year and based on no prescribed curriculum or syllabus. In practice, however, there were serious difficulties both technical and educational.

Let us take the less fundamental difficulties first. The 1953 convention established only the right of the foreign student to present the diploma gained in another member state as a qualification for entry to the university as a whole: it did not require the university to accept him, but only to guarantee that he would not be refused admission simply on the grounds that he had a foreign qualification. Thus students could always be refused because they did not have the qualifications in specific subjects required for entry to a specific faculty (e.g. Latin for entry to some medical schools) or because their applications came too late. In many countries the expansion of universities had fallen far behind the expansion of qualified applicants. This led to the imposition of the *numerus clausus* and the turning away of qualified applicants simply because there were not enough places left. All students holding foreign diplomas were likely to be disadvantaged, but Atlantic College students especially so for three reasons. The first was that they were not really 'foreign' students, but French or German or other students seeking to enter their own universities with a foreign qualification. This did not cause much trouble in Germany because the Federal Government was co-operating in the experiment and had sponsored the initial selection of students, but it did mean that they had to take an additional German examination called 'nos-trification'. In France, however, the importance of passing the *baccalauréat* was still so great that the only concession made in respect of French holders of foreign diplomas was in cases where the parents—not the student—had been living abroad for some years and so unable to enter their child for this *baccalauréat*. Consequently the only French boys from France who could come to Atlantic College were either exceptionally gifted ones, who had passed their *baccalauréat* already, or academic drop-outs who never expected to pass it. There were similar problems in other countries.

The second reason was that whereas throughout Europe the results of the university entrance examinations were published in early July, the British GCE A-level results did not come out till mid-August, when the European universities had already completed their admission processes.

The third, and educationally much the most important, was that the English sixth-form course leading to A-levels was by far the narrowest and most specialised in the world. Students presenting a diploma which included either no foreign language or no mathematics were likely to find themselves in trouble with faculty requirements, even if the 1953 convention specifically ruled out any attempt to discriminate between diplomas as valid qualifications for entry to the university as a whole on the grounds of their 'substantive content'.

All these were important technical objections to using the GCE as the common curriculum of an international college. But there were fundamental educational objections to using the national curriculum and examinations of any one country and then relying on 'equivalence'. From the point of view of curriculum all countries provided, very naturally, programmes with a strong national bias: none was internationally oriented. This, as the designers of the European Baccalaureate and of the International Baccalaureate subsequently found, affected all subjects, even mathematics, to a certain extent, but was particularly apparent in history and languages. Why should French or Swedish or Italian students, coming to an international college in Wales, find themselves expected to follow courses which concentrated heavily on the history of England as presented to the English? Even as a young schoolboy in England I had been puzzled by the story my history books told me of how the English appeared to have won every battle in The

[2] Kurt Hahn, *The Young and the Outcome of the War* (London: The Lindsay Press, 1965).

[3] Atlantic College. *First Appeal Document* (Llantwit Major, 1961).

[4] Atlantic College. *Atlantic College Handbook* (Llantwit Major, 1981).

[5] Marcel Proust, *Time Regained* (London: Chatto and Windus, 1931), 122.

[6] Frank Bowles, *Access to Higher Education* (Paris: Unesco, 1963).

[7] Council of Europe. *Equivalence of Diploma leading to Admission to Universities: Declaration on the Application of the European Convention of 11 December 1953* (Strasbourg, 1953).

[8] Atlantic College. *Prospectus and Plan of Studies* (Llantwit Major, 1962).

2
THE FOUNDING
OF THE INTERNATIONAL
BACCALAUREATE

The International School of Geneva, known familiarly as Ecolint, has a justifiable claim to be the oldest of modern international schools. Founded in 1924 to meet the needs of employees of the original League of Nations, it was the only major international school to survive the Second World War. It numbered among its pupils Indira Gandhi, later Prime Minister of India. It was at Ecolint, within a year of its foundation, that the first idealistic call for an international school-leaving examination came in 1925. On the instructions of his Board of Governors, the then Director of the School, Paul Meyhoffer, circulated to 17 European leaders in the educational reform movement a questionnaire testing their reactions to a proposal to establish a *maturité internationale*. The recipients included such people as Albert Thomas in France, Edouard Chaparède in Switzerland, and J.H. Badley of Bedales in England, but no one outside Europe. There is no record of their replies. The project appears to have been still-born, probably because, although it may have fired the imagination of some post-war idealists, it did not, as it did after the Second World War, respond to a widely-felt need. There were in 1925 very few international schools and very little student mobility. Nevertheless, some of the questions posed raised issues, such as the relationship between 'general' and 'specialised' education which were still relevant 40 years later and which are discussed in Chapter Three.

At the end of the Second World War Ecolint again took the lead in the founding of the International Schools Association, set up in 1951 to help the growing number of international schools, all over the world, with their common problems. One of the most pressing of these problems, already for Ecolint and increasingly for the newer schools, as they added senior high schools, sixth forms, or *classes terminales* to their primary and middle schools, was that of preparing their older students for entry to universities. This time the only realistic solution seemed to be the establishment of an international baccalaureate.

It had not been a problem between the wars. The sons and daughters of the expatriate community, if French, French-speaking, or interested in learning French, were educated in *lycées français à l'étranger*, by far, and rightly, the most prestigious chain of schools for a foreign community. They were, as their name implies, French schools, not international schools, and they had their channel to the university through the French *baccalauréat*. If the families were English, whether in the colonial territories, or very widely in South America, they had a chain of English schools, not government-sponsored to anything like the extent of the French *lycées*, but teaching the English system and with their own examination channel in the 'Cambridge Overseas' GCE. Americans used the tests of the College Entrance Examination Board, in so far as anything beyond a high school diploma was necessary. These schools were supported by the US State Department on condition that they provided an 'American' rather than 'international' education. A small number of Goethe or Leonardo Institutes catered for German or Italian nationals. There was no need for an international examination because each nation looked after its own and there were very few 'international' schools. The 'international community' and genuinely 'international schools' are a phenomenon of the second half of this century. Moreover, in the interwar period entry to universities was considerably less academically selective and more dependent on the ability of parents to pay the fees. This most expatriates could easily do. They did not have to worry much about their sons and daughters passing university entrance examinations.

After 1945 things were very different. Government subsidies had opened the universities to a much wider social-economic range and entry became increasingly competitive, based on grades in school-leaving or university entrance examinations. To compete successfully in these examinations it was necessary not merely to have a sound general education, but to have followed the national syllabus of the country to which the student hoped to go to college. Thus when I first visited Ecolint as a consultant, I found students doing advanced physics for entry to science faculties divided into four small groups, one following the syllabus for the Swiss *maturité fédérale*, one that of the English GCE A-level, one that of the French *baccalauréat*, and a fourth preparing for the American College Board Advanced placement.

This was not only immensely wasteful of resources but offended against the international spirit of the school by dividing students into national groups, while the 'minority nationals' had to sink or swim as best they could. In languages there were all the problems of translation and in social studies of national bias that we have seen plaguing Atlantic College. The creation of an international baccalaureate had ceased to be solely an internationalist idea and became a practical necessity.

In 1948 the Conference of Internationally-minded Schools, a loose grouping not unlike the recipients of the original 1925 questionnaire, passed a resolution calling on Ecolint to resume its initiative. In 1955, Van Houtte, founder of the European Community Schools, made a similar plea, directing it in this case to the newly-formed International Schools Association, which was being given house room by Ecolint. These moves aroused increasing interest among both the teaching staff and the board of Ecolint but it was not until the appointment of Desmond Cole-Baker as director of Ecolint's English-language section in 1961 that action was begun to translate the idea into a reality. A committee of sponsors was formed, drawn from members of various international organisations based in Geneva, but the driving force in the transition from an idea, to which so many people had paid lip-service, to a reality was not international organisations nor, as in the case of Atlantic College, a group of influential opinion leaders with royal patronage, but the teachers at Ecolint, led by Cole-Baker.

There were times when to this small group of teachers who campaigned for it throughout the sixties it must have seemed like a pipe-dream. By now more than ten thousand students of over a hundred different nationalities have entered universities from Harvard to Heidelberg and Kyoto to Budapest with this qualification—a remarkable example of what a few peoples' initiative at the grassroots can achieve.

As a result of the co-operative efforts of this group, 1962, the year of the foundation of Atlantic College, also saw the first small conference in Geneva, organised by the teachers in Ecolint's social studies department, under their Chairman Bob Leach, which made specific mention of the words "International Baccalaureate". Bob

Leach, a widely-travelled American Quaker with long experience of international education, had been seconded to ISA. He was first concerned, as had been the teachers at Atlantic College, with the difficulty of teaching history in an international school; but while they were facing the problem for the first time, he had been living with it for years.

Ecolint had neither continuing funds of its own for curriculum development, nor, like Atlantic College, substantial backers, but it did have some very enthusiastic teachers prepared to give up their own time for the cause they believed in. Unesco was at that time engaged on a "Major Project" on "The Mutual Appreciation of Eastern and Western Cultures". Under the auspices of the International Schools Association, Leach was able to get a grant of $2,500 from Unesco to mount a small conference of social studies teachers in international schools to explore "The Social Studies programme in international schools appropriate to the preparation for an International Baccalaureate". It was a fairly small gathering with working papers prepared entirely by teachers at Ecolint; but observers were present from Unesco and the European Schools, and the initiative justifies to some extent Bob Leach's claim to have been 'the original promoter of the International Baccalaureate' although, as we have seen, he was one of many.[1] Unesco was sufficiently interested to continue a further series of small contracts with ISA to study other elements in the international school curriculum, but the scale of this operation is indicated by the fact that the total Unesco funding, secured by four small grants, was $10,000. This sort of funding could never have made possible more than 'discussions'. It was enough to enable a few more teachers from other schools to come together for an interesting day or two, but not enough to maintain an independent office or a secretary, nor enough to prepare adequate papers for meetings nor to do anything to follow up between meetings. ISA had not, and never has subsequently developed, the kind of resources that would enable it to undertake a major project in international education such as the IB, and Ecolint itself was in severe financial difficulties at the time. It actually looked to Leach that "unless some rationalisation was achieved, the oldest and most important of international schools may well go bankrupt".[2]

These difficulties were partly produced by the one serious flaw in Ecolint's structure, the fact that it was and still is divided into separate English and French sections. A determined effort to unite the school in a single bilingual institution was made at that time by Desmond Cole-Baker, but it failed. In doing so it increased the conviction of some of the 'outsiders', who had begun to be interested in the idea of an IB, that neither ISA nor Ecolint alone would ever be able to bring the project to fruition. ISA was in any case inclined to withdraw, because the second Unesco contract was for "a study of the possibility of an interchangeable curriculum between and among international schools". Most ISA members were more concerned with primary and middle school education, and reluctant to spend time on what still seemed the visionary and for them largely irrelevant dream of an international baccalaureate.

The next step forward was therefore a decision at the 1964 annual meeting of the ISA that a separate organisation be set up to continue work on the IB project. This organisation continued to be sponsored by Ecolint in spite of Ecolint's own financial problems, but was designed to have an independent legal status, similar to that of ISA itself, as an *association* under Swiss Law. The name chosen for it, the 'International Schools Examination Syndicate', was presumably suggested by some Cambridge-educated Englishman, since the Cambridge GCE board is called a 'Syndicate': for a bilingual organisation it was an unfortunate choice since *syndicat* in French means trade union. ISES operated unofficially from June 1964, but was in fact, as had been true from the start, essentially a Geneva-based group of Ecolint teachers and other supporters.

These supporters included John Goormaghtigh, the Belgian director of the European Office of the Carnegie Endowment for World Peace, Georges Panchaud, Professor of Education at the University of Lausanne, and Jean Siotis, the Greek assistant director of the Carnegie Endowment Office. Panchaud was the first educationist with an international reputation and contacts to join ISES/IBO and Siotis played a valuable role not only in the Council, but as chairman of the first examining board, which examined candidates for Ecolint's experimental examinations in contemporary history.[3] The debt which the whole project owes to John Goormaghtigh, however, is incalculable. At the time when he accepted the chairmanship of ISES he was chairman of the Board of Ecolint, but he soon relinquished that post to concentrate on ISES/IBO. He remained president of the IBO Council until 1980 when, at a meeting of the Council held in Siena, he handed over to Dr. S.M. Sy, Rector of the University of Dakar who, in his turn, handed over in 1984 to Dr. Piet Gathier, Director-General of Secondary Education in the Netherlands. It was, of course, a great advantage for IBO to have as President of the Council a distinguished international lawyer when, in 1974 and 1975, it began to appear that the experiment was proving a success and would need a new long-term international status: but that is insignificant compared with 15 years of leadership marked by a deep and intuitive concern for international education, a capacity for understanding across cultural boundaries whether in Europe or Africa, and a gift for personal relations. No director-general of a new and hazardous project can ever have worked with so congenial a chairman. It is of some interest in view of accusations that the IBO is 'too Anglo-Saxon' that the first three chairmen have come from Belgium, Senegal, and the Netherlands.

In January 1965, ISES was formally incorporated as an *association* empowered to receive and administer funds. So far, so good. It had been clear for some time that the dream could only be turned into a reality if it had a secure source of funds over a number of years and an efficient and continuing administrative structure, which could channel into practical activity the individual enthusiasm that had been aroused. ISES was an improvement in terms of organisation and personnel, since it had already been proved that neither foundations nor multi-national corporations nor governments were prepared to grant the sorts of funds that would be needed either to ISA or to Ecolint. But ISES still needed a backer, as Atlantic College had done. In 1964 he appeared in the form of Georges-Henri Martin, editor of the influential *Tribune de Genève* and a trustee of the Twentieth Century Fund.

In August 1964 the Twentieth Century Fund offered to ISES a grant of $75,000 for an investigation into the feasibility of an international university entrance examination. Since the foundation was research-oriented, the form of the grant was tied to further investigation of the practicability of the project, combined with an assignment to Martin Mayer to write a report on the outcome of these investigations. It meant that for the first time the promoters, now in the form of ISES, could plan a programme of development, establish an office and executive secretary, and finance a tour by Martin Mayer and Gene Wallach (an Ecolint teacher) of international schools in parts of the world where interest in the project seemed likely. The increased seriousness of the commitment also meant that a number of more influential people interested in international education were attracted to join the Council, as the planning group of ISES was somewhat grandiloquently termed. To those who then joined in the project, or who later read either Martin Mayer's report or Bob Leach's book, the proliferation of councils, assemblies, executive committees, pedagogic committees, and technical committees, to administer an as-yet non-existent examination, recalls the worst excesses of voluntary organisations, caught up in the trammels of international co-operation in either of the two Unesco capitals, Paris and Geneva. Mayer, in attempting to describe it, recalls Keynes's description of international discussions concentrating on "the determination of how many votes Brazil should have on a commission where decisions would not be taken by voting". "Nevertheless," he goes on, "the meetings were sometimes productive of important discussion, and even of decision."[4]

It is these productive discussions with teachers involved in the day-to-day problems of international education which remain so pleasantly in the memory. The stimulating discussions of how history or languages or science should be taught in an international context, with Bob Leach, Nansi Poirel, Nan Martin, Reg Unitt, and above all Gérard Renaud, the philosophy teacher at Ecolint who had spent some years teaching in French schools overseas; the whirlwind energy and deep humanity of Ruth Bonner who joined ISES from ISA and a lifetime of work both in international education and in womens' international organisations; the convivial dinners at the Rallye at the end of the day, when everyone paid his own shot, since no one in those days received anything from the non-existent funds; all these are unforgettable and made up for the administrative frustrations.

I had been drawn into the circle, partly through the Atlantic College connection but more importantly because the two main centres of research interest in the Oxford department were then the structure of the sixth form curriculum in England and comparative education.

In 1960 we had published *Arts and Science Sides in the Sixth Form*, based on the findings of research funded by the Gulbenkian Foundation, which sold more than 3,000 copies. This was followed by three conferences at Oxford between October 1960 and April 1961 which brought together more that 300 teachers from schools and universities to discuss possible reforms of the excessively specialised and polarised English curriculum and marked the beginning of what proved to be a 25-year period of abortive discussions at a national level.

Shortly after, we negotiated with the Council of Europe a project for the comparative study of upper secondary curricula and examinations in the member states. This was carried out by Dr W.D. Halls, then tutor in comparative education in the Department, and a leading consultant to ISES/IBO. The findings were published by the Council of Europe in a series known as *The Oxford Council of Europe Studies in Curriculum and Examinations* (OCESCE). It was not surprising therefore that, quite apart from my own connection with Atlantic College, the Department became more and more involved in the Geneva project to research the feasibility of an international baccalaureate. When I first visited Geneva in the autumn of 1964 the grant from the Twentieth Century Fund had at last made it possible to plan a more realistic investigation. The need was as apparent as it had been in planning the Atlantic College curriculum. Ecolint had not, and could not have, adopted the highly unsatisfactory Atlantic College solution of preparing everyone for the same national examination and relying on equivalence. But this meant that Ecolint had no common language policy and that even in apparently neutral subjects like physics the 16-18-year-olds were divided, at great cost and to the detriment of their international contacts, into the four small 'sets' already mentioned.

As early as 1964 Cole-Baker and the Ecolint group had started to enquire about the chance of larger-scale support from the Ford Foundation. The Foundation was, in principle, interested, because they were investing several million dollars in providing a new building for the United Nations International School (UNIS), set up in the tradition of Ecolint as the international school for the UN in New York, which was operating from the buildings of an abandoned high school on Second Avenue. The visits of certain members of the Ecolint teachers' group had led both UNIS teachers and Ford officials to think that perhaps the right curriculum for the upper section of UNIS would be one based on this new international university entrance examination, if it ever became a reality. They therefore suggested two additional members for the ISES Council, Desmond Cole, the Director of UNIS and Harlan (Harpo) Hanson, then Director of the College Entrance Examinations Board's Advanced Placement Program. The addition of these two new members, who were not only not Geneva residents but who brought in a transatlantic dimension and a specialised knowledge of examinations, had dramatic effects. They are best described in the contemporary words of Martin Mayer's report to the Twentieth Century Fund:

"From mid-1965 to mid-1966 IBO [the new name for ISES adopted actually in 1967] staggered through a series of personnel crises, questionable financial allocations and unsatisfactory panel meetings, while the Council resisted any expansion of the membership which would diminish the influence of Geneva. . . . In 1966 when negotiations for a larger grant from the Ford Foundation began to lag, Oxford moved reluctantly but firmly to take over the project. Peterson agreed to serve as director of IBO, part time until January 1967 and full time (on his sabbatical leave) for six months thereafter."[5]

My own memory of the 'move' by Oxford is not so much of a calculated takeover as of a co-operative rescue operation. It is based on a conversation outside the Café de Remor in Geneva between Desmond Cole, Harpo Hanson, and myself at one o'clock on a summer morning after one of the frustrating administrative sessions.

"This thing will never get off the ground," said Desmond, "unless someone can take it on full-time."

"I've got a sabbatical coming up," I replied, "and I'd do it myself, but I'm committed to teaching at Berkeley."

"I'll fix Berkeley," said Harpo.

The fix which he negotiated with the faculty of Education at Berkeley was that I should teach one semester only in the summer of 1967. Since my only remaining full-time commitment at Oxford for 1966 was the eight-week Michaelmas Term from October to the beginning of December, that gave me nearly a year to devote full-time to launching the IB.

The first thing to do, without which nothing else would be possible, was to clinch the Ford Foundation grant. This Harpo and I were able to do in New York in the course of a one hour interview with Shep Stone. Much preliminary discussion had, of course, gone on and it was probably just the reassurance given by the more solid commitment of Oxford and of the College Board which determined the foundation to take the gamble. For it was a gamble. We were still engaged in action research to establish whether an international baccalaureate could be feasible. Nobody could say whether it would be. "Well, boys," said Shep Stone, as we went out, "you're going out of here with $300,000. I wish you

had just directed a massive study of 'Access to Higher Education' for Unesco, and Ralph Tyler. Additional members who joined the Council in 1966 and 1967 were Dr Andren, Rector of the University of Stockholm; Mohammed El Fasi, Rector of the Moroccan Universities; Heinz Fischer Wollpert, Rector of the Goethe Gymnasium in Frankfurt; Lord Hankey, former British Ambassador to OECD; Senteza Kajubi, Director of the Institute of Education at Makererè; Charles Sa'd, Principal of Choueifat National College, Beirut; and Madame Zakowa, an inspector in the Polish Ministry of Education.

With this extension of the Council went a great simplification of the organs of the IBO, which were now to consist of a council, meeting annually, an Executive Committee of five members, and later a Board of Chief Examiners, responsible for the annual examinations, from 1969 onwards under the Chairmanship of Professor Hans Boesch, Professor of Geography at the University of Zurich and for many years Secretary-General of the International Geographical Union.

The five objectives were of course interlinked and progress towards them was stimulated by a fairly strict deadline. The Ford Foundation had been pressing for a major international conference at which the IB proposals could be presented and Madame Hatinguais offered to host this at the Centre Internationale des Récherches Pédagogiques at Sèvres in February 1967. This was not to be another gathering of such teachers and sympathisers as chose to attend, but a carefully-structured conference of persons invited as representatives of the countries and interests whose support would be needed if the project were to take off. Leach points out that it was the first time that the American director of the CEEB Advanced Placement Program, the English Secretary of the London University GCE Board, the French Director of the Office du Baccalauréat, and a retired Director of the Swiss *Maturité Fédérale* had ever sat round the same table.[7]

In preparing for this conference I had two continuing consultants, Gérard Renaud, who remained on the staff of Ecolint until he joined the IBO as Assistant Director in 1968, and Bill Halls, who was conducting the OCESCE studies for the Oxford Department.

After a brief meeting of this troika in Oxford to plan our work in preparation of the conference, I set out on a tour of international schools in the Middle East, Africa, and South America in order to be able to present to the conference a reasonably well-distributed pilot group which would be prepared to participate in trial examinations. It included a swing through Nigeria, Ghana, Uruguay, Chile, and the USA. The schools visited were largely those which had been identified as 'possibles' by Martin Mayer on his previous tour and at the 1967 conference IBO was able to present the following list of schools prepared to co-operate in an experiment: Atlantic College, British Schools Montevideo, Ecolint, Goethe Gymnasium, International School Ibadan, Iranzamin (Tehran), *Lycée International de St Germain*, Santiago College (Chile), and UNIS. All these, except Iranzamin, are still entering candidates for the IB at the time of writing, though Santiago College had to drop out for a few years. For one week, during the height of the revolutionary period, Iranzamin was the last school in Tehran, public or private, to remain open. Some of its students and teachers in exile participated in the founding of what is now International School Spain in Madrid which offers the IB today.

Other schools which I visited at that time, for instance the Französisches Gymnasium, and the John F. Kennedy in Berlin, and St George's Rome, decided, sometimes after a lot of discussion, not to adopt the IB. The process of decision is a complicated one and was then much more complicated since the IB was an untried venture. Often there is in a school a group of experimentally-minded teachers who initiate discussions, but are in the end unable to carry with them a majority of their colleagues. In the initial group of schools the deciding factor was usually a convinced and convincing principal. Even when the decision has been taken, it may be difficult to win immediately the support of all parents, particularly when the school has been offering the national examination, English GCE, or French *baccalauréat*, which meet the needs of some among its many national groups. In such cases a number of schools have started by offering the IB as an alternative track, while continuing to prepare those who wanted it for the GCE A-Level. This is almost as extravagant of resources as the four-track system then operating at Ecolint, and in the three schools with which I have been closely involved as a member of the governing body—Ecolint, St Clare's (Oxford), and Singapore—the result has been the same. The GCE track has slowly withered and died as more and more students opted for the IB. The last bastion of the GCE at Ecolint was not in fact the British parents but Commonwealth parents from formerly dependent territories.

In December I moved from Oxford to the first IBO Office, in a room made available by Ecolint, with Ruth Bonner as administrative assistant and Lucette Donche, who is still working for IBO after 20 years, as book-keeper. Meanwhile the two other members of the troika, Gérard Renaud in Geneva and Bill Halls in Oxford, were pressing ahead with the finalisation of a curricular pattern and syllabuses for individual subjects. A first draft of the curricular pattern had been presented by Gérard Renaud at the first curriculum conference in March 1965 and agreed between Atlantic College and Ecolint at a language conference in October. IB was designed for the last two years of pre-university education and at this stage, which was increasingly being seen as the last of 'general education' and the first of subject-oriented specialisation, there were already four different traditions to consider. The first was the conservative tradition of general education which required that all students should continue to study the same wide range of subjects with approximately the same time allocations as they had studied throughout secondary education. This was represented by the West German *Abitur* and the Swiss *maturité fédérale*. At the other extreme was the English GCE, narrowed down to three subjects only, related to the student's future choice of specialisation at the University, and supplemented only by the fiction that one quarter to one third of the time allocation would be devoted to unprescribed and unexamined "general studies". In between were the reformers in France and Germany who were moving from the conservative pattern towards one of different tracks for the *baccalauréat* or *Abitur* which recognised a gradual movement towards the student choosing one or another line of specialisation, while continuing a substantial and prescribed element of general education, by varying the time allocation between major and minor subjects. In North America the requirements for a high school diploma had already been so far diluted in intellectual terms that the phrase 'twelfth-grade slump' was becoming familiar and the Advanced Placement Program had been introduced to restore some element of academic challenge to what remained essentially a 'cafeteria style' curriculum.

The curriculum conference in March 1965 was the first to which the French Ministry sent one of their *inspecteurs généraux*, André van Smeevoorde, the chief inspector for languages. It was after discussion between him and George Bruce of the London GCE board about whether candidates should be allowed to choose their subjects, that, in one of those late-night discussions which were often so fruitful in the early days, he and Gérard Renaud hit on the compromise, which Gérard presented next morning on the blackboard and which has remained the basis of the IB *schéma général* ever since. The key to this was that no individual subject save two languages and mathematics should be specified, but that candidates would be compelled to choose at least one subject from certain specified groups. The picture on the blackboard was then one of six subjects, a first language (probably either the mother tongue or the language of instruction of the school), any second language, mathematics, one subject chosen from a group then called 'Social Science', but now 'Study of Man in Society', one from a group then called 'Laboratory Science', but now called 'Experimental Sciences', and one from a 'sixth group'. Much argument about the number of subjects, which was at one time proposed as seven, and about different levels, was still to go on. This will be treated in chapter three, but there is little doubt of the historic importance of this blackboard presentation. If Bob Leach can claim to have been during this phase the first promoter of the IB, Gérard has some claim to have been its architect. Van Smeevoorde became more and more interested in the IB, accompanied me on my visits to schools in the Middle East, and became IBO's first Chief Examiner in Languages.

The interest of the French Ministry of Education was very marked at this time, no doubt increased by the readiness of ISES to present their international examination as a bilingual baccalaureate in which all papers could be taken in either English or French and all documentation was published in both languages. Three *inspecteurs généraux* attended the second curriculum conference at Atlantic College in October 1965. Leach attributes to this meeting the first presentation of the *schéma général* 'package deal'.[8] In this I believe he is wrong, although we have already seen that the resemblance between it and the existing Atlantic College curriculum was very close. At a meeting between Gérard and Monsieur Tric, the *inspecteur général* for philosophy, one of the most successful innovations of the IB was developed. In the design of the European Baccalaureate, France had successfully insisted that philosophy should be a compulsory subject, as it then was in the French *baccalauréat*. Gérard succeeded in persuading him that philosophy, as a substantive subject, should be simply one of the options in the third group, but that all students should follow a restricted course in the Theory of Knowledge. The nature of this course is described in the next chapter.

By the end of 1966, then, ISES/IBO was ready for the International Conference at Sèvres. A curricular pattern and syllabuses in two languages were ready, as were proposals for the nature of the examination with specimen examination questions on which Bill Halls had been working at Oxford. A group of schools had agreed to start teaching the syllabuses and enter candidates for trial examinations. What we hoped to achieve over the next year or two, as a result of the conference, was the agreement of enough universities, whether autonomous or controlled by their ministries of education, to co-operate in the experiment by giving at least provisional recognition to the IB diploma as an entry qualification. Then and then only could IB examinations begin to replace national ones.

Membership of the conference included governmental delegates from Bulgaria, Britain, Cameroun, France, two of the Federal German *Länder*, Poland, Sweden, Switzerland, and Tanzania, together with representatives of universities, of OECD, Unesco, the Council of Europe, and the national examining bodies of the countries concerned. The conference lasted three days, breaking up after the first plenary session into Commission A on the 'Structure, Standards and Syllabuses of the Courses', chaired by Dr Fischer-Wolpert with Gérard Renaud as consultant, and Commission B on 'The Organisation and Procedure of the Examinations', chaired by Robert Blackburn with Bill Halls as consultant. Many of the features of the examination discussed in the next chapter, the six-subject schéma, the higher and subsidiary levels, and the principle of 'compensation', were quickly accepted. The most important new principle was proposed by Desmond Cole, Principal of UNIS. He was concerned lest the introduction of the IB might have the effect of splitting off the IB course, as an élite (super-'College Bound') group within the school. Could the IB not offer something to every member of the sixteen-to-eighteen age group? The French, and indeed the Europeans generally, but not the English, remained wholly opposed to the IB becoming a 'subject' examination, rather than a 'diploma' or 'package' examination. Cole's proposal that the 'package' concept should be retained for the IB diploma, but that individual 'certificates' for achievement in individual subjects should also be awarded to students who did not qualify for the diploma, was accepted by everybody. It was of crucial importance for the future.

The proposal advanced in the final plenary session had been suggested by Ralph Tyler. It was that for an experimental period of six years from 1969 the universities and national authorities in as many countries as possible should undertake to recognise the IB as an entry qualification for not more than 500 students a year from a group of schools inspected by ISES/IBO and approved by their governments. There was a dramatic moment when Professor Nikolov from the University of Sofia rose to announce that "Bulgaria accepts", but most delegates had not come empowered to make such a decision. The conference did, however, end with strong expressions of support and willingness on all sides to co-operate in seeking the official endorsement of their ministries or autonomous universities.

By the time that I returned to Oxford at the end of my sabbatical year, retaining the overall direction of the experiment, but leaving Gérard Renaud, who resigned his teaching post at Ecolint, in charge of the Geneva office, two of the countries with centralised systems, France and Sweden, had agreed to co-operate, as had some autonomous universities, 14 British, three Swiss, and many American. By 1970, after two years of trials, the first 29 students used the official IB examinations for university entrance.

This is, perhaps, the appropriate place to say a word about the contribution made by the Oxford department. Because it was essentially concerned with the post-graduate training of teachers, a large proportion of whom were preparing to teach in this upper secondary age-range, the faculty included specialists in exactly the fields with which ISES/IBO was concerned. Through the OCESCE studies these specialists in the teaching of mathematics, languages, science, history, and so forth, were being kept in touch with the latest trends in their subject in Europe. Since the six-year experiment was accepted by the university as a valuable piece of action research in the department's particular field, I could provide from the department's resources the sort of secretarial and administrative support that was never forthcoming from ISA. Some of the Department specialists provided the first examiners and in time became deeply committed to the whole project.

Let me close this chapter, therefore, so much of which records things which would never have happened without the initiative of individuals, with one more anecdote. Philip Heafford, tutor in physics in the Department and a specialist in science teaching in developing countries, was due at a subject panel meeting at Sèvres, at a period when a series of strikes at airports and seaports had severed communication with France. I remember that the rest of the world smiled at the typical English headline: "Continent Isolated".

Philip, who was a keen mountaineer as well as a physicist, went down to Dover, bought a bottle of brandy, and walked along the quay waving it until he saw a French fishing boat.

"Can you give me a lift to Calais?"

"Only if you're a mountaineer, Monsieur."

"Why that?"

"I can't take you into Calais. But I could land you on the rocks at the base of the light-house, if you can manage the climb."

So the science panel got its full complement.

Notes to Chapter Two

[1] Robert Leach, *International Schools and Their Role in the Field of International Education* (Oxford: Pergamon, 1969).

[2] Ibid., 38.

[3] Martin Mayer, *Diploma: International Schools and University Entrance* (New York: Twentieth Century Fund, 1968), 225.

[4] Ibid., 220.

[5] Ibid., 225.

[6] Ibid., 219.

[7] Leach, op. cit., 70.

[8] Ibid., 67.

3
FROM EDUCATIONAL AIMS
TO A CURRICULUM
AND EXAMINATIONS

Confusion and debate about the aims of education is not peculiar to the closing years of this century. Aristotle's analysis is not very far from the brief that might be given to a commission of enquiry today: "In modern times people's views about education differ. There is no general agreement about what the young should learn either in relation to moral virtue or to success in life; nor is it clear whether education should be more concerned with training the intellect or the character. Contemporary events have made the problem more difficult and there is no certainty whether education should be primarily vocational, moral or cultural. People have recommended all three. Moreover there is no agreement as to what sort of education does promote moral virtue."[1]

At the beginning of this century Dr Alington, later to become headmaster of Eton, was asked by an aggressive parent: "In a word, Dr Alington, what are you educating my son for?" "In a word, Madam," he replied, "Death." In which he may have been quoting from Montaigne's Essay.[2]

I was once asked, at a Council of Europe seminar in Salerno, to give a brief description of the educational aims of the IB programme. I could not quite match the brevity of Alington, but I tried to encapsulate them in a single sentence thus: "to develop to their fullest potential the powers of each individual to understand, to modify and to enjoy his or her environment, both inner and outer, in its physical, social, moral, aesthetic, and spiritual aspects."

I still find this a fairly adequate one-sentence summary, though such generalised statements of aims tell us little. They must be judged by their translation into a curriculum and, in the case of

IB, into a series of examinations which can be administered within the constraints prevailing at the time. What is important in this statement of aims is the concept of general education as process rather than content which is implied; but before turning to that it may be as well to outline the context and constraints.

In seeking to achieve our translation from educational aims to a curriculum and examinations, those who planned the IBO were faced with a series of interlinked problems arising from the special context, but they also benefitted from one special advantage as compared with national systems.

In terms of aims, we were seeking to design a genuinely international curriculum to meet all the various needs of those sixteen-to-eighteen-year-olds in international schools who were seeking entry to different forms of higher education all over the world. We believed that those needs and interests included the moral, aesthetic, and practical education of the whole person and thus extended far beyond the purely intellectual and academic preparation normally sanctioned by university entrance examinations. But in what sort of context were we working? National systems can, if they decide to do so, include this education of the whole person, as well as of the academic scholar, in the total curriculum without including it in the examinations. They can prescribe a curriculum by law, promote its implementation through their system of teacher-training and control any failings through inspectors. International schools and the IBO had no inspectors, no common system of teacher-training, and no powers of prescription, apart from mutual consultation, except through the regulations for the examination. Such a situation was reasonably familiar to the British, for whom the curriculum at this stage is controlled by the examinations, but less so to those from other countries. This we may call the first problem. The second was the one raised at the Sèvres Conference in 1967 by UNIS. At first sight the problem of translating aims into examination procedures might have seemed much simplified by the fact that we were concerned with a very specific group, the intellectually able and academically motivated candidates for university entry. But, as UNIS pointed out, if the introduction of the IB were not to split the eleventh and twelfth grades in international schools by creating a 'super-college-bound' élite, the IBO must also provide courses for other students. The decision, noted in the last chapter, to award 'certificates' for performance in individual subjects to these who did not take the full diploma was only the beginning of a solution to this problem, but it was significant. I remember in the very early days the Guidance Counsellor from UNIS telling me of the pride with which a student of very limited ability, describing her very practical and 'life-oriented' programme, concluded by saying: "And I'm taking IB subsidiary biology." This problem is one which has concerned a number of European countries, where traditionally students who did not intend to seek entry to higher education left school at sixteen or before but now increasingly remain in school. It had to be faced by IBO from the first. Young people of this age in their own country in the late 1960s could and did leave school and start a job or take up some sort of vocational training. They could not do so if their families were living in a foreign country. So they tended, much more than in national systems, to stay on in the international school. How could their needs best be met within a curriculum which was primarily designed for those who were seeking to enter universities? It seems probable, as we shall see later, that the solution may lie in the nature of the IB subsidiary-level syllabuses.

The third problem for those seeking to realise a pedagogic ideal was that each syllabus, particularly for each of the higher-level subjects, which students normally expected to continue at the university, had to keep reasonably close to that of national systems: otherwise the examination results would be suspect to university admissions officers, and misfits might occur at the beginning of those university courses (by no means all) which assumed direct continuity with school courses. It was one of the oddities then, as it largely is now, that university courses in some subjects, such as accountancy, anthropology, and architecture, required no previous acquaintance with that specific discipline, while those in others, such as biology, botany, chemistry, and classical languages, selected for entry only those students who had followed a standard course in the relevant subject in the upper secondary school. For such courses the planners had to ensure that the 'fit' was reasonably good for the full range of European universities.

It may be appropriate here to make an initial comment on a criticism which is often made of the IB curriculum, that it is 'too Eurocentric'. There are two senses in which this criticism can be made. It may be asked why, in taking account of this 'fit', so much attention was paid to the entrance requirements of European universities. The answer to this question is a practical one. Students in international schools working at the IB level, even Third World students, if they sought entry to higher education, were overwhelmingly seeking to enter colleges or universities in Europe or North America. In North America entry to higher education did not depend on performance examinations but on the scholastic aptitude tests, the SATs (see chapter six). The question of 'fit' was almost entirely confined to the European universities and here we had the advantage of being able to draw on the OCESCE studies. Even in Third World countries university courses were, at this time, based on European models.

The other sense in which the IB curriculum has been criticised as too Eurocentric is in the content of the syllabuses. Here it may well be that, although the content of the curriculum in mathematics and the experimental sciences is relatively culture-free, that of the languages, study of man in society, and aesthetic groups suffered initially, and still suffers to some extent, from this Eurocentric bias. This is discussed in the final chapter.

The problem of 'fit' has become steadily easier as European countries have moved to a pattern more like that of the IB.[3]

A fourth problem shared with national authorities, was that although educators in all countries have reiterated that examinations must not dominate the curriculum, that what is taught and learnt should be the first concern of planners and examinations come second, yet, in practice, as soon as examinations become selective and the grade achieved becomes of crucial importance to the individual, planners find themselves concentrating more and more on what can be most fairly and accurately examined rather than on what is most educationally desirable. The 'Tyranny of Testing'[4] is not relevant solely to the American multiple choice tests.

The fifth problem (we are now reaching the end of this formidable list) was the likelihood that if the IBO were to develop genuinely innovative syllabuses, the schools would still not choose to offer them, because they had no teachers who had been trained, or felt competent, to teach them. Leach records his view of Ecolint that "there is too much Swiss influence, too many British staff, too many American students."[5] This comment reflects an unrealistic purism, which affected ISA, about what an international school should be. After all one would expect a special influence of the host country and a student body that reflected the local composition of the expatriate community. But the point about the staff is of some importance. We have already seen that the francophone international community is served by the *lycées français*. Almost all other schools catering for this community as a whole use English as the medium of instruction. The IB is now offered in English, French, or Spanish. Out of more than 6,000 candidates of 121 nationalities who took the May 1984 examinations, 90% took them in English, 6% in French, and 3.5% in Spanish.

One would expect, therefore, a high proportion of the teachers in international schools to come from English-speaking countries. Among these teachers the predominance of teachers from the UK at this stage over those from North America or from countries, such as Scandinavia or the Netherlands, where many teachers speak English, is probably due to two factors. The first is that British teachers are more accustomed than others to teaching for external examinations; the second is that British teachers at this level are accustomed to lower salary scales than those of North American or other European countries. The American principal of a school in the Gulf put it to me very succinctly at an IB conference in Bahrein in 1984: "For what I have to pay an American teacher with three years experience I can get a good English teacher with ten years experience." But these British teachers had been trained and accustomed to teach the conventional subjects normally found in the British sixth forms of the period. Very few had spent long enough in an international school to develop the interest and capacity to teach anything else. International schools, if one excludes such leaders as Ecolint, UNIS, and the United World Colleges, rely very heavily on teachers on two-year contracts. The teachers themselves are often reluctant to stay for more than two such terms lest they compromise their prospects in the career structure at home. It has always seemed to me that the organisation of a long-term career structure and training system for teachers in international schools is one of the greatest needs of international education and might have been a better use of Unesco's funds than some of the conferences and speech-making which have recently absorbed them.

Nevertheless, the great advantage which the IBO has enjoyed over national systems has been the willingness of teachers, particularly those who have spent some considerable time in IB schools, to experiment. We shall see later in this chapter how difficult it has proved to introduce reform in Federal Germany because the teachers were not ready for it, and it is my personal view that the failure of eight successive attempts to rectify excessive and premature specialisation in England has been due to the same factor.

Innovative and committed teachers often think that if only control of education were handed over to the teachers, change and reform would be easy. They forget that the majority of their colleagues are not innovative and committed, and that when the silent majority reckon that reform is imminent their instinct is to close ranks in favour of the more comfortable alternative: keeping things as they are. The IBO has been reasonably free from the effects of this syndrome. As we saw in the last chapter, those schools where the majority of the staff were against innovation, although they may have considered introducing the IB when some enthusiasts suggested it, yet when the time for decision arrived, came down against it. The teachers involved in the IB have been mainly self-selected innovators.

Let us return now to the concept of general education which, in this context and under these constraints, we were seeking to embody in a curriculum and examinations.

General education, *culture générale* or *allgemeine Bildung*, had long been the avowed aim of upper secondary education in Europe and of the early years of college in North America. The way in which this aim had been translated into a curriculum throughout most of Europe in the nineteenth and early twentieth centuries represented education as essentially the transmission of knowledge or information and general education therefore as the transmission of general knowledge over a wide range of subject-areas. Gradually, throughout this period, the width of this range increased. There were added to the old classical curriculum of Latin, Greek, and mathematics, first history, then the natural sciences, then subjects of the kind that Guizot in France once called 'an education for grocers': geography or economics. In continental Europe this had led to 'encyclopaedic' curricula such that at the peak of the movement the German student preparing the *Abitur* for entry to the University was 'learning' as many as 13 different subjects for one or two periods a week. Indeed the Gymnasium was nicknamed the 'thirteen subject school'.

The great objection to this kind of encyclopaedism is that the 'learning' involved tends inevitably to a superficial memorisation either of information or of what Whitehead called 'inert ideas', that is, prestructured interpretations of information given by the teacher to the student. Montaigne wrote: "If the student embraces

Xenophon's or Plato's opinions by his own reasoning, they will no longer be theirs; they will be his. . . . He must imbibe their ways of thinking, not learn their precepts. And let him boldly forget, if he wishes, where he got them; but let him know how to make them his own."[6] An encyclopaedic general education leaves no time for the student to make any ways of thinking his own before he hurries on to the next one-hour session of absorbing unrelated information about chemistry, French, or geography in his crowded week.

The English response had been different. Unwilling to dilute the 'grand old fortifying curriculum' in the Classics, they had divided the sixth form, that is the last two years of upper secondary education, into 'sides' or sections, leaving the Classics untouched, but adding first a 'Science Side' and then a 'Modern Side'. General education was left to unexamined and unprescribed courses in 'General Studies', which might be anything from German for 'Scientists' to art history for 'Classics'. The fiction, constantly reiterated by the apologists for the system, was that these General Studies occupied 'one quarter to one third' of the students' time. In fact, every independent survey has shown that, except in some of the best schools, they occupied less than one fifth of the class contact hours and none of that private study or homework which is so vitally important in this stage of education.[7] Neither school nor students were prepared to devote much time or effort to what did not count in the increasingly important examinations.

In the USA, General Education was the traditional function of the college. To Europeans the relation between Harvard or Columbia College and Harvard or Columbia University seems strange and unfamiliar. We Europeans forget the extent to which we have 'pushed down' the bachelor's degree (baccalaureate) or the 'first MB' in Medicine to the schools, leaving the universities to concentrate on specialised courses in single disciplines. I remember being warned, when we first discussed the use of the IB in North America, that we might be sued for false pretences, since we were using a term, 'baccalaureate', to sanction completion of a high school course when its normal use belonged in higher education.

The controversy about placing responsibility for general education either in secondary or higher education was going on in the US at the time when the IB curriculum was being planned. Daniel Bell in *The Reforming of General Education* (1966)[8] pointed out that the role of the college was being challenged at both ends: the better high schools were introducing 'enriched' or 'advanced place-ment' courses which duplicated the first year of college, while within the university the graduate schools were pushing back into college more and more specialist courses related to their own dis-ciplines. There was one other notable respect in which American concepts of general education differed from European. This was in the content. The content of this stage of general education in the US has been the subject of much debate since the introduction of the new Columbia College programme at the end of the First World War, through Hutchins's reforms in Chicago in 1936 to the Harvard 'Red Book' at the end of the Second World War. Where it has consistently differed from European practice has been in designing special and substantial general education courses, whether based on 'Great Books' or 'Contemporary Civilisation', rather than simply continuing the study of a wide, 'general' pattern of secondary school subjects.

The dispute between high school or college as the proper place for general education, which was going on at the time when the IB was founded, was less relevant in the European context. One of the most cogent arguments brought forward by Daniel Bell against the supporters of the high school was that while intellec-tually able and motivated high school students might well be ca-pable of 'college level' work in languages, mathematics, and the natural sciences, a real understanding of the humanities and social sciences needs a greater personal maturity and is better developed between the ages of eighteen and twenty-one.[9] Young people do not mature at a steady rate that suits educational systems, and in many European countries the highly questionable procedure of 'repeating' classes had led to pupils being still in the upper sections of secondary schools at an age when in America they would have been completing the second year of college. When the IB was founded, the usual age at which German students completed their *Abitur* was 20-21.

It was the English, with their tradition of accelerated promotion, entry to universities as soon as the necessary examinations were passed, and early specialisation, whose general education was most neglected. Even so I can remember, as headmaster of a country grammar school in the 1940s, a boy who celebrated his twenty-first birthday in the sixth form, whereas I had entered Oxford as an undergraduate one month after my eighteenth.

What is common to all these concepts of general education and to their articulation through curricula and examinations is that their generality lies in their subject matter. The group of reformers who were planning the IB saw things rather differently, and this difference is expressed in that single-sentence statement of aims. We sought not to ensure that as 'generally educated men and women' our students should have acquired a wide range of knowledge, but that they should have developed, as far as they were able, their power and desire to engage in a wide range of what Montaigne called "ways of thinking". In other words, to quote Edgar Faure, a French Minister of Education, that they should "learn to learn".

This theory, that the aim of general education was not the acquisition of general knowledge, but the development of the general powers of the mind to operate in a variety of ways of thinking, had a profound effect on the planning of curricula and methods of assessment. Let us take history, one of the most problematical subjects in an international context. To an encyclopaedist approach it was unacceptable in a national programme that the student should not have covered, let us say, the Saxon monarchies, the Norman Conquest, The Wars of the Roses, or the Great Revolution. In an international context this sort of encyclopaedic knowledge became impossible. If it were unthinkable to know nothing about the French Revolution, what of the American Revolution, the Russian Revolution, the Chinese Revolution, the Mexican Revolution? How, then, were students to get a general education, not in the sense of acquiring general information in order to forget it, but in experiencing ways of thinking in order to understand? To learn history not in order to know some specific 'facts', but to learn to think historically?

The first attempt to formulate this concept of general education in the context of the present study is to be found in the Oxford University Department of Education report on *Arts and Science Sides in the Sixth Form* (1960).[10] This report draws to some extent on the Crowther Report (1959)[11] but had in fact been largely completed before the publication of that report. Indeed, as the preface to the Oxford report states, it contains "a complete divergence of opinion on the merits of what the Crowther Report admits to be the unique English system of concentrating specialisation in either the Arts or the Science field".

The key paragraph is the following: "We shall not solve the problem of combining general education with specialisation until we cease to think of general education in terms of general knowledge. It is not a sign that a man lacks general education if he does not know the date of the Treaty of Utrecht, the latitude of Singapore, the formula for nitro-glycerine or the author of the *Four Quartets*. It does denote a lack of general education if he cares nothing for any of the arts, confuses a moral with an aesthetic judgement, interprets the actions of Asian political leaders in terms of nineteenth-century English parliamentarianism, or believes that the existence of God has been scientifically disproved."

The report goes on to propose a reform of the English sixth form curriculum by extending the range of specialised subjects from two or three to four, spread over both arts and sciences. To this was to be added a fifth block of time devoted to religious and physical education, the creative arts and a new course, occupying no more than 60 hours a year and designed to help the student to 'make a unity' of his or her whole learning experience. To quote once more: "The fifth block should therefore include a course, similar to the best and not the worst of the *'classes de philosophie*, on the methodology of the subjects. It may be suggested that this is beyond the capacity of the average sixth former. I do not think so. It is certainly not beyond their interests. If it were beyond them it would be a condemnation of all our present programmes. For we have agreed that it is not the factual knowledge but the 'learning to learn' which is the real purpose of these programmes; and if the pupils cannot understand the methods and limitations of the subject even when they are discussed and explained, it is not likely that they will absorb them without understanding and without explanation. After all we are not concerned that the sixth form historian, or physicist, or classicist shall in adult life be able to answer examination questions in history, physics, or classics, but that he shall have acquired in those studies an intellectual capacity and outlook which he can apply to managing a business, a colony, a newspaper, or a parish."

It is not difficult to see in this pattern the first sketch of what, seven years later, had become the *schéma général* of the International Baccalaureate. The use of a "colony" as an example was not very far-sighted and the references to "methodology", where something like 'underlying epistomology' might have been a better term, produced conflicts and misunderstandings between French and English in relation to the IB Theory of Knowledge course. The proposal that an experiment should be undertaken with 50 schools using this five-block course as an alternative to two or three A-levels was not taken up any more than the proposal, made 19 years later by a working party set up by the Schools Council, that 50 schools should experiment with the IB.

Meanwhile in France, Jean Capelle in *Contre le baccalauréat* was inveighing against encyclopaedic programmes and examinations based on recall of memorised information: "The pupil is not required to enter a garden abundantly full of flowers in order there to compose for himself a personal bouquet: in essence he is required to store and bring back one example of each species in order to be able to produce on demand the specimen required by the luck of the examination"[12] (my translation). Just as the Oxford report proposed an increase in the number of disciplines studied for the terminal years of secondary school in England, so Capelle proposed a decrease for France: "One prepares better the acquisition of a general education by study in depth at secondary level of half a dozen subjects sufficiently diverse in their nature (which avoids specialisation) than in skimming over a dozen different fields of knowledge solely in order to be able to recall something about each of them on the day of the examination." As *Rebâtir l'école* justly remarks, the quantitative accumulation of items of knowledge required destroys the quality of study. "It is the old story of the 'tête bien faite', which we praise without really seeking to produce it, and the 'tête bien pleine' which we deplore but make in fact the object of our examinations."

What seems to me today particularly interesting in Capelle's argument is the insistence that it is the student and not the curriculum planner who must use his academic studies to form his own mind in his own way.

Given this consensus that able and well-motivated students at this age should concentrate on not more than five or six diverse subjects if they are to study in sufficient depth to achieve that understanding and commitment which promotes further learning, Daniel Bell's objective of general education *through* specialisation becomes feasible.

But how was the IBO to plan a whole curriculum in which the actual syllabus in each of the half-dozen subjects would exemplify this principle? And how to examine in such a way as to encourage the teaching of 'minds well formed' rather than 'minds well stuffed'? At this stage we benefitted greatly from the advice of Hellmut Becker and the German concept of 'paradigmatic learning'. Even within a single discipline, such as physics or history, if the objective is rather to teach a student to learn, to think and to imagine, than to teach a body of knowledge, then it is better to select certain examples, where elements of the discipline can be studied in depth, than to attempt to cover a whole corpus of knowledge, even if that corpus is restricted to the established (and probably out-dated) body of knowledge deemed appropriate for pupils in the upper secondary school. Of course these paradigmatic examples must be related to a common core of content, but much of this will have been acquired between the ages of thirteen and sixteen and this can be strengthened in the final syllabus, while still leaving plenty of time for the study in depth of the paradigmatic examples. It is of course possible to go too far in one's fear of the mere acquisition of information. You cannot teach students to think historically unless they have something to think about; and this means some historical 'facts' taken on trust. Nor can they learn to think and imagine historically and critically unless they can relate their special subject of historical study to its wider, though less intimately understood, context.

Individual IB syllabuses were therefore often drawn up, as can be seen from the current issue of the general guide, in the form of an outline common core of the discipline with a choice between a number of special options for study in depth.

Such an approach was then new to many teachers in national systems and produced some inevitable tensions between teaching and examinations. Becker himself, writing in 1979 of his experiences in the reform of education in the Federal Republic of Germany says:

> The change from a general encyclopaedic education to a paradigmatic one, in which there can be no set canon, but rather changing emphasis, was not understood and accepted by the teachers and therefore not brought into practice. Even though in this age of knowledge explosion it must theoretically be clear to them that encyclopaedic education is impossible, they will plan their lessons in a way as if a Leibnizian approach was still possible. That means, then, that the 'courage to leave gaps', much advocated in pedagogic theory, has not been adopted in the classroom.

In speaking specifically of the upper secondary school, he writes:

> Then in the Bildungsrat (German Educational Council) I participated in the drafting of 14 versions of recommendations on these issues. The 14th version was accepted. I subsequently read what the Minister of Education formulated as a uniform recommendation to

the various State authorities, on the basis of our recommendations. They proposed the introduction of a core and option system for the senior forms of the Grammar School (*Gymnasium*) as had long been the practice in Anglo-Saxon countries and in Scandinavia.[13]

If England and Wales are Anglo-Saxon countries I think this is giving them too much credit. Certainly in the IB planning we owed much to Germany, if not to her practice, then to her thinking.

This pattern of academic study of six subjects, so distributed that they provided some experience of mankind's main tools of thought and ways of thinking, provided the framework of general education through specialisation. But more needed to be added. In order to take one step even further the experience of what individual study in depth is like and to provide an intellectual outlet for what Kurt Hahn called the grand passion, every candidate for the IB diploma is now required to conduct a substantial piece of individual work on a topic of his or her own choice, related to one of the six subjects chosen and recorded in an 'extended essay' of approximately 4,000 words. This work is undertaken in the student's own time, usually spread over four to six months in the middle of the two-year course and under the guidance, which of course will vary, of one of the teachers. It is assessed by an outside examiner. Feedback from students very soon convinced us of the value of this element in the total curriculum. Of course some dreary stuff was submitted just 'to fulfil the requirement', but many students have quoted it as the part of the IB experience which helped them most when they reached the university. The stimulus to the grand passion was more dramatic. We very soon found that we had to put back the date for submission of the extended essay to some months before the completion of the course, because schools complained that too many students were becoming so deeply involved in their extended essay topic that they were neglecting the rest of the course and might fail their diploma examinations.

To ensure that some part of the total curriculum included learning from direct experience rather than academic study and to stimulate the social service aspect of Kurt Hahn's philosophy was more difficult to achieve through the medium of examination regulations. Here it seemed that we must rely on the growing enthusiasm among the schools themselves and that the most the IBO could do was to 'hinder hindrances to the good life'. The main hindrance we saw in current national systems was not any lack of interest among the students and teachers, but the sheer pressure of competition for better and better grades in the academic examinations on which entry to universities depended. I remember, when I was headmaster at Dover College, the following conversation:

"I'm afraid I shall have to give up playing in the orchestra next year, Sir."

"But why? You're our best violinist and you love it."

"But Bristol University is asking for two As and a B for entry to Chemistry and I can't spare the time."

All that the IBO could do was to ensure that within our system this kind of competition for the student's time did not squeeze out experiential learning. Hence the regulation that every school entering candidates for the IB examinations must guarantee that they have the equivalent of one half-day a week free for engagement in some sort of creative aesthetic or active social service activity— the so-called CASS requirement.

There was from the first a wide variety in what schools did both within this minimum and beyond it. Many students engaged in both aesthetic and social service activities, and students at the United World College and some other schools devoted much more than one half-day a week to them. Most schools now go far beyond just guaranteeing that the time is available and plan a wide and varied range of such activities in which students are encouraged to engage. Such experiential learning cannot be externally assessed, but it does play some part in the whole profile provided to university admissions officers, in the form of an annex to the IB Diploma. Some of the forms of activity developed by different schools are described in later chapters. It may be of some interest that something like the CASS requirement is advocated in Ernest Boyer's report on the American High School (1983) as the "New Carnegie Unit".[14]

Finally we come to what was to many the crown of the whole course, The Theory of Knowledge course. Here we were lucky in having as our chief collaborator and, in so far as performance in the course was assessed, our first examiner, Madame Dreyfus, a French *inspectrice* for philosophy.

We have already seen in the Oxford report *Arts and Science Sides in the Sixth Form* a first sketch of what this course was to become, but it was the French input, first from Gérard Renaud and then from Dina Dreyfus which gave it its initial form, from which it has diverged little in the fifteen years of the IB's history.

The aim of the course was to counteract two weaknesses which we saw in the pre-university courses of most European countries. The first was the tendency which most students had to study their different subjects in watertight compartments. Not only did they fail to relate apparently disparate subjects such as physics and history to each other; they often did not seem to see connections between literature and psychology or history and literature. Their teachers often did not seem to have the time to help them to see such connections, possibly because the form of the examinations positively discouraged it. Yet we have to remember that only about five percent of all those men and women who spend their formative years in academic work actually become professional academics in specialised fields. For the remaining 95% the ability to see inter-connections between different specialised approaches to an intellectual problem is very important.

The second weakness was the failure to make explicit in the minds of students the differing forms which academic learning and knowledge take. To quote from an earlier statement of aims:

> Finally the International Baccalaureate included in its requirements two somewhat novel features which spring directly from the educational philosophy which this chapter tries to express. It is a requirement that every pupil must follow a course in the theory of knowledge and that every pupil must have the chance to spend some part of his school time in creative and aesthetic activity or in social service, or indeed in both.
>
> If the whole philosophy underlying the distribution requirement is that what matters is not the absorption and regurgitation either of facts or of predigested interpretations of facts, but the development of powers of the mind or ways of thinking which can be applied to new situations and new presentations of facts as they arise, the same philosophy is exemplified in the treatment of individual subjects, and it is through them that we seek to give general education. By the serious study of history we hope not that the pupil will memorize, although he needs to memorize as a means to an end, but that he will learn to think historically so that when faced with a problem in politics, or commerce, or literary criticism, or any other human predicament, he will not neglect, but will be able to assess, the historical element in his situation. Why else should those who are not going to practise as professional historians learn history at school, in order to forget it when they leave? But all the findings of educational psychology lead us to think that this transfer of training, this application of principles learnt in one situation to the problems of a new situation, does not take place unless the principles themselves are made explicit in the mind of the learner. To have learnt to think historically about the seventeenth century, without realizing what thinking historically means, may not help the young administrator or the labour-relations officer in a large factory to think historically about *his* problems at all.[15]

The rationale of introducing into upper secondary education a unifying and reflective element of this kind has been well expressed by Jerome Bruner, Professor of Psychology first at Harvard and then at Oxford:

> Teaching specific topics or skills without making clear their context in the broad fundamental structure of a field of knowledge is uneconomical in several deep senses. In the first place, such teaching makes it exceedingly difficult for the student to generalise from what he has learned to what he will encounter later. In the second place, learning that has fallen short of a grasp of general principles has little reward in terms of intellectual excitement. The best way to create interest in a subject is to render it worth knowing, which means to make the knowledge gained usable in one's thinking beyond the situation in which the learning has occurred. Third, knowledge one has acquired without sufficient understanding to tie it together is likely to be forgotten. An unconnected set of facts has a pitiably short half-life in memory. Organising facts in terms of principles and ideas from which they may be inferred is the only known way of reducing the quick rate of loss of human memory.

The intention of the course was to help the student to think about the questions which underlie the nature of knowledge as presented in the school disciplines and his daily life, about such questions as the grounds for accepting as valid a proposition in logic, in mathematics, in physics, in sociology, or in history; as the importance and limitations or quantification in different academic disciplines; as the basis and interrelation of moral, aesthetic, and religious beliefs; and so, using Jean Capelle's image, to bring back from the garden of his studies his own bouquet, his own deepened understanding and enjoyment of his own experience, rather than a collection of individual flowers unrelated to each other and selected by an outside arbiter on the basis of the boundaries of the 'disciplines'.

The sections of the Theory of Knowledge course in the fourth edition of the General Guide to the International Baccalaureate were as follows:

1. Logical symbolism (now revised to Language and Logic)
2. Scientific activity and the formation of scientific concepts (an example)
3. Mathematics and Reality
4. The constitution of a human science (an example)
5. Historical knowledge
6. The nature and basis of moral and political judgement
7. The nature and basis of aesthetic judgement
8. Opinion, Faith, Knowledge, Truth.

The current programme of the Theory of Knowledge Course will be found in appendix one.

In designing a series of examination and assessments on the basis of which to award an IB diploma for so inclusive a course, we had both an obligation and an opportunity to take into account the differing techniques of assessment used in those countries to whose institutions IB candidates were mostly seeking entry. The position was complicated by the fact that, just as with the upper secondary curriculum, the examination systems in Europe were in a state of flux.

Examinations at the end of secondary education commonly serve one or more of three different purposes: certification, selection, and motivation. The pre-war tradition of the *baccalauréat*, *Abitur*, or *matura* in continental Europe was one of certification. Success in the examination certified that the student had completed the secondary course and was 'ripe' for entry to the university. All those who passed such examinations had, therefore, a right to enter the university and to study in any faculty they chose. The old 'school certificate' and 'higher school certificate', or 'matric', in England performed much the same function, though conferring no absolute right of entry. Those who exercised this right were those who could afford to. The expansion of state aid to secondary and higher education after the Second World War and the consequent opening of the universities to a much wider socio-economic range soon produced a situation where there were far more students completing the secondary course and seeking entry to higher education than the traditional universities had room for. This meant that the examinations were forced to assume a function of selection as well as certification. There are certain conflicts between the two functions. An examination designed, like the pre-war German *Abitur*, to certify 'ripeness' tends to sum up a whole battery of achievements and to be taken when the student is ready to take it: on the other hand it does not need to attempt a fine discrimination between students, certifying that one is 'riper' than another, or to place them in rank order. But this capacity for fine discrimination and placing in rank order is essential in an examination which is to be used for selection. The effect of this tension between the two functions can be most clearly seen in the tortured history of the West German *Abitur*, which retained throughout the concept of a global assessment, feeding into the computer a whole range of variables designed to certify ripeness, but receiving from it a single grade, calculated to the first decimal point, on which the candidate's chance of entry to his or her chosen faculty depended.[16]

Confusion about the function of the examination was compounded by the changes in the structure of the upper secondary course, to which reference has already been made. In France, although not in Germany, entry to certain faculties began to depend not merely on the global mark in the *baccalauréat* but, as in England, on marks in the subjects on which the candidate had concentrated.

Meanwhile in North America, entry to college of some kind was virtually open to all who could pay or work their way through college. Scholarships or entry to the most favoured colleges depended upon SATs and personal records, while subject examinations of the European type, provided by the College Entrance Examination Board, were relevant only to placement in more advanced courses when the student actually arrived at college.

In a study carried out in 1970 for the Council of Europe I identified five factors which should enter into the design of an examination system: validity, reliability, 'backwash' effect, cost, and speed, and summed up what was then the essence of our thinking in the International Baccalaureate Office thus:

> Reviewing the state of research and innovation in Europe, it would seem that the most promising line of development is the *examen bilan*. What is needed is a process of assessment which is as valid as possible, in the sense that it really assesses the whole endowment and personality of the pupil in relation to the next stage of his life, but at the same time sufficiently reliable to assure pupils, parents, teachers, and receiving institutions that justice is being done. Yet such a process must not, by its backwash effect, distort good teaching, nor be too slow, nor absorb too much of our scarce educational resources.[17]

The phrase *examen bilan* we also owed to Jean Capelle.

A good example of the process by which the IBO sought to reach a compromise between national traditions and the best achievable balance between the five factors was the establishment of the examination system for languages. For Language A, the student's 'best' though not always 'native' language, the national model clearly was the examination in the mother tongue which at this level is largely literary. A two-day discussion was held in Paris, in which examination experts from Britain, France, Federal Germany, and the USA participated. On the curriculum side there had been general agreement that a course in language and literature at one or other of the two levels was an essential part of general education, with special implication for both moral and aesthetic education. It was also agreed that this was certainly one case where the purpose of the examination was to assess what the student could do and not, as in some traditional examinations, what he or she did not know. For the purpose and outcome of this discussion, let me quote again from a more contemporary source:

> All representatives at the international panel were agreed on the objectives of the course and the kind of literary skills both in expression and appreciation which it sought to develop through a wide reading of original literary works. When it came to discussion of the methods used for assessment, however, the divergence was very wide indeed. The English commonly examine this (A-Level English literature) by asking the candidate to write answers to as many as four or five questions, often of some sophistication (e.g., '"Poetry begins in delight and ends in wisdom". Robert Frost. Indicate from your own experience of reading poetry how far you agree with this opinion', or 'Milton's Satan moves us . . . because he alone is able to convey dramatically what goodness is. Discuss.'). Since the total time allowance is two and a half hours, each of these questions has to be answered, allowing for some time spent in reading the paper and choosing which questions to answer, in less than thirty minutes. Apart from anything else, this attaches considerable value to the capacity to write a fast, neat, and legible hand. At the other end of the scale the French and Germans often examine this by asking for a single composition, or critical analysis of a short, previously unseen poem, for which four or five hours are allowed (under examination conditions, needless to say, much less rigid than those of the GCE), supplemented by an oral examination.[18]

Perhaps half-way between them came the American suggestion of asking for more general literary essays, but three of these with a time allowance of one hour each.

Given the known unreliability of oral examinations and of general essays, the English method could probably claim the lead on the reliability scale. Its validity also seemed comparatively high if, but only if, the main object of the examination was to test the extent to which the candidates had actually read the comparatively narrow range of literature in the syllabus and remembered both it and the more important critical theories applying to it. If, however, the objectives of the course were conceived as the awakening of a life-long interest in and critical reading of good literature, the development of a precise and personal style of expression, and the maturing and refinement of the moral and aesthetic judgement, the question immediately arose whether a method of assessment which relied so much upon testing recall was really valid. It was argued that, faced with questions of such complexity and so little time in which to answer them, the average candidate could not possibly write anything valuable which he originally felt or thought at that moment, but was forced into reproducing his previous thoughts or, even worse, the thoughts from a textbook or a teacher transmitted in note form, and that this explained why English examiners so regularly complained that the candidates answered, not the question asked, but the nearest equivalent to which they had already memorised an answer. To this it was replied that there were some people who did respond very quickly to a fresh point of view or a new interpretation posed to them in the form of a question and who did their best work, including original thinking, under the sort of pressure which the GCE examinations exerted.

But it was when the backwash effects of this type of assessment were considered that the International Baccalaureate panel became most convinced that it should be rejected. Granted that there were a few candidates for whom it acted as a stimulus to original thought, the 'good examinees' of the English tradition, it seemed probable that for the great majority preparation for tests of this kind would encourage pupils and teachers alike to treat the course as if quick factual recall of the content of the 'set books', and of the standard views of critics upon this content, was the objective of the course. It was felt that this would have so harmful an effect on teaching that the genuine reliability and somewhat fictitious validity of the method were inadequate reasons for using it. Even if the oral and the long essay or appreciation, with adequate time given for a pupil to produce his best, were less reliable tests, they did encourage a 'dialogue' form of teaching and the composition of more deeply felt or considered written work, while a properly structured oral provided a less dangerous way of controlling that the texts had actually been read and appreciated. Since the margin of error in assessing this type of course is always likely to be great, it seemed more important to ensure that the examination would not inhibit good teaching than that it should measure with a lesser degree of inaccuracy something other than the objective of the course. The International Baccalaureate examination in Language A at Higher Level, therefore, consists of one written paper of four hours, which may either be devoted to the composition of a single essay, in which the candidate will naturally draw upon the literary experience which the course has given him, or be divided between a rather shorter essay and critical appreciation of a previously unseen passage of poetry. To this is added an oral examination intended to provide an assessment of his capacity for oral expression, his quickness in responding to a new idea or interpretation, and the depth of his acquaintance with the literature which he has studied."

Originally, the 'extended essay' mentioned above was also a compulsory part of the Higher Level examination in Language A, but this can now be submitted in any of the disciplines studied and has been replaced in Language A by a 20% allocation of marks for internal assessment of 'guided course work'.

It will be seen that in this case rather more weight was given to 'backwash effect' among the three major factors. Cost and speed did, however, have considerable influence on attempts to improve reliability. There seems little doubt that the reliability of marking literary essays can be increased and the marker-subjectivity reduced by multiple marking. Three markers grading the essays independently and then aggregating their marks are more likely to be consistent than a single marker. But this is costly and unless they all live in close proximity likely to be slow. It may be significant that the panel found it in use in Luxemburg, but it did not seem practical for the IB. The English system of improving reliability by drawing up an agreed 'marking scheme', based on the analysis of a first sample of scripts by a meeting of examiners, was also rejected, partly on the grounds that it was too 'content-based', assuming that examiners should know in advance what the 'right' answer to a literary question was, but mainly because of the time involved. It is often overlooked that in most continental European examination systems the question papers are the same for all candidates, but the grading is undertaken by a series of independent juries, who complete their work in two or three weeks. In England on the other hand there are eight different examination papers set by the different independent examining boards, but the scrupulous procedure for ensuring the maximum possible reliability means that the results do not come out for a couple of months. We have already seen that one reason why Atlantic College was finding so much difficulty in using A-level for entry to European universities was that they needed the results on which they based their admission procedures long before the A-level results were available. The continental system of the oral examination was retained. There were many reasons for this. In assessing a student's use of language and appreciation of literature there are elements which are much better revealed in an oral dialogue. Professor Panchaud summed them up thus: "la vivacité d'esprit du candidat, son habileté à se tirer d'embarras, sa façon de s'exprimer, la solidité de ses connaissances, son émotivité, etc."[19] As a check on whether the candidate has read and appreciated the literature on which the course has been based, I have found them more useful than the typical A-level questions. Three minutes out of a thirty-minute interview with two candidates in New York convinced me that one of them had not read *The Mayor of Casterbridge* and that the other had been so excited by *The Waste Land* that she had taken the trouble to read Jessie L. Weston. The following dialogue with a candidate in Tehran on the subject of Dostoyevsky's *Crime and Punishment* is an illuminating example of what some IB candidates are like:

"Of course, I had an advantage because I read it in Russian."

"Oh you're Russian are you? Your English is so good I took you for an American."

"No, no. I'm not Russian, I'm Iranian. My mother is Russian."

"So are you taking Farsi as your Language B?"

"No, I'm taking French."

To be quadrilingual at the age of eighteen may be one of the advantages of an international education, though of course both this girl and her situation were exceptional.

By bringing in a different examiner of different skills to the total process of assessment I think we also achieved some small improvement in overall validity and reliability. For the IBO in particular, above all at this stage in its development, there was an additional advantage that every school would be visited each year by an IBO representative and every candidate personally meet an IB examiner. Whenever the possibility of abandoning the face-to-face oral on grounds of cost was discussed with students their opposition was vehement. To them one of the attractions of involvement in the IB was the feeling that they were participating with students of schools in far-away countries in a world-wide network. The oral examiner was the living embodiment of this participation. For a student in Montevideo to talk about what he or she had been reading directly to an examiner from Paris or Oxford was a privilege that such students were reluctant to forego. This preference for meeting an IB examiner face-to-face has been maintained even though it is now very rare for the examiner to have come from overseas.

There were of course great penalties in costs. As the number of schools in distant countries, many of them with only a handful of candidates in their early years, grew, we had to rely more and more on locally-based examiners, and inevitably there were cases where the reliability of the oral became very questionable. It is, when taken by itself, probably the least reliable and most costly element in any battery of examinations, just as the multiple-choice test is the most reliable and, once sufficient numbers are involved, the cheapest. Retention of the oral for Language A is justified by the value of its inclusion to the battery as a whole, by its contribution to backwash effect and to validity, and by the personal contact it involves between schools and what too easily could become a remote and impersonal examination board.

Multiple-choice tests, along with a considerable battery of other tests, were accepted as a valuable part of the examination in Language B, for most students the first foreign language. Here the examination was assessing not so much literary skills and sensitivity as actual command of the language. This command has been identified as the ability to hear and understand, to speak, to read and to write. These different skills we aimed to assess by auditive tests, oral tests (in this case recorded on cassettes), reading comprehension tests, and written compositions. To these we added a multiple choice test designed to survey the candidate's command of idiom and lexis more widely than could be done through any of the others. It has already been mentioned that we could not employ translation, which was just as well, since this is the most sophisticated of language skills and questionably suitable for high school students.

There was at first some objection from both ends of the spectrum to the multiple choice tests. There were still some Europeans who distrusted them as an 'American' importation with very harmful backwash effect. This was fairly easily dissipated when it was realised what a small part they would play in a battery otherwise well-designed for backwash.

At the other end of the spectrum were those who objected because a proper degree of pre-testing and quality control could not be exercised, partly because the IBO could not afford it and partly because no comparable population existed on which to carry out pre-testing. Consequently the quality of our first multiple choice tests was certainly not up to the standard expected by, for instance, the Educational Testing Service or GCE Boards. This led to a good deal of quite justifiable condemnation of certain items. We were saved from abandoning the use of such tests by Professor Fletcher Watson of Harvard who asked:

"Let me see. This suspect item is one of 40 in the Language B examination. What weight within the Language B examination does the multiple choice test carry?"

"One fifth of the total marks."

"And Language B is one of the six subjects, graded on a 1 to 7 scale which make up the IB diploma total?"

"Yes."

"Then we are talking about one fortieth of one fifth of one sixth of the candidate's total assessment. Gentlemen, I don't think you should worry too much about it."

Multiple choice questions were, in the early days, the most expensive form of testing for the IBO. As student numbers have grown such tests have become increasingly cost-effective, and because of their reliability (even though imperfect) and their validity for testing certain ranges of skill, knowledge, and even to some extent understanding, I am sure we were right to include them from the first.

Similar problems had to be discussed in relation to the examinations in the other subjects. It was one of the attractions of the IB project that such international discussions on a technical level had never gone on before—certainly not in a context where the outcome of the discussions would not be theoretical but embodied in examinations which would actually be taken by real, individual students and provide their pathway to higher education.

Taking the examinations in the different subjects as a whole, the complete range of assessment methods was as follows: face-to-face orals, orals tape-recorded on cassettes, multiple choice questions, 'short answer' questions, essay questions, practical examinations, assessments of projects, assessment of extended essays, teachers' assessments of course work. A much more detailed description of the individual tests can be found in *International Baccalaureate*, chapter three.

Such, then, was the battery of tests, the *examen bilan* with which the IBO entered upon its six-year experiment. It was designed to provide the admissions officers of universities with evidence of general education and the admissions officers of faculties with evidence of sufficient preparation in those disciplines where a specific level of preparation was required. It sought, as the European Baccalaureate did, to provide a numerical basis of selection based on general 'ripeness', but also, as the European Baccalaureate did not, on a basis of performance in specific fields. How much weight would be given by any particular country or any particular university to the general as compared with the specific was beyond the control of IBO. We would have liked great weight to have been given to the total score, but were aware that in some universities it would be the score in certain higher-level subjects that counted. Above all, the battery had been very consciously designed with special attention to backwash effect. We were trying to design a curriculum which would realise certain educational aims: it was a practical necessity that those who followed it should be able to take an examination recognised for entry to higher education on an international scale. But it was the curriculum which came first. Ruth Bonner used to keep a notice or 'text' up in her office: "Stop working for examinations."

Some modifications have been made in the system over the last 15 years, mainly dictated by considerations of cost and speed, as an *artisanat* project initially involving nine schools and 29 candidates grew to a bureaucratic one involving nearly 300 schools and 6,000 candidates. These are described in subsequent chapters.

How far can the IBO claim that the pattern of curriculum and examinations which it presented to the students, the schools, and the universities did in fact conform to the educational aims from which it started? In the field of understanding we had made an attempt to ensure that every student who completed the diploma had studied to some extent the two great tools of thought, the natures and uses of language and mathematics. We considered the possibility of a course in general linguistics, but rejected it in favour of the study of a second language. This was partly because not to include a second language in an international course seemed unacceptable and partly because it is easier to motivate students to study a second language than to study theoretical linguistics. But the argument that the study of a second language gives as good an understanding of the nature of language as the study of linguistics seems to me suspect, unless it is taught more specifically for that purpose. Probably we need to do more thinking about Language B.

We had tried, too, to see that every student had some experience of the natural, experimental sciences and some of the study of man in society. We considered and rejected the proposal that history should become compulsory—although there are some epistemological and social grounds for that—because it would have either extended too far the range of subjects or excluded the whole range of social sciences. If ever an alternative IB with two higher and five subsidiary subjects were to be introduced, as some delegates at our last Study of Man conference proposed, there might well be a case for it.

We had made some provision in the subject syllabuses, but mostly in the Theory of Knowledge, for the discussion of moral, aesthetic, and religious judgements and we had allowed for the student who wanted, in composing what Capelle called his personal bouquet from the garden, to give special emphasis to art or music.

But had we done enough to develop the powers of the individual to modify his environment as well as understand it? There is, I hope, a creative element as well as an interpretative one in many of the syllabuses, and the CASS requirement ensures that it will not be entirely neglected, but I cannot feel that we have yet done enough.

Finally, had we done enough to develop each student's capacity to enjoy his environment? Some educationists may question the importance of this aim. At the Salerno conference, with which this chapter began, I was asked by a Dutch delegate whether I meant that students should be encouraged to go fishing, to which I answered "Yes, but not in lesson time." It must surely be true that a complete education of the whole person should include increasing the capacity to enjoy leisure. In the Anglo-Saxon tradition perhaps too much attention has been given to team games and spectator sport, but there have been other traditions. It was an Englishman who wrote:

> I want to know a butcher paints;
> A baker rhymes for his pursuit,
> Candle-stick maker much acquaints
> His soul with song, or, haply mute,
> Blows out his brains upon the flute.[20]

This kind of enjoyment has to be learnt, and learning it is part of education; so is fishing or water-skiing; but they are not a part of education that can be contained in an examination syllabus. What an organisation like the IBO can do, and we have striven to do, is to ensure that the demands of 'swotting for exams' or *bourrage de crane* leave adequate time for learning to enjoy leisure and that the course of study is itself, as far as possible, enjoyable. You do not make young people good university students of physics or history by making them hate physics or history at school and in the long run it is better that a student leaves school with a love of good literature and an inadequate knowledge of contemporary critical theory than vice versa. To quote one of the most recent surveys of curriculum development: "However successful a teacher may be in developing the pupil's ability to make technical analyses of classical literary works or of scientific phenomena, the educational process cannot be considered successful if it leaves the pupil with a dislike for such material".[21]

It is almost impossibly difficult to establish whether students enjoy their courses and even more difficult to know whether, if they do, that enjoyment will carry over to intellectual enjoyment in later life. Much will depend on the teacher rather than the syllabus—and the influence of a teacher can last almost a lifetime. What we have tried to do with the IB is to give more chance to good teachers by introducing the teacher's assessment into the examination result, to give more chance to good students by a reasonable variety of options, by as much relevance as we can achieve to the variegated world they are going to grow up in, and by as much opportunity as we can contrive for them to find and express their own enthusiasms. I have no proof: I can only say that from my necessarily limited experience of student reactions at our 'consultative conferences', they prefer the IB courses to the alternatives that are offered to them.

Notes to Chapter Three

[1] Aristotle, *Politics* Vol. VIII:2. My translation.

[2] Michel de Montaigne, Essai XIX 'Que philosopher c'est apprendre à mourir', *Essais* (Bordeaux, 1595; later edition, Paris: Lefèvre, 1826).

[3] A.D.C. Peterson, *International Baccalaureate* (London: Harrap, 1972), 94-95.

[4] B. Hoffman, *The Tyranny of Testing* (New York: Collier-Macmillan, 1964).

[5] R. Leach, op. cit., 38.

[6] Montaigne, op. cit., 25.

[7] A.D.C. Peterson, *The Future of the Sixth Form* (London: Routledge & Kegan Paul, 1973), chapter two.

[8] Daniel Bell, *The Reforming of General Education* (New York: Columbia University Press, 1966).

[9] Ibid.

[10] Oxford University Department of Education. *Arts and Science Sides in the Sixth Form: a report to the Gulbenkian Foundation* (Oxford, 1960).

[11] Central Advisory Council for Education, *15 to 18: A Report* (London: Her Majesty's Stationery Office, 1959).

[12] Jean Capelle, *Contre le baccalauréat* (Paris: Berger-Levrault, 1968).

[13] Hellmut Becker, 'Initiating and Implementing Reforms: The Case of the Federal Republic of Germany', in *The Future of Formal Education: The Role of Institutional Schooling in Industrial Society,* ed. Torsten Husén, Proceedings from the International Symposium at the Royal Academy of Sciences, Stockholm, 1978 (Stockholm: Amqvist and Wiksell International, 1979).

[14] Ernest Boyer, *High School* (New York: Harper and Row, 1983), chapter twelve.

[15] A.D.C. Peterson, *International Baccalaureate*, 40-41.

[16] Jill Spence, 'Access to Higher Education in the Federal Republic of Germany: The *Numerus Clausus* Issue', *Comparative Education,* vol. 17, no. 3 (1981): 285-292.

[17] Peterson, *New Techniques for the Assessment of Pupils' Work* (Strasbourg: Council of Europe, 1971).

[18] Peterson, *International Baccalaureate*, 68-70.

[19] G. Panchaud, et al., *La Valeur objective des Examens* (Paris:Payot, 1969).

[20] R. Browning, *Collected Poems* (Oxford: Oxford University Press, 1905).

[21] Daniel and Laurel Tanner, *Curriculum Development: Theory into Practice* (New York: Macmillan, 1975).

4
THE SIX-YEAR
EXPERIMENT WITH THE IB

The International Baccalaureate team left the Sèvres conference of 1967 with a small network of international supporters and widespread encouragement to embark on the proposed six-year experiment. The desirability of providing a common curriculum for international schools leading to examinations which would enable their students to cross national frontiers and enter universities in many parts of the world was not questioned. The question was whether it would prove feasible.

Within this consensus, however, there were initially certain divisions of opinion about the nature of the experiment, some of which have persisted throughout our history. There were also great practical difficulties to be overcome which the reader will find recurring again and again. Let us deal with the differences of opinion first. There were some members of the Council, notably Professor Panchaud, who initially conceived of the experiment mainly as a piece of applied educational research. For this purpose it seemed desirable that the number of schools involved should be strictly limited and the performance of students, the predictive validity and reliability of different examining techniques and the effects of an international and multi-cultural curriculum most strictly monitored, perhaps in a few selected universities. There were others, notably, of course, the representatives of the schools and particularly of Atlantic College, who saw the permanent establishment of an IB as the solution to what was for them an urgent and otherwise insoluble problem. They regarded the six-year experiment as the introductory phase of something which simply must, by one means or another, become permanent. To them any opportunities for pedagogical research, either in curriculum or examinations, would be a minor spin-off.

This difference of opinion was reasonably quickly resolved and by 1973 Panchaud himself was urging that we should give a higher priority to serving the needs of the international community than to research. If the IB had been confined to a small, select, and highly concentrated group of schools and universities, where close monitoring would have been practicable, the experiment would have provided evidence neither of its general applicability nor of its financial viability.

The additional argument sometimes advanced against the potential contribution of the experiment to more general research, that the group of students involved was not only too small to be statistically significant, but also an unrepresentative sample, has always seemed to me to have been based on a misunderstanding. It was true that they were either the children of relatively rich parents, being educated in their local international school, or those selected for scholarships to Atlantic College. What was not adequately recognised was that this did not make them an unrepresentative sample. Students who at that period remained in school after the age of sixteen were, in Western Europe and even more in the Third World, also either the children of relatively rich parents or the winners of scholarships. Nor were they, any more than the university-bound cohort in national schools, an 'intellectual elite'. Indeed the students at Atlantic College, and later at the other United World Colleges, were selected for scholarships on a wide range of criteria, many of them much more concerned with character and commitment than with purely academic promise.

It may well be that the potential contribution to research, particularly in countries where there is an interest in developing either a more coherent or a better balanced upper secondary course, is greater now than it was during the experimental period. At least, this seems to be indicated by the increasing use of the IB in selected schools within national systems. But the main reason why national governments have supported it is not as a 'test-bed for research', but for the service it renders to the international community and the mobile student.

Another difference of opinion which has had a more lasting influence on the policy of the IBO has been based on political rather than pedagogical values. There were some who held, and still hold, the view that if the IB is an experiment in international education then the languages in which it is available must, as far as possible, be extended to all the world's main tongues; the cultures on which it is based must as far as possible represent the main world cultures; and the IB schools should as far as possible be equally spread throughout the world, with no one area predominating.

The more pragmatic among us were more concerned with meeting existing needs and made continual use of the saving clause "as far as possible".

It was inevitable, in view of the large part played by French educators and by the French Ministry of Education in launching the whole project, that a Geneva-based office should operate in French: on the other hand it quickly became very clear that the overwhelming majority of schools which wished to adopt the IB operated in English. None operated in Chinese, Russian, or Arabic. From the first, therefore, the IBO was bilingual rather than multilingual. But even so we were not funded like a UN agency, and soon realized the heavy cost of publishing everything even in just two languages. Simultaneous translation for all meetings and not merely for the annual meeting of the Council is still beyond our resources. In any case an early experience of its use in a panel of mathematicians, held in Paris, convinced me that in highly technical subjects it was a doubtful blessing. We therefore started by relying on the fact that all our collaborators, or at least the great majority of them, if they did not speak French and English fluently, at least understood both languages, especially when spoken by those who spoke their own language with a foreign listener in mind. John Goormaghtigh and Gérard Renaud were particularly adept at speaking French in this way, but the greatest artist I ever heard was Madame Hatinguais, who lectured in French at the Oxford Department of Education and appeared to me to be understoood by everyone in the room. This system worked reasonably well so long as the teachers needed to participate in subject panels came mainly from a small group of international schools in Europe. As soon as the IB spread to North America, Asia, and anglophone Africa, the language problem became more difficult. Pragmatism has usually found a way. Either the English speaker who does not understand French, or his French counterpart who does not understand English, is seated next to a neighbour who translates for him, or the convener of the panel seeks to find sufficient bilingual colleagues when assembling the team, although this may be at the expense of other qualities. One is reminded of the story of the Canadian life-guard on one of the beaches, thanking another swimmer for carrying out a very efficient rescue:

"But you're the life-guard. Why didn't you do it?"

"Oh, I can't swim."

"You can't swim? How on earth did you get the job?"

"I'm bilingual."

The question of introducing a third language did not arise during the period of the six-year experiment. The first school in Spain, Viaro near Barcelona, did not join until 1973 and the two Latin American schools, The British Schools, Montevideo, and the Colegio Colombo Britannico, Cali, were operating in English as well as Spanish.

If we could not for economic and administrative reasons adhere strictly to political imperatives in the matter of administrative languages, we could at least do something for the individual candidates. This led to a regulation that although the examination questions would be set only in English or French, a candidate could apply for permission to write answers in a third language: and this permission would be given if the examiner or, as the numbers grew, a member of the examining team, could read papers in that language. This, too, worked well enough in the early days. Erwin Baurmann, our first chief examiner in physics, was happy to read papers in German as well as French or English. Now, as we shall see later, it is beginning to be questioned, not on economic grounds but by the docimologists (examination experts). Although our use of languages for administration and for the whole battery of examinations was thus politically rather less than truly international, we did at least ensure, as a matter of principle, that a student of whatever nationality should be able to offer his mother tongue as one of the two required languages. Such students usually offered their mother tongue as Language B and the language of instruction of the school as Language A. This meant that it was easy for them to get a high grade in Language B and some of us thought this unfair, but the prevailing view was that this no more than compensated for the disadvantage they suffered from studying all their other subjects in what was for them a foreign language. Nor did we think that university admissions officers would be falsely impressed by seeing that a Thai student had got a high grade in Thai as Language B. The problem of dialects, presented for instance by a West African girl who told me that her mother tongue was only spoken in her own group of villages and that she would prefer to offer Latin as Language B, was solved by ruling that we would only examine in languages which had a written literature. This led to a strange conversation when I was first asked if we would examine in Wollof. The West African Examinations Board then had an office in London, so I consulted them.

"You're lucky," they said. "Our Wollof examiner happens to be in London so I'll put you on to him."

"Can you tell me, Sir, if Wollof has a written literature?"

"Not yet," came the reply. "I am writing it."

These languages were usually maintained by students through private study, though we tried to ensure that the schools always found a coach for the individual student. This was not too difficult in international cities. At first we called them 'rare' languages, until a very charming Chinese lady, sitting next to me at one of the language conferences whispered: "Chinese would be medium rare, I suppose." This led to a revised designation of 'Infrequently Offered Languages'. Policy on languages remains and is likely to remain an area of divergent opinions. We shall come back to it in chapter seven.

Policy about dispersion, whether the IBO should seek to recruit an internationally balanced group of schools in which no cultural area predominated or should simply respond to demand, may have roots in Professor Panchaud's original concept of the project as a whole. For purely pragmatic reasons it hardly arose during the first six years. We would have liked a genuinely international distribution, but the first essential was to recruit a sufficiently large and diverse group of schools to demonstrate that the project was feasible and filled a need.

Let us turn now to the practical problems. They were all interrelated. We needed to extend the number of schools using the IB both absolutely and in terms of geographical spread and variation of type. Within those schools, particularly those day schools like Ecolint and UNIS which hoped to use IB as their sole pre-university course, we had to persuade any remaining groups of parents who were reluctant to entrust their children's futures to an untried experiment. In order to do that we had to secure acceptance from an ever-widening group of universities. We had to set up an administrative structure which would see us through six years. All this was going to cost a lot of money, but all of it depended on the degree of success we could achieve in establishing a curriculum and examinations of the kind described in the preceding chapter, and this became the first task of the new administration. The interrelationship between the problems helped a lot. The response of the universities reassured the parents, and the enthusiasm of the schools was a potent factor in raising money, as UNIS had demonstrated in relation to the Ford Foundation grant. We shall return to Finance and Administration at the end of this chapter, but meanwhile it is worth recording one great stroke of good fortune which affected all our inter-related problems. It was one of those coincidences of timing which often decide the success or failure of new initiatives. I do not refer here to the fact that the period of our experiment, 1967-1975, coincided, initially at least, with the most recent period of Western prosperity, when money for good causes was relatively easy to raise, but to a crucial development among the international schools.

In February 1968, one year after the Sèvres conference, Lord Mountbatten agreed to become chairman not just of Atlantic College, but of a more widely internationalised group of such colleges, which he was determined to establish, as his final contribution to the avoidance of World War Three. To this chain he subsequently gave the name of the United World Colleges. I had known Mountbatten during the war; I was seconded from the Special Operations Executive to serve on his staff when he was Supreme Allied Commander, South East Asia. My somewhat strange appointment as Deputy-Director of Psychological Warfare and the secret nature of some of my duties meant that I met him from time to time on a more informal basis that was usual for a comparatively junior officer and this contact probably made subsequent co-operation between IBO and UWC easier. I can remember a conference on the United World Colleges at Princeton when he told the audience: "If you want to know anything about this International Baccalaureate, you can ask Alec Peterson. He's one of my wartime spies," and added with true naval authority: "You can recognise him by his scruffy beard." Mountbatten very quickly realised that his grand design for a world-wide chain of United World Colleges depended on the success of the IB experiment and the continued existence of the examinations. His success in establishing that chain forms the subject of the next chapter, but it is worth recording here that on three occasions when IBO seemed to be heading for the rocks of financial disaster, he intervened personally to save us. I am as sure that without this help and the input of students and teachers from the United World Colleges, the IBO would have foundered, as I am sure that without the IB, the United World College fleet could never have set sail.

The first practical problem to be tackled was of course the establishment of an administration and the preparation of examinations. In 1968 the IB office moved from its first home at Ecolint to a charming villa in Cologny on the outskirts of Geneva. An officer experienced in examinations, Jim Sellars, was appointed on eighteen months' secondment from the Inner London Education Authority. It had been agreed that after my sabbatical year I should return to Oxford, but spend two or three weeks at Christmas and Easter in Geneva and five or six in the summer, acting as a part-time Director-General. With the aid of the Ecolint team, Gérard Renaud, Ruth Bonner, and Lucette, and the Oxford unit under Bill Halls, we were able to provide a full range of 'trial' examinations for the early summer of 1969 and promise the first 'real' session for 1970. This involved the gradual recruitment of an international Board of Chief Examiners and a growing number of assistants.

There were some reservations about the quality of the first trial examinations both at Atlantic College and UNIS, Atlantic sticking for the moment to A-levels and UNIS to Advanced Placement; but both were determined to go on with the experiment. In 1970 the first 'real' examinations, carrying the promise of university recognition, were held. The gradual growth in the number of candidates over the six years is shown in the following table:

year	certificate candidates	full-diploma candidates	pass rate for diploma
1970	696	29	
1971	681	76	70%
1972	631	151	63%
1973	840	311	79%
1974	634	386	80%
1975	840	377	75%

The limit set by the universities and national ministries of not more than 500 university candidates each year was never exceeded or even reached during the six-year period, since those who entered for individual certificates only were not using them as entrance qualifications, but either for exemption from similar freshman courses in American colleges or simply for personal satisfaction. The general pass rate for the full diploma, although based on criterion referencing rather than norm referencing, stabilised after the first three years and has generally remained between 72% and 80% ever since. This pass rate was slightly higher than that expected either in the GCE A-level or the French *baccalauréat*, which in 1970 varied for the different *filières* between 55.5% and 74.4%. This seems justified since a 'pass' represented the absolute minimum for university entrance and there was always a preponderance of United World College students, who had been initially selected as capable of achieving this. At Hammersmith and West London College of Further Education which, rightly in my opinion, practised open entry to its IB course, the pass rate was always significantly lower than the overall average. That the standard represented a level acceptable to universities is evidenced by their continued acceptance of it after the end of the six-year experiment and by the results of the statistical analysis of correlations between IB and final degree results in the United Kingdom carried out by the Schools Council in 1979.

Negotiations to secure the co-operation of universities had started immediately after the Sèvres Conference, since it was clear that if the six-year experiment were to start in 1970 it was essential that the recruitment of a representative group of participating schools should be accompanied by assurances from a wide range of universities that the new diplomas and certificates would be genuinely recognised for entry or placement. This did not prove as difficult as some people had expected. The growing mobility of students meant that most universities were already accepting a small but regular intake of students on the basis of foreign qualifications. The IB might be new and untried, but it did at least offer the university authorities a chance to collaborate in a limited experiment which might provide a more convenient method of assessing a candidate's qualifications than the attempt to analyse and compare twenty or thirty different national qualifications. It was as much in their interests as in ours that the experiment should succeed.

The universities to which the great majority of students from international schools wanted to go were those of Europe and North America. For the very few from Eastern Europe our Polish Council Member, Madame Zakowa, made it clear that within these national systems the secondary school-leaving certificate merely entitled the student to enter for the quite separate university entrance examinations and was not used as the basis for university selection—just as in England the GCE A-level was not used for selection to Oxford or Cambridge. What was needed, therefore, was simply the recognition of the IB as a secondary school-leaving certificate, after which the mobile student could compete in the normal university selection on equal terms with those who had attended national schools at home. In practice this presented no difficulties and a trickle of students was soon entering such universities as Warsaw or Budapest and finding their IB preparation perfectly adequate. It was to universities in the United States that the largest group of IB students sought entry. Here also results in the IB examinations were not directly relevant to university entry. This was based on SATs and other factors and had been completed in the early months of the year, long before the IB examinations were taken. Gradually, as the IB became better known, the fact that a student was enrolled in a full IB course could affect an application for entry, but the actual results of the examination were used for placement after entry or for exemption from specific freshman courses. Decisions on such recognitions were, of course, the responsibility of each university, as they were in England, and we sometimes found it difficult at this period to explain to our continental European colleagues that there was no authority covering the USA or England with whom they could discuss the conditions for entry to university.

Desmond Cole and Harpo Hanson did a great job of explaining the project at individual universities, and the fact that first Harvard and then Princeton were prepared to offer holders of the full IB diploma a direct entry to the sophomore year did much for our reputation in the US. In actual practice, however, offers of this type of full advanced placement have not been very often taken up. Students have preferred to enter the freshman year with their contemporaries and to use their IB qualifications to secure exemption from specific freshman courses, thus widening or accelerating their total university courses.

The next largest group of potential candidates was those seeking entry to British universities. Here, of course I was able to make quite a lot of contacts myself, but in order to ensure that every university was approached, we secured in June 1968 the part-time services of Leslie Stephens, who had just retired as headmaster of a small 'public school', to act as our Universities liaison officer. By March 1969 he or I had contacted every university in the UK and all but seven had accepted. Leslie continued to play a great part as an IB consultant.

There remained the continental European universities where decisions lay with a central authority rather than with individual universities. The response of the French Ministry of Education was crucial, but their co-operation in the whole project had been so close that a first step, in the form of recognition for foreign students and French students whose parents had lived abroad for more than two years, was almost immediate. This was all right for the normal mobile student in an international school but not enough for Atlantic College, since in their case it was the students and not the parents who had lived abroad. Thanks to the tireless efforts of Mountbatten, this hurdle was also surmounted and in 1974 a decree was passed extending the equivalence to all UWC students irrespective of nationality. The remaining problem, as we shall see in so many other countries, was recognition of the IB as an alternative entrance qualification for French students educated in France. This had caused no difficulty in Britain or the US where decisions on admission rested with the individual college or university, but presented and still presents a major problem in countries where this rite of passage is controlled by a central authority and competition for university places is so sharp a political issue that anything which looks like 'back door entry' is unacceptable.

The solution eventually found in France was to authorise certain schools to offer the IB and to recognise this for entry to French universities only for students from these schools, but initially at least French students at the Lycée International de St Germain had to prepare to sit both examinations.

In other continental European countries the first step had sometimes been taken by direct negotiation between a school and University authorities for a special dispensation. This procedure had been adopted by the Goethe Gymnasium in Frankfurt and Vigbysholm outside Stockholm. Our policy was to seek to extend these arrangements to cover IB schools as a whole and by 1969 Lord Hankey, who had previously been British ambassador in Stockholm, with the help of his colleague on the IB Council, Dr Andren, had achieved this in Sweden, while in Germany a special 'nostrification' process had been agreed for all students from the three founder schools, Atlantic College, Ecolint, and UNIS.

All these arrangements were, of course, provisional and covered the six-year period only. By the end of 1973, 20 countries had accorded a general and others a partial recognition on this basis and IB students were already attending 175 different universities in 25 countries.

From what sort of schools, then, did this growing number of students come? In establishing a policy about the recruitment of new schools we were naturally concerned to ensure that they should be capable of teaching the IB programme successfully, but the requirement to demonstrate the range of its applicability pressed two other considerations on us. We sought diversity of type and we sought diversity of location. The standard type was of course the private fee-paying international school, created to meet the needs of an international community, such as Ecolint in Geneva or UNIS in New York. But we sought also to show that an international baccalaureate would have something to offer to schools in the publicly-maintained systems which either served to some extent a multi-national intake or were authorised to experiment with a more internationally-oriented curriculum. Schools of this type in the founding group were the Lycée Pilote de Sèvres outside Paris and the Goethe Gymnasium in Frankfurt, though neither entered very many candidates. One bright idea which proved to be an illusion was that newly independent countries, which were in the process of abandoning curricula and examinations based on those of former colonial powers, such as the GCE or the *baccalauréat*, might wish to adopt the IB, at least temporarily, since it would continue to give their students access to foreign universities which a new national examination might not at first. I spent a week in Malta during this period, discussing such a project with the Maltese Ministry of Education, but in the end Malta, like many other 'new nations', preferred to develop its own national system.

One restriction that we did adopt was that we would not make the IB available to 'proprietary' schools, that is, to schools conducted for private profit. I think our reasons at the time were, first, that other schools had a prior claim in a period of restricted expansion and, second, concern for our image. Some sceptics or adversaries at first tended to dismiss this 'Geneva baccalaureate' as being obviously intended for Swiss 'Girls' finishing schools'. We felt we had to scotch that one.

Now that the IB is more firmly and widely established it may prove that this decision was one of our early mistakes. There is some force in the argument that if the IB programme is the best

available education for students of this type it is unfair to deny it
to them because of the financial organisation of their school. Moreover it is in practice quite difficult to establish the criteria which
identify a 'proprietorial' or 'profit-making' school. There are many
grey areas in the definition of 'not for profit' in the tax legislation
of different countries; and if in any one city the only international
school available to students is one which fails to satisfy these
criteria, should they then be denied the IB?

As a sample of the range and type of school involved during
this six-year period, let me attempt brief pen portraits of seven
schools, representing a wide range of both type and location.

I have not included in this group the three 'founders', Atlantic
College, Ecolint, and UNIS since reference to them occurs throughout this book. Nor shall I deal here with new United World Colleges nor new schools in Canada or the USA since they form the
theme of the next two chapters.

Iranzamin

The first school in the Middle East to enter candidates for IB
examinations was Iranzamin. This school, under the leadership of
a remarkable principal, Dick Irvine, had been formed as a break-
away from the American Community School in Tehran with the
intention of giving an international rather than an American education. Dick struck me as one of those quiet, non-proselytising,
but firmly principled former missionaries who have so often won
the confidence of Eastern communities for their schools. When the
Chinese mission was expelled from the Shah's Iran, the school
inherited the former Chinese embassy and their first science laboratory was converted from the embassy greenhouse. The international character of Iranzamin made the IB obviously appropriate
and helped the school to attract a growing number of Iranian
pupils. The French Ministry wished the school to be inspected and
I visited it first with van Smevoorde, the French Inspector-General,
in 1968. We combined the job of sorting out some of the problems
involved in adapting the IB to the situation in Tehran with conducting the trial oral examinations in English and French. The

problems, as might have been expected, were concerned with languages, history, and economics, and with the general question of the admission of Iranian nationals to Iranian universities on the basis of the IB rather than the national examinations. The first and the last were solved by a compromise which IBO might well not have been prepared to extend indefinitely. Iranian students took the national examinations in Farsi (Persian) language and literature, and their grades in these examinations were accepted as grades in Language A by the IBO. History and economics did not present as great problems as we had feared. Once the Iranian authorities were assured that although Marxism appeared on the syllabus we were teaching *about* Marxism and not attempting to proselytize, no further objections were raised. This may have been because they already knew and trusted Dick Irvine or it may have been because they knew that if there were any indoctrination going on they would find out about it very quickly. In conversation with Western or Westernised students I was told: "Of course there are Savak agents in the school and we know who they are. But they don't bother us and we don't bother them." Dick told me that the only time he had ever had a phone call on that sort of issue was when the school film society showed *Battleship Potemkin*. The police knew within 24 hours and asked why he was showing Russian propaganda, making it clear that this was going a bit far; but nobody suffered.

On a second visit to Iranzamin I was able to combine the roles of oral examiner and fund-raiser. About half-way through the six-year period, it was beginning to look very doubtful that we should have the funds to complete it. Mountbatten had therefore secured for me an audience with the Shah in the hope that he might offer some help.

It was an alarming prospect. As I approached the palace I had visions of being led into a throne room and being expected to bow three times before opening the conversation with some such words as 'May your Imperial Majesty live for ever.' In fact it was very different. I had passed through a few corridors and waited not more than five minutes in an ante-room when a small man, looking to me more like a university professor than a King of Kings, opened the door and asked me in. We sat and chatted very pleasantly about education for about three quarters of an hour. Mainly, I must admit, he was telling me about his educational plans for Iran rather than I him about the IB. "What I would really like", he said, "would be to set up a chain of boarding schools in Iran like your English public schools." Then, perhaps remembering the swinging sixties: "not like they are now of course, but like they used to be. The schools that built your Empire—oh, but of course, one doesn't use that word now."

However, I did get in a few words about the IB and we seemed to part on very amicable terms.

That evening at my hotel, I got a telephone call from the Minister at Court which asked me one of the most difficult questions I have ever had to answer: "His Imperial Majesty would like to make a grant to help the International Baccalaureate. How much do you want?" Ask for too little, one would never forgive one's self: ask for too much, one might get nothing.

With ten seconds to think, I replied: "one hundred thousand dollars". And in due course, by installments, it arrived.

National College, Choueifat

The other Middle Eastern school, National College, Choueifat (a suburb of Beirut), did not actually enter candidates until 1971, but the Principal, Charles Sa'd was already a member of the IB Council. He was a great believer in education as a builder of bridges between communities, religions, and nations. The school had been founded by his father in 1886 and numbered many Arabs from outside Lebanon among its former pupils, although its background was Maronite. In those happy years, almost incredible today, Lebanon was known as 'the Switzerland of the Middle East', partly, I suppose, because of a shared interest in banking and commerce, but mainly for the success in harmonising different cultural, religious, and linguistic traditions. In such circumstances the school flourished and was able to do much towards achieving the sort of aims which it shared with the United World Colleges. I visited it on my Middle Eastern tour with van Smevoorde in 1968 and we were impressed by the quality of the education. Approval by the Lebanese Government and recognition of the IB were, of course, essential and this involved a visit to the Prime Minister. As soon as we entered his room he rose from his desk with genuine smile of welcome: "Ah, Charlie, my old teacher." From that moment Sa'd was Charlie to me also. He had a quality of warmth which extended not only to those who sympathised with his views, but also to pupils, past and present, of the school. When the troubles began, I saw on the records of two Choueifat candidates, in the section where the teacher recorded any special factors which might affect the students' performance: 'These two boys took their examinations under mortar fire.'

The one problem which even the goodwill of the Prime Minister could not solve for us was the recognition of the IB as an entry qualification to Lebanese universities for Lebanese students educated within Lebanon. In vain we argued the importance of the foreign students at Choueifat not being separated from the Lebanese and thus losing the cultural contacts with the host country which should be one of the main advantages of an international education. The arguments which had made the French Ministry so reluctant to concede this acceptance prevailed also in Lebanon, reinforced perhaps by the fear that any concessions made to the IBO might be seized upon as a precedent by other special interests.

As the violence of the conflict within Beirut increased, Choueifat became virtually untenable and the school moved out. This was not a flight into exile like that of the teachers and students from Iranzamin who ended up in Spain, but a planned move. New 'daughter schools' were opened, first in Sharjah, and later in Abu Dhabi and Al Ain. The latest in this chain is the International School of Choueifat UK, near Chippenham, England. Presided over by Charlie's widow, Leila, the Choueifat Schools have kept alive and growing Charlie's vision and the name of Choueifat.

The British School Montevideo

The British School Montevideo was opened for eight pupils on 8th October, 1908. It was originally intended to develop as a preparatory school for children of the British community resident in Montevideo, Uruguay. Within a short time it expanded rapidly and in 1925 moved into its first purpose-built school building. Further expansion brought with it the incorporation of the first Uruguayan students (now the vast majority), co-education from 1936, and the first Uruguayan national secondary courses in 1940.

By 1958 there were already 700 pupils in the school and a further move was initiated to the present site, acquired some years previously, in the suburb of Carrasco. By 1965 the whole school was accommodated on the Carrasco site, and by 1970 was reaching its current capacity of some 1,000 pupils. External examinations were originally taken only by pupils taking the full range of subjects in English, but in the latter part of the 1960s those in the Uruguayan *liceo* started being prepared, first for GCE O-levels as was the case for the English side, and then from 1970 for the International Baccalaureate. It was the first school in the Southern Hemisphere to start working for the IB. The school had also attracted a considerable international clientele which made the switch to IB particularly suitable. In this bilingual school on the cultural frontier between the Latin and the Anglo-Saxon, the IB was a great success from the start, and today all students at the top of the school are being prepared for either the diploma or certificates. Peter Stoyle, who was headmaster when I visited the school, moved some years later to St George's Buenos Aires and has long been the highly successful regional officer for both IBO and UWC in South America.

Lycée International de St Germain-en-Laye

The Lycée international de St Germain, in one of the most beautiful and historic suburbs of Paris, owes its origin to the school established by the French government to serve the children of NATO personnel when NATO headquarters were in Paris. When France withdrew from NATO, St Germain took on a new role, serving the international community of Western Paris. It remained a state school with all the facilities, accommodation, and overheads provided by the French Ministry of Education. Bilateral agreements were, however, drawn up with Federal Germany and the Netherlands by which those governments undertook to continue appointing and paying teachers for St Germain. Unfortunately no such agreements were forthcoming elsewhere. Consequently the British, American, Swedish, and Danish parents all formed what amounted to private companies to collect fees and oversee all expenses for the continued running of their sections. These sections had been established by the Proviseur, Edgar Schérer, an inter-nationalist, in the NATO days, so that the whole school could follow a common core programme with French as the language of instruction and each national section having in addition lessons in the national language and culture.

It is not surprising, therefore, that Schérer quickly saw the po-tential of the IB as a unifying factor in the academic structure of the school, with each national group educated in the earlier stages both in French and in their national language. I remember on my first visit being enchanted by the purity of their French, when I listened to some of the smallest English primary school children singing French songs, and wishing all children could have a bilin-gual education.

Schérer had played a leading role in the negotiations leading up to the Sèvres conference and candidates were entered for the first examination session in 1970.

From its inauguration in 1977 until 1983 he served as one of the heads of schools representatives on the IBO Council, while Madame Bardinet, the IB Co-ordinator, contributed substantially to the curriculum panels. Joined later by representatives from the French-American School in San Francisco and the École Active Bilingue in Paris they formed an active group maintaining the French contribution to the developments of the IB.

The main difficulty in using the IB as a unifying factor was, as in so many other countries, the reluctance of the national author-ities, in this case the French Ministry of Education, to recognise the IB as an alternative track for their own nationals.

English, Dutch, Italian, or Scandinavian students could form combined IB classes, but French students still had to prepare the French *baccalauréat*. Fortunately there was enough similarity be-tween some of the programmes for students to work together for much of the time although preparing for different examinations and some enthusiasts actually sat both examinations, although for them only the *baccalauréat* was required.

Subsequently, in the late seventies, this situation was modified and the IB was accepted as an alternative track to university en-trance, even for French students, from St Germain and three other authorised schools. This situation is again under review as a result of the introduction of the special international option of the French Baccalaureate. One of the great disadvantages of the IB for French students, whether in an international school in those cities where no *lycée français* exists, or in a United World College or in authorised schools in France, is that although the IB enjoys 'equivalence' for entry to French universities, possession of a national *baccalauréat* is a requirement for entry to posts in government service and here an 'equivalent' qualification is unacceptable. It may be that this barrier has been responsible for the fact that very few French students are to be found in United World Colleges.

Hammersmith and West London College of Further Education

In 1972 the IB was introduced for the first time not in an international school nor an experimental school, but in one of the colleges of further education forming part of the public educational system provided for London by the Inner London Education Authority. In such colleges no fees are paid and the age of the students may range from 16 to 60. Most of the IB students were between 16 and 20 and I saw a lot of them because, when in 1973 I finally took early retirement from Oxford in order to concentrate on the IB, I joined the staff of Hammersmith and West London as a 'part-time lecturer' teaching the IB Theory of Knowledge course. In return for this, the College gave me the use of a minuscule office and the services of a part-time secretary, who became a great enthusiast and recruiting agent for the IB.

The decision of the college to join this barely-fledged experiment was, as usual, due to a number of personal factors: The principal, Bill Bonney Rust, had done some research in the Oxford department on his sabbatical year; the teacher in charge of international education, Gabriel Green, had read about IB in the educational press and conceived a burning enthusiasm for the project; E.H. Briault, the enlighted director of the Inner London Education Authority, had been deeply involved in the abortive attempts to broaden the English sixth-form curriculum and was glad to authorise one of his colleges to experiment with an alternative.

The college, now magnificently housed on the old site of St Paul's School in Kensington, was then dispersed over a number of small campuses and the IB was taught at Hugon Road near Wandsworth Bridge. For me it was a bit of a change, after years of a ten-minute drive to a rather well-appointed office in Oxford, to take a series of buses across London to the largish cupboard which served IB as the 'office of the Director-General'. I was much better off during the weeks which I still spent in Geneva. But we could not afford anything more, and I was very grateful both for house-room and for the chance to teach real IB students. They were a splendid mixture: the son of an academic (whom I later met as head of a Cambridge College), bored with the rigidity of his conventional school and A-level courses; drop-outs from the North London comprehensive where Gabriel's Jamaican wife was a teacher; an unforgettably pretty French girl who had run a beauty salon in fashionable Chelsea and who explained her decision to come back to college when her boutique failed by saying "I knew all about beauty, but I didn't know how to run a business, so I thought I'd better get some education". A large proportion, though not by any means all, were either foreign or immigrants and teaching that part of the Theory of Knowledge course which deals with moral codes and religion to a mixed class of Christians of many varieties, Buddhists, Moslems, and those who claimed to be 'nothing' was a fascinating experience.

John Horne, an inner-city high school teacher from Los Angeles, wrote recently (*Los Angeles Times*, October 13, 1984): "Last year I had the privilege of teaching ancient history to two classes of tenth graders. Two dialogues of Plato, the *Apology* and *Crito*, were what the kids enjoyed most. Even one of my most turned-off students, 'Grumpy Rochelle' stayed after class to tell me how much she had enjoyed reading them. And why, you doubters may ask, did minority group kids in an inner-city high school enjoy Plato so much? I believe it is because Plato has given them a new hero, a fellow by the name of Socrates. The story of Socrates' trial and death is one that transcends time, social class and race."

Reading this recalled vividly almost exactly the same experience I had had with a similar group at Hammersmith and West London. Dina Dreyfus had recommended the *Euthyphro* as reading for the Theory of Knowledge course and we got it in a Penguin Classics edition called *The Last Days of Socrates* which also included the *Apology*, *Crito* and some extracts from the *Phaedo*. The reaction of my mixed race students in London exactly parrallelled that of his in Los Angeles.

The college started with a restricted range of IB options, as had many schools, but in time growing enrolments made a wider range possible. Enrolments did grow as first a Spanish and then a Scandinavian school, which could only provide education for their nationals up to the age of sixteen, began sending their students on to Hammersmith and West London for the final two years. For the last five years HWLC has regularly entered 40-60 candidates for the IB diploma.

International School, Moshi (Tanzania)

This school was founded by the Good Samaritan Foundation in 1969 with capital grants from the Board of World Missions of the Lutheran Church in America. Moshi lies at the foot of Mount Kilimanjaro; a primary purpose of the school was to provide education for the children of expatriates working in the Kilimanjaro Christian Medical Center. It adopted the IB in 1973, because, as its brochure (1983-4) says, "we find in the International Baccalaureate programme the ideal framework for our programme of studies and extra-curriculum activities". Moshi's student body has always contained a sizeable number of Scandinavians because of the Lutheran connection; the following extracts from a letter from a Finnish student to Ruth Bonner give something of the feel of the pioneering days:

> Dear Mrs. Bonner:
>
> I do not know if you remember me, since you meet so many foreign students but I am the fellow who visited the IB office towards the end of July this year. You surprised me by giving me the IB diploma which I thought I had not earned. You also helped me to find a place where I could stay overnight and introduced me to a previous IB student with whose friends I spent a nice evening talking about things, mostly education.
>
> Thanks for everything you did for me at that time. Thanks also for the IB organisation for providing me among others the chance of acquiring a secondary school diploma while studying abroad. If I would have had to complete my Finnish secondary school in Tanzania by correspondence, I would have been in a very unpleasant situation. Studying the IB courses in the International School in Moshi, I could be among other students and share their problems and they mine. Thank you very much.
>
> The entrance examinations for the Science department in the Helsinki University were very easy. The IB course, namely, was much wider both in chemistry and physics than the corresponding courses in Finnish high schools. I got just about the top marks in both tests.

I selected to study chemistry as my major subject, and started mathematics as one of the minors. Other minors I haven't decided yet since I'm not sure how I will specialize in chemistry. Right now I think I will specialize in biochemistry next year.

My other future plans include also studies abroad but yet I have no ideas of the site and time. I guess I will study here in Finland for a couple of years and then start to think about going abroad for longer studies. Financing those studies will be the major problem. I guess I must hunt for scholarships when the time comes. Working and studying at the same time is not very effective but even that would be interesting for a while, say for three months in summer. Therefore I ask if the IB organization with its international ties knows anything about scholarships available or laboratories providing work and at the same time practical training for foreign students of chemistry. Maybe there is an organization in Geneva that specializes in these matters. With any information I would be greatly thankful. Just as thankful as I am for the IB.

Apart from Scandinavians the student body is drawn from a wide range of different countries (approximately 30 in 1980) with strong contingents from Britain, Germany, and India. The Tanzanian government does not encourage African students to attend private international schools, but there has usually been a fairly large group of Tanzanian Indians. The school as always made a special effort to integrate with the local community and the Tanzanian principle of self-reliance is exemplified in its philosophy and its IB 'Cass activities'. Students work on the *shamba* or school farm, help with maintenance and support services at the medical centre, bring children from the local orphanage to the school swimming pool, help with local road and bridge building and have cleared trails and built a climbers' hut on Mount Kilimanjaro. All these activities are co-ordinated by the Students' *Ujoma* or Community Service Council. Although a Christian foundation, it includes among its students Hindus, Muslims, and Sikhs. The school maintains close ties, including teacher exchanges and visits, with the United World Colleges, in particular with Waterford Kam-Hlaba in Swaziland.

Colegio Colombo-Britannico

The Colegio Colombo-Britannico in Cali is a private, Catholic co-educational school founded in 1956 by a group of Colombians who wanted to provide for their children a bilingual education.

Although it is a comparatively recent foundation its name associates it with the long-established chain of schools in South America offering a British type of education and one of the founders was the honorary British Consul. The student body are 95% Colombian but the curriculum is genuinely bi-lingual and about a quarter of the teaching staff is British on the usual two-year contracts. At present it has nearly one thousand pupils, between six and eighteen.

The present Director, Jack Cushnan, who is also British, took over the school in December 1972. He was seeking a programme less encyclopaedic than that leading to the Colombian *bachillerato* and less specialised than the English GCE. Among the papers left by his predecessor (who is, by a curious coincidence, the present Director of Examinations of the IBO) he found a brief note suggesting that the school should investigate the IB, which was at that time being introduced in the British Schools, Montevideo and in Santiago College, Chile. The decision was quickly taken and the first two candidates, both girls, completed their full IB diplomas in 1976, scoring very good grades.

One of the advantages of the IB to Colegio Colombo-Britannico, as to many other schools in Latin America, was that it provided pupils with a sense of participation in a wider world and an opportunity to match their performance against more widely recognised standards than the local ones of the Colombian *bachillerato*. It is probably this sense of responding to a challenge which has led to an increasing enthusiasm among them for participation in the IB programme, although this involves a heavy work-load, since they have also to fulfil the curricular requirements of the *bachillerato*. By 1984, ten years after introducing the programme, more than half the graduating class of about 40 are normally involved in it, with a quarter taking the full diploma. Some have used it for entry to top-rank American colleges or British universities, but the great majority continue to go on to the university in Colombia, where on academic record the college is regularly ranked in the first ten of Colombian schools. For Colegio Colombo-Britannico, as for many IB schools in other parts of the world, the greatest step forward would be recognition of the IB as an alternative university entrance qualification to national universities for Colombian citizens educated in Colombia.

And so, finally, to the sixty-four thousand dollar questions, finance and administration. One thing we most certainly did not do when presenting the IB project to the Sèvres conference of 1967 was to submit detailed estimates either of the cost of the six-year experiment or where we expected the rest of the money to come from. Like the founders of Atlantic College, we were convinced that the idea was right, that in the long run it would prove financially viable and that in the meanwhile we would chance our arm. Those who backed us were investing in an idea and in people, not in detailed plans and projections.

The first two and a half years were very busy, setting up the organisation and providing first the trial and then the real examinations for 1970. On the other hand the expenses were not high and we were able to rely for funds almost entirely on grants from our first sponsors. The Ford Foundation was sufficiently satisfied with the outcome of their initial investment to confirm the follow-up grant of $200,000 in 1969 and the Twentieth Century Fund also provided a second tranche of $75,000, but it was understood that these grants were to be terminal. New support came in the form of £5,000 a year for seven years from the Dulverton Trust in the UK, a major supporter of Atlantic College, and £41,500 spread over five years from the Calouste Gulbenkian Foundation, which had financed the Oxford Departments 'Arts and Science Sides' investigation. Part of this sum was linked to a specific research project and could not be used for general expenses. In Europe we were also helped by the Atlantic College contacts in securing smaller grants from the Agnelli Foundation and The Wenner Gren Foundation. Significant for the future was the first small annual government contribution, from the Department of Education and Science in London.

Although these sources of funding enabled us to start on the six-year experiment, two financial problems were clear from the beginning. The first was that if the experiment were to be successful we needed to demonstrate, at least two years before it was completed, how the continuation of an International Baccalaureate was to be financed: educational foundations may support limited experiments; they cannot be expected to fund permanent institutions. The second was that, since we could not expect to establish this long-term financing until the experiment had been concluded, we would still need a further injection of funds about half-way through the project and must meanwhile control expenditure as tightly as possible.

Both problems were discussed at the IBO Council meeting following the first academic year of the experiment. The long-term solution which at that time I advocated was that, since after 1975 regular governmental support would become absolutely necessary, this should be sought through some sort of association with Unesco, the IBO either becoming an organ of Unesco, like the International Bureau of Education in Geneva, or becoming a function of the IBE. An application should be made for a substantial grant from Unesco in the 1972 budget and a further resolution concerning the final integration of IBO as a function of IBE/Unesco could be presented to the General Assembly of 1974.

I now think that this was an ill-judged proposal and it will be seen from the course of the subsequent negotiations that it was also impractical. Nevertheless at the time it seemed to have a sort of logic about it. What more appropriate form of activity for Unesco than providing simultaneously a model international curriculum and an international examination serving the needs of mobile students including refugees?

Gérard, in addition to managing the Geneva office, had nobly taken on the position of treasurer, though quite how stressful this was to prove for a teacher of philosophy few of us realised at first. There must have been many times when he had to draw on the stoicism of his great love, Spinoza.

The short- and medium-term financing did not look too bad. The financial picture which he presented to the Council in 1970 after the first of the six years showed that, unless disaster struck, we had reasonable hopes of meeting our obligations over the first four of the six years. This was based on an originally estimated maximum annual expenditure of $163,000 reduced by an 'austerity programme' to an actual expenditure of $124,775 for the first year and an estimate of $144,700 for the second. Against this, by dividing the income from pledged grants into equal tranches spread over the period of the grant, he was able to show an assured income of approximately $130,000 for each of the first three years and just over $100,000 for the fourth. Additional income would have to be found to cover the shortfalls but the chances of doing so looked reasonably good. Even this degree of reasonable hope, however, had only been made possible through two interventions by Mountbatten in November of that year. After a dinner at the White House, given in his honour by President Nixon, Mountbatten persuaded Henry Ford and McGeorge Bundy to authorise the offer of a 'supplementary matching grant' of up to $100,000 from the Ford Foundation, to match pound for pound what new funds we were able to raise in the UK. Later in the month, at a dinner given by Walter Annenberg, the US Ambassador in London, Mountbatten persuaded Annenberg to divert a donation of $25,000, which he was offering to the United World Colleges, to the IB. The Ford offer was exceptionally generous after the conclusion of a terminal grant and I remember being warned that 'after this the doors of the Foundation are not merely closed to IB, but locked, bolted, and barred'. Nevertheless it did unlock to us, through matching, good opportunities in the UK and enabled Ford, who had made the whole experiment possible, to ensure its ultimate success. Tight control of expenditure was not easy, but we were greatly helped in the early days by those who worked for the IBO either for nothing or for no more than expenses and by Gérard's capacity for economising by taking on so much work himself. One of the problems of international organisations seems to be a built-in escalation of wage costs. The political reasons for the choice of Geneva as a headquarters were strong, but all organisations based in one of the world's 'international' cities, such as Addis Ababa, Brussels, Geneva, Nairobi, Paris, Vienna, or Washington, find themselves faced with a common financial problem. If you want to achieve a genuinely international balance in your staff, a classic example of which is Unesco, you have to pay rates at least equal to those which staff members would expect to get in the home country. Thus if you want to include Ruritanian examiners in an examining team you have to pay the whole team at Ruritanian rates, even if these are above what the others would receive for similar work in their own countries. Added to that is the fact that rates of pay for full-time staff in international cities tend to rise well above normal through the competition of lavishly-funded international employers. The city itself then becomes a high-cost (and high lifestyle) centre and staff expect, not unnaturally, to be paid at rates which enable them to live at the same level as their peers, just as they would at home. For poor countries the extreme case of this syndrome is probably the diplomatic world.

For the IBO fairness demanded that for our full-time staff we should either pay Geneva rates or establish ourselves, as the World Federation of the Teaching Profession had and as World University Service considered doing, in a cheaper and less prestigious city. The political argument for remaining in Geneva and the need for continuity prevailed, probably rightly. We therefore decided to tie our rates of pay for the permanent full-time staff to those of one of the existing international organisations and for this we chose CERN (Centre Européen des Recherches Nucléaires) whose chief administrator was a member of the IB Council and whose wife, Paddy Hampton, served for some time as Gérard Renaud's assistant. There was, however, the possibility of a compromise.

The compromise, for which I argued strongly from the first, was that we should decentralise some part of our operations to a less expensive area. The obvious area was the UK. We already had a commuting or peripatetic part-time Director-General, with an office provided, first by Oxford University and then by Hammersmith and West London College, at virtually no cost. The obvious operation to transfer was the administration of the annual examinations. The actual content of the examinations remained, of course, in the hands of the international board of examiners, whose membership is described below, but as the number of candidates increased, so the administrative task of printing, checking, translation, and distribution of the examination papers, arranging the visits of oral examiners and assembling the results, became more and more formidable. Since 90% of the examinations were taken in English an English speaking-staff was needed and the obvious place to recruit and employ them was not a francophone international city. Moreover an operation of this kind needs, in addition to the regular staff, a lot of part-time English-speaking clerical staff at the peak periods, who would not be available in Geneva.

In recommending this decentralisation I was encouraged by the example of the US College Entrance Examination Board, which, although maintaining control of the curriculum through its own headquarters in New York, contracts out the administration of the annual examinations to the Educational Testing Service in Princeton. Another parallel was the Cambridge Examinations Syndicate which had delegated to a separate administration the conduct of the Cambridge Overseas Certificate.

For examiners we adopted a compromise from the start, paying them rather more than they would have received for similar work in England, but rather less than they would have received in the USA or Scandinavia. Initially, at least, those who examined for the IB undertook the work because they were interested in the project, and these differentials had little or no effect. It is possible, however, that as the IBO has become more institutionalised and less of an adventure, they have begun to contribute to the preponderance of English assistant examiners.

Reducing the cost of the annual examination session was the more important since it is from the excess of the examination fees paid by the candidates over the costs of setting and grading the examinations that an examinations board is normally financed. With so few candidates and a highly complicated international exam, IBO could not hope to achieve anything like this in the first six years: but we had to show that we were on the way to funding at least a substantial part of the operation from this source. The first objective was to reach a position where once all the fixed costs, including the cost of producing a full set of examinations, were met from general revenue, the cost per candidate of actually administering and grading the examinations was less than the examination entrance fees paid by the candidate. Only then could we argue that as the number of candidates grew the need for subsidies from other sources would diminish. This situation was achieved by 1972, although the 'profit' on the examination session, less than 10,000 Swiss francs, was hardly a significant element against a total expenditure of 657,000 Swiss francs. Income generated by our own operations, that is examination fees and sale of publications, did, however, increase from virtually nothing in the first of the six years to approximately one quarter of total expenditure in the last. The small annual grant from the UK was followed by 10,000 guilder from the Netherlands, 25,000 deutschmark from Federal Germany, 21,000 Swiss francs from France, and 15,150 Swiss francs from Canada, but these were more earnests of goodwill than significant contributions to funding. Unesco also manifested goodwill. G.V. Rao, Director of Budget, had been a member of the Council from the first and in September 1971 M. M'Bow paid a visit to the IB office. It was clear, however, even before the half-way mark of 1973 that new sources of revenue would have to be found. Then, in that year, disaster did strike. It struck the whole Western economy and within it one tiny project, the IB. For the IBO the disaster had three elements: inflation, the chaos of exchange rates, and the drying up of financial support either public or private for idealistic or international initiatives. It has always seemed to me something of a miracle that we survived.

Inflation hit us mainly because, while expenditure naturally tended to rise, the main source of our income still consisted of annual instalments of grants negotiated in the pre-inflationary period. A minor factor was that we did not feel able, as an experimental examination still relying on the goodwill of our customer schools, to raise the fees for our services sufficiently quickly in line with inflation.

The effect of unstable exchange rates was well described by Gérard in his treasurer's report for 1973: "IBO was seriously affected by the monetary fluctuations. While 80% of its income is in US dollars or in pounds sterling, the currencies most hit by devaluation in the past twelve months, 90% of its expenses are in Swiss francs, the currency which floated upwards."

In some ways things had seemed to be going well when the financial crisis struck. More and more schools were interested and a new United World College was due to open next year in Canada. Students were being accepted by universities on an increasingly world-wide scale. Above all the examinations were now running better. Increasing numbers were clearly going to demand strengthened administration, but the academic quality and international character were vouched for by the following representative board of Chief Examiners:

Professor H. Boesch, Chairman (Geography)
    Geographisches Institut der Universität, Zurich
Dr H.R. Christen (Chemistry)
    Kant. Oberrealschule, Winterhur
Dr R.F.S. Creed (Biology)
    University of London
Mme D. Dreyfus (Philosophy)
    Inspectrice d'Académie, France
Dr S. Furhammar (Psychology)
    Gymnasieskolan, Boras, Sweden
Professor P.K. Ghosh (Mathematics)
    Former Principal of Nizam College, Osmania University, India
A. Klein (Physics)
    Oberstudiendirektor, Köln
Dr G. Lienhardt (Anthropology)
    University of Oxford
Dr L.Th. Maes (History)
    Université d'Anvers
Professor G. Mautschka (Music)
    Hochschule fr Musik, Frankfurt

J.B. Morgan (Mathematics)
  University of Reading
M.G. Ruffino (Latin, Greek)
  Collège de Genève
Dr A. Strassenburg (Scientific Studies)
  State University of New York
Dr J.J. Thompson (Physical Science)
  University of Oxford
M.C. Troger (Plastic arts)
  Professeur d'art, Paris
Professor J. Vaizey (Economics)
  Brunel University, London
M.A. van Smevoorde (Languages)
  Inspecteur général, France

assisted by

T.A. Carter
  University of Southampton
H. Decker
  Goethe Gymnasium, Frankfurt
J. Grunenwald
  Inspecteur pédagogique, France
M.G. Ruffino
  Collège de Genève

At the Council meeting of 1973 some very difficult decisions had to be taken. Fortunately two new appointments had been made to the IBO Council who were able to play important roles in these decisions. The first was Leo Fernig, an Assistant Director-General of Unesco who had recently been appointed Director of the International Bureau of Education in Geneva: the second, Piet Gathier, Director of Secondary Education in the Netherlands and now President of the IBO Council. Leo Fernig had reported in 1972 that the Board of IBE had voted in favour of including the general budget of IBO in its own operations as a long-term solution, but by a very narrow majority. It was therefore very important to mobilise support at the General Conference of Unesco in the Autumn. I was inexperienced in the ways of Unesco and surprised both by the ease with which delegations could be persuaded, even in the corridors, to subscribe to general resolutions

of support and by the difficulty and time-scale of subsequent negotiations to get these general expressions of support translated
into any agreement on action, particularly action that was going
to cost money. By the time the council met in 1973 it was clear
that we could not hope to have settled the long-term future with
Unesco before the Autumn of 1974. Since IBO was morally committed to providing examinations for students once they had entered on the two-year course, I was compelled to recommend that
the six-year experiment should be extended for a further year to
provide examinations in 1976 as well as 1975. The moral obligation was accepted, but John Goormaghtigh pointed out that we
had not secured funds to cover the additional year. This addition
to our commitments naturally intensified the financial strain. True,
some additional funds had been secured to cover 1974 and 1975.
The Ford matching grant made possible a gradual company-by-
company approach to banks and trading companies in the UK
with overseas interests which ultimately produced a further
£20,000; in Federal Germany where these things were centralised
the Stifterverband Deutschen Industrien contributed 75,000
marks; and two new British Foundations £10,000. The most significant new source of support, however, was the $20,000 from
the Hegeler Institute in the US, negotiated by Blouke Carus, who
subsequently joined the IB board and became the first Chairman
of International Baccalaureate North America. Blouke, like many
other long term supporters of the IB, had first heard of it through
an article in the press, in this case the *Herald Tribune*. His enthusiasm led me to a number of visits to North America and ultimately
to the great expansion of the IB in the US and Canada which is
described in chapter six. But this was for the future. For the present
costs were rising both because of the world financial crisis and
because of that expansion of activities which afflicts projects which
are the 'victims of their own success'.

To some extent I was myself responsible for these growing costs.
On the eve of my early retirement from Oxford I was foolish
enough to fall off a ladder and condemn myself to three months
in hospital covering the interval between the closing of the Oxford
office and the opening of the Hammersmith one. If I were to
operate at all, I needed a private room and a telephone. To the
cost of this the IBO, in its old family tradition, very generously
contributed. This was an unexpected expense, but there was another built in to the new plan. Apart from the six months of my

sabbatical year, as long as I remained Director of the Oxford department and the 'experiment' with the IB my major research interest, I cost IBO nothing but travelling expenses. Once I retired, however, it had been agreed that IBO would take over payments into a pension fund. Fortunately, there was very soon to be a saving in travelling expenses. In 1976 I succeeded Tony Besse as Chairman of the UWC International Board. This involved a round-the-world trip in that year and again in 1977, visiting the colleges and national committees, discussing with governments projects for new colleges, and negotiating wider acceptance of the IB for returning students. Mountbattèn wrote (15th December, 1976): "Thank you so much for your letter of 7th December enclosing your report on your Far Eastern and North American tour, which I have read with the greatest interest. It certainly was obviously of the greatest value for the IB and, as you know, anything you can do to enlarge the acceptance of IB will be very helpful to UWC." The UWC and IBO also helped each other by sharing the costs of representation in South East Asia and Latin America.

We still hoped, although with decreasing confidence, that some form of Unesco association would provide the long-term solution. But clearly we had to start now, within our own administration, those reforms which would transform it from a band of colleagues and friends, committed to an ideal and reacting to every new problem by improvisation, into a bureaucracy, hopefully a humane bureaucracy, which could perform efficiently and economically much wider and longer-term tasks which might be entrusted to it. The first stage in this administrative reorganisation was the complete transfer of responsibility for providing the language examinations from Geneva to the UK.

It had been clear from the first that by far the most complicated part of the examinations would be those in foreign languages. This was not only because of the IBO's policy with regard to the spread of languages examined, but because it was in the teaching and assessment of foreign languages that we had the best opportunities for research and innovation.

Here, again, a British university provided the necessary centre for co-operation. Tom Carter, who, as Head of Modern Languages at Atlantic College, had played a leading role in all the conferences leading up to the establishment of the IB, had recently been appointed Director of the Language Centre at Southampton University. Since research and development in new methods of teaching and examing foreign languages was one of the functions of the centre, he was able, much as I had been doing at Oxford, to draw on the resources of the University and the interests of his colleagues for action research, making use of the IB as a 'test bed'.

Initially the service performed at Southampton was simply the composition of a battery of tests of reading and listening comprehension in the four major languages, English, French, German, and Spanish, Tom's position being that of one of the assistant examiners in languages, working under the general direction of van Smevoorde. In 1974 the first step in transferring the administration of the examinations from Geneva to the UK was taken. The IBO entered into a contract with the university, by which additional space was made available in the language centre and a small staff recruited to concentrate, under the general guidance of Tom Carter and administrative direction of Dianne Williamson (a science teacher with international experience), on the provision of the annual language examinations for the IBO.

By 1977, the first year after the conclusion of the experiment, we were examining in 24 languages as language A and 29 as language B.

Economies in the administration of the examinations were one response to the crisis, but they were not enough. Already a series of austerity budgets had meant that the IBO was doing less than we saw as desirable and doing it with an often overworked staff. In the examinations the cost factor was forcing us to abandon methods of assessment, such as listening comprehension tests in languages which we had introduced because of their significant contribution to validity. Some new source of regular income was needed.

We were still hoping to achieve a Unesco/BIE solution, based on the transfer to BIE of responsibility for the curriculum development and general administration of the IBO based in Geneva, with the conduct of the annual examinations contracted out to an examinations office, self-supporting on candidates' examination fees. This, I thought, might remove one of Unesco's apprehensions, that if they assumed full responsibility, complaints from parents or teachers or accusations of cheating might enter that highly political arena. The plan of action which Leo Fernig proposed was the proposal of a resolution at the General Conference of Unesco in 1974, to be followed by a small contribution from BIE in 1975 and inclusion of the infrastructure of the IBO in the BIE budget from 1976. The following resolution was duly proposed in 1974 by Canada, Egypt, Great Britain and Northern Ireland, Iran, Switzerland, Malta, Morocco, Mauritius, Mexico, Nigeria, Tanzania, and Togo, and unanimously adopted by approximately 70 delegations present at the time of voting:

> Amendement au Projet de programme et de budget pour 1975-1976 (document 18 C/5)
>
> Titre 11—Exécution du programme
> Chapitre 1—Éducation section 1.32—Enseignement supérieur 1505 à La Conférence générale,
>
> Prenant acte des progrès realisés par l'Office du baccalauréat international dans l'harmonisation des programmes de l'enseignement secondaire supérieur et dans l'élaboration d'un système international d'évaluation pour l'accès à l'université.
>
> Estimant que l'expérience est de nature à offrir aux systèmes nationaux un moyen efficace de développer et de rénouver les programmes d'enseignement ainsi que les méthodes d'évaluation.
>
> Souhaitant que le service ainsi rendu à la communauté des nations soit renforcé et poursuivi sous contrôle international.
>
> Invité le Directeur général à examiner les dispositions qu'il serait possible de prendre à partir de 1977 pour contribuer à la continuité du travail de l'Office du baccalauréat international et, en consequence, à soumettre les propositions appropriées à la Conférence générale lors de sa dix-neuvième session.

Armed with what seemed a strong expression of opinion by member states, we proceeded during 1975 to serious discussions with senior Unesco officials. In the course of these discussions, costs naturally played a large part and since we had to make provision also for a fall-back plan should the discussions with Unesco fail, we put forward, both for our own plan and for discussion with them, a new source of regular income.

This was that in addition to the examination fees paid by the individual candidates, schools authorised to take the IB should pay an annual subscription. This recognised the fact that the value of the IB to international schools was now sufficiently well-established to convince their boards of management that it was worth paying a small annual subscription to ensure its survival. The plan was accepted by the schools, at the rate of initial affiliation fee of 1,000 Swiss francs and an annual subscription of 2,000 Swiss francs. Together with the first instalment of a grant of US $30,000 a year for three years from the US State Department, it enabled IBO to survive.

By the end of 1975 it was becoming increasingly unlikely that any form of integration with, or regular financial support from, Unesco would prove acceptable. As a fall-back, John Goormaghtigh set about drawing up plans for alternative methods of securing intergovernmental involvement and Piet Gathier persuaded the Netherlands Minister of Education to call a conference, to be held at The Hague in February 1976, at which those governments interested in the future of the IB could discuss its future. Meanwhile, as an emergency measure representatives of ten of the schools most concerned to keep the IB going met in London and agreed 'in order to save IBO' to quadruple their annual subscriptions.

It was the Hague conference which really marked the end of the 'experimental period' and the launching of the IBO on the international scene. For me it began with a symbolically farcical episode. As our aircraft was approaching Amsterdam the pilot came through on the intercom: "I've just been warned that there is a bomb on this plane. I expect that it's just a hoax, as usual, but as a precaution we shall touch down on the edge of the tarmac, and I must ask you to evacuate as quickly as possible by means of the emergency chutes."

This we did. I had often wondered how they would work, and there was something splendidly childish about all the solemn bureaucrats and their wives, clutching brief cases and bags as they slid down the chutes like children in a playground. Everyone remained calm, even bored, with the exception of the air hostess who did not think we were taking it seriously enough and kept trying to speed up the flow of those collecting their belongings by saying: "Hurry up. It's an emergency." Once out, we stood lethargically round the machine until someone suggested that if there really were a bomb on it, perhaps we had better move away. It all reminded me vividly of all of us in the IB, meeting one threat of bankruptcy after another over the six years with the continued conviction that somehow or other the final disaster would never happen. Nor did it.

The conference which averted it was attended by the ministers or secretaries of state for education of five countries—Belgium, Italy, Morocco, the Netherlands, and the UK—and by senior officials from Cameroon, Canada, Denmark, France, Federal Germany, Iran, Roumania, Sweden, Switzerland, USA, and Unesco.

The presentations we gave concentrated on the service which the IBO was making to the internationally-mobile community and the absolute necessity of governmental support if this service was to be continued and expanded with the objective of ensuring that there should be at least one school offering the IB in every major international centre.

The long-term plan put forward by John Goormaghtigh was the one which was under discussion with Unesco; that Unesco should set up a 'staff unit' in Geneva which would take over responsibility for research and curriculum development, while the existing IB foundation, with possible amendments to its constitution under Swiss law, would continue to operate the annual examinations. "It goes withouy saying", he added, "that the closest possible links should be maintained between these two organisations". Meanwhile, and with an eye to the future, governments supporting the IB should be represented on the IB Council. In the short term, that is until 1978 when it was hoped that the long-term plan would be finalised, the IBO would need considerably increased financial support from individual governments.

At the conclusion of the discussions Dr van Kemenade, the Netherlands Minister of Education and Science who had chaired the meeting throughout, put three questions to the delegates.

The following is an extract from the official record of the meeting:

> 3. In reply to the Chairman's *first question*:
>
> "Are a number of countries prepared to support the Director-General of Unesco if he includes in his 1977-1978 program curriculum development at the upper secondary level with special reference to the provision of a continuing service to the development of the International Baccalureate?", the majority of members, while recognising the problems, which might arise from a division between curriculum development and the operation of an examination, confirmed their support for the proposed pattern of co-operation between Unesco and the International Baccalaureate Office as an interim solution for the next two years, while reserving their position for the future.
>
> 4. In reply to the Chairman's *second question*:
>
> "Are a number of countries prepared to make a financial contribution in 1977 and 1978 to enable IBO to carry out the necessary examination activities?", representatives of nine countries among the 15 countries represented at the Conference replied in the affirmative, mentioning in one or two cases that such commitments should be regarded as matching Unesco contributions or were subject to the

processes of budgetary approval in the countries concerned. Representatives of some other countries indicated the possibility of such support but were not empowered at this stage to commit their governments.

In considering the scale of contributions it was agreed that these might fall into three categories: normal contributions, symbolic contributions from countries which wished to indicate support but could not engage in significant financial commitments, and augmented contributions from countries with greater resources or a special interest in the project.

In the light of the statement of delegates, the meeting agreed, while not wishing to impose or limit the scale of contribution by any government, to suggest the following general guidelines for the scale of annual contributions to cover the years 1977 and 1978.

> symbolic contributions : $1,000
> normal contributions : $8,000-$10,000
> special contributions : $15,000

Delegates were invited to confirm to the International Baccalaureate Office, Palais Wilson, Geneva, the scale on which their governments were prepared to contribute, if possible before April 1st, in order that the information might be available to the Executive Board of Unesco at its meeting at the end of that month.

It was further agreed that the IB Office should approach the countries participating in IB activities but not represented at this Conference, with the aim of giving them the opportunity to lend their financial support.

The meeting was also of the opinion that other member-states of Unesco not represented at the conference should also be invited to join the contributing countries. Depending upon the response to this invitation, the amounts of normal and augmented contributions could be reduced in subsequent years as the number of contributing countries increased.

Finally it was also agreed that the Council of IBO should be reconstituted to allow for the representation of all contributing countries.

5. In reply to the Chairman's *third question*:

"Are a number of countries prepared to promise aid now for the years after 1978 or to discuss the continuation of the IB again in 1977?", there was unanimous agreement to discuss the question again in 1977, but members felt that it was too early to consider now detailed questions of aid in the years after 1978. There was considerable support for the view that in the intervening period serious consideration should be given to other patterns of relationship between Unesco and the IBO than that envisaged for the next two years, and that the possibility of creating a new inter-governmental agency should not be excluded.

The meeting concluded with renewed expressions of gratitude to the Netherlands Government and general support for the International Baccalaureate.

As it turned out, the doubters were right. Unesco finally rejected the IBO proposal, possibly because there is no tradition within Unesco of actually operating in the field of education, as it does in the fields of science and culture, through independent organisations either existing or set up for the purpose. Unesco seems always to have regarded education as a matter for the member—states and its own role simply as provision of information and the promotion of conferences, discussions, and exchanges of view. Fortunately this outcome did not adversely affect the attitude of individual member-states, and the second conference proposed at the Hague was duly held on February 15th 1978 at Lancaster House, London, jointly sponsored by the British Government and the Commonwealth Secretariat. It was opened by His Royal Highness The Prince of Wales and presided over by the Secretary of State for Education and Science, Mrs Shirley Williams. This time more than double the number of nations were represented and, although consultative status with Unesco was maintained, the IBO retained its legal identity in Switzerland, with the additional backing that one third of the members of its council were now to be nominated by a 'Standing Conference for the International Baccalaureate' set up by the supporting governments, an elaboration of the structure which John Goormaghtigh had envisaged from the first, should the Unesco negotiations fail. A third such conference was hosted by the Belgian Minister of Education in Brussels in 1981. This, and the fourth conference at Trieste in 1985 are described in chapter seven.

5
MOUNTBATTEN AND
THE EXPANSION OF
THE UNITED WORLD COLLEGES

Atlantic College had hardly been opened before the first tentative steps were taken towards setting up further Colleges on the same model in other parts of the world. Two areas were of particular interest: Germany and Canada. Both had shown strong support by sending students to Atlantic College, but it was in Canada that the idea of a second college first took root. Towards the end of 1963 Sir Lawrance Darvall and Robert Blackburn visited Canada to encourage the setting up of a Canadian national committee, which would stimulate a flow of Canadian students to Atlantic College and undertake the selection process. They met with a very friendly reception from the Prime Minister, Lester Pearson, one of the great advocates of international co-operation and a Nobel Peace Prize winner. One sentence from his acceptance speech has almost become a United World College motto: "How can there be peace without people understanding each other, and how can this be if they don't know each other?" A target was soon set up of two students from each province and in the course of the discussions Darvall and Blackburn met Senator Donald Cameron, the founder and Director of the School of Fine Arts at Banff, in the Rocky Mountains National Park. Cameron suggested that this school, like the original St Donat's Castle, might provide a suitable base for an Atlantic College in Canada and after a brief inspection of the site the UWC representatives enthusiastically agreed. The idea of a second college in Canada had obvious attractions. It seemed at first to exemplify the 'Atlantic' nature of the project, with the almost mystical element of the sea acting as a bridge between nations and an impersonal challenge to humankind. It was always hoped, in the early days, that the college would be a joint Canada-USA project, but the interest of the Prime Minister and Canada's special interest in anglophone-francophone relations made a Canadian site particularly attractive.

By the end of 1964 the Canadian Atlantic College Committee had been formally constituted with Senator Cameron as Chairman. In the aims, set out in its constitution, "establishing a residential educational institution in Canada to be known as 'The Atlantic College, Canada' took precedence over increasing and strengthening Canadian participation in the first Atlantic College".

Prominent members of this committee were the Rev. Cedric Sowby, then headmaster of Upper Canada College, and Ken Rotenberg. Both did much to make Atlantic College known throughout Canada and to encourage and select a Canadian entry to Atlantic College. In particular Ken Rotenberg's driving energy and refusal to contemplate failure did much to carry the project through when prospects looked at their darkest.

In 1965 The Minister for Northern Affairs and General Resources made it clear that he would not approve the Banff site or the establishment of any new permanent institution within the National Park. At first, Cameron continued to press for his scheme, hoping that the objection might be lifted if and when there was a change of Minister. By this time, however, certain divisions of opinion were growing up between the Canadian committee and the Council of Atlantic College, which was still the only organ of the budding international movement. Some members of the Council had never been really happy with the Banff project, which had no link with the sea, and now Lord Hankey, who had made two visits on behalf of UWC, was impressed by the growing interest in British Columbia. At the same time Sir George Schuster, by then Chairman of the Atlantic College Council, was increasingly concerned that the financial viability of Atlantic College was not yet finally assured, that the Canadian Committee did not realise the magnitude of the fund-raising task involved in establishing a new College and that their growing commitment to this project was inhibiting the vital supply of funds and students from Canada and the US to Atlantic College.

Schuster's alarm was understandable. It had always been clear that deficit financing would be necessary until the student numbers in the college grew to a 'financially viable level'. Exactly what that level is may be a matter of doubt and depends upon the range and variety of academic and other activities regarded as desirable. My general experience has been that if you ask the headmaster of an English independent boarding school what he regards as the ideal number, the most usual answer will be '$x + 50$', x being the number currently in the school. At Atlantic College the first 'target' was 300, subsequently raised to 350. This involved not only a considerable period of deficit financing, but a massive fund-raising campaign to provide the dormitories, classrooms, laboratories, and other specialist facilities for art, music, drama, sea rescue, and so forth. Schuster's achievement in bringing the college through this development period has long been acknowledged as one of the high points in its history. Indeed it is not too much to say that without him Atlantic College might have foundered.

From the first, the main contributors to Atlantic College were British banks and industries—in the earliest days mainly the steel companies in Wales. By 1983 nearly five million pounds had been raised but of this only 100,000 from the UK and 72,000 from Federal Germany were in the form of government grants. By far the largest single benefactors were Mr and Mrs Maresi, who had responded to the initial plea for a girls' dormitory and over the years contributed nearly one and three quarter million pounds for special projects. The two main charitable foundations were the Dulverton Trust and the Bernard Sunley Charitable Foundation, but The Ford Foundation, Grant Foundation, Leverhulme Trust, and finally the Mountbatten Memorial Trust made very substantial contributions, as did the two 'anonymous donors'. But looking down the list of those who contributed more than 10,000, one finds the names of more than 20 British industrial corporations. A very small proportion came from governments and virtually nothing from outside the UK.

Nevertheless the Council of the Atlantic College passed a resolution on 16th October 1966 which greatly encouraged the Canadians. Its terms were that the Council:

> (a) reaffirms its faith in the original wide conception of the Atlantic College project for the establishment of colleges in a number of countries;
>
> (b) considers that the development of the first college at St Donat's has so clearly established the value of the original conception as to justify immediate consideration of the establishment of colleges in other countries;

(c) decides that for working out a programme for the wider development of the project the Council should appoint an International
Action Committee to formulate proposals.

Although this resolution may have seemed to endorse the principle of setting up new colleges, the committee disposed of no
regular funds with which to assist the process. As a sub-committee
of the Atlantic College Council it was still concerned with the need
for scholarships to that college, where there were at that time eight
Canadian students, but all of them on a full fee-paying basis. On
9th November, Hankey, who was a member of the committee,
wrote to Sowby as follows: "I must tell you that we are still rather
disturbed here about the question of scholarships. As I understand
it the Atlantic College idea is fundamentally intended to enable
boys of the most diverse types to work, play and live together and
to engage in common activities, thus promoting their real sense of
understanding. This is not only an international affair, but is also
intended to operate right across social distinctions of class, income
and origin. The scholarship system enables boys to come, provided
they are of adequate intellectual merit and general character, irrespective of whether their parents can pay the quite considerable
fees."[1] This letter is of interest not only because it states the scholarship policy as one of opening entry to all social classes rather
than of removing the colleges from the 'private sector', but also
as an indication of the committee's order of priorities. At first it
was even contemplated that these priorities should be communi-
cated to the Canadian committee by letter as being, first, to establish the permanent viability of Atlantic College through scholarships; second, to found a new college in Germany; third, to
found a new college in France or possibly Canada. Fortunately
wiser councils prevailed and money was somehow found to enable
Hankey to make a two-week visit early in 1967, in order to consult
with the Canadian Committee, albeit with these priorities as his
brief. Not surprisingly, little progress on the new college came of
this visit, except the maintenance of good will between the two
committees and considerably increased knowledge of the project
throughout Canada. Government objections to the Banff site were
maintained but not unwelcome to the International Action Committee. On the other hand, the committee's arguments for going
slow on the Canadian College were not unwelcome to Senator
Cameron, when it became clear that building a college elsewhere
might involve raising more than three million pounds. There was,

however, some improvement in scholarships and the number of Canadians entering Atlantic College in September 1967 rose, from its long established average of four, to eleven. At the end of the visit what proved ultimately to be a second *ignis fatuus* lit up the horizon. In effect it led its followers to their ultimate destination. It was reported that one of the Canadian Defence Colleges, situated at Royal Roads, eight miles West of Victoria on Vancouver Island, might soon become redundant to defence needs and could conceivably be made available for a Canadian college. This news reached him too late for Hankey to visit the site, but the sea-coast, western location was infinitely preferable to the Action Committee, and a subsequent inspection showed that the accommodation and facilities would be ideal. There was a great attraction in this beating of swords into ploughshares, as the prospect of the Royal Air Force site in Singapore exemplified later. For the next three years all attention was concentrated on Royal Roads and the West Coast. Hankey had been accompanied on this second trip by his wife Joanna, who was a former Director of Programmes under the Indian Advisory Act for British Columbia. Her friends and contacts produced both scholarships and commitment from the provincial government.

Meanwhile, the Action Committee turned its attention to the country which it considered to be the first priority in the establishment of new colleges—Germany. This choice was probably due to three factors: the concept of the colleges as organs for the promotion of reconciliation and peace; the enthusiastic support for Atlantic College in Germany, both through donations and scholarships, and the personal commitment of Kurt Hahn.

In January 1968, Hahn visited Sylt and Cuxhaven, accompanied by David (now Sir David) Wills and Desmond Hoare. David Wills and Lord Hankey played decisive parts in the expansion, under Mountbatten's leadership, which led to the establishment of the next two colleges, and much of the finance needed for the exploration of these projects came from David Wills's charitable trusts. Sir Eric Berthoud, former British Ambassador to Poland, who subsequently did so much for the United World Colleges in Eastern Europe, had established good relations with the German Ambassador in London and with the *Studien Stiftung* which supported German students.

This German initiative soon proved premature. The assumption that a college must be based on the sea was still strong and the group concluded that Cuxhaven or Sylt provided the only two possible sites on the German North Sea coast. The local authorities were co-operative about providing possible sites for building but two factors inhibited further action: Hellmut Becker wrote to advise strongly against attempting anything in Germany until the acceptance of the IB for entry to German universities had been fully established, and enquiries in two countries which strongly supported Atlantic College indicated that it was too soon after the Nazi occupation to expect Dutch or Norwegian families to send their children to a college in Germany. Partly for these reasons and partly because they did not believe that it would be possible to raise the two million pounds needed for buildings, even though the Cuxhaven authorities had offered a 55-acre site, admirably situated, the German National Committee reluctantly turned down the project. It was a deep disappointment to Kurt Hahn and David Wills who felt that a great opportunity was being missed, but the project for a German College was not abandoned: it was shelved.

In the following month, Lord Mountbatten, who had been instrumental in getting support for the build-up of Atlantic College from both Conservative and Labour governments, agreed to take on the direction of the project and was elected Chairman of the Atlantic College Council. He made two conditions, that the project should be more internationalised and that an International Office, working for him and separate from the administration of Atlantic College, should be set up. What he inherited was one college now manifestly successful but still in need of funds, two 'prospects' for which no serious funds were available, an international 'movement' which had neither form, nor funds, nor base, and a group of experienced, energetic, and influential enthusiasts who were prepared to give a lot of their time, and in some cases a lot of their money, to turning the dream into a reality. Mountbatten himself saw it as the best contribution which he, the last surviving Supreme Allied Commander from World War Two, could make to preventing World War Three. With this as his main aim he threw into it his immense capacity for organisation and the mobilisation of support. The confidence with which he faced his formidable task reminds one of a remark attributed, I hope not apocryphally, to Lester Pearson in a similar context: "We've got a great idea, we've got a great bunch of people. What are we making all this fuss about a little money for?"[2]

With this backing and these supporters, but from his restricted base, he launched into this international project. Within a short time it had a new name 'United World Colleges', chosen by Mountbatten after discussion with U Thant; a new International Council of which Mountbatten served as President for nine years; and an international office.

From then on the United World Colleges were his main interest in life. In 1969, for instance, he seems to have taken a month off in June, but every other month of the year included at least one UWC activity, including visits to Sweden, France, the Netherlands, and Italy. Prince Bernhard in the Netherlands and President Saragat in Italy agreed to become national patrons and Olivier Giscard d'Estang and Admiral Eric Af Klint, chairman and secretary of the French and Swedish national committees. Meetings were held with Senator Cameron and Malcolm Muir, chairman of the US national commission. Of all these appointments the most important in the subsequent history of UWC was probably that of Ambassador Migone, who had been introduced by Signora Agnelli, honorary secretary of the Italian Committee. An invitation from the College led in 1971 to a visit by Gianfranco Facco Bonetti, the first secretary at the Italian Embassy in London. In the train going back he struck up an immediate rapport with Desmond Hoare and the two dreamed up a plan for a new college on the shores of the Adriatic near Trieste.

Many, many young Italians owe their education at one of the colleges to Migone's efforts and his name is commemorated in the library of the College of the Adriatic. I remember at a Council meeting in Singapore, when the hopes of a college in Italy were being discussed, that Migone, getting slightly confused over his English idiom, said:

"I think, Lord Mountbatten, they have given us the red light."

"Surely you mean the green light, Migone?"

"No, no. In Rome when we see a red light we accelerate."

It was not a bad description of the way Mountbatten himself treated all obstacles. By 1972 he had set up national committees in France, Sweden, Netherlands, Italy, Malta, Switzerland, Malaysia, Australia, Belgium, Spain, Luxemburg, Bahamas, in addition to existing committees in Canada, Denmark, Germany, Norway, and USA. He had also completed the structural reorganisation of incorporating the international movement in a company registered as United World Colleges (International) Ltd. The company had its own board of directors, of which he became the first chairman, entrusted with the task of implementing the policies of the International Council. The governors of Atlantic College (and of subsequent Colleges) were represented on this Board by their chairmen.

Of course many of the individuals involved in the new structure were the same people as before. When, after a couple of years, Mountbatten vacated the chairmanship of the board he was succeeded for the next two years by Tony Besse, and the two following that, by myself. He "stole", as he said himself, Robert Blackburn, the deputy headmaster of Atlantic College (now renamed the United World College of the Atlantic) to become his chief staff officer and run the International Office. Through the good offices and financial support of David Wills, initial office space was provided in London House, a graduate Hall of Residence for Commonwealth and later EEC students, from which, in offices now considerably extended and rented by the International Company, UWC still operates. Robert records that one of the first things Mountbatten did was to sit down and design a logo for his new command, just as he had done in South East Asia.

It was typical of Mountbatten's method of working to set up a small personal staff whom he trusted completely, to whom he gave personal access at any time, and whom he worked ruthlessly. The role of his private secretary, John Barratt, in the development of UWC is often ignored and underestimated. The link between Broadlands and the International Office was extremely close. In eight years no letter was written, no speech drafted, no visit planned or fund-raising event arranged without the closest contact between the very few staff in both offices, with Mountbatten inspiring, directing, and interfering on a daily and often hourly basis. Not infrequently the International Office would find itself involved in tasks not directly linked with international education—transporting a Labrador retriever to Sandringham for the shooting, or assisting to plan an exhibition in Singapore commemorating the capitulation of the Japanese forces in SEA Command!

Mountbatten's methods in setting up national committees and securing support have been vividly described by his biographer, Philip Ziegler.[3] No head of state or minister of education, cornered at a government reception or private dinner party, had much chance of escape. The only one I can remember hearing of was Hubert Humphrey who, in 1969, declined the honour of becoming chairman of the North American Founding Committee because of other commitments. But the electric force of Mountbatten's personality did not always survive the initial charge for very long. Looking through my report of a tour of the South East Asian countries some seven years after he had set up national committees for the benefit of the Singapore college, I find such phrases as "strictly speaking the National Committee does not exist and the Minister of Education has long forgotten that he is chairman". On the other hand, when a man of influence, like Sir Kenneth Ping-fan Fung in Hong Kong, became really committed, the National Committee produced a steady flow of scholarships. The United World Colleges' two 'roving ambassadors', Berthoud and Hankey, had quite a job following up Mountbatten's lightning committee foundations.

The first principle on which the proposed chain of colleges was to operate was quickly established. Within the guidelines agreed by the movement as a whole, each college was to have its own board of governors and be responsible for its own policy, finance, and administration, with the International Office lending such assistance as it could, mainly in the raising of scholarships. It took a bit longer to work out how the International Company and Office should be financed and the form of co-operation between the individual colleges and the 'movement' as a whole is part of the developing story of this chapter. The autonomy of the colleges, however, meant that their financial viability depended, as with all independent schools, on raising capital for infrastructure and on fee income from students for recurrent costs.

But the United World Colleges were to be no ordinary independent 'schools for rich kids'. The form of education that they were to give—an international pre-university course with all the added features developed at Atlantic College—was inevitably expensive; but the new council and board were determined that, following the example of Atlantic College, the provision of scholarships should be so generous that no sixteen-year-old selected on merit from any country should be denied access because the family could not pay. To quote the International Council's guidelines, a UWC should provide "a significantly international student body and teaching staff, with entry open to all students and teachers, irrespective of race, nationality and religion, who accept and support the ideas of the UWC movement. Selection of students for entry from the widest possible range of social and cultural backgrounds based on merit alone and irrespective of the family's financial resources".[4]

The way in which this 'scholarship policy' was initially conceived is worth recording. As is clear from Hankey's efforts in Canada, there was no intention at first that all students should receive scholarships although all would be selected on merit. Desmond Hoare, in a letter written in 1973 to Larry Huddart, who was setting out to establish national committees in South America mainly on behalf of the Canadian College, wrote: "I am sure that we can continue a 70% scholarship entry in Atlantic College and in the Pacific school." Mountbatten repeated the same figure of 70% in his planning letter of 4th July 1974. It was not envisaged that these scholarships should cover the whole costs of boarding and tuition. Scholarships awarded by public bodies, such as the Local Education Authorities in England, the *Studien Stiftung* in Germany, or local authorities in Norway, were adjusted according to their normal practice, to the financial resources of the family. Scholarships to Atlantic College awarded by the Canadian National Committee were for fixed amounts, initially $3,000 but then reduced to $2,500, which did not cover the full expenses.

In adopting a policy of scholarships similar in pattern to that commonly found among 'private' schools such as Eton or Andover, but on a much more generous scale, it seems to me that the United World Colleges were initially trying to open entry to all social classes, but later sought to use their scholarship policy to emphasise that they were not 'private schools', but in some way part of a new world system of public education. This might have been consistent with the objective of rapid expansion into a world-wide chain, had they in fact been set up by an inter-governmental agency such as the UN, with the governments of different countries accepting an obligation to treat education in their United World College as part of the national and therefore free system of education. For a series of linked private charitable foundations, it was not compatible with that objective. Mountbatten, in discussions with government officials, national or provincial, who were often precluded from giving financial support to private secondary education, tried to argue that the United World Colleges were not private schools because they were sponsored by an 'international movement'; but it did not carry weight. One could I suppose call these two concepts of the UWC, as nationally-sponsored colleges or as a diverse chain of independent schools, the 'strong' and the 'weak' concepts of the movement.

There is an interesting parallel here with the long-drawn-out attempts of the IBO to integrate with Unesco and a similarity in the solutions, at present adopted by both UWC and IBO, of securing not general intergovernmental support at the UN level, but the support of individual national governments, in the case of UWC, those of Canada and Italy.

Whatever solution was found to this problem it was clear that the colleges must and could meet their recurrent costs from the income, whether in fees or scholarships, provided by the students. But how was the 'movement' as a whole, with its International Board and office to be financed?

There seem to have been three stages in solving this. The first, in the days of the International Action Committee was really living from hand to mouth, relying on the good will of 'anonymous donors' (who usually turned out to have been David Wills or James Whitaker) for specific activities and of those who travelled in their normal course of business (like Eric Weiss) to fit in some work for Atlantic College. This could clearly not have supported the kind of planned and ongoing expansion that Mountbatten saw as necessary. He therefore set to work to raise funds, through his wide range of personal contacts or through fund-raising 'events', to provide for the needs of the International Company and Office. One of these 'events', the 'Night of Nights', for which he secured world-wide TV coverage since it brought on to the same stage Princess Grace of Monaco, Bob Hope, and Frank Sinatra, followed by a supper party at St James's Palace for friends of UWC, raised two and a quarter million pounds—possibly a record for any charitable occasion in Britain. Two thirds of this went to Atlantic College and one third to the International Office.

The third stage we owe to Tony Besse who argued consistently, against a good deal of opposition from the individual colleges, that the International Office must have an assured, regular source of income and that the only source from which this could come was a levy on fee income from the individual colleges, by this time three, with a fourth in sight.

One of Mountbatten's first visits, within a month of his appointment, was to the Canadian Defence College at Royal Roads. It still seemed very doubtful whether these buildings were really going to become available, but he urged strongly that the committee should hold on to the hope. To some, no doubt, the fact that the main building was 'in Scottish baronial style' was an attraction, just as many years later was the existence of the 'castle', when Montezuma was chosen for the site of the College of the American West. Mountbatten also persuaded Lester Pearson to become Honorary Chairman of the Canadian national committee. Joint US-Canadian planning, however, was set back when Cameron found that the US Commission, based in New York, was 'flabbergasted' at the scale of fund-raising that might be involved and was also, unlike the Canadian Committee, not empowered under its constitution to raise funds for such a purpose but only for scholarships.

The remainder of 1968 and 1969 Mountbatten devoted to establishing national committees, strengthening the finances, changing the name, and setting up the administrative machinery. It was not until 1970 that the momentum towards the setting up of new colleges was resumed. Early in that year it was finally confirmed that Royal Roads would not become available, but General Kitching, the new secretary of the Canadian committee, expressed his enthusiasm for 'building from scratch' rather than continuing to look for ready-made solutions.[5] Canada was on the way, but meanwhile she had been overtaken in the race by a new contender.

A new political development, the British military withdrawal from 'East of Suez' changed the perspective, particularly for Mountbatten. It meant the handing over to the Singapore government both of the British Army school, St John's, and a large RAF base at Changi which included both a school and a hospital. Mountbatten had a strong personal commitment to Singapore from his days at SEAC and the possibility of securing a complete school 'ready-made' as a new United World College in that area seemed too good to miss. After discussing the possibility at a UWC meeting in London in March 1970, he wrote to the Singapore Prime Minister, Lee Kuan Yew, with whom he was on good terms. His suggestion was that the best use for St John's would be as a United World College, serving primarily the countries of South East Asia, and so enhancing Singapore's position as a cultural, economic, and educational centre for the region. At the same time Hankey wrote formally to the British Foreign Office seeking support for the project. Before the Foreign Office reply could reach him, Lee Kuan Yew had replied to Mountbatten that St John's had already been offered to the British European Association as an international school for the expatriate community. He suggested that some form of co-operation might be possible between this new school and the United World Colleges, and recommended Mountbatten to get in touch with the newly-formed Singapore International School Study Committee. The chairman of this committee was Roy Bennett, the immediate past chairman of the International Chamber of Commerce. In July he and two of his colleagues on the committee visited London for discussions with UWC. Just a month earlier the Canadians had taken the dramatic step of appointing a headmaster for the college they now intended to build. In Singapore there seemed to be a clear basis for co-operation. The study committee were doubtful whether there would be enough demand from the expatriate community to fill the school at an economically viable level. St John's had places for one thousand students of whom 320 were boarders. In particular the committee was very doubtful whether the school could support a sixth form, that is, grades eleven and twelve. Educational thinking in England was indicating that below a certain level of total enrolment the provision of sixth-form education was uneconomic. We had also found in the IB that many international schools took pupils only up to the tenth grade. The possibility that UWC might co-operate in providing some sort of sixth form college which would be a separate part of the school and bring in boarders from outside Singapore, seemed a solution well worth examining. At the same time the Singapore government was anxious to press ahead with a private international boarding school which would diminish the pressure from Malaysian Chinese for places in Singapore's own school system.

At a meeting in July it was agreed that a three-man mission from UWC, consisting of Robin Hankey, Desmond Hoare, and David Wills should visit Singapore in the following month to discuss possibilities on the spot. It is worth noting that this group included the two UWC representatives who had been most deeply involved in Germany and Canada.

The visit of the three-man commission produced a sudden change of front on the part of UWC. The commission agreed that there was not enough room at St John's to accommodate a separate United World College as well as the International School and that far the best site for a college would be provided by taking over a large section of the RAF site at Changi. This site and its buildings would provide not only classrooms and accommodation for 300 students and faculty, but 'three beautiful playing fields', two swimming pools and easy access to the sea. Moreover a recent article in the *Straits Times* had drawn attention to the urgent need for beach and sea rescue services in the area. It seemed tailor-made for a replica of Atlantic College. Exactly as in Canada and Germany, this vision of a second Atlantic College dominated our thinking at that time. The Minister of Education seemed not averse.

The commission recognised that there would be a problem about the capital costs of adaptation. Desmond Hoare's 'guestimate' was 83,000 before opening, with a final figure of 275,000. It was not clear where this money was to come from, except that it was agreed, as so often happened subsequently, that it must not be sought from sources which might otherwise be supporting Atlantic College. It could not be expected to come from Singapore itself. There was some talk of a substantial grant from the British government, which might induce the Australian and New Zealand governments to follow suit, but a quarter of a million at 1970 prices was a lot of money to find from the country which was already responsible for Atlantic College and it was soon made clear, even before the Changi plan had been abandoned, that it would not be forthcoming from either the Foreign Office or the Ministry of Overseas Development.

With hindsight it now seems that the vision of an Atlantic College replica at Changi was even more illusory in terms of recurrent costs. Atlantic College was at last financially viable because, after passing through the perilous period described earlier during the build-up of numbers, it had reached a stage where it could support itself on the original pattern of scholarships and fee-paying.

It seems most unlikely, however, that a second Atlantic College at Changi could ever have hoped to build up such numbers or even the smaller target of 200 adopted in Canada and Italy, even if various proposals made by Desmond Hoare to reduce the cost per place had been adopted. Almost all the students would have had to be boarders, since the policy of the Singapore government was not to allow Singapore citizens to attend private schools. Hankey did succeed in persuading the Minister of Education, who remained very much in general favour of a UWC in Singapore, to make an exception for ten Singaporean scholarship holders, in view of the great importance to a UWC of some participation from the host country; but the rest of the students would have to have been boarders. Where would they have come from? And who would have paid for their scholarships when the cost was so much higher than in local schools? Lee Kuan Yew suggested that the college should aim not just at South East Asia but at East Asia as a whole and so draw heavily on Japan. This might have produced a small entry, though it cut across the plans for the new College in Canada, now firmly planned for the West Coast with an orientation towards the Pacific and Japan; for both political and financial reasons it now seems extremely unlikely that scholars in any numbers would have come from Malaysia, Indonesia, Vietnam, or the Philippines. European families or donors, given the choice of Canada, the UK or Singapore, could hardly have been expected to choose Singapore much more frequently than they do now for the existing UWC of South East Asia. Finding scholarships to fill 300 places in a College at Changi which replicated Atlantic College would now be a financial nightmare for the UWC movement as a whole.

Fortunately, we were rescued from that by the decision of the Singapore government that they could not spare so large a slice of 'their tiny island' for such a project. In October, at a dinner party given in London, Mountbatten made one last attempt to revive the Changi option, but got a very firm shake of the head from Lee Kuan Yew, who said that he regarded it as unrealistic and urged a return to negotiations with Roy Bennett for co-operation with St John's. Changi as a site proved an *ignis fatuus*, just as had Banff.

The original concept of this co-operation from the side of UWC who had, after all, sought to acquire the whole school, was for the establishment of a separate UWC sixth-form college on part of the site, which would provide for a limited number of students 'coming up' from the lower forms of the International School but would draw mainly on students selected by the national committees which Mountbatten proposed to set up throughout the region.

In a letter to Lee Kuan Yew of August 1970, before the Changi option had been raised, Mountbatten made it clear that UWC was not then intending to be involved at all with the earlier stages of education. The Singapore High Commissioner in London also stressed the importance of the UWC sixth-form college being truly international and separate. As the new negotiations progressed, it became clear that the Study Committee, now developing into the board of governors of the Singapore International School, did, after all, want the school to provide sixth-form education for expatriates. They therefore saw co-operation with UWC and the admission of boarders from Malaysia as the means by which they could achieve adequate numbers. The British High Commissioner, Sir Arthur de la Mare, in a series of letters to Hankey made it clear that although both governments were strong supporters of the UWC involvement, the first priority for Singapore was the establishment of St John's as an effective international school. His analysis of the problems of transition from a British Forces school to an international school typifies the process which was beginning all over the world of 'national schools overseas', whether of American, British, or other origin, gradually developing into international schools, as the national composition of the fluctuating, mobile international community changed. "As regards complications in the attitudes of expatriates here", he wrote, "I think the main problem is likely to be a certain conflict between on the one hand the predilections of the British community for a school on the British Public School model and on the other the fact that the school will have to adapt its curriculum and methods to the needs of pupils of very mixed race and nationality preparing themselves for universities in many different countries".[6] It is not surprising that Hankey should have already cleared with Brigadier Mullins of the Army Education Corps, who was acting as a consultant to the new school, that he saw no objection to the introduction of the IB.

A pragmatic bargain was soon struck and before the end of October it had been agreed that Singapore International School as a whole should become an 'Associate School of the United World Colleges' and that UWC would be responsible for providing a flow of scholars into the sixth form, selected and financed by national committees to be set up in the area. During these negotiations, Hankey made what he called "the revolutionary suggestion" that the whole school might become a UWC. Desmond Hoare went out to Singapore in January 1971 and arranged that Atlantic College should provide two of its senior housemasters, Meurig Owen as Headmaster and John David as Director of Studies, together with four ex-students, a girl from Finland, and young men from Canada, India, and Peru, to act as assistant teachers in the international sixth form. He soon reported that co-operation had got off to a good start and that the first UWC students would enter in September 1972, but one decision of the new board bitterly disappointed Hankey. This was that it would be politically unwise to press the Prime Minister to implement, for SIS, as an associate school, the offer to allow ten Singaporean scholars to enrol in a UWC. One can understand both Hankey's disappointment and the delicacy of the political situation since SIS was undoubtedly a private school. Robert Blackburn recalls Lee Kuan Yew explaining to Mountbatten that Singapore must concentrate on national education to create a new nation-state before it could afford the luxury of international education.

Singapore International School began the new academic year in September 1972 in a very different situation from that which had been expected. Far from being underfilled, it had a total enrolment of nearly 1,200, considerably more than St John's had had. This was mainly due to an unexpected residual demand from the military. The sixth form had expanded from 50 in 1971 to 120 and its British percentage declined from 42 to 39. It included nine UWC scholars, six from Australia and one each from Italy, Spain, and the UK, but none from South East Asia. The curriculum was based on the same combination of GCE A-levels and college subsidiary subjects which had been used at Atlantic College before the adoption of the IB.

In March 1974 Mountbatten again visited Singapore and SIS, including the Jungle Centre in Johore which SIS had established with financial support from UWC. As a result of this visit he concluded that there were only two options possible, either to bring to an end the 'association' or to admit the whole school as a United World College. He therefore wrote to the newly-formed Executive Committee of the UWC International Board, strongly recommending that SIS should become a full member of the United World Colleges—Hankey's "revolutionary suggestion" made during the earlier negotiations.

The proposal was indeed revolutionary and of very great importance for the UWC movement as a whole. As recently as 1967 Hankey, on one of his early visits to Canada, had been instructed to insist that only a school on the Atlantic College pattern could be accepted within the movement. Nevertheless when the board met in May the force of Mountbatten's personality and the growing realisation among many members that a world-wide chain of 'Atlantic Colleges' would be a miracle that not even he could achieve, produced an initially favourable reaction. The Executive imposed only two conditions, the introduction of the IB and an increase in the number of UWC scholars. A formal resolution to recommend to the International Council the acceptance of SIS as the United World College of South East Asia was taken at the board's meeting in November 1974.

The IB had by then been introduced. In speaking to staff and parents' meetings during 1974 I found, as at Ecolint, the main reluctance coming from parents, not necessarily British, who had been relying on the Cambridge Overseas GCE as a channel to British or Commonwealth Universities. As at Ecolint, the IB was therefore first introduced as an alternative track to GCE A-levels, but again as at Ecolint, the preferences of the students and the complication and cost of running two tracks led to the final abandonment of the GCE and a single curriculum based on the IB.

The acceptance as a United World College of what, for the majority of its pupils, was an all-age, all-ability, international secondary day school, serving, like other international schools, the expatriate community of a large international city, undoubtedly caused misgivings among some well-established members of the UWC movement. There have always been some who have felt that Singapore and the second school of this type, the United World College of Southern Africa in Swaziland, are not 'real' or 'pure' United World Colleges.

It is true that they do not replicate the characteristics of Atlantic College. The students as a whole have not been selected on merit, nor are the great majority there because they have chosen commitment to an ideal of education for international understanding. They are mostly sons and daughters of families who happen to be working in the area and, having chosen this as the best school available, pay fees to go there. These are very different schools to the tight-knit communities of sixteen-to-eighteen year olds, living together, working together, and adventuring together, which Kurt Hahn envisaged.

Yet, on the other hand, it must be allowed that they provide an opportunity, perhaps just as great as that of the 'real' colleges, to spread the ideals for which the UWC stands. To a certain extent the pure or classic type are preaching to the converted, while the other type are actually doing the converting. I found, and this was confirmed by the principal and also, I believe, in Mountbatten's experience, that the enthusiasm for the ideals of UWC at Singapore was every bit as great among the ninth and tenth grade as among the eleventh and twelfth. It is unfortunately true that the flow of UWC scholars to the upper school has never been as substantial as either the college or the International Board would have liked,[7] but provided that there is enough commitment within the school to keep the flame alight, is there so very much difference between the educational experience of a young German or Italian who comes as a UWC scholar and that of a young German or Italian who comes because his parents are working in Brunei and choose this school?

The final acceptance of the United World College of South East Asia took place, on the recommendation of the Board, at a meeting of the International Council held on Vancouver Island in April 1975 for the official opening of the Lester B. Pearson United World College of the Pacific. The race, if it was a race, for the title of the 'second United World College' therefore ended in a dead heat. To understand how that happened we must return to Canada, but before doing so a word is needed about a third contender, Italy. The idea put forward by Gianfranco Facco Bonetti, after his discussion with Desmond Hoare, that a college should be founded in the neighbourhood of Trieste met with an enthusiastic response from the regional government of Friuli-Venezia-Giulia· which set up a consortium of influential Italians, led by Avvocato Pacia. Within a few months they had produced a possible cliff-top site at Sistiana just north of Trieste. In his planning letter of July 1974 Mountbatten actually mentioned 1976 as the opening date for the college. As so often happened, the first site ultimately proved to be neither very suitable nor even available, but, as in Canada, this turned out in the long run to be a blessing.

In June 1974 the Italian founding group and UWC International Office organised an educational conference, held at the Castello Duino, just up the coast, where Rilke wrote the first two Duino Elegies. This historic setting, with a mediaeval castle overlooking the sea, was far more attractive—and extraordinarily like the site of Atlantic College. The purpose of the conference was to discuss the whole programme of a United World College in Italy. It was assumed that the academic programme would be based on the IB and I therefore chaired the academic panel, while David Sutcliffe, who had succeeded Desmond Hoare as principal, sent over two teachers and a group of students from Atlantic College to investigate the opportunities for social service and life-saving activities. The students' report was used as the basis for the Italian college's activities programme when it finally opened. From this time on Gianfranco Facco Bonetti became project manager for the college.

The education panel, recognising the historic importance of Trieste as a cross-roads of Italian, German, and Slavonic cultures, included members from Austria, Federal Republic of Germany, Hungary, Italy, Malta, Netherlands, Switzerland, UK, USA, and the EEC. Its main recommendations were: that the language of instruction should be English, but that all students should include Italian as one of their IB languages and learn enough Slovene to communicate in the neighbourhood; that a strong department of Arabic studies should be set up and efforts made to attract a student intake from the Eastern Mediteranean; and that an International Centre for Adult Education should be linked with the College. The students also were enthusiastic about the opportunities for adventure and social service in the neighbourhood. Sailing, skiing, mountain climbing, and pot-holing were all available, with their concomitant opportunities for rescue training and service, although the coast was not a dangerous one as at Atlantic College. They even suggested that the College might provide the village with something which at the time it lacked, a local fire brigade. Most important, perhaps, the conference revived the already growing interest of the Prince of Torre e Tasso, the owner of the castle. He still lived in the main part of the castle, but there were some buildings dating from the eighteenth century which had long been unoccupied, and the possibility of grouping the college around these and other contemporary buildings in the centre of the village made Duino itself the ideal site. Perhaps even more important was the recruitment to the founding consortium of Corrado Belci, a former member of Parliament for the region and a man of great influence in both Trieste and Rome. The role that he played in the founding of the College of the Adriatic is curiously similar, as we shall see, to that played by John Nicol in Canada.

All looked well set, but in May 1976 the earthquakes in Friuli, which rendered 70,000 people homeless, called for all the energy and resources of the extremely energetic regional government. For the next three years work on the college project had to be put aside and Bonetti was given the task of organising the relief works, taking on the post of Consul in Capodistria, at considerable risk to his career prospects, partly in order to remain in contact with UWC proposals.

In Canada, however, things were moving rapidly to a climax during the negotiations in Singapore. In 1971 Senator Cameron, who was in bad health, resigned as chairman of the national committee and was succeeded by Colonel Robert Houston, who had been on the committee from the start and had also served on Darvall's staff. The college project was now firmly committed to the West Coast and three very bold decisions were taken: to set up a separate, Western-based, founding committee and ultimately governing body for the college, to appoint a headmaster who could play a leading part in its design and to purchase from the Defence Department at a very favourable price a virgin site on Pedder Bay, fourteen miles from Victoria. The key to the success of this great gamble lay, as usual, in people.

For the founding committee Mountbatten was able to persuade Jack Clyne, an influential West Coast businessman and political figure, to give his active support. Unfortunately this appointment coincided with one of the many false trails which occasionally diverted Mountbatten's attention. The US Commission, which had for years taken no substantial part in the development of a North American college, came up with another proposal to found a North American UWC by acquiring a ready-made college, in this case an existing school in Vermont. The project soon proved to be one of the least acceptable of the many suggestions of this kind, but by the time Mountbatten and the board had realised this, largely through the influence of Lola Hahn, the harm was done. The Canadians were deeply hurt that all their work had been jeopardised in this way.

At this stage Lester Pearson came to the rescue by persuading the Hon. John Nicol, an immensely influential Western politician, who had masterminded his own campaign for the premiership, to take over responsibility for getting the college founded; Jack Matthews, the headmaster of Lakefield School in Ontario, who had been an active member of the National Committee from its early days and had spent a year at Gordonstoun, gave up his post to become director of the as yet nonexistent college; and David Wills provided the seed money to make this advance work possible and also nearly 90,000 to purchase the site at Pedder Bay.

John Nicol was in those days rather like a second Mountbatten, with the same capacity for getting things done, the same tendency to bulldoze his way through obstacles and the same combination of charm and conviction, that made it almost impossible to say no to him. It is said that he had the bulldozers into the forest at Pedder Bay before the funds to build a college had been raised, and it was even hinted that this was before he had title to the land.

His powers of conciliation were shown in averting the danger of a clash between East and West coasts, which seems almost inevitable in North America. After a visit to British Columbia, Cedric Sowby came back with all his misgivings allayed: the national committee remained based in Ontario and got on with its highly professional selection and funding of Canadian students for Atlantic College, while the founding committee assumed responsibility for the Canadian College. Largely, of course, this consisted of fund-raising for capital projects and John Nicol and Jack Mathews must have been one of the most effective fund-raising teams in educational history. They were ably supported by Jim Coutts's scholarship fund committee.

In David Sutcliffe (who is now Director of the Italian College and Vice-President of the IBO Council) and Jack Matthews the first colleges had two very remarkable leaders. I have known a great many school principals in my day but never any under whom I would rather have served or studied. Jack was able to plan his college from the start and saw it, not as the familiar campus of classroom blocks and halls, but as a village in the forest in which students of all nations would live, study, and serve their local community as well as the wider world. Regular student meetings were even known as 'the village meeting' and he was 'Jack' to each student. Yet they studied hard and, though perhaps getting less intensive classroom teaching, got just as good grades in the IB. One day, walking the nature trail above the College, I came face to face with a splendid girl from Sierra Leone:

"Are you the International Baccalaureate?" she said in a deep African voice.

"I suppose I am."

"You are a terrifying monster."

"Why am I a terrifying monster?"

"Because you make me do mathematics."

But I learned later that the terror diminished and she got her IB diploma in the end.

The IB was even more essential for a college in Canada than for Atlantic College. There was no Canadian system of national examinations, and no university outside Canada would have accepted a Canadian high school diploma alone as an entrance qualification. But by the time that the decision to build at Pedder Bay was taken, Robin Hankey had contacted almost every university in Canada and ensured the acceptability of the IB.

The death of Lester Pearson seemed at first yet another blow to the hopes of a college, but Mrs Pearson, who had accompanied him on his visit to Atlantic College, knew how much he had cared for the college in Canada, as a contribution to peace and understanding. She and John Nicol were able to convince the Canadian government that the most appropriate national memorial to her husband would be, not a statue or a building, but generations of young people coming to Canada to learn the art of living together as inhabitants of one world. The Canadian college, renamed the Lester B. Pearson United World College of the Pacific, thus became the first college to exemplify to the full the 'strong' concept of a college. Not only did the government recognise it as officially Canada's national memorial to a great Canadian and contribute substantially to the capital costs, but this recognition made the raising of loans and capital funds for a rapid building programme very much easier. Above all, the federal government agreed to endow 40 scholarships each year for foreign students— nearly half the student entry.

John Nicol, in his address to the Senate on 15th February 1973, had made one particular statement of very great importance to the movement as a whole: "To begin with I should like to tell you what it is not. It is not a private school for the children of rich people. We are aiming for 100 percent scholarship enrolment. We realise that this is extremely difficult, but that is what we are aiming for."[8]

This very 'strong' statement has affected, not only the policy of Pearson College, but that of the whole UWC movement, ever since, and its implications will be discussed in the final chapter. At the time it was made it was clearly important to his hearers, but I doubt whether any of them asked themselves whether "100 percent" meant that every student at the college would be receiving a scholarship, or that every scholarship would cover the full cost of tuition, board and lodging, or perhaps both.

The opening ceremony, carried out by Mountbatten and Mrs Maryon Pearson in April 1975, with the first 100 students already at work in the 'village', was a triumph of determination and perseverance. Among the dignitaries present was Prince Sadruddin Aga Khan, the High Commissioner for Refugees, representing the United Nations.

The two colleges which formally joined the movement on that day could hardly have been more different. Pearson College, with its simple buildings of local redwood is very unlike the mediaevel core of Atlantic College, but I have never been quite able to decide which site is the more physically beautiful: UWC South East Asia has fine functional buildings but as little natural beauty as the rest of Singapore. Pearson is like a timber village in the midst of a forest: South East Asia is like any good international school in the midst of a great commercial city. Pearson, with its hundred percent scholarship policy, exemplifies to the full the concept of UWCs as being not private schools but part of a new government-sponsored system of international education: South East Asia, with an average of twelve UWC scholars entering in each of the last five years, thus hardly 'dominating the sixth-form boarders' numbers', is essentially a private international school, in which the UWC movement plays an important animating role. Have they enough in common to justify calling both 'United World Colleges'? Or did Mountbatten make a mistake when, in his determination to expand, he pressed for the change from 'associate school' to full United World College? I think not, but the issue is discussed more fully in the final chapter.

The next two colleges to join the movement, Waterford KamHlaba United World College of Southern Africa, and the United World College of the Adriatic at Duino, were to some extent examples of the two concepts. I place both in this chapter, because, even if neither became a full United World College until after his death, Mountbatten played so great a part in the acceptance or foundation of both, once looking forward to opening the Adriatic College in 1976, that they belong here.

Waterford School was founded as a multiracial school, situated at Mbabane, capital of Swaziland, because it would have been illegal in South Africa. The founders were a group of South Africans led by Michael Stern who had been headmaster of a school in Johannesburg. Despairing of providing the kind of education he believed in within the apartheid system, he threw up his job and set out to create a new school in which students of all races could—as they subsequently did—study together and co-operate in service to the local community. It was given its extra name KamHlaba, which means 'world in miniature', by the King of Swaziland on the occasion of his visit. It opened in 1963 with one classroom, six teachers, and 16 students; one year after the opening of Atlantic College, there were two schools with very similar ideals at opposite ends of the Earth.

Waterford was not, therefore, like Singapore, a typical international school serving the mobile business community, but a school expressly founded in the spirit of the UWC. On the other hand it was an all-age school, most of whose students were fee payers sent there because that was what their parents wanted. By 1975, when Waterford first came in contact with the UWC movement it had 300 students, roughly half boys and half girls, half 'white' and half 'black or brown'. Most of the whites were children of South African families who wanted multiracial education. Its academic standards were high, using the Cambridge Overseas O- and A-levels. On the other hand, as Christopher Newton-Thompson, chairman of the governors, made clear in proposing 'associated school' status on the pattern of Singapore, the school felt itself isolated in Swaziland and believed it would have much to gain by the international contacts which association with the UWC movement would give and much to contribute in the field of community service.

Since the association of St John's in Singapore, there had been much discussion of what should be our policy in increasing the number of associated schools. There were those who felt that the cost in time, effort, and money of establishing new colleges on the classic Atlantic College model was so great that the movement might stagnate. It seemed to them that the only chance of exerting a world-wide influence was to recruit around this nucleus an inner ring of perhaps a dozen associated schools, which would work in close collaboration with the other colleges and with the International Office. Beyond this, an outer ring would form itself of hundreds of IB schools round the world, since the IB curriculum embodied much of the UWC philosophy in its internationally-oriented syllabuses and CASS activities, although not, of course, the same degree of commitment to adventure training and community service, and nothing approaching the UWC scholarship policy. The advantage to the associated school was seen as being a remedy partly for isolation, as at Waterford, and partly for lack of continuity. The rapid turnover of staff at international schools has already been mentioned: for many this extended to Directors and governing bodies also. There were some schools where the staff or governors felt that formal association with the UWC would give the school a more lasting commitment to its educational objectives.

On the other hand it was argued that each new associated school would, if the association were to have real meaning, increase the costs of the international office, and there seemed no likelihood of the schools themselves being able or willing to meet these costs. Moreover, those who had welcomed the transformation of the Singapore International School somewhat reluctantly, on the grounds that it was not a 'real' United World College, strongly suspected that any other school which was accepted as an associated school would follow the same path and within a few years be knocking on the door for acceptance as a full United World College.

The Board, therefore, determined to proceed rather cautiously with proposals for association. At the meeting in October 1977 it agreed that existing "acceptable" schools should be encouraged to come into association, but that a decision on formal membership should be preceded by "a period of informal linking of appropriate length between these schools and existing United World Colleges". No doubt individual members of the board had their own ideas of what length would be appropriate. The first two informal links of this kind were established between Waterford and Atlantic College and the British Schools Montevideo and Pearson College.

This was the situation on 31st December 1977 when Mountbatten, who had always announced that he would retire from the presidency on reaching the age of seventy-five, handed over, actually a year later, to his great nephew, His Royal Highness the Prince of Wales. Before doing so Mountbatten had strengthened the International Office in a way that is perhaps best described in his own words: "In 1975 when I realised that I really must go I wanted to get a Chief of Staff for my successor. As Colonel Commandant of the Royal Marines I knew that the best Commandant General the Royal Marines had ever had was going to retire as four-star General at a very early age. So I persuaded him to come at a salary about half what he would have got in industry to be the first full-time Chairman of the Executive Committee. As you know it was Sir Ian Gourlay. His new title will be Director-General. Without the help and support of these three—Ian Gourlay, Robert Blackburn, and Nina Little—I would never have been able to do half of what has been put in that book—not half." The "book" was a record of all that he had done as President of the United World Colleges. His public farewell was made at a meeting of the International Council at Atlantic College on 13th April 1978, attended by national committee representatives from Australia, Bahamas, Belgium, Brazil, Canada, Caribbean, Egypt, France, Finland, Federal Republic of Germany, Hong Kong, India, Ireland, Italy, Kenya, Mexico, Netherlands, New Zealand, Norway, Singapore, Spain, Sweden, Switzerland, United Kingdom, USA, and Venezuela.

In his farewell speech Mountbatten paid warm tributes to all those who had helped him over the last ten years, first to Sir George Schuster, then to the 'anonymous benefactor' whom he at last revealed as David Wills, to Sir Eric Weiss, who both personally and through his company, had helped both UWC and IBO, to Desmond Hoare, Tony Besse, David Atterton, who had succeeded Sir George as Chairman of the governors, the three headmasters, Roy Bennett, Bob Lutton and George Thomson from Singapore, and finally John Nicol and Page Wadsworth from Canada. He also reiterated his sense of the common interest of UWC and IBO. In thanking Robert Blackburn, who had served him throughout as his Chief Staff Officer, he said: "Robert Blackburn has gone to join the International Baccalaureate as Development Director and I don't hesitate to say that there is nobody in the world more qualified to help the IB in their development. . . . but what we have lost on the swings we appear to have gained on the roundabouts. The former Director General of the IB has just been elected as Chairman of our International Board." It was, in fact, at this time that I took over from Tony Besse who remained as one of two vice-chairmen, the other being Sir James Whitaker who subsequently became chairman of the Atlantic College governors.

During this historic meeting, which included the unveiling of a plaque commemorating Kurt Hahn, Newton-Thompson made with great eloquence the case for admitting Waterford KamHlaba as an associated school without prolonging further the period of informal linking. There were still some doubts among the faithful, but Mountbatten's conviction and enthusiasm overrode them all and the motion for immediate admission was adopted unanimously. This, almost the last of his services to the movement, was by no means the least and was typical not only of his vision but of his capacity for grasping an occasion and carrying others with him.

Those who had assumed that an associated school would very quickly become a full United World College were soon proved right. At the week-long conference at Ditchley Park in 1980, held to review the whole future of the UWC under the new President, it was decided to examine urgently what steps should be taken to bring this about. There were two obstacles: finance and the introduction of the IB. There were some of the usual objections to the IB from teachers accustomed to the heavy degree of specialisation in their subject inherent in the English GCE, but the real problem was that, being in the Southern Hemisphere, with many students going to South African universities, Waterford worked to a different academic year and needed an examination session in November. It is a mark of the close co-operation between UWC and IBO that, although a November session of the IB was clearly foreseen as a long-term goal to serve schools in Australasia and South America, IBO agreed, in spite of the considerable expense, to phase it in earlier than intended for the benefit of Waterford. It was at the same time a gesture on the part of IBO towards the recommendation of the Brussels conference that we should seek to find ways of helping the developing countries, and it allowed us to make some return to Mountbatten for the number of times he had rescued us from bankruptcy. The financial arrangements were agreed in negotiations carried out during the summer of 1981 and the final agreement incorporating into the movement the Waterford KamHlaba United World College of Southern Africa was signed early in 1982. It was a pace of development which Mountbatten would have heartily approved, though he did not live to see it.

Nor, too, did he live to preside, as he had once hoped, at the opening of the United World College of the Adriatic. The founding consortium did not allow itself to be daunted for very long by the earthquakes and in 1977 Pacia was able to report that, with the aid of the National Committee, they had been able to get the legislation concerning the improvement of Higher Education in the Trieste area which included the College, merged with the Friuli-Venezia-Giulia Recovery Bill. This would have given immediate central government backing to their plans, but unfortunately members of Parliament from the Communist Party, which was strongly supporting the project locally, were comparative strangers to it in Rome, and demanded more information. On 5th October that year Belci, Bonetti, Migone, Pacia, and de Antoniis, a consultant to the IBO, met with two Communist MPs and all was satisfactorily explained. A sum of 700 million lire (roughly $800,000) was earmarked by the Fondo Trieste for the project and to this was added the equivalent of a further $1.3 million by the regional government.

From then on negotiations on the UWC side were taken on by Tony Besse, as one of the deputy-chairmen of the Board, and David Sutcliffe. Both made frequent visits to Duino for consultation with members of the consortium including Belci, who finally accepted the Chairmanship at the unanimous request of his colleagues.

David had by now a very clear idea of the kind of college it should be in terms of environment and social life. From Atlantic College he took the model of a historic castle as the core. To this the regional government added the old custom house, dating from the 18th century, almost at the gates of the castle, and a former village elementary school which has been converted admirably into a classroom and laboratory block, known as the Mountbatten Academic Centre. From Pearson College he took the model of the 'village college', but it was a different kind of village. One of the criticisms which have been made of both Atlantic and Pearson colleges is that their extremely beautiful sites are too isolated. The college of the Adriatic was also to be in a beautiful environment, but, instead of having an isolated campus, its residential buildings were to be scattered about the village, rather as Oxford colleges are scattered about Oxford. First-year students were to be housed in the restored castle foresteria, or guest wing, getting their own breakfast, but the plan was that second-year students should get bed-and-breakfast in local boarding houses during what was the 'off season' of a tourist resort. This was a concept which I first came across during the planning of the University of Sussex, the first of the new twentieth-century Universities in England. The cost of building 'halls of residence' was to be saved by lodging the students with 'seaside landladies' whose brief summer season co-incided with the university vacation. In Duino it was conceived not just as a device for saving capital cost (though that was at-tractive) but as part of a deliberate policy of fostering the closest possible contact between the students of many nations and their host community. Instead of acres of playing fields, a sports centre, with facilities for swimming and sailing, was to be developed in a nearby village both for the college and for the local community. The library, named in memory of Ambassador Migone, would be in the old custom house building, and, although highly efficient in terms of electronic retrieval technology, smaller than in other colleges. So arrangements would be made for students to have library facilities at the University of Trieste. Unfortunately the 'seaside landlady' plan did not work out in practice any more than it has in Sussex, but the interaction with the village is still greater than at other colleges.

With a planned proportion of 25% Italian students, this close involvement with the host country reproduced to some extent the pattern of Waterford KamHlaba and at present the proportion of Italian students is actually higher.

As in Canada, the various provinces of Italy were persuaded to fund scholarships, beginning with ten from the region of Friuli-Venezia-Giulia, while the central government funded ten scholarships for students from developing countries. As a result the college was from the start 'one hundred percent scholarship' and, perhaps even more than Pearson College, a part of the national system of education, rather than a 'private school'. The delays imposed by the earthquakes meant that it was necessary to renegotiate the agreements reached with the Prince of Torre and Tasso about the use of buildings in the castle, and changes in the Italian government imposed some further delays and caused some hesitation among board members. But by 1981 Tony Besse reported that negotiations with the Prince had been successfully concluded, while both regional and central governments were enthusiastic. He therefore proposed that an opening date of September 1982 should be accepted as a firm commitment. There were still some legal formalities to be completed, but any further delay would mean a risk of losing the money included in the budgets of the Fondo Trieste and the Regional Authority. This forward policy was strongly backed by Migone. It was a gamble, but a gamble that had to be taken. The Board therefore set up a Duino-based steering committee, consisting essentially of the consortium with Tony Besse, who was empowered to negotiate for UWC, as chairman. The job of this committee was to continue to move forward the project for an opening date in September 1982, to appoint a director and to complete the legal formalities for setting up a governing body of the college, into which it would then merge. The pattern was very like that which had been followed in Canada and Singapore.

David Sutcliffe, who had served 13 years as headmaster of Atlantic College, accepted a very warm invitation from the Italian sponsors to come over as the first rector of the new college. His first brochure, setting out the plans on which the steering committee had been working, ended with a reminder both of the castle's history and of the fundamental purpose of a UWC: "On the 27th of June 1914 the Archduke Franz Ferdinand of Austria spent his last night at Duino castle before leaving for Sarajevo, where his assassination led to the outbreak of the First World War. This event is itself a challenge to us to ensure that future generations passing through Duino have a happier influence on world affairs."

Building plans never go quite according to schedule, but the first students did enter the college in September 1982. This was made possible by yet another gesture of the regional authorities, who made available the Europa Hotel, a few miles up the coast, to provide both working and living space, while the renovation works were still going on. By the time of the formal opening—by the Prince of Wales in October 1984—of the Mountbatten Academic Centre and the Migone Library, the renovations of the foresteria, of the old custom-house, and of the elementary school had been completed and the dream, at least in its first phase, had become a reality.

The last time I saw Mountbatten was in 1978, the year before his death. At a luncheon party given by Sir Eric Weiss, a group of his friends and admirers met to discuss a project which some of us had thought up to celebrate his eightieth birthday: the establishment in London of a permanent memorial in the form of a 'Mountbatten Center for International Education' (an outline of which, as subsequently submitted to the UWC Board, will be found in Appendix 3). It was decided that I should call on him and test his reaction. He liked the proposal, partly, I think, because it appealed to him as another new initiative by UWC, partly because the idea of housing the UWC and IBO offices in a common building with shared technical facilities, financed in part by rents from other co-operating international organisations, appealed to his engineering and practical side and partly because he liked the idea of exploiting his own old age in one more great fund-raising exercise for the cause. Just as he had once planned in the greatest detail his own funeral, so he set out to give me detailed instructions on how potential supporters of his memorial were to be approached. No one was to say that 'they represented Lord Mountbatten', but in writing to his friends in America we could ask for an interview to discuss 'a matter which concerned Lord Mountbatten' and then disclose in conversation that the scheme had his approval.

But the eightieth birthday never happened. On 27th August 1979 he and his family were out lobster-fishing off the coast of Ireland when a bomb, planted by the IRA, blew up the boat. He, one of his grandsons, and a local fisher-boy were killed instantly; the rest dreadfully injured. To murder in so horrible a way an old man who had spent the last ten years of his life working for peace was a strange way to promote a political cause; but for Mountbatten himself it was a good end. To quote his biographer: "To die with no time for fear or regrets, doing what he enjoyed most with the people who were above all precious to him, escaping the horrors of increasing decrepitude or senility, to end not with a whimper but with a bang that reverberated around the world—that truly was the fate Mountbatten would have chosen for himself. But for the tragedy of the other victims, it could be said that he was the most fortunate of men."[9]

Notes to Chapter Five

[1] Letter from Lord Hankey to the Rev. Cedric Sowby.
[2] Private communication.
[3] Philip Ziegler, *Mountbatten* (London: Collins, 1985), 663-666.
[4] United World Colleges, *Guidelines* (London, 1984).
[5] Letter from General Kitching to Robert Blackburn, 6 April 1970.
[6] Letters from Sir Arthur de la Mare to Lord Hankey, 1971.
[7] Desmond Hoare, in his newsletter to former students of 1 January 1971, wrote: "UWC entries will, I believe, dominate Sixth Form boarders' numbers from the 1972 entry onwards."
[8] *Record of Proceedings of the Canadian Senate*, 15 February 1973.
[9] Ziegler, op. cit., 700.

6
THE INTERNATIONAL
BACCALAUREATE
IN NORTH AMERICA

The growth in IB programs in the USA and Canada came as something totally unexpected to the European founders. The following table, showing the number of schools and colleges authorised to teach the IB in Asia, Africa, Europe and North America, dramatically illustrates the course of this new development:

	Asia	Africa	Europe	North America
1977	9	3	29	10
1978	9	5	37	19
1979	14	4	41	24
1980	17	5	42	40 (including 12 Canadian)
1982	21	6	57	65 (including 22 Canadian)
1984	27	10	66	126 (including 36 Canadian)

The rates of growth were, as expected, more or less equal for the first three years after the conclusion of the 'experimental' period. Then, suddenly, in 1980, North America began to leap ahead. The bare figures, however, conceal a more complicated process than appears on the surface, resulting from two of the 'false trails' which appear so often in this history. We began, as anticipated, with a small core of international schools which have participated throughout: UNIS, Washington International School, whose co-founder and Director Dr Dorothy Goodman played a leading part in the councils of the IB over the next decade, the Anglo-American

School (New York), and the French-American School (San Francisco). To them were later added the two United World Colleges: the Lester B. Pearson United World College of the Pacific and the Armand Hammer United World College of the American West (New Mexico). These were the schools that the founders might have expected.

The first false trail that we followed was to approach some of the Ivy League preparatory schools. Harpo Hanson and I spent some time in discussion both at Andover and Exeter. Although we found very considerable interest among the staff, as I did subsequently at Eton, Shrewsbury, and Uppingham in the UK, the exercise proved fruitless. Andover did commit some resources to a serious study of the IB, but came to the conclusion that in pedagogical terms they could produce as good a curriculum themselves, while, for placement at university, students with the backing of Andover and the College Board Advanced Placement credits were probably doing better than they could have done with the IB. There might have been a better case for the IB in England, where such schools are more constricted in designing their own curricula by the demands of the GCE, but today there is only one such school in England, as in the USA, which offers the IB.

The second false trail pointed in the direction of the community colleges. The situation in American education in the mid-seventies seemed to make the IB attractive to community colleges, particularly on the East and West Coasts. Such colleges were awarding a two-year degree, the Associate in Arts, for which a programme of general liberal education seemed well suited. Similar patterns were being tried out in Europe, the Diplôme d'Études Universitaires Générales (DEUG) in France and the Diploma in Higher Education (Dip HE) in England. The rationale underlying these developments was presumably that if tertiary education was to be opened to a much larger percentage of the age group, as many people advocated,[2] only a small proportion of the intellectually-able and academically-motivated would either want to go on to four-year degrees in Liberal Arts or benefit from doing so. The American system benefitted from a degree of transferability to which Europe was not accustomed. Students who completed a well-recognised AA degree in a community college were accepted into the third year of a four-year degree course in many state universities, where they replaced those original entrants who had dropped out at the end of two years.

This road to higher education attracted in the mid-seventies a small but significant number of good students who could not enter four-year colleges directly either because of demographic pressure on places or because they could not afford to spend four years away from home. A community college AA degree combined with an IB gave access to a full bachelor's degree at a four-year college, either a state university or a private university, such as Harvard, which recognised the IB as conferring sophomore status at least.

The man who took the lead in introducing the IB to the community colleges was Seymour Eskow, then President of Rockland Community College, north of New York City. At a meeting of the Board of Directors of IB North America (IBNA) in October 1976 he indicated that there were three areas which attracted American institutions to the IB, the nature of its liberal curriculum, the internal US mobility it permitted, and the two-way flow it created between the US and other countries. For himself and for Rockland it was the third that was the most important. For other institutions it has proved to be the first or, in fewer cases, the second.

Rockland tried two experiments which seemed to have considerable attractions. The first was a 'study year abroad' in which a group of Rockland IB students spent one year of their course at Hammersmith and West London College. This happened during the years in which I was based at Hammersmith, and my impression is that the failure of the experiment was due to inadequate planning and experience in what were still the very early days of the IB. Hammersmith and West London was situated at that time in rather run-down buildings in a run-down area of London, with much less cohesion as a community than Rockland Community College. We did our best to give the 'Rocklanders' a welcome and an international experience, but I don't think we realised how great the culture shock would be, nor how much careful planning and special attention would have been necessary to make a success of this first experiment. In retrospect I can well understand why neither the authorities at Rockland, nor those at Mercer College which also participated, were satisfied with the experiment. I ought to have done more about it myself, being on the spot. The second experiment, carried out in collaboration with the local school board, was to give early admission to the IB course at the college to able and motivated high school students at the end of the eleventh grade on the basis that they would receive their high school diplomas at the end of the first year of their IB course, and Associate in Arts degrees at the end of the second. This seemed an ingenious way of accelerating progress to both the AA degree and the IB but it depended on harmonious co-operation between the college and the school board, which was not always forthcoming. Meanwhile the demographic and economic factors which had made this path to a degree attractive were changing, and the flow of talented students to support it proved inadequate. This was accentuated by a concerted move in the high schools to oppose accelerated transfer in order to maintain their own falling enrolments. In 1977 the IB Annual Bulletin showed five community colleges authorised to enter candidates for the IB, but only one Public High School. By 1980 the last of the community colleges had withdrawn, but the public high schools numbered 22 in ten different states: Connecticut, Massachusetts, Michigan, Ohio, Nevada, New Jersey, New York, Tennessee, Texas, and Wisconsin. In Canada, also, the expansion within the public system had begun, with high schools adopting the IB mainly in Alberta, British Columbia, and Nova Scotia. Today the five international schools in the USA and one in Canada, have been joined by 130 Canadian and US public high schools.

The community college trail had petered out, but expansion within the public high school system went far beyond anything that the IBO Council had ever anticipated. We had, of course, often claimed that the IB provided national systems with a 'test bed for innovation', a useful possibility of experiment with new developments in curriculum and examinations which it would be difficult to try out within nationally-controlled systems. This function is still recognised, even in France, which, although deeply involved in the birth of the IB has become less interested since developing its own *option internationale* within the *baccalauréat*.[3] In a number of countries—Australia, Denmark, France, Federal Germany, Mexico, Netherlands, Norway, Sweden, and the UK— one or two schools in the state system have been authorised to offer the IB and their experience is probably watched by the educational authorities. But the degree of such involvement on a nation-wide scale that happened in North America was something different. What made it possible and what promoted it?

It could only have taken place in countries where there was no central control of either the curriculum or the standards of achievement. In most countries the central government controls both; in the UK there is no central control of curriculum, but at this level both curriculum and standards of achievement are effectively controlled by the GCE examining boards. Only in North America was control of the curriculum left mainly in local hands and control of standards of achievement in the hands of the individual schools and school districts. Such a situation, in which the transition from secondary to higher education presented unique problems, had long created a precedent for private initiatives in the US, though not in Canada. In a country as enormous as the US, with an almost infinite variety of school districts having considerable control over the secondary school curriculum, those responsible for the tertiary stage of education, beginning with such colleges as Harvard or Columbia, clearly needed some criterion of admission which would at least screen out such applicants as were manifestly incapable of following academic courses. The alternative could only have been selection by nepotism or wealth. As we have seen, this screen was provided in Europe by examination systems, more or less centrally-controlled, which, by their very nature, controlled the curriculum. The Constitution of the United States ruled out such a single Federal system and no State government, except to some extent Pennsylvania and New York, felt inclined to meddle in such a matter. It is difficult to see how they could have.

It was left, therefore, to private initiative. As early as 1900 a group of the more prestigious colleges and secondary schools had set up the College Entrance Examination Board, which at first set conventional subject examinations, and supplemented these from 1926 onwards with the Scholastic Aptitude Tests (SATs), so familiar to most American high school students. It must be remembered, however, that the SAT sets out to measure the candidate's 'aptitude' for higher education, not the acquisition of any prescribed skill or body of knowledge. "Although the abilities that the Scholastic Aptitude Test measures are developed abilities, those abilities normally develop rather slowly over a long period of time and under the influence of factors not well understood. This means that students cannot, late in high school, hope to improve their performance on the SAT by studying for it, despite the claims of coaching schools to the contrary."[4] This manifesto against 'swotting for exams' or *bourrage de crane* meant that, except for approximately one third of candidates, who also took achievement tests, the College Board exercised no influence on the curriculum of the eleventh and twelfth grades of high school and even the achievement tests were deliberately made as bland and unobtrusive as possible. This was left entirely to the mercy of the democratic process, through elected school boards and appointed superintendents. For seniors, who were told that they could not improve their SAT scores by study and who had already completed all the credits necessary for graduation, it is not surprising that a form of intellectual apathy should have developed called 'twelfth grade slump', as they waited through the year to start work again at college. It was this slump which Eskow had tried to by-pass by early admission to the IB course in the college. In any case the Board itself estimated that up to 1950 its examinations were not being taken by more than five percent of High School graduates.[5] Perhaps one of the first indications of the growing concern both of the colleges and of the public was a quadrupling of this proportion by 1960. But the SAT was only a screening device and, in a context in which it was assumed that 80% or more of the age-group would soon be going on to tertiary education, it provided no stimulus to curriculum planners, teachers, or students to seek higher levels of achieved academic excellence.

The 'College Board' re-entered the area of curriculum and standards in the mid-1950s with the creation of the Advanced Placement Program. This programme, to quote from the Board itself, "grew out of a concern focused first at the Ford Foundation and given later impetus by Sputnik and by schools threatened by plans for early—that is before high school graduation—admission of their more talented students to college".[6] It was, in fact, the high school's answer to 'twelfth grade slump' and contributed to the controversy discussed by Bell in *The Reforming of General Education* (see chapter three). By 1970, 55,000 students were taking three-hour examinations for AP, 'doing college level work while still in high school', and working to programmes externally prescribed and externally set. The AP 'syllabus' in a subject has never been as detailed or prescriptive as the GCE A-level, but the parallel is quite close.

A precedent had, therefore, been established for the provision to high schools of parts of a curriculum externally designed and leading to examinations externally assessed, not for entry to college but for placement. The fact that the director of the AP program became one of the earliest members of the IB Council was of great importance to the recognition of the IB in North America and co-operation has been close and friendly ever since.

So much for the conditions which made the widespread adoption of the IB in North America possible. What, then, were the factors which made it actually happen? There is a strand of educational thinking in America which has always regarded a liberal education as 'liberating' and thus sought experiences which opened to students horizons wider than those of their home towns, but in more specific terms I would list the main factors as three: public dissatisfaction with the decline in 'standards of excellence' in high schools throughout North America, with a consequent interest in any programs which offered a way of restoring them; the fact that IBNA was separately incorporated as a not-for-profit corporation in New York, with its own board of directors, its own fund-raising capacity and its own budget; and extremely efficient promotion through introductory seminars and teachers' workshops introduced by Gilbert Nicol, who succeeded Charles Rose as Executive Director in August 1977. Let me try to deal with these factors in chronological order.

Ever since the shock of Sputnik there had been increasingly serious concern about standards of education in North America. This concern may have started at the elementary level with such influential books as *Why Johnny Can't Read*, but since the early fifties James Koerner had been exposing the academic weakness of many teacher-training programmes, and Jacques Barzun the lack of intellectual rigour in much college education. With both of these men I had a number of conversations about possible remedies. In 1956 the Council for Basic Education was set up, initially more concerned with elementary education, but gradually extending its interest to the high schools. In 1962 Admiral Rickover, then very influential in the councils of defence, published a fierce indictment of the high school curriculum and standards of achievement, comparing them with those of Switzerland, a country whose strongly decentralised cantonal system and commitment to democracy in a multi-cultural and multi-lingual society seemed to make it more comparable with the USA than other, more centralised European countries.[6] I met Rickover at this time at a luncheon party arranged at his request by the First Lord of the Admiralty in London, and Rickover's passionate interest in all plans for educational reform, such as the IB, was very apparent. There were, of course, those who defended the very leisurely pace and absence of 'elitism' or academic competition in the North American system, pointing out that American PhDs were every bit as good as European—only it took them longer to get there, which was something that a rich nation could afford.

Nevertheless concern about the lack of intellectual challenge to the talented and motivated in the high school persisted and it was hard to argue that twelfth grade slump was a stimulating experience. Throughout the seventies and early eighties a series of enquiries, such as the President's Commission on Foreign Language and International Studies, highlighted the areas of greatest concern. They culminated in a spate of reports in 1983-4, of which one of the earliest and most comprehensive was that of the National Commission on Excellence in Education, published in April 1983 under the title *A Nation at Risk*. Six hundred thousand copies of this report were sold and it was reprinted so much in large-circulation journals that the final estimate of its circulation is well over six million.[7] Another was the Report on Secondary Education in America by the Carnegie Foundation for the Advancement of Teaching, published under the title of *High School*, which has already been mentioned in chapter three.

In terms of the curriculum, the recommendations for a core curriculum of these two reports are very close to the IB pattern. *A Nation at Risk* proposes for the college-bound: four years of English (Language A), at least two years of a foreign language (Language B), three years of mathematics, three years of social studies (Study of Man in Society), three years of science (Experimental Sciences) and half a year of computer science. The five compulsory subject areas are the same as those of the IB, and computer science is an optional topic in the IB. *High School* covers a broader spectrum of the whole high school course, but all the five areas are there; to these it adds "Service, the New Carnegie Unit" the equivalent of IB's CASS requirement and for seniors the " 'Senior Independent Project', a written paper that focuses on a significant social issue and draws upon the various fields of study in the academic core", the equivalent, that is, of the IB's 'Extended Essay', with perhaps some element of the Theory of Knowledge objectives included.

It is not difficult to see why in such an educational climate some high schools concerned for academic excellence began to think of introducing an IB track. Because of the decentralisation of the American system they were free to do so. They soon found that although the IB examinations were based only on a two-year course

Meeting of Executive Committee of UWC at London House. 1986. Left to right: three office staff, Jack Matthews, Gianfranco Facco Bonetti, Sir Michael Parsons, Dr Armand Hammer, Professor Thomas Symons, The Hon. Kingman Brewster, the author.

The three planners of the Café de Remor (see Chapter 2) twenty years later.

H.R.H. The Prince of Wales chatting with students at the Lester Pearson United World College of the Pacific. (See Chapter 7.)

At an IB Executive Committee meeting, La Mainaz, Switzerland. 1981. Left to right: John Goormaghtigh, Piet Gathier, the author. (See Chapter 2.)

A rescue boat manned by students of the United World College of the Atlantic. Such boats have saved some two hundred lives. 1978. (See Chapter 7.)

Students at the Waterford KamHlaba United World College of Southern Africa, Swaziland. 1985. (See Chapter 5.)

Presentation of the 10,000th IB diploma by Signora Falcucci, Italian Minister of Public Instruction to Jaako Personen, a Finnish student from International School, Moshi, Tanzania. (See Chapter 7.)

Mountbatten presenting the first IB diplomas in the Greek Theatre of the Geneva International School. 1971. (See Chapter 4.)

covering the eleventh and twelfth grades, the necessary preparation for entry on these courses stretched down, and so affected the whole school through the aspirations of students who hoped to enter the IB track in their junior year. In European languages, for instance, the standards of the IB courses and examinations had been based on European practice which assumed the study of a foreign language for a minimum of four years.

It was possibly this influence of the IB not only on the whole curriculum of the eleventh and twelfth grades but on the academic pattern of the whole senior high school that led a number of high schools to experiment with the IB rather than simply to introduce or expand AP courses. There were, of course, other reasons. AP was by now very familiar and widespread throughout the country. For schools anxious to be in the forefront and particularly for 'magnet' schools, such as Rufus King in Milwaukee or Lincoln Park in Chicago, seeking to offer something distinctive, it was particularly attractive. Some of those who already had flourishing AP courses and then introduced the IB as well may have benefitted from a 'Hawthorne Effect'.

Nevertheless the IB did offer something more: a coherent curriculum based on a positive, though flexible, concept of education, a sense of excitement for both students and teachers deriving from participation in an international co-operative project and a challenge deriving from matching themselves against international standards. It was well put by Daniel Tyson, a teacher at the Armand Hammer United World College of the American West, in an editorial originally published in *Independent Schools*, a publication of the National Association of Independent Schools: "In 1982 almost 142,000 students wrote one or more Advanced Placement examinations . . . in that same year 1,449 students in North America entered two-year programs leading to the IB . . . A natural question is 'Why introduce the IB to challenge good students when the AP program already provides this opportunity?' One answer is the kind of challenge each provides. It is one thing for students to prepare for AP examinations in subjects they like and do well in. It is another kind of challenge to prepare for external examinations that cover an entire curriculum, integrate one's learning in the Theory of Knowledge course, write an extended essay and perform community service."[8] One sees here an echo of the controversy between group certificates and subject certificates in the UK, but one also senses an obligation on the IB planners to make each element in the course as little distasteful as possible. Robert Birley, who ultimately became a great supporter of the IB at Atlantic College, originally opposed it because he had watched German students studying mathematics and hating it. If this involvement of the whole curriculum was what attracted some schools and stimulated their teaching faculty to great co-operative efforts, it was to others the reason for deciding against the IB or withdrawing from it after a few years of experiment. There is no doubt, from teachers' experience reported again and again, that, just as the introduction of the IB course involves some financial cost to the school, so to teach an IB course involves a lot of intellectual input as well as a lot of sheer hard work from the teachers. But again and again they have reported that it has been worth it. Their participation in the teachers' workshops discussed later in this chapter confirms this.

We shall return later to the experience of some public high schools which have joined in this experiment, but a word is due here to the pioneer. The first high school to introduce the IB was Francis Lewis in the Borough of Queens, New York. The Principal, Mel Serisky, had read about it in the press and after attending a conference on education for the talented and gifted, and visiting IB classes at UNIS, decided to introduce an IB track at Francis Lewis in 1977, the first year after the conclusion of IB's 'experimental period'. I remember him saying at the time: "I had programmes for the ethnic, programmes for the handicapped, programmes for the deaf, programmes for the semi-literate, special programmes in computing, but no programme for the brightest students aiming at the best colleges. The fact that IB would admit them to universities overseas was simply a bonus." Mel Serisky and I became firm friends and accompanied each other in presentations about the IB from Niagara Falls to Miami Beach. The school and a bunch of enthusiastic teachers played host to a steady stream of enquiries from other high schools who wanted to see how this new programme worked. UNIS had been the pioneer in introducing the IB to the educational world in the USA: Francis Lewis was the pioneer in introducing it to the public high school.

Belief in the contribution which the IB could make to solving a national problem in education led to the chartering of the International Baccalaureate North America as a separate not-for-profit corporation in New York in 1975, the year in which the IBO's 'experimental' period officially ended.

It was clear that if the possibilities inherent in the IB were to be brought to the notice of school boards and public high schools throughout North America considerable funds would be needed. IBO in Geneva could not have been expected to provide such funds, even if it had had them, which it did not. On the other hand a number of educational foundations were prepared to prime this pump for the benefit of American education, but not to channel funds into an international organisation in Geneva, which might or might not use them in North America. The establishment of IBNA as something not unlike a subsidiary of IBO, marketing the product—that is the curriculum and examinations—in North America, and raising funds in North America for use in North America, seemed a neat solution. Gérard Renaud objected very strongly at a later period to this metaphor of 'marketing a product' and of course the relationship of IBNA and IBO was always much closer and more subtle than that of an agency operating a franchise. IBNA is in spirit, if not legally, a part of IBO as much as an arm is of a body. The Americans who serve on the IB Council or Executive do so as 'ad personam members', not as representatives of IBNA, although of course the fact that they do transmit the views of the IBNA board to Geneva and those of Geneva to the Board is extremely valuable. The role of American examiners on the Examining Board is in no way different from that of British, French, or German examiners.

This was always recognised in New York and Gil Nicol put it well in an early activities report during one of our frequent cash flow crises (June 1978): "Because IBNA is an integral part of IBO and has, in effect, if not legally, no separate existence, the Executive Committee agreed that IBNA should do all in its power to help IBO to make up the balance of the projected deficit. Unhappily IBNA is no more prosperous (despite the widely held misconception that America is the land of never-ending surpluses) than IBO." The fact is that in the last years of the seventies both organisations faced the possibility of close-down. But these difficulties affected only financial, not academic, matters. The continued academic quality of the IB was ensured by the fact that the curriculum and examinations remained under international control in Geneva, although individual Americans naturally participated in this academic control, as did those from other countries, and as they always had. On the other hand the establishment of IBNA as a not-for-profit corporation in New York relieved potential donors, often of quite small grants, of the restrictions placed on their support of a foreign not-for-profit organisation. At the same time it reassured them that their funds would be used, not for the general purposes of that foreign institution, but for the promotion of excellence in American education. For the IBO it meant that the expansion of the IB in the US and Canada could go forward without any substantial commitment of our general funds and would ultimately bring in general revenue in the form of examination and affiliation fees. Moreover, the establishment of a close and continuing link between IBNA in New York and the wide range of colleges to which IB students world-wide might be expected to apply would replace the more formal negotiation of the acceptability of the diploma with Ministries of Education in more centralised European systems. For IBNA it made it possible to recruit to the Governing Board men and women of a level of distinction who would never have been available to a 'regional office' of IBO and to set up a structure of committees to oversee the different aspects of the programme of expansion. To have as members of the Board and of the School and College Relations Committee a former New York State Commissioner of Education, the Directors of Admission of Bryn Mawr, Cal. Tech, Harvard, McGill, Michigan (Ann Arbor), and Wisconsin, as well as the Director of Advanced Placement at the College Board, gave IBNA a national standing in its own right. To have an eminent lawyer as its president and the finance director of a major publishing house as its treasurer guaranteed its seriousness.

The initiative in this establishment of IBNA as a separate entity came from Blouke Carus, whose negotiation of the initial grant to IBO from the Hegeler Institute was mentioned in chapter four, and who became Chairman of IBNA in January 1977. As Chairman of Open Court, with a strong commitment to arresting the decline of academic standards (and of the American language in the reading material currently being fed to the young), he had sponsored a series of conferences on educational reform in which the very distinguished members of the company's editorial advisory board took part. The papers delivered at these conferences, published in a regular series, contributed to the discussions on reform to which I have referred. It was a privilege to be invited to these conferences and to have the chance of discussing American problems in education with such people as Jacques Barzun, Cleanth Brooks, and Albert Levi. One never knew who one was going to meet. I remember on one occasion arriving early for a conference at Starved Rock, Illinois, and running into an old man in the lobby. We spent a very pleasant and to me a fascinating hour walking round the gardens and talking, but without introducing ourselves. Indeed, for all we knew, either of us might have been the janitor: when we checked in it turned out that he was Isaac Bashevis Singer.

Blouke quickly saw the potential in the IB for actualising some of the reforms he had been advocating, but he also saw that this would depend on an effective promotion campaign in the US. I do not think either of us realised at first the similar role that the IB could play in Canada, nor quite the extent to which it would expand in the US. Indeed, I remember saying to him once that if ever the number of US schools offering the IB reached 50 it might be necessary to hive off the US operation as an entirely separate concern. This figure was, in fact, reached before the end of 1981 and today there are more than 100.

In the traditional pattern, adopted first at Ecolint and then in Hammersmith, IBO had first accepted the help of Rockland Community College in setting up a regional office for the USA within the college under an enthusiastic teacher, Howard Berry.

The community college track, however, was petering out and two things needed to be found quickly if the IB were to serve the high schools: a separate office and a full-time officer. The College Board offered to provide, on a temporary basis, a desk and telephone at a nominal rent of $125 per month. Dr Charles Rose, essentially an art historian, agreed to serve at least temporarily as executive officer and was succeeded in August 1977 by Gilbert Nicol who has continued as Executive Director of IBNA ever since and to whom, more than any other person, the successful launch of IB in North America is surely due.

Gil Nicol, after serving in Military Intelligence, took his BA at Amherst in 1947 and his Bachelor of Laws at Columbia in 1950. His subsequent career had been passed in college and university administration, including three years as Associate Director of Development at Princeton and five years, from 1971 to 1976, as Executive Director of the Society for College and University Planning. He was, therefore, very experienced in the world of educational planning and fund-raising. He was also sufficiently committed to the cause to be prepared to work very hard in conditions which many people might have found intolerable.

Immediately before he took over from Charles Rose there had

been a number of interim arrangements proposed for setting up a more permanent office but with part-time staff, based either at Harvard (as the London office was later based at London University), UNIS, or the College Board. It was, I think, fortunate that all these were rejected in favour of a full-time Executive Director (for whom a salary would have to be found somehow) and an independent office.

This original office of IBNA, consisting of 200 square feet, partitioned off from the reception area on the ninth floor of an office block on 680 Fifth Avenue, reminded me vividly of the enlarged cupboard which had formed the office of the Director-General at Hammersmith and West London College. How Gil, assisted later by Stephanie Isler, managed to carry on the business of the growing IBNA from such cramped quarters continually amazed me; but they did, and the spectacular growth in the number of schools offering the IB program in North America started well before the move, in May 1983, to more commodious and functional offices at 200 Madison Avenue.

The address may have had its disadvantages and contributed to the myths, which gradually gained credence among some IB principals, that IBNA was a rich organisation flourishing at the expense of other IB schools and of the IBO as a whole. It takes a New Yorker to realise that a Fifth Avenue address can mean anything from affluence to penury. Nothing could have been further from the truth than this myth and its origin really lies in the fact that in the late seventies both IBO and IBNA were struggling desperately to keep their heads above water. It is not surprising that in such circumstances 'headquarters' and 'the field' should have been in occasional dispute about the allocation of resources. In my own experience, in war and peace, I can hardly remember an occasion when headquarters and the field were not in dispute at some level. Unfortunately, voluntary organisations devoted to fostering international understanding are quite as capable of such misunderstandings as anyone else. Dame Margaret Miles, writing of the Council for Education in World Citizenship at a time when it also was desperately seeking funds to keep afloat, records: "The separation from the United Nations Association was not the result of disagreement over policy, but simply of the sheer difficulty of getting money and suitable accommodation. . . . the sight of organisations pledged to the promotion of international harmony and tolerance bickering and squabbling among themselves was neither seemly nor conducive to a confident public image."[9] Some disagreements and disputes were understandable, but there were times when the many men and women of good will in the IBO and IBNA must have felt much the same about some of the suspicions and misunderstandings that arose within our family.

What I would call the reasonable disputes mainly arose over three issues: the proportion of fees paid by schools in North America which should be retained by IBNA to finance its own operations; the fixing of the dollar/Swiss franc exchange rate; and delays in the transmission of dues from one office to the other, arising, in the early days of IBNA, from acute cash flow crises in one or both of the offices.

From the point of view of not-for-profit status it was essential that IBNA should be a separate legal entity responsible solely to its own board of directors and transferring money to IBO Geneva only in return for services received. By far the most important of these was the setting and grading of the annual examinations, but there were other elements in IBO's world-wide operations, such as curriculum development and university recognition, which benefitted IBNA and the North American schools as much as they did schools in other parts of the world. When IBNA was set up, IBO was just moving out of the period of relying on foundation support to that of tripartite funding through examination fees, school subscriptions and regular government support. The first agreement on resources which I tried to negotiate in 1975 was that IBNA should retain all school subscriptions from North American schools, should raise and spend foundation grants within the USA, but should pay over to IBO for services a sum not less than the total examination fees of North American candidates. In 1976 the IBO executive committee found this a little too generous to IBNA and a 1:4 split of school subscriptions between New York and Geneva was agreed. Until both organisations were more financially secure, disagreements about allocation, exchange rates and cash flow were almost inevitable, but were contained by good will. Occasionally, because of my real liking for America, I found myself defending the American point of view in the international forum of Geneva, just as, because of my real liking for France, I found myself defending the French point of view in London or New York.

In 1980 Blouke Carus, with considerable foresight, announced that he wished to retire as active chairman of IBNA in order to devote more of his time to IBO, of whose International Council he had long been a member. His former role was assumed by Tom Hagoort, the present president, who had been involved both in the founding of the Washington International School and of the relocation of UNIS.

It was in February 1981 that the first signs of a possibly serious rift between IBO and IBNA appeared and here there really did seem to me to be an element of unreason.

The annual conference of IB Heads of Schools had been scheduled to take place in New York that year, hosted by UNIS. These annual conferences sprang out of the reconstitution of the IB Council with one third of its membership representing the schools and elected by the schools themselves. They have alternated between Geneva and one of the other major cities—Vienna, New York, Madrid, and Quito—but this was the first to be held on the American continent. They have proved very valuable for the discussion of issues of mutual interest and enhancing the feeling of comradeship among the IB schools. I shall not easily forget the choir of San Estanislao Kostka school outside Madrid singing 'The Hymn of the International Baccalaureate'. The conferences have also proved valuable in providing an opportunity for airing in public myths and misconceptions which have been gradually rankling in private. Gil Nicol had not been present in Vienna in 1979 but had reported some "misrepresentations by several persons who argued that IBNA was a separatist organisation that threatened the future of IBO".

In New York Gérard Renaud forewarned us. At a meeting of the IBNA Board held the day before the conference he reported growing concern about 'the potential Americanisation of the IB programme'. The IBNA office was considered to be too highly-financed and well-paid, and some of the heads of schools present for the conference considered that the cost of IBNA was escalating and constituted too great a drain on the total resources of IBO. Hagoort explained the fallacy involved and the Board decided to hold itself in readiness to correct any misunderstanding which might arise at the following day's conference.

Nevertheless I was astonished to find myself approached on the following day by the headmaster of a school in Asia who claimed to have worked out to his own satisfaction, and to that of some of his fellow principals, that the present system of allocating resources between Geneva and New York must ultimately lead either to a collapse of the whole IBO or to a complete take-over by the

Americans. When these suspicions were voiced in open conference Hagoort invited the protagonists to discuss them with a special session of the IBNA board and the misunderstanding was cleared up. It was on occasions like these that the standing and authority of IBNA board members were so valuable.

It is very difficult to avoid jealousies and misconceptions of this kind in an international organisation whose members rarely meet or visit each other's countries. No one who had actually seen the working conditions at 680 Fifth Avenue could have harboured such illusions for a moment and differentials in salary between such cities as Geneva, London and New York are inevitable, as I have tried to make clear in chapter four.

Later in the year both Blouke Carus and Tom Hagoort attended a meeting of the newly-formed management committee of IBO in London, and allocations were amicably worked out between the two bodies, including a special 'grant' of 20,000 Swiss francs from IBNA to IBO to help with one of the cash flow crises. This precedent was followed in 1983 when IBO faced its greatest and hopefully last financial crisis with a 'grant' of $30,000.

Tom contended at this time that if IBO as a whole was to become financially viable without depending on foundation grants, which would never be made on a continuing basis, it must seek a swift and substantial increase in the number of IB schools, and that under current conditions such an increase could only be found in North America. He has surely been justified. The Brussels Ministers' Conference of 1981 envisaged the finance of IBO coming in equal parts from three sources: examination fees, school subscriptions, and government contributions. Of the three, government contributions have fallen steadily behind and school subscriptions gone steadily ahead. The distribution of income figures for 1984-5 were: examination fees 27.0%, school subscriptions 51.5%, and government contributions 10.3%. There can be little doubt that without the 300% growth of North American IB schools between 1980 and 1985, a period when the number of IB schools in the rest of the world grew by approximately 33%, IBO as a whole might have foundered. If there is one financial principle which international voluntary organisations such as IBO should work on it is surely that of cross-subsidisation. If once we started to calculate the relative cost-benefit of admitting a school in a new part of Africa or one more in a European or American city where we are already working, we should be lost.

It is more than time to return to the progress achieved by IBNA and the Executive Director over the last decade. IBNA faced very much the same financial problems in North America as IBO had done during the first six years. Until a large enough group of schools could be enrolled to fund its operations from school affiliation fees, the initial promotion would have to be funded from grants. These were sought, as IBO had sought them mainly in the UK, from three sources: governments, educational foundations, and business corporations. The US and Canadian governments both contributed, but there were difficulties in both countries arising from their federal structure. In the US the grant, initially $15,000 per annum in 1975, rising to $30,000 in the sixth year, was made first through the State Department and then through the United States Information Agency, of which the State Department bureau supporting IBO became a part. After six years this grant was terminated, but fortunately by this time the Armand Hammer United World College of the American West was being founded and I was able to persuade Dr Hammer to 'pick up the tabs for the USA' for a further three years. In Canada also an annual grant of 5,000 Canadian dollars was made by the External Affairs Department, but all attempts to supplement this from the Council of Education Ministers of the provinces failed, although Alberta individually did contribute. In general the IBO Standing Conference of Governments has found that there are likely to be more problems in negotiating continuing support from countries where education is a state or provincial responsibility than from those with a central Ministry.

Another source of at least semi-official help was International Schools Services, an agency which serves American Schools Overseas and which made grants totalling more than $17,000 in the early years; but for really substantial and continuing support IBNA had to turn, as IBO had during its launching period, to educational foundations, and to a lesser extent, to industry. Here the experience of the two organisations was very clearly parallel. Both had to face the difficulty that foundation aid was almost entirely concentrated in the field of higher education rather than secondary education. Both found repeatedly that foundation officers were attracted by the project but 'regretted that it fell outside the terms of their grant policy'. Both, in the end, found the solution in support coming mainly from one or two foundations, like Dulverton and Gulbenkian in the UK, with which the IBO or IBNA promoters had previous connections.

For IBNA the first major support after the initial grants from the Hegeler Institute came from the Andrew W. Mellon Foundation and was negotiated by Harpo Hanson. By sheer coincidence during Gil Nicol's first year in office the Exxon Education Foundation, with which he already had relations, decided to undertake a limited venture in secondary education and responded to his appeal with a grant in 1978 of $50,000 over three years. In the same year through another old contact The Geraldine Dodge Foundation was persuaded to make its first grant of $25,000. In total, over the launching years, Mellon contributed $330,000, Exxon $100,000, and Dodge $85,000. The whole policy of IBNA was, like that of IBO, to reach self-sufficiency without foundation support (except for special projects such as the support for science development funded by the Alfred P. Sloan Foundation) as quickly as possible, but this could never had been achieved without the help of these three major supporters. As in the UK they were backed by a number of smaller contributions, often at the rate of a thousand dollars a year for some years, from corporate donors such as the Anderson and Company Foundation, Dresdner Bank, New York Times Foundation, and Western Electric. Finally the growing interest in Canada brought grants approximating $10,000 from Gulf Canada and Imperial Oil.

All this may sound like a success story, but as anyone who has ever tried to raise funds for general secondary school curriculum development, as opposed to buildings for an individual school, will know, it was not an easy success. The ratio of successes to applications in appealing to alumni for a new building must always be higher than in appealing to the general educational world for a curricular innovation—or even worse an examination! The two Canadian grants mentioned above were, for instance, the outcome of 21 applications.

These resources, together with the proportion of school fees allocated for retention by IBNA, enabled Gil Nicol to launch his campaign to bring the IB to the attention of schools throughout the US and Canada. Apart from publicity, much of which was generated by the schools themselves, the operations through which he achieved this were short conferences of two types, the 'Introductory Seminars' and 'Teacher Training Workshops'. In his progress summary in 1983 he wrote: "IBNA's Introductory Seminars and Teaching Training Workshops are without doubt the principal consideration in a school's decision to apply for authorisation (i.e. to introduce the program). 21 out of 39 schools applying in 1982/3 had sent representative teachers to the introductory seminars in the last two years. The receipt of 26 applications in June is largely attributable to the schools wanting to send teachers to the September 1983 Teacher Training Workshops."

The introductory seminars were one-day conferences intended simply to introduce administrators and teachers to the programme. Toward the end of the 1978 school year notices of the first seminars were sent to 6,600 school boards, addressed to the associate superintendents for curriculum and instruction, and to 1,500 independent schools. In 1979 nine such seminars were held in the following cities (numbers attending in parentheses): Atlanta (8); Boston (4); Calgary (13); Chicago (12); Houston (21); Los Angeles (8); New York (10); Portland Oregon (15); and Toronto (11). Normally the presentation of the IB was undertaken by one or two people, either from New York or from a school or college in the locality. It depended very much on the availability of people and in the New York seminar both Harpo Hanson and I took part.

Gradually these special seminars were replaced by presentations on the IB made at the annual meetings of teachers or administrators. Here it was often possible to contact far more people who were already assembled for the main conference. Thus in 1980 IBNA was represented at meetings of the American Association for International Education and the American Association of School Administrators at Atlanta, and at those of the National Association of Independent Schools in Boston and the National School Boards Association in Dallas, where over a hundred people attended the IB presentation.

Even though expansion was by now beginning to go even faster in Canada than in the US, no introductory seminars were held in Canada in 1980, simply because the joint meeting of the Canadian Association of School Administrators and the Canadian Educational Association in Vancouver provided such an excellent forum. This proportionately faster and greater expansion in Canada than in the US may have been due to two factors: that Canada had no equivalent to the College Board's AP program and that Canada had a United World College, a sort of demonstration school, which at that time the US did not.

More important in the long run may have been the teacher training workshops. The introduction of the IB to a North American School depended more on the enthusiasm of the teaching staff than on anything else. Some schools which had given serious consideration to the project rejected it because the teachers felt that the extra effort which it demanded from them was not compensated for by the advantages that the school and the students would gain. We have seen this situation before in other contexts and also the great advantage that the IB gained from the fact that where it was introduced it could count on an enthusiastic involvement of the teaching staff. If they were against it, then IB was not introduced.

But the teachers did often feel that even if they were supportive they needed some support themselves. To them, as to the students, the sense of being involved, with schools all over the world, in an international movement was important, but they also valued the contacts and advice that they derived from meeting with teachers in other schools, which had even a little more experience than they had of teaching the programme.

The first teacher-training seminars were introduced in 1978. At the two week-end meetings 97 teachers were enrolled, coming from 26 schools. Some of these were clearly schools not yet enrolled in the programme. Four years later, in 1982, there were 283 from 54 schools and in 1984 four such workshops, held in Calgary, Chicago, New York, and Las Vegas, enrolled 579 teachers from 106 enrolled schools and 19 from seven 'prospective' schools.

Those who conducted such seminars were initially teachers from schools already teaching the program. In 1978, for instance, two workshops were held in Milwaukee and New York and an introductory seminar in Victoria (British Columbia). In Milwaukee two teachers from UNIS, two from Francis Lewis and one from Pearson College took part, in New York eight teachers from UNIS and two from Francis Lewis, in Victoria four from Pearson College.

Recognising the importance to the schools of these teacher training workshops, IBNA tried to minimise the expense from the school's point of view by paying the cost of board and lodging at the centre for up to three teachers from each school and also subsidising travel for these up to a maximum of $150, depending on the distance from the school to the centre. Only in 1979 did lack of funds make it necessary to cancel these subsidies and the effect on attendance was disastrous. IB was already an expensive programme for any school to introduce without involving un-budgeted expenses. As funds began to improve again and the sup-ply of experienced teachers in other schools to build up, it was possible to relieve UNIS of part of the burden which its faculty had so nobly borne. Even more important, it became possible to involve at least one examiner in each subject panel, some of them chief examiners brought over from Europe. In 1983 three chief examiners from Europe, one from America, and one moderator for the Theory of Knowledge course in anglophone schools were involved. Tom Winnifrith, the Chief Examiner in English as Lan-guage A described the program of Las Vegas, Calgary, Chicago, New York as "the flying circus".

All this, of course, cost a lot of money and may have sparked off the jealousy of schools in other continents for whom few if any such workshops were being provided. But it has to be remem-bered that it was only in the free and unregulated system of North America that expansion of this kind in the public system was possible and that it was from this expansion that the money was being provided.

What sort of schools, then, did this promotion in the public sector attract? Gil Nicol in his progress report for 1981/2 gave the following analysis:

"IB Schools in North America seem to have little in common except a consensual interest among teachers and administrators in the aims of the IB program. This is certainly true of the most recent group of admitted schools and is probably just as true for those who have joined in past years. At the risk of over-generalization, it is the case that some schools serve rural areas, others small municipalities in out of the way places, and a number of them urban centers or the surrounding suburbs of major metropolitan areas. Their 11th and 12th grade enrollments range from less than 100 to more than 600. Their communities range from those that are affluent to those with sizeable portions of their populations below or near the poverty level. Some have had long years of experience with challenging academic programs like AP and others have not. Still others, like the new IB school in New Mexico, The Armand Hammer United World College of the American West, with all its students in the IB program, are part of independent school communities that have had previous experience and exposure to the IB program. Some IB schools have achieved national recognition, but many are unknown outside their immediate vicinity. Almost all IB schools have had honor courses in the upper grades in one guise or another, but only 62% of those in the United States authorized in 1981-82 had been offering one or more College Board Advanced Placement examinations."

This very varied pattern seems to persist today.

In order to put a little flesh on the bones of these generalisations let me conclude this chapter with pen-portraits of a handful of schools representing the full IB range, as I did in chapter four.

Southfield High School

Southfield Senior High School, Michigan, established in 1951, first affiliated with IBNA in 1979 at the suggestion of William Kritzmire, Associate Superintendent for Instruction of the School District at that time. The school has currently an enrolment of more than 3,000, multi-ethnic, multi-racial and multi-religious in character. It offers language courses in French, German, Hebrew, Spanish, and Latin. Kritzmire was looking for a programme which would meet the needs of the academically talented students and hit upon the IB, as others had done in different parts of the US. For this group Southfield offers both IB and AP courses to its eleventh and twelfth grade population of nearly 700 students, but the IB seems to fit particularly well with the five 'concerns' expressed in the published philosophy of the school: concern for a sound and thorough background of academic study, based upon learning to learn; a well-rounded programme of extra-curricular activities; a political awareness leading to understanding both of the merits and the shortcomings of the American way of life; a conscious process of socialisation; and provision of a range of vocational skills and experiences.

Although approximately 65% of Southfield graduates go on to some form of higher education or training, the IB and AP courses, which lead not simply to college entrance but to advanced placement, naturally enrol a comparatively small proportion of the twelfth grade. The largest single AP group in 1984 was 25 in American History, and the largest IB group, 19 in English as Language A at Higher Level. The school entered eleven candidates for the full Diploma in 1984 and nine for individual certificates. Of the Diploma candidates eight were successful, which is very close indeed to the world-wide success rate of 75% achieved in that year by more than 2,000 candidates of 121 one different nationalities.

Most IB or AP graduates from Southfield go on to higher education at the University of Michigan at Ann Arbor, with the occasional move East to such colleges as Cornell, Dartmouth, or Harvard. It might seem, therefore, that there is nothing very 'international' in the experience of the IB in middle America. My own very limited and now out-dated experience of talking to students at an IB Consultative Conference at Princeton makes me doubt this. There is, after all, a strong international element in the programmes and, for some students at least, a stimulus to the imagination in following the same courses as their peers from 120 different nations.

In February 1984 Southfield was one of 202 high schools to be recognised nationally by the federal government as an 'exemplary high school'. In bestowing this honour, the Secretary of Education stated: "Southfield High School is one of the nation's unusually successful schools in which faculty, students, and community have demonstrated a commitment to excellence and are dedicated to maintaining that commitment at all times."

The predominant response to *A Nation at Risk* was encouragement of the 'exemplary' school and Southfield is a fine and typical example of one type of high school which adopted the IB in a reasonably affluent suburban area.

Rufus King School for the College Bound, Milwaukee

Rufus King represents a type of IB High School very different from Southfield. When Milwaukee moved to desegregate its schools it adopted the 'magnet school' system rather than bussing. Each of the city's 15 high schools was given a special characteristic in the hope that students would be attracted to cross the boundaries of 'catchment area' and racial community to attend the school of their choice. Rufus King, which in 1978 was an all-black school in a predominantly black neighbourhood, was designated as an academic high school 'for the college-bound', 'college-bound' meaning any post-secondary program. As part of its new characteristic it introduced the IB.

Five years later Milwaukee's assistant superintendent for curriculum and instruction, who had been principal of the high school when the programme was introduced, summed up the experience thus: "We made it work because we had to make it work: but most of all we made it work . . . because the students wanted it to work." A staff writer for the *St Petersburg Times*, concerned with the introduction of the IB in Florida, listed the following changes that had come about at Rufus King in the first five years:

"This year 55% of the 907 students enrolled at Rufus King are white—showing that the school is successfully acting as a magnet to attract whites. In addition blacks make up almost 24% of the students participating in the IB program, showing that blacks are not excluded."

"Ninety-eight percent of the students in the IB program during the last five years have gone to College."

"Last year Rufus King had one of the best discipline records of any Milwaukee high school. Only 28 students were suspended and none was expelled. In comparison twelve Milwaukee high schools had more than 1,000 suspensions each."[10] As in most IB schools of this type the growth of the IB has been gradual and only a small proportion take the full diploma. In the first year only five students took IB exams; by 1983 it had risen to 40, and in 1984 there were seven candidates for the full diploma and 79 for certificates. Rufus King was also recognised by the Secretary for Education as an 'exemplary high school'.

Other high schools of this type which have found the IB a bridge over ethnic separation are Lincoln Park in Chicago, another exemplary high school whose IB program was mentioned in a speech by President Reagan, and Harlingen High School, Texas. It was a former guidance counsellor at Harlingen who read about the IB on an aircraft and came straight to see me in my office in London. He was the kind of counsellor who seemed to be known as 'Granpa' to half the youth of this small town near the Mexican border and he saw in the IB a bridge leading out from their high school rather than into it. "Half my kids are Mexican Americans," he said "and some of them are very bright—particularly on Math. They ought to be getting into the best colleges, but what admissions officer is going to pay much attention to a transcript or diploma from a small town they've never heard of deep in the heart of Texas? So I want your programme for them." In 1984 Harlingen had two candidates for the full diploma and 20 for certificates. An earlier diploma graduate had received a scholarship from Cal. Tech and the University at Texas in Austin was actively recruiting Harlingen's IB candidates.

Ashbury

The first independent school in Canada to adopt the IB was Ashbury. Founded in 1891 to provide in Ottawa an education modelled on the principles of the English public school, its original 17 pupils had grown to 450, including boarders. There is a tendency in schools founded on this model to remain closer to it than their prototypes do in the 'home country'. The late Shah of Iran, who, it may be remembered, was attracted by that model, would have been impressed by the recent experience of an IB examiner visiting such a school in a Central American republic, who asked the principal, with some sympathy for his isolated position—doing the IB in the midst of insurgency and counter-insurgency:

"I'm afraid you must have an awful lot of problems here. Is there anything you'd like to consult me about?"

"There is one thing that's worrying me a bit. Do you think the boys ought to be made to wear ties?"

Canada also has its spots of Victorian nostalgia—like the Empress Hotel in Victoria—which strike the English visitor, but I did not find Ashbury one of them. Perhaps this is due to a student body which, although predominantly Canadian, contains students from the Caribbean, China, Eastern Europe, Hong Kong, Latin America, Malaysia, Middle East, Scandinavia, UK, and US. In this it is typical of many schools in capital cities.

Ashbury introduced the IB in 1975. Some of the attractions to the school were well summed up by the principal in an article in the 1980 issue of the school magazine: an increase in student motivation to work outside the classroom; a greater challenge to gifted students; international standards of achievement and international recognition; advanced placement at universities; and a structured programme. "The IB should be viewed as a system of education and not a series of examinations."

The almost complete decentralisation and teacher-assessment-based requirements of the Ontario system of high school graduation made it easy for Ashbury to fit the IB into the provincial requirements, so that students following common courses could secure both an Ontario and an international qualification at the same time. Owing to the enthusiasm of a particular teacher, Ashbury became one of the leaders in the teaching of the Theory of Knowledge course and developed it into a 13th-grade course in Philosophy which was accepted for credit by the Ontario Ministry of Education. Ashbury, like other schools in North America, developed its full IB diploma course as the core around which were grouped a number of students taking individual IB courses and examinations as part of their Ontario high school graduation courses. In 1985 the teacher responsible for the IB programme recorded, at the end of a ten-year period, 12 IB full diploma candidates in his 12th grade with 64 registered for examinations in individual subjects. Pre-registration for 1986 indicated a possibility of 20 full diploma candidates. Out of a total 12th grade enrolment of 60 that is a significant proportion.

Ashbury, is of course, what those who use that terminology call a 'school for rich kids' although it has a small scholarship scheme. What it shares with Rufus King, which is emphatically not a school for rich kids, through the medium of the IB, is a commitment to academic excellence.

The French-American International School, San Francisco

Jumping into a cab in the centre of San Francisco, I gave the address, somewhere far out on the outskirts of the city, of what was then the French American Bilingual School.

"Why," said the cab-driver, "that's the French-American school. That's a fine school. My kids go there." I have always thought this one of the best welcomes and recommendations I have ever received on visiting an IB school.

The school was founded in 1962, the same year as Atlantic College, by progressive leaders of San Francisco's international community, as an elementary school with 22 pupils. Today it has a total enrolment of 425, of whom 54 are in grades 9-12 where the IB is offered. Instruction, except for those who enter the later high school grades with inadequate knowledge of French, is in both languages, as in the École Active Bilingue in Paris. Consequently, their seven candidates for the full diploma in 1984 all earned the 'bilingual diploma'.

Of the student body 25% come from French-speaking countries, and the total range of nationalities represented is over 30. The faculty also is international with eight different nationalities represented.

In 1976 Bernard Ivaldi, then secondary school division head of UNIS, was appointed Director and introduced the IB for the school's first 11th-grade class, making it the first IB school on the West Coast. The role of UNIS in helping other schools to introduce the IB has not been limited to North America and other UNIS staff have gone as principals of IB schools in both Hamburg and Vienna. French-American IB graduates have gone to many American universities and also to the universities of Bordeaux and Cologne.

For this school the IB with its bilingual curriculum and examinations was an obvious choice although the number of its IB diploma candidates in 1984 did not yet rival those of the Washington International School (24) or the Anglo-American School of New York (15).

Bernard Ivaldi contributed an article to the discussion on the role of the IB in French education published in *Dialogues* 1984, which is described in the next chapter.

Valley High School, Las Vegas

Within the public high school system one of the pioneers in the West has been Valley High School, Las Vegas, Nevada, founded in 1965 to serve a full range of students from a middle-class suburb on the outskirts of Las Vegas. It now has an enrolment of 2,400. The IB was introduced as part of a committment to providing a challenging general education for the college-bound covering the whole range of the curriculum rather than merely individual subjects. Students who have maintained above-average grades in the Junior High School are encouraged to take an algebra course in

Grade 8 and the first year of a foreign language (Spanish, French, or German) in Grade 9. This leads to a pre-IB course in Grade 10 which includes Advanced English II, Advanced Science I, Foreign Language II, and Algebra II/Trig. On entering the formal IB course in Grade II, students have a preparation comparable to that of their peers world-wide and are able to take the IB language B examinations after four years continuous study of the language. Valley High School also offers AP programmes, and in some classes IB and AP students will be taught together, but these words from the school's introductory brochure for students considering enrolment in the IB course are worth quoting: "This program offers an additional criterial advantage. It does *not* require a student to make a commitment to any particular field of study. The IB graduate will have the background, the discipline, and the *flexibility of choice* to consider several career possibilities in divergent fields as a result of participation in this 'well-rounded' secondary program." (The longer preservation of this flexibility of choice is one of the objectives of the many, so far unsuccessful, attempts to broaden the upper secondary curriculum in England and Wales.) Valley High School, like Rufus King, is proud of things like its 95% attendance record, its wide range of services, and the role it has played in the promotion of the IB in the organisation of teacher training workshops for the Southwest.

Bellaire High School, Texas

Another IB school which has been honoured as an 'exemplary high school' by the federal government is Bellaire High School in a suburb of Houston. The Senior High School enrolls 2,400 students in grades nine through twelve, mainly neighbourhood students from a reasonably affluent suburb, but with a sprinkling of transfer students from every part of the city, attracted by its 'magnet' programmes. The ethnic mix is 71% white, 13% black, ten percent Hispanic, and six percent Asian. Eighty-five percent are college-bound.

Bellaire introduced the IB in 1980 as an addition to existing honours and AP programmes. The languages taught include Spanish, German, French, and Hebrew to fifth level, with Chinese, Russian, and Latin to fourth. A course in Arabic has just been introduced. Students are encouraged to take either AP or IB examinations. Most IB students still take individual certificate examinations, in numbers approximately equal to those taking AP, but since the end of the first two-year IB course in 1982, 27 students have earned the full diploma.

Bellaire provides a good example of the American tradition with regard to IB 'CASS activities' of treating these as a series of student-organised rather than teacher-sponsored programmes. The IB fits well into the long-standing goals of the school, which are described thus: "to offer an academic background which gives graduates a head start in college; to offer an elective program that allows students to explore areas of interest; to offer a broad program of foundation courses that helps students to become an integral part of our common social, cultural and economic community; to prepare students for adult life by helping them assume responsibility for themselves, their fellows and the school; to allow students to work and be a part of the world of work while attending school; and to encourage students to participate in classroom situations that call for logical and creative thinking".

Notes to Chapter Six

[1] IBO Annual Bulletins. (Geneva: International Baccalaureate Office).

[2] E. McGrath, ed., *Universal Higher Education* (New York: McGraw-Hill, 1966).

[3] Philippe Bréant, Interview in *Dialogues, Revue de l'Enseignement Français l'Étranger* (French Ministry of Education, December 1984).

[4] Report of the Commission on Tests. *Part One: Righting the Balance* (New York: CEEB, 1970).

[5] Ibid.

[6] Admiral H.G. Rickover, *Swiss Schools and Ours* (Boston: Little, Brown & Co., 1962).

[7] Gerald Holton, 'A Nation at Risk Revisited', *Daedalus*, (Fall 1984): 1-27.

[8] Daniel C. Tyson, 'A Test of Character: The International Baccalaureate in America', *Independent School*, vol. 44, no. 1 (October 1984): 55-56.

[9] Derek Heater, *Peace Through Education: the Contribution of the Council for Education in World Citizenship* (London: Falmer Press, 1984).

[10] Barry Klein. In *St Petersburg Times*, February 13, 1983.

7
THE SECOND DECADE
AND TODAY

Both the IBO and the UWC ended 1985 with a conference which was in some sense a summing up of the progress in the second decade. The fourth inter-governmental conference on the IBO was held in Trieste in October, and a full meeting of the UWC International Council, the first for five years, at Atlantic College in June. In this chapter, I outline the developments leading up to these two meetings and what I think of the current standing of theses two projects, launched nearly a generation ago. In the final chapter, I raise some questions which seem to me important for their future.

Let me repeat, therefore, the warning with which I began, and which becomes more and more necessary in discussion of the present and the future, that this is no official history. The facts are as accurate as I can make them, but the views that I put forward are my own and not necessarily endorsed by either the International Council of the IBO or the International Board of the UWC. From both of these bodies I shall have retired by the time this book is published.

Both the IBO and the UWC were much concerned during their second decade with issues of public or private status and with those of centralisation and decentralisation. For the IBO, a significant step forward was taken at the third inter-governmental conference held in Brussels in February 1981 and hosted by the Belgian Ministers of Education. The conference was attended by the Ministers of Education of Belgium, Côte d'Ivoire, Malaysia, Netherlands, Nigeria, and Sudan; other governments represented were those of Australia, Brazil, Canada, Denmark, Federal Republic of Germany, Finland, France, Iraq, Ireland, Italy, Japan, Mexico, Morocco, Norway, Poland, Portugal, Senegal, Seychelles, Spain, Sweden, Switzerland, UK, USA, and Venezuela; observers attended from the British Council, the Commonwealth Secretariat and the EEC. Apart from approving, in principle, a ten-year development plan, the main act of this conference was to establish formally the Standing Conference of Governments as one of the three elements making up the International Council of the IBO. A constitution was approved for the Standing Conference, and an annual contribution by governments in membership was recommended, to be fixed normally at 40-50,000 Swiss francs. In recommending this pattern of governmental support John Goormaghtigh said: "I would like to stress that we are not asking you to make a donation to a worthy cause, but we are asking you to contribute to the funding of an international public educational service which has proved its worth."

As a result, 19 governments joined the Standing Conference and representatives of the following countries were the first elected to serve on the IBO Council: Belgium, Canada, Denmark, France, Netherlands, Japan, Sudan, and the UK. The Standing Conference has met annually ever since and in 1984 the IBO Council was expanded to 27 members in order to facilitate triennial rotation among its constituent membership.

The only two countries, apart from the US, in which IBO ever contemplated setting up a separate national presence in collaboration with the national authorities, as opposed to regional offices directly controlled from Geneva, were France and the UK. When, after the London conference of 1978, the principle of financial support to the IBO from governments was first accepted, the French Ministry of Education proposed that instead of making a purely monetary contribution, they should make a slightly smaller contribution in cash, but supplement this by seconding an expert from the French educational service to strengthen the administration in Geneva. This meant that the total value of the aid given to the IBO would thus be greater than that contributed by any other government, but John Goormaghtigh and I deliberated for a long time as to whether we should recommend acceptance of the offer. There was no doubt in our minds that with the rapid expansion of the project the administration in Geneva did need strengthening, but we feared the kind of conflict of loyalties and internal dissensions which do arise in the case of such secondments. In the event our fears proved justified and the situation was made worse because it proved impossible to secure a work permit for the seconded expert to reside in Geneva. The experiment was therefore brought to an end in October 1981 with inevitable adverse effects on the previously cordial relations between the IBO and the French Ministry of Education. Subsequently a reverse experiment was tried by setting up an office in Paris to serve France and francophone Africa, not in this case by establishing a separate legal entity on the lines of IBNA, but by collaborating with an existing French institution operating in the same field of international schools. Unfortunately the institute chosen, the Mission Laique, soon suffered itself from an internal crisis which led to conflicts with the IBO and seriously affected the credibility of both organizations with the Ministry of Education. This experiment also was therefore terminated.

From that time on, French interest in the IB has declined and been replaced by the development of the *option internationale* in the *baccalauréat*. One great advantage of the *option internationale* is that it will give access to the professions as well as to the universities. The French government has never been prepared to extend this to the IB on the grounds that the IBO is not a government institution. Access to the professions has only been accorded to the European Baccalaureate and to the Franco-German Baccalaureate, both of which are under joint governmental control; but the European Baccalaureate is only taken in the handful of schools set up by the EEC and the Franco-German Baccalaureate only in one or two schools jointly controlled by the two partner governments.

From the point of view of the international schools, the disadvantage is that it is a return to the principle of bilateral agreements. In the *option internationale* the structure of the course and the bulk of the examinations will consist of the normal tracks of the French *baccalauréat*, but the foreign language and history/geography section will be designed and examined in co-operation with the 'partner' nation. For students in an international school using French as the medium of instruction, therefore, this will involve separate groups preparing, for at least part of their time, the Franco-American, Franco-British, or French-Spanish option. The whole issue is discussed at length in the December 1984 issue of *Dialogues*, the *Revue de l'Enseignement Français à l'Étranger* to which Bernard Ivaldi, principal of the French-American School, San Francisco, contributed. Hope is expressed that it may be possible to arrive at a degree of co-operation through which a student could prepare or be awarded a French *baccalauréat, option inter-*

nationale, and an IB diploma simultaneously, and this matter was further discussed at the fourth intergovernmental conference in Trieste.[1]

The situation in England and Wales was rather different and in one feature, the degree of dissatisfaction with the existing system, very like that in North America. Since 1958 there had been a widely accepted consensus that the structure of the curriculum in the sixth form, the equivalent of the eleventh and twelfth grades in North America, was much in need of reform. This, as I hope I have shown in chapter three, was part of a general European movement, but, whereas in France and Federal Germany substantial changes were made by the two governments, the English tradition precluded such direction from the centre. Proposals for reform had, therefore, to come from one of the 'partners' in the educational system and be accepted by the others. There was no disagreement about the nature of the reform needed. All proposals had the same two objectives, to reduce the degree of specialisation on either an 'arts-side' curriculum, which contained no Mathematics or Science, or a 'science-side' curriculum, which normally contained no foreign language, and to postpone the age at which the choice between the two sides was made.

The first proposal for reform was put forward by the universities in 1962, but rejected by the schools on the grounds that its broader-based programme of general education would favour the rich independent schools and the larger grammar schools with more broadly qualified staff. Two years later the government, in an attempt to introduce at least a machinery for reform, created a single national advisory body to advise on both curriculum and examinations, known as the Schools Council. In 1966 this body produced a report (*Working Paper No. 5*)[2] recommending the introduction of major and minor subjects in the GCE, not unlike the IB Higher and Subsidiary. When this was also rejected by the schools, the Council withdrew it and substituted in 1967 (*Working Paper No. 16*)[3] a pattern of two A-levels and from four to six one year elective courses, internally designed and assessed by the schools, rather more in the tradition of the USA or Federal Germany. To this it was the universities that objected. It seemed clear that the only hope of reform lay in proposals that would command the support both of the schools and of the universities.

A joint committee was, therefore, set up of representatives from the Schools Council and the Standing Conference on University Entrance. It worked long and hard to produce an agreed report recommending that the sixth form curriculum should be divided into 'qualifying' and 'further' courses (the 'Q and F' Proposals). This was met by a violent campaign of rejection from the teachers and finally rejected by a full meeting of the Council in 1971. It was replaced, again with the agreement of both partners on the joint committee, by the 'N and F' Proposals, a five-subject pattern with a 'normal' standard slightly less demanding than the existing A-level, and two subjects carried on to the 'further' level. These proposals were published by the joint committee in 1973 (*Working Paper No. 46* and *No. 47*),[4] but the response of the Schools Council, based on very detailed examination of their implications was not available for discussion until the Autumn of 1977. One is reminded of a phrase which shocked the educational world of Federal Germany in 1967: "two decades of non-reform".[5]

I had been campaigning since 1960 for a limited experiment with one of the reform proposals, which might have produced some empirical evidence on which to base further discussions and at least have disposed of some of the more fanciful objections.[6] The N and F proposals were, like those put forward in *A Nation at Risk* for the USA, very close to the pattern of the IB. Five subjects with two at Further level compared pretty closely with the IB's six subjects with three at Higher, while the IB's Theory of Knowledge, CASS, and Extended Essay were represented by the traditional 'one quarter to one third of the time' devoted, in theory, to unspecified and unassessed 'general studies'. Although the proposals did not contain, as the IB did, a distribution requirement, they did 'encourage' schools to impose this themselves. The two patterns were so close and the IB was now so widely acceptable to universities and professional bodies in England (more than a thousand IB students have entered British Universities) that in 1979 we persuaded the Schools Council to set up a feasibility study to investigate the possibility of conducting a nationally-monitored experiment with the IB in 50 schools and colleges, well-distributed both by type and location, over a four-year period. This study was financed by the Schools Council, with the help of a small grant from the 'Cambridge Overseas' Board which also had an interest. It was conducted by a working party including representatives from the Department of Education and Science, the Schools Council, the Standing Conference on University Entrance, the National Foundation for Educational Research, and the Universities of London and Cambridge.

After a year's work they presented their report. They had identified 45 schools and colleges prepared to co-operate in the experiment; a survey of university performance of the admittedly inadequate sample of those who had by then entered British universities on the basis of the IB and completed first-degree courses indicated that far from being disadvantaged, they obtained slightly better results than the average of A-level entrants; and they recommended that the experiment, which was estimated to cost £20,000 a year for the four years, should be undertaken. The examinations committee of the Schools Council rejected the recommendation.

So ended the IBO's second attempt to work with the educational authorities of one country. I was told, afterwards, that the reason for the rejection was that the Schools Council had committed all its resources to a series of other major projects, including the reform of the examinations at 16-plus, and was unwilling to commit itself further to the apparently endless process of 18-plus reform.

I was not too disappointed myself, because the rejection came at a time when the IBO was again in financial difficulties and I rather doubted whether a grant of £20,000 a year for four years would enable us to carry out the experiment without committing additional resources in what seemed likely to be a period of galloping inflation. My personal involvement in these negotiations was in my capacity as Vice-President of the IBO Council, since on July 31st 1977 I had retired as Director-General, being succeeded by Gérard Renaud who had, for so long, been in charge of the office in Geneva and the day-to-day administration of the IBO.

From then on the structure adopted has developed as one of a central administration based in Geneva, controlling a separate examinations service based in the UK and regional offices—in Buenos Aires for Latin America, in Singapore for the Far East, in London for Europe, Africa and Asia. In regions where the IB was not yet widely developed we appointed regional representatives—in Jamaica for the Caribbean, in Mexico City for Mexico and possibly Central America, and in Adelaide for Australia. IBNA remained anomalous only in legal and financial terms, but in academic terms was comparable with the other regional offices.

Of these regional offices that in London was by far the most important. Shortly before I retired I had negotiated an agreement with London University's Institute of Education similar to that which Tom Carter had agreed with Southampton University for the Language Examinations Office. As we have seen in chapter five, Robert Blackburn joined the IBO in 1978 as Director of Development and Deputy Director-General, and this became his office. He and Gérard got on well, but probably better running separate offices and meeting frequently than they would have done had Robert moved to Geneva, even if the work-permit problem could have been solved. Moreover London had great advantages as a centre for the further worldwide development of the IB, quite apart from the very much lower cost. It was clear, by now, that anything between 80% and 90% of new IB schools would be using English as the language of instruction and communication; for the Scandinavian countries and the Netherlands, London was an easier centre to deal with than Geneva; for the Middle East, the Far East, and Africa, other than francophone Africa, communications were easier, and close co-operation was possible with the Commonwealth Secretariat and with the headquarters of the European Conference of International Schools. By an informal arrangement, dealings with Spain and Italy were at first carried on direct from Geneva, with the rest of Europe delegated to London. Possibly the greatest advantage of locating the main regional office in London, however, was the possibility it provided for close contacts with the UWC office in London House. This kind of co-operation extended also to other parts of the world. In South America Peter Stoyle, former Headmaster of the British School, Montevideo, and then IBO regional officer, working from St George's School Buenos Aires, became also the UWC liaison officer with their national committees throughout South America. Travel costs were shared and the support of both organizations ultimately made it possible to set up a regional office. In South East Asia UWC agreed that John Goodban, their regional officer working from the United World College in Singapore, could also look after the interests of the IBO. It has sometimes been questioned whether in areas like these we ought to be using expatriate regional officers. This seems to me to be another of those times where theoretical and practical considerations clash, at least for the present. In theory, it is easy to say that the IBO regional officer should be a national of one of the countries of the region. In practice, so long as the majority of the schools using the IB are either schools for expatriates or, as they often are in South America, schools originally based on an expatriate or binational tradition, an expatriate with a lifetime's experience of the region may be more widely acceptable than a national of any one country in the region.

The areas which present the biggest problems today in providing a full service of and to IB schools are probably Australia and Africa. In both cases the main problem is distances and communications, compounded in Africa by the lack of communication between anglophone and francophone countries. The IBO secured a grant from the Leverhulme Trust in 1981 to carry out a comparative study of the upper secondary curricula of francophone and anglophone schools in West Africa, in the course of which the possibility of introducing the IB on an experimental basis in one school in Senegal and one in Côte d'Ivoire was discussed, but up till now the francophone IB has not yet been established in Africa. Nor has it been possible to provide schools in Africa as a whole with anything like the back-up services, such as teacher-training workshops, which have been developed in other parts of the world, although the London Office, following the IBNA example of combining IB workshops with the annual meeting of large associations of schools, has been able to provide at least one workshop each year in Africa, the Middle East, and East Asia.

For the United World Colleges also the second decade produced new developments in terms of objectives, of public and private status, and of decentralisation. Of these the most fundamental was in the field of objectives and owed its initiative to UWC's new president, the Prince of Wales. To Kurt Hahn and to Mountbatten the contribution that the United World College movement could make to world peace and international understanding lay in educating a generation of potential leaders or 'animateurs' at all levels who had the understanding and the commitment to work for these causes, particularly in international relations, and who, through the rescue services, 'the moral equivalent to war', had developed their common love of all humanity and their readiness to face a challenge; but things were changing. Some people saw the long-term danger of war more in the spread of hunger and in the tension between the rich countries of the North and the poor countries of the South than in traditional conflicts between developed nation-states which might be avoided through diplomacy. Others wondered whether there were not other things than death by water or cliff from which men and women needed rescue. Could not the UWC movement contribute more directly to tackling some of the world's great human problems?

One of the first actions of the new president was to summon the conference at Ditchley Park already referred to. At this those who had long been involved in UWC discussed with the newcomers the whole range of our philosophy and activities. Two quotations from the report of this conference, colloquially called the 'Indaba', show the way in which thoughts were moving:

"Statements of aims should demonstrate UWC's practical concern with understanding between people rather than governments, particularly through the life-long activities of former students."

"The importance of rescue services should not be over-emphasised; the crucial considerations are the provision of services that are really needed and the fostering of good links with the local community. There is need for broad and progressive interpretations of the role and nature of service, particularly of the ideas of rescue and challenge, which might mean rescuing the disadvantaged from social problems."

Such considerations may have been among those which led the Prince of Wales, on a state visit to Caracas in March 1978, after meeting with a group of ex-students, to discuss with the President of Venezuela the establishment of a United World College of Agriculture, as a contribution, however small, to tackling the problem of world hunger. The President's reaction was extremely favourable. The planning of such a college, provisionally entitled the Simon Bolivar United World College of Agriculture, was entrusted by the Minister of Agriculture to Dr Luiz Marcano, an expert on tropical agriculture, who was about to spend a sabbatical year at Reading University and who would be able to work closely with the UWC. Marcano saw a gap in the provision for increasing the production of food throughout tropical America and the Caribbean, a gap between schemes to assist the peasant farmer at one end of the scale and schemes to develop large agro-industrial estates on the other. The real shortage, he believed, was of trained managers for small- and medium-sized farms with the scientific and technical knowledge to get the best out of the land and the economic and social skills to market their produce. In this he was echoing Simon Bolivar himself who once said: "Doctors and engineers abound among us, yet we sorely lack good mechanics and farmers who are those required by our country in order to move forward in prosperity and well being."

On the UWC side there was considerable enthusiasm for the project, which was discussed at the Indaba, but also considerable doubt about the role that the UWC should play and about whether this sort of diversification was in the best interests of the movement as a whole. Sir George Schuster in a memorandum of 9th May 1978, warmly welcoming the proposal, put his finger on the essential point. "The first practical question", he wrote, "is with what final objective is this possibility to be followed up? Is the objective to be: A) the establishment of a United World College in Venezuela or B) to establish a Venezuelan National College with the assistance and advice of the UWC organization?"

"In this note I assume that the objective is A."

He went on to refer to the phrase in the UWC objectives about "providing an education suited to the needs of the times" and argued that "in Venezuela, as in most of the Third World countries, the chief need of the times is to create conditions improving the standard of life, especially by improving agricultural production; and in the matter of education the essential need is that work in the country-side should be regarded as providing an honourable career." The whole memorandum is yet another example of the far- and clear-sightedness of a man then approaching his hundredth birthday. To those who questioned whether the proposed college would be sufficiently international he might have quoted another resolution of the Indaba: "No individual college can be truly international: it is bound to—and it should—reflect its own regional location. Therefore an overall geographical and political balance has to be sought in the project as a whole." In other words, if the UWC movement was to be represented in tropical America and the Caribbean it must be by a college which provided "an education suited to the needs of the times"—and of the place.

Things moved fast in 1978. By August, Luiz Marcano's appointment had been officially confirmed by the Ministry of Agriculture and a committee set up with initial finance. A first draft of an agreement between this committee and the UWC was drawn up for submission to the UWC Board and two UWC representatives, Peter Stoyle and Dr Kerdel Vegas, Chairman of the Venezuelan National Committee, added to it.

During this period three factors emerged which had a continuing influence on the final outcome between Sir George Schuster's A and B alternatives: first that the whole of the finance for the founding of the college would be raised, as with the other colleges, by the Venezuelan founding committee, UWC's commitment being limited to the costs of consultancy; second that there were likely to be bureaucratic difficulties within Venezuela arising from the fact that three separate Ministries, Agriculture, Education, and External Affairs, were involved; thirdly, that there were some members of the UWC Board who, as in the cases of Singapore and Waterford, were hesitant about whether UWC should be involved beyond giving advice, and questioned whether the college, when fully established, would be 'a real UWC'. They were more attracted, in fact, by the B alternative.

In 1979 there was a change of government in Venezuela and the first sign of inter-ministerial difficulty arose, when the Ministry of External Affairs expressed some hesitations about the UWC connection. These were resolved without difficulty, however, and by the time the UWC International Council met at Pearson College in July 1980 the chairman of the committee, Dr Francisco Morillo, was able to report that the new government was equally supportive and that the agreement with the UWC had been signed in 1979, not on behalf of the committee but by the Minister of Agriculture. This agreement between a private organisation and a government department committed the two parties to collaboration in a feasibility study, to be carried out immediately by the Venezuelan committee, leading to the establishment of the college by the Venezuelan government.

The agreement makes it clear that the college would have a dual purpose: to provide a practical training for farm managers and to promote international understanding by the inclusion in its courses of elements designed to this end, such as world policies in agriculture and the problems of population and nutrition on a world scale. One half of the student places were to be made available to non-Venezuelans, mainly though not exclusively from South America and the Carribbean. The teaching language would be Spanish.

It was one of Marcano's principles that the college diploma should specifically *not* meet the requirements for entry to higher education (which might have increased the production of economists or even lawyers, rather than farmers) and it was clear that the IB had no essential role in such a college, though we did discuss whether some IB subsidiary courses such as English Language B or Economics might be adapted for inclusion in the curriculum, so as to encourage interchange of teachers and students with other colleges.

The negotiation of the Venezuelan agreement was my last function as chairman of the UWC international Board. When I accepted the chairmanship in 1978 I was already seventy, an age which in my younger years I had regarded as well beyond the limit at which people should 'make way for younger men'. I therefore stipulated that I would serve for only two years, as Tony Besse had done, and that I would regard it as one of my main tasks to find a successor. It is one of the few tasks that I feel reasonably confident of having carried out with triumphant success. Professor Tom Symons, who was elected in 1980 and then re-elected for a second three-year term in 1983, might have been regarded on his record as ideal for the post. Founder Vice-Chancellor of Trent University, Ontario; Chairman and then Treasurer of the Association of Commonwealth Universities; the first Canadian to receive the Distinguished Service to Education award of the International Council for the Advancement and Support of Education; he had an unrivalled and continuing experience of the world of international education. But it has not been his record or his experience which have made him so valuable to the UWC movement or won him so many friends in it. It has been his wisdom, his humanity, and above all his patience in office. Ever since serving under Colin Mackenzie in South East Asia during World War two I have always rated patience, a quality I sorely lack myself, as supremely important for a chairman, particularly of an international board or committee. To watch Tom steer a meeting through to conclusions, which in the early stages seemed impossible to achieve within the allotted time, without appearing to hurry anyone, has been an unforgettable experience. In announcing the election at the meeting of the International Council at Pearson College in 1980, I was able to recommend UWC to the invited guests as an organisation with epitomised the history of their country, with a Frenchman as its first Chairman, a Scot as its second, and a Canadian as its third. In 1986 Tom Symons, having served two three-year terms was succeeded by an American, the Hon. Kingman Brewster, former president of Yale and US Ambassador in London.

The UWC played a considerable part in the Venezuelan feasibility study. Marcano was anxious to draw on the educational experience of the farm institutes in the UK and in 1981 we were able to arrange a three-week visit to the site by Peter Brown, Chief Inspector for Agricultural Education, as well as visits by Sir Ian Gourlay, Jack Matthews, and Gary Fletcher, a teacher from Pearson College. The site made available by the Venezuelan government was a farm of 742 hectares, two kilometres from the town of Ciudad Bolivar—potentially rich farming land, diversified by its proximity to the Andes foothills and thus eminently suitable for the teaching of a wide variety of farming practices. A second visit from the Prince of Wales, on his way back to London from Australia maintained the momentum.

On June 9th, 1981, a non-profit foundation, known as FUNDACEA, was set up to develop and administer the college. The founder-members included both individuals and organisations, such as FUSAGRI, the service to farmers foundation, UWC, and some of the foundations which have given support such as the Shell Foundation, Vollmer Foundation, and Eugenio Mendoza Foundation. The President of the Executive Committee, of which Luiz Marcano and Francisco Morillo are members, is Senora Maria de Burelli.

This was considerable progress in the first three years with the foundation of a completely new type of college. Possession of the site with some buildings and the appointment of a director-designate made it possible to continue with the planning of the course and the practical on-site development of technical assistance to local farmers. This latter was of particular importance in view of the emphasis laid on the UWC principle of service to the local community. On the other hand the more formal process towards opening the college recalls the long series of disappointments about opening dates experienced both with Pearson College and the College of the Adriatic. Jack Matthews, on his visit in 1981, commented that it was hoped to open the college in 1982 and that the UWC would be called upon to help with the selection of students from outside Venezuela. In 1982 it was remarked how very appropriate it would be if the college could open in 1983, the 200th anniversary of the birth of the Great Liberator, but again difficulties with the Ministry of External affairs (not unconnected perhaps with the Falklands/Malvinas conflict?) supervened. Leonard Mayer, Chairman of the UWC Mexican Committee, who had at times been one of the sceptics, paid a visit to the site in this year and returned with an enthusiastic report to the UWC Board meeting in November.

The most appropriate occasion for the formal admission of a new college to the movement is a meeting of the International Council and when a meeting of the full Council, which has become a fairly rare event, was convened at Atlantic College for June 1985, there were some hopes that this might be marked by a firm opening date for what had now become 'The Simon Bolivar United World Institute of Experimental Agriculture'. Alas, the best that Luiz Marcano could report was that they expected to receive the permit from the Ministry of Education very shortly and hoped to be able to open the college either in January or August 1986.

There were many other new proposals for United World Colleges during the Mountbatten period and later, of which the most generous was the offer by the Filipinas Foundation not only of a suitable site but of a generous endowment to cover the costs of the initial build-up period. It was turned down in the end for three reasons: because of the political instability of the area, because we doubted whether such a college would be able to recruit enough students on a regional, much less an international, basis and because it was felt that it would compete for scholarship funds and for students with the college in Singapore. Other areas explored at one time or another were Japan, Thailand, and Sri Lanka, but the three projects which recurred again and again in our planning were for colleges in Germany, in India, and in the USA.

After the collapse of the Cuxhaven proposals described in the last chapter, a number of other possibilities were examined in co-operation with the German national committee. Of these the nearest to achieving success was for a college in Rheinland Pfalz near Edenkoben based on the Schloss Ludwigshohe, a former summer residence of King Ludwig I of Bavaria, and an adjoining hotel, then used by the Bundeswehr as a training centre—another sword in this case not beaten into a ploughshare. In 1972 David Wills visited the site and reported favourably on it, though there were some who maintained that rescue services on the Rhine were more needed against pollution than drowning. The hope was that finance would come mainly from land and Federal government sources and the scheme enjoyed high-level government support in Germany. Two warning signs, however, appeared as early as 1974. One was the German Ambassador's reason for support—that there was a real need for suitably trained Germans in the international field; the other was contained in a letter from Peter Lubben, the secretary of the founding committee, to Ruth Bonner at IBO Geneva: "Our negotiations with the Cultural Ministry of Rhein-land—Pfalz seem to have reached a promising stage now: we must now prepare detailed syllabuses on the basis of the IB and the German curriculum." Nevertheless Ruth in her reply referred to "the Edenkoben College which is to open its doors next year, I believe". This typical piece of optimism on opening dates I found in the files marked by someone with a double exclamation mark. In 1975 the Cultural Ministry of Rheinland Pfalz reported that no funds would be available over the next two years and that part of the castle would in any case be needed for a picture gallery. Yet it was not until 1976 that the scheme was finally dropped, when it became apparent that half the student places would have to be reserved for Germans and that these students would require a third year after completing their IB, since the German authorities were still not prepared to recognise the IB as a substitute for the *Abitur*, then normally taken at a considerably later age, for German students educated within Germany. Attempts to find a non-governmental sponsor for a German college came to nothing.

In the US when the time came things went very differently. This was due entirely to the intervention not of a government but of one man.

Shortly before his assassination, Mountbatten had aroused the interest of Dr Armand Hammer, Chairman of Occidental Petroleum and a philanthropist in the tradition of Andrew Carnegie, in the United World Colleges and introduced him to his successor as President of UWC, His Royal Highness The Prince of Wales.

UWC had long been convinced of the need for a college in the USA, but our fingers had been burnt in Vermont; since when no one had been able to see a way forward. This meeting changed everything. The two men hit it off, the contact was maintained and once Dr Hammer had visited Pearson College and was convinced of the value of the project, he had, to a quite unparalleled extent, the resources, the energy, the organising capacity, and the generosity to make it happen. The speed with which it did happen contrasts sharply with the long gestation of other UWC projects and would have delighted Mountbatten. It was only possible because Dr Hammer put behind it not only his driving energy but the resources of the Armand Hammer Foundation and of Occidental Petroleum. Even so the fact that Jim Pugash, his special assistant for the project, could announce in August 1981 that he had inspected more than one hundred possible sites, having been given the assignment only in May, indicates a remarkable speed of operation.

One of the immediate results of Armand Hammer's initiative was a transfer of interest to the West Coast. The first suggestion for a possible site was the renting and possible subsequent acquisition, of part of the campus of the US International University, a private college based in San Diego with 'outposts' in Kenya, Mexico, and the UK. This, among other possibilities, was considered at a meeting presided over by the Prince of Wales in Washington on May 1st, 1981, but rejected. No immediate decision was taken on a site at this meeting, but a search committee was set up consisting of Professor Symons, Dr Hammer, Ambassador Brewster, Ted Lockwood (the retiring President of Trinity College), John Nicol, Jack Matthews and two representatives of the US Commission for the UWC in New York: George Franklin and Russell Palmer. Jim Pugash, as Secretary to this committee, was sent out on his travels. At this meeting Dr Hammer assured the future of the college by making three commitments: to purchase the site when found, to cover the college's deficits during his lifetime, and to provide an endowment at his death.

Jack Matthews and Blouke Carus had visited the site at San Diego and found certain attractions in the proposal, but there were nagging doubts about the wisdom of the American UWC being set up in association with an existing institution rather than in complete independence, and when Ted Lockwood recommended strongly against the association, attention passed first to a site at Scotsdale, Arizona. Then, before the end of May, Jim Pugash found what seemed to him the ideal site at Montezuma, a small village six miles from Las Vegas, New Mexico. By June the search had been narrowed down to Scotsdale or Las Vegas. Ted Lockwood visited Las Vegas, where 'the castle', a magnificent nineteenth-century 'railway hotel', built to exploit the hot springs and subsequently used as a Jesuit seminary, now stood empty. He was very much in favour of New Mexico which he described as having "what remains of the old South West", a fascinating area to study, close to two large Indian reservations; plenty of opportunity for wilderness and mountain training and wild life conservation; a local population with a tradition of hospitality to strangers; and good opportunities for contact with local hospitals and the Highlands University. Dr Hammer records that when he saw the site he simply said "This is it!" and bought it for a million dollars (I believe the asking price was 1.8 million). On August 26th 1981, at a meeting in Albuquerque, he secured the enthusiastic support of the governor, Bruce King, and of the state superintendent of schools, who promised 'to cut through any red tape'. On the following day, at a meeting of the Working Group, Tom Symons proposed that the group should now be wound up and replaced by the governing body of the college, thus bringing it into line with the other colleges and following a precedent set by Pearson College. A board of governors was set up under the chairmanship of Dr William McGill, a former president of Columbia University. Dr Hammer said he hoped to see the college opened within twelve months and was supported by John Nicol, who recalled the speed with which they had been able to work at Pearson College 'once the bull-dozers were in'. By September Ted Lockwood had accepted the post of Director: he was assisted in planning the college by Jack Matthews, who acted as a consultant and during the summer of 1982 by Andrew Maclehose, who came from Atlantic college as Dean of Studies, and by groups of students from Pearson College who came down to help with landscaping the campus and restoring old buildings. By February 1982 they were recruiting faculty and getting roughly 25 applications for each of the eleven posts advertised. The first intake of students duly arrived in September 1982, including 19 Americans, 19 each from Europe and from South and Central America, seven each from Africa and the Middle East, and five from India and Nepal. The fact that they also included two each from the USSR, Poland, and China was due to Dr Hammer's personal connections. On October 27th in a colourful dedication ceremony, conducted by the Prince of Wales and attended by a full meeting of the International Board of the UWC, this group of young people from 46 countries gave the college a wonderful send-off. One of my colleagues remarked that, as on a number of similar occasions at other colleges, the most reassuring thing was the capacity of the young and the old to relate to each other. The oldest was almost certainly Dr Hammer himself.

In 1983 Ted Lockwood gave his first report: in general an enthusiastic record of success, with only two main reservations, first, the very heavy workload on the faculty and the need for faculty housing on the campus, a problem which had faced Atlantic College in its early days, and second, some concern that American students were hardly ready in academic terms for the challenge of the International Baccalaureate. The second problem was not surprising when one remembers that American high schools which adopted the IB as an honours program had found that it involved changes in the academic content of the ninth and tenth grades. It led to a decision to encourage the entry of American students who had completed the eleventh rather than the tenth grade. It will be interesting to see how this works out in practice. My own experience leads me to believe that the powers of able and motivated students to 'catch up' on step-by-step programmes are far greater than teachers imagine. Nevertheless, though the grade distribution of the first two graduating classes was well above the average of all IB schools, there was a considerable improvement in the performance of the 1985 class over that of 1984. It was a disappointment that, just as at Atlantic College, the Chinese and also the Russian students gave up the IB in order to concentrate on improving their English.

In 1983, after six years' service in the post, Gérard Renaud resigned as Director-General of the IBO, though continuing to serve as a consultant on the pedagogical side. He had served the IBO with single-minded devotion for nearly 20 years, a long and difficult period, beset by financial worries, the growing pains of an organisation expanding more rapidly than anticipated and the almost inevitable conflicts within the IBO itself between functions, such as curriculum and examinations, between cultures, between regions and between interests. In all these conflicts respect for Gérard's personal qualities of friendship, integrity and devotion was one of the mitigating factors. If there were feuds within the family, the family surmounted them. As my French steadily got worse after leaving Geneva, so Gérard's English got better, and we worked very harmoniously together.

He was succeeded by the present Director-General, Dr Roger Peel, another real internationalist, English by birth and education, American by experience, trilingual in English, French, and Spanish. After serving as assistant professor of Spanish at Yale, he had, as Vice-President for foreign languages at Middlebury College, administered a chain of foreign language schools in Europe and was well acquainted with the European scene. Roger inherited an organization which on the pedagogic side was healthy, though ready for further development, but on the financial and administrative side was facing its most serious crisis yet.

On the pedagogic side the most satisfactory development of the first decade seems to me to have been the relative success of the

IB's most innovatory features, the Theory of Knowledge Course, the Extended Essay, and the CASS requirement. Since most schools belonged to the anglophone tradition, to which the inclusion of anything which appeared to be 'philosophy' was unfamiliar, we learned much in the development of the Theory of Knowledge course from our French collaborators, who saw clearly that the nature of the course was not a history of ideas, nor a course in epistemology, nor one in symbolic logic, and yet drew to some extent on all three. In Sue Bastian at UNIS and Lubor Velecky at the University of Southampton we had excellent interpreters of the course to less familiar teachers in schools of the American or British tradition. But what made the course the success which I believe it has been was the enthusiasm of the teachers, evidenced by their regular participation in summer schools in different parts of the world with an average participation of between 35 and 40 students and teachers. I have little doubt that this enthusiasm was partly due to the great degree of freedom which schools enjoyed in designing their course and the permission accorded to them to leave out sections of the syllabus which, for local cultural reasons, they found inappropriate. Yet this freedom had its disadvantages.

In the very early days some schools tended to confuse the course with a rag-bag service of lectures on 'current affairs' and its history over the initial 20 years has involved a substantial amount of in-service teacher-training as well as a process of continuous discussion among the IBO's academic advisers. The current outlines of the course will be found in Appendix A. One great problem was how performance in all these three areas could be made to enter into the final assessment, on which the issue of the diploma was based, and to what extent this assessment could, as in the six subject areas, act as a control to ensure that the course was being properly covered. My own experience with the way in which the unspecified and unassessed 'general studies' area in the English system was 'often neglected and wasted' led me to the view that in systems where terminal examinations dominated, it was fatal to divide the curriculum into two sections, one of which counted in the examinations while the other did not. Both teachers and pupils were inevitably tempted to concentrate on the first and neglect the second, as they did in England. On the other hand, we were determined that the Theory of Knowledge course should not degenerate into a 'seventh subject'.

The solution we found was to give it a weighting which affected the points scored for the diploma as a whole, but not those of any individual subject. Since each of the six subjects studied for the diploma was graded on a seven-point scale with four as the pass mark, the minimum total required for the diploma, with some provision for cross-subject compensation, was 24. To these it was agreed that a student could add one bonus point for excellent work in the Theory of Knowledge, while one point would be deducted for a complete failure to participate. This looked after the question of incentive, but how to exercise control? With the rapidly growing number of IB schools world-wide, inspection was clearly impossible. The best teachers were strongly opposed to an external examination, as being too near the procedure for a seventh subject, but it was not the best teachers we were worried about. After many experiments we settled for a common examination, externally set but internally graded, with external moderation, as part of a battery of assessments on which the school awards the bonus or minus point. I remember a fascinating meeting in Paris with Dina Dreyfus, the French inspectrice who was the first examiner responsible for this course, at which we drew up the common examination. The purpose of the examination was quite as much to give teachers in new schools some idea of the issues which we hoped would arise in the course as to help with assessment. It may clarify, therefore, the nature of the course if I quote some of the questions which have appeared: "If moral codes are simply the conventions of the society in which they operate, does it make sense to strive for a more just society?" "Does reading historical novels help us to understand history: if so, how?" "In what ways can language hinder thought? Illustrate any general point with an example." "Discuss and illustrate with examples the role of theory in the activity of any one science." The development of this course has probably involved more discussion and more substantial teacher-involvement and teacher-training than that of any other part of the IB curriculum, but the support for it continues to grow. In the 1985 examinations, out of 2,227 diploma candidates, 620 got the bonus point and 58 suffered the deduction of the penalty point. In 1985 the common examination was abandoned in favour of internal assessment moderated throughout submission of samples of course work.

My own last involvement in it was to chair a teacher-training workshop in Bahrain in 1984, when fascinating questions about the teaching of such a course in an Islamic context were raised.

The second innovation, the extended essay, also presented some problems in development, but is now well established. Students had initially to be counselled not to choose subjects which were far too wide—such as 'Russian Foreign Policy in the Twentieth Century' or for which the relevant material was simply not available where their school was situated. Another general weakness was prolixity and it was some time before students realised that they would really be penalised if their essays over-ran the 4,000-word limit. Their tendency at first to over-concentrate on the essay has already been mentioned, but also their report that this part of the course really built a bridge between secondary and higher education. The nature of the essays has of course varied widely. R.S. Bourne, who conducted a survey of extended essays in 1977, noted of the history essays that there were too many that took one figure of the recent past and "slung a pseudo-historical study around it" (for example out of 81 essays, 15 dealt with Hitler and Nazism; 16 with Russian revolutionaries; and 11 with other 'strong men' of the contemporary period). Another favoured type was those which dealt, from a strongly personal angle, with the problems of racial minorities. Such choices can be defended on the grounds of personal involvement, but a gradual training in attitudes of scholarship has been necessary. Some, such as 'Cannes à travers la Révolution Française' or 'Agricultural and Food Marketing Systems of Sri Lanka' were serious pieces of local history.

Essays written in the scientific subjects were often reports on individual fieldwork or experiments conducted over longer periods of time than is available in school 'practical' sessions. One or two were of a very high quality and achieved publication in scientific journals. The claim that they prepared students for more serious work at university level may be borne out by the experience of Alan Hall, the biology teacher at Atlantic College. Attending the Nordic Conference of Physiology and Pharmacology in June 1985, he found that papers were being presented by three of his former pupils from Atlantic College, one from 1973-5, one from 1976-8, and one from 1978-80.

Assessment of extended essays is carried out by external examiners, who receive also a report from the teacher-supervisor. It can contribute one or two bonus points, and failure to put in a serious effort can incur one minus point. In 1985, 1,471 candidates received one bonus point, 310 received two bonus points, and 234 suffered the deduction of a point.

The initial problems involved in any form of control or assessment of CASS activities have been indicated in chapter three. The IBO's initial position was that to make participation in active social service or creative aesthetic activities compulsory for each individual would be counterproductive and that, the regulations having ensured that time was left available, we should leave the way in which that time was employed to the enthusiasm of the students, stimulated and guided by that of the teachers. I believe that this worked well at first, but that problems have arisen with the expansion in the number of schools in different parts of the world.

In the early days I used, as Director-General, to receive a number of enquiries from schools as to what should count as a CASS activity: "Playing football?" "No, but organizing a youth club football team would." "Going to an Art Gallery?" "Not unless it was part of a regular club activity." As the number of schools increased, such personal contacts became less and less possible and the addition of the words "or physical" to the original recommendation of "creative aesthetic or active social service activities" opened the way for the comment made at the IB conference in Nairobi in 1984 that a school *could* claim that its students were fulfilling the CASS requirement by playing football and going to the cinema. I do not suggest that there are many, or indeed any, schools which do claim this, but there does seem to be a case for re-examination of this part of the curriculum and more help from IBO to those teachers who are striving to make it a reality for as many as possible of their students.

In the course of such re-examinations the question of greater control and assessment is usually raised. If the IBO considers CASS activities an important part of the students' total education, which it certainly does, should they not be in some way enforced? It is necessary here to make a distinction between two senses of such a proposal.

If it means that IBO should compel all students to engage in such activities and deny them the diploma if they do not, then it seems to me both educationally unsound and administratively impractical. To force the small minority of adolescents who cannot be encouraged into such activities and are actively opposed destroys their value both for minority and majority. They will, of course, go through the motions of doing something which they will claim satisfies the requirement, if their diploma depends on it; but the effect of this, both on themselves and their companions, who are genuinely participating, will be to do more harm than good. You can lead a horse to the water but you cannot make him drink, and force-feeding produces nausea. As an incoming headmaster, I once inherited such a system and before abolishing it I consulted a very experienced inspector, who told me this story. He had been visiting a primary school where the head, impressed by the value of 'hobbies' for young children, required that every child should have one. In the rainy playground he met a little boy, weeping bitterly, and the following conversation ensued: "Come, come, my little fellow. It can't be as bad as that. Tell me what's the matter. Are you being bullied?" "Oh, Sir. I do so 'ate my 'obby."

Moreover, how could IBO, with no inspectorate, realistically monitor such a requirement? If it means that the school should impose it, that must surely be left to the authorities of the school and in schools like the UWCs, where students choose to come with that commitment, it is clearly possible. Does the proposal then mean that the IBO should control more tightly the degree of provision for such activities and encouragement to engage in them in each IB school? Again, if by 'control' is meant the kind of control imposed in national systems through detailed regulations and inspection, that would seem to me neither desirable nor practical. What does perhaps need improvement is a better system of guidance for teachers both in stimulating such activities and in encouraging them by assessment, not, as in the case of the other two elements, by bringing them within the points system but by attachment to the diploma of a more detailed 'profile'.

During 1984-5 the Examinations Office carried out a survey of the CASS programmes in operation. The poor response, only 54 schools out of 134 entering diploma candidates, may have been due partly to a genuine misunderstanding of what was required of them, but also, I suspect, to a suspicion that such a request coming from the examination office indicated the possibility of a proposal to start examining this part of the curriculum and awarding grades. The survey did, however, reveal certain factors which would need to be taken into account in any improved system.

a) The tradition in North America is that such activities, often promoted by clubs, are stimulated and organised by students, not by teachers. In such circumstances there might be difficulties in any scheme for assessment of performance in them by teachers.

b) In Third World countries there is a danger that social service activities may be regarded as 'paternalism'.

c) In some countries the involvement of school students in social service activities is frowned upon.

My own impression is that none of these present insuperable obstacles—as indeed many schools in the categories quoted have shown— but that a re-examination, is desirable.

It is true that in those United World Colleges of the 'classic' Atlantic College type, CASS is likely to work best, since they are boarding schools which students have chosen to enter knowing the important part such activities play in a student's life there. But it is worth remembering another feature affecting all the other IB schools: that the IB has only been introduced in schools when the teaching staff were in favour of its introduction, including the commitment to CASS. The appointment of Alec Dickson, the founder both of Voluntary Service Overseas and of Community Service Volunteers, as consultant on CASS activities at the request of the Heads of Schools conference was an indication of their serious commitment.

Dickson, in an article reprinted for *Interact*, the regrettably defunct IB schools journal, listed 40 different social service activities being carried out by CSV volunteers, as examples which IB schools might follow, particularly in locations where the traditional rescue activities pioneered at Atlantic College are neither needed nor practical. Nevertheless, such activities do still go on and it is worth quoting as an introduction to any survey of CASS activities, the following report from Atlantic College:

"The inshore life-boat unit and the coast guard unit were also called out at 3:30 a.m. on a Saturday in March 1985 to assist in search for a 30 foot vessel which had sent out a mayday distress call off Aberthaw. Two college boats joined in the search with the Barry lifeboat, a Trinity House vessel and two fishing boats, as well as a helicopter. Four of the missing crew members from the boat that had sunk were picked up at sea, two of them by the college B boat."

Similar dramatic mountain rescues have been recorded from the College of the American West, but for most IB schools the social service activities have been either in the field of nature conservancy, as in Colombia or Tanzania, or the kind of help to the aged, the sick, and the disadvantaged which can be given by young people in the big cities, teaching crippled children to swim or simply visiting the aged and infirm. Sometimes it is difficult to arouse as much student enthusiasm for these simple day-to-day kindnesses, but it can be done and the learning experience seems to be genuine. As a social worker in Montevideo said in talking to the students: "Perhaps in a home for the aged, in a hospital, or even in a small school for deprived children, Tuesday is the highlight of the week for the residents, the sick or the little ones: when a group of young people arrive and do their rounds in the area of service. Perhaps when talking to an old person you wonder just how far you are getting through to them; perhaps the game of draughts or chess or scrabble seems very mundane to you, but then let us look on the side of the person you are helping; for them it is something to look forward to every Tuesday. Be assured that each *anciano* visited by you looks forward to this day; when we have to tell them that you are not coming, a great disappointment shows on their faces, and it seems that Wednesday is a long time coming." It may be asked whether the element of 'challenge' is adequately represented in such activities, but it is worth remembering that challenges are psychological as well as physical and that between the ages of sixteen and eighteen there are many kinds of fear to be overcome which are best overcome in company with one's peers.

The regular syllabuses in the subjects included in the six group pattern have been reviewed by a series of general conferences in the Study of Man subjects, hosted by the English Department of Education and Science in London in May 1982, in the science subjects hosted by the Japanese government at Tsukuba in 1984, and finally in languages in a series of regional conferences held in 1985 in Cali/Quito, Chicago, Paris, and Bangkok, with an input on Arabic from the Bahrain conference of 1984, to be followed by a general conference in 1986. A particular interest of my own was the development of new 'applied' subjects at the subsidiary level, the rationale of which is discussed in the next chapter.

On the side of finance and administration the situation which greeted the new Director-General on arrival was not so good. The preliminary budget estimates presented in 1983 showed an anticipated deficit of more than half a million francs, a situation which, unless rectified within the year would have led to the closing down of the organisation under the laws governing charitable foundations in Switzerland. A drastic reappraisal was clearly needed and with the chairman of the council tied both by his university duties in Dakar and his responsibilities in the francophone universities world-wide, an appeal was made to John Goormaghtigh in Strasbourg to chair an emergency committee. Thanks to his efforts and the tireless energies and world-wide travel of the new Director-General, the crisis was surmounted, partly through a deliberate, though temporary, moratorium on curriculum development and reduction in the Geneva Staff, partly through negotiation of more favourable terms with the now prosperous IBNA, and partly through the familiar, though now, I hope, obsolete, 'rescue operations'. The UWC helped by persuading Armand Hammer to continue his annual contribution of $30,000 for a further year and a similar sum was contributed as a 'special grant' by IBNA. As a result of all this activity the budget for 1983-4 was brought back into balance while that for 1984-5 showed for the first time a substantial allocation to reserves.

In August 1984, the long saga of the location of the examinations office reached its end. After the transfer of the language examination from Geneva to the University of Southampton in 1974, the next step had been the transfer of the other examinations to offices in London, provided by London University in the same building as the London Regional Office. The whole examinations office was then put under the control of the present Director of Examinations, Derek Goulden, former headmaster of Colegio Colombo-Britanico, who had been working for the UN in the Caribbean. The split was obviously undesirable, though less undesirable than the split between Geneva and Southampton. After a brief flirtation with another *ignis fatuus*, in the shape of the projected Mountbatten Center, and a series of proposals to repatriate all the Examinations to Geneva, it was decided at last to seek a single centre outside the high-cost capital cities. Co-operation with universities in the UK had long proved its value, both for the academic contacts it provided to IBO staff and because Oxford, Southampton, and London had in turn provided accommodation and services at less than commercial cost, through their interest in the project. The decision to concentrate in one provincial centre coincided with a period of university contraction in England and two universities, Sussex and Bath, offered very favourable proposals, using accommodation that seemed, for the moment at least, superfluous to their needs. In both cases there were already established personal links through IB examiners and a tradition of admitting IB students. In the end the decision was made in favour of Bath, which was better placed in terms of rail and air communications and had excellent computing facilities. The Examinations Office employed in 1985 more than 20 full-time staff and recruited four or five part-timers at the two peak periods of packing and script-checking. Considering that 90% of the work was carried on with schools that operated in English and the difficulties encountered in securing a work permit for even one foreign employee in Geneva, it was surely just as well that the proposals for 'repatriation' had never won the day.

For an operating centre as opposed to a political headquarters or centre of policy-making, it seems doubtful whether Geneva is well suited to the needs of non-governmental international organisations. The great difficulty lies in recruiting staff with the requisite language qualifications. Since most Swiss citizens need already to command two languages, German and French, those who are fluent in English as well are scarce and command high salaries. Yet the IBO, for all its commitment to two and later three official languages, had in practice to operate mainly in English since that was the working language of 90% of the schools. To recruit enough bilingual staff outside and bring them to Geneva was not possible even if we could have afforded it, since they would not have been granted work permits. Organisations such as the IBO are therefore compelled to seek administrative staff among the wives of UN or other officials, whose right to reside and work in Geneva depends on their husbands' positions. Sometimes this turns out very fortunately as for the IBO it did with Ruth Bonner and Paddy Hampton, but it does limit recruitment in any labour-intensive function to a very limited and sometimes transient field. In the long run I am sure that the decision to decentralise was right.

The tenth meeting of the International Council of the United World Colleges, held under the presidency of the Prince of Wales at the United World College of the Atlantic from 19th to 21st June, 1985, assembled the largest gathering of the movement's supporters in its history. In addition to a full attendance of the International Board and representatives from the embassies of Ivory Coast, Hungary, Poland, and Senegal, the British Council, CIDA, the EEC, IBO and the UN High Commission for Refugees, there were delegates from the UWC national committees in: Argentina, Belgium, Canada, Chile, Colombia, Costa Rica, Denmark, Ecuador, Finland, Federal Republic of Germany, Ghana, Hong

Kong, India, Ireland, Italy, Jamaica, Japan, Kenya, Mexico, Namibia, Netherlands, Norway, Pakistan, Peru, Portugal, Senegal, South Africa, Spain, Sweden, Switzerland, United Kingdom, United States of America, Venezuela, Zambia, and Zimbabwe.

The strangest omission from this list is that of France. How far this is due to the failure, so far, to arrive at a satisfactory pattern of integration between the *option internationale* of the French *baccalauréat* and the IB I do no know. But that one of the great, perhaps the greatest culture of the Western World should be so sparsely represented in the network of 6,000 former students of the United World Colleges seems to me little short of tragic—both for France and for the rest of us. Federal Germany has sent 392 students to UWCs, Norway 243, but France only 59.

The President in his opening address raised many of the issues which recurred again and again throughout the meeting: the need to re-emphasise our long-term goals while diversifying the structures through which we sought them, the need to reconsider our sources of funds (including, 'dare I say it', greater contributions from families of students) the need to reach out to new cultures, notably the Islamic, the need to make more effective and better known the work of the ex-students' network. The report of the meeting forms the most complete and up-to-date description of the present state of the movement. It was, I think, the near-unanimous impression of those who took part in the meeting that the high point of the eight sessions was the seventh, on the ex-student network. Under the Chairmanship of Mr Ray Crotty (Atlantic 1966-8) the senior ex-student on the Board, four ex-student members of their national committees, Ms Gloria Andrede, Ecuador (Pearson 1976-8), Mr Jens Henick Jensen, Denmark (Pearson 1978-80), Mr Glyn Roberts, Mexico (Atlantic 1966-8), and Ms Ulrika Stuart, Sweden (Atlantic 1975-7) gave an account of this experience at a UWC. All agreed that it had 'changed their lives'. The same remark was made recently to my daughter-in-law by a Polish student at a craft conference in Warsaw, who had taken the IB at Hammersmith and West London College, but had no idea of any family connection. They did, however, while welcoming the computerised data-base, urge that the network needed to be better organised and that the college courses should do more to help students to understand major international problems and how they themselves could help to put the ideas of the UWC movement into practice.

The fourth inter-governmental conference on the IB, hosted by the Italian Ministry of Public Instruction, the Regional Government of Friuli-Venezia-Giulia and the Province and City of Trieste, on the 29th and 30th of October, 1985, also assembled a record number of participants. Apart from Signora Falcucci, the Italian Minister of Public Instruction who chaired the meeting, the education ministers of Lesotho, Kenya, and Pakistan attended in person, while the US Secretary of Education sent Blouke Carus as his personal representative to read a very supportive message. Other governments represented are listed in appendix four.

There was also a strong representation of observers from the International Council of the IBO and school representatives from Bahrain, Colombia, France, Federal Germany, Italy, Japan, Netherlands, Tanzania, UK, and USA.

The purpose of the conference was to consider the IBO's development plan proposed for the next five years and in particular to strengthen the governmental participation, both in terms of finance and educational development. In introducing the plan, the Director-General pointed out that on the financial side the government contributions had remained static at around 500,000 Swiss francs, the figure achieved at the previous conference in Brussels in 1981. As a result of both inflation and the rapid growth of the IB this now represented only just over ten percent of the IBO's income, rather than the approximately 33% envisaged at Brussels. In order to maintain the degree of governmental, as contrasted with private, influence in the IB, he asked government representatives to agree to raise the standard contribution of governments in membership of the Standing Conference from 40-50,000 Swiss francs to 75,000 Swiss francs, with provision for bi-annual reviews, and to co-operate actively over the next five years by sending experts to curriculum review panels and assisting, where possible, in development projects. As at the first IB conference at Sèvres in 1967, few of the government representatives had come mandated to approve financial commitments, though there was general agreement that in view of the IBO's services to the mobile community the sums involved were not, even in the present hard times, very great. At a subsequent meeting of the members of the Standing Conference, the representative of the Council of Europe offered in co-operation with the Belgian government to host a meeting in Strasbourg in a year's time at which government representatives would be able to return to the financial issue after having consulted their respective Ministries. Another major item would be recognition of the diplomas in Europe.

This had been discussed at length in the conference with particular reference to two countries, France and Federal Germany. We have seen that negotiations were already going on in Paris about the possibility of enabling international schools to provide courses which would lead either to the *option internationale* or to the IB. These were carried further at Trieste and opened up, to me at least, some interesting lines of thought. In terms of an ideal education, it seems to me an attractive concept that in the progression from national and patriotic education to international education as conceived in the founding of the UWCs, described in chapter one and further elaborated in chapter eight, there should be a period of bicultural education as in the *option internationale*.

In terms of practicalities, however, though there are some schools, those in areas of large mono-cultural immigration, for instance, or of the original 'American Overseas' type, where a bicultural education may be both educationally desirable and administratively possible, there are others, the genuinely international schools with 30 or 40 different nationalities represented in the student body, where this is not so. One of the dramatic ceremonies at Trieste was the presentation of the ten thousandth IB diploma by Signora Falcucci to a Finnish student who had received his education in Malaysia, Thailand, and Mozambique, with brief periods at home in Finland, before taking his IB at the International School, Moshi, in Tanzania. For such students biculturism is not an 'option'.

The problem posed in Germany was rather different. Essentially it is the old problem of recognition of the IB as a university entrance qualification for nationals of the country educated within the country, which I first encountered in Lebanon in 1966. The argument against recognition is familiar: that it provides, for instance, for German students in Germany, usually the children of affluent parents, a back-door entry to the university, avoiding the fierce and public competition of the *Abitur*. The argument in favour of recognition is equally familiar: that in every country today there are bound to be a number of international schools serving the international community; if nationals of the country are debarred from attending these schools then the possibility of cultural contact between the international students and the host country is broken off—to the detriment of both.

It seems to me that the best solution to this problem is that originally worked out in France and now operating in a very wide range of other countries, by which the IB is recognised for nationals educated within their own country in a small number of specifically authorised schools—including, of course, UWCs.

In Germany, however, it seems that this problem is intensified by two factors: the fact that in Germany the age of transfer from upper secondary school to university is still higher than in other countries and the IB course therefore shorter than the normal *Abitur* course; and the fact that in a number of cities throughout the world, German schools offering courses leading to the *Abitur* have been established, thus extending the back-door argument even to some German students educated outside their own country.

It would be naive to suppose that a solution to the problems in these two countries can be easily found, yet it is surely important that in the interests of those students who find themselves in cities where the national courses and examinations are not available, in the interests of continued German and French participation in the UWC movement and in the interests of international education and cultural contacts within their own borders, a solution should be found. It was one of the great benefits conferred by the Italian government in calling and hosting the Trieste conference that it made possible widespread discussion of what such solutions might be.

Notes to Chapter Seven

¹ *Dialogues*, December 1984.

² *Schools Council Working Paper Number 5* (London:Evans/Methuen Educational, 1966).

³ *Schools Council Working Paper Number 16* (London: Evans/Methuen Educational, 1967).

⁴ *Schools Council Working Paper Numbers 46 and 47* (London: Evans/Methuen Educational, 1973).

⁵ Saul B. Robinshon and Kaspar Kuhlman, 'Two Decades of Non-Reform in West German Education', *Comparative Education Review*, no. 5 (1967): 311-330.

⁶ Peterson, *The Future of the Sixth Form*, 77-85.

8
SOME ISSUES
FOR THE FUTURE

I have taken part in the victory celebrations after two World Wars—though admittedly only as a Boy Scout in 1919. It is from that sort of time perspective that I would like to discuss with the reader some of the issues affecting the future of these two experiments in international education.

Let us group these issues under three headings: analytical, educational, and political. In other words, first, what do we mean, the reader who has persisted as far as this may ask, by international education and is it desirable? Second, if desirable how should it be taught and to whom? Third, who should provide it?

It would be possible to argue in favour of the International Baccalaureate simply as an administrative device, rendered necessary by the growth in the internationally-mobile population. A certain international character in the course would then follow automatically for purely administrative reasons, in order to make it possible for schools to include enough students of different nationalities in the same class. This argument has, indeed, been used, is valid, and has been the basis of some of the support which the IB has received. The international education which it implies could be negative (the avoidance of national idiosyncrasies), informative, and synthetic (the attempt to maximise skills and procedures incorporated in as many as possible of the national systems): but without specific international intention. International education of a purely informative type has long been regarded as useful for those whose business brings them into contact with people of another culture. Even during the two World Wars there were 'know your enemy' courses and it helped the eighteenth-century slave traders to know enough about the social systems of Africa to understand the inducements by which certain rulers could be persuaded to sell their people into slavery. Today, in a commercial world increasingly dominated by the search for 'competitiveness' with other nations, it is advantageous that the entrepreneur should know enough about his competitors, their language, and their customs and markets, to ensure that it is they and not he who suffer from the competition. The national interest, we are told, demands it. There were, however, many among the supporters of the IB who saw international education as something more than that. Prominent among these were the original founders, the teachers and the students.

Even if the course, as designed by the founders, had been of a purely negative, informative, and synthetic nature, the teachers and students would have turned it into something more positive; but in fact there was no divergence. What, then, was and, in my opinion, should continue to be, our common intention?

Let us go back to the concept of general education, as the fullest development of the powers of the individual mind, within which we were working. No such education of the whole person worth the name could be purely informative. To fructify, information must lead to understanding and understanding of other nations and cultures is impossible without some degree of sympathy. It worried the Allied military during the Second World War, who were then busy trying to type-cast the Japanese as monsters, that there was a great shortage of people who spoke Japanese and understood Japan and that most of these were, in their opinion, pro-Japanese—in other words that they thought of Japanese as fellow human beings and not as monsters. The progress from international knowledge to international understanding is implicit in the nature of education. Moreover there are aesthetic as well as moral elements involved.

T.H. Huxley, one of the great pioneers of Science Education, wrote:

> The man who is all morality and intellect, although he may be good and even great is, after all, only half a man. There is beauty in the moral world, but there is also a beauty of the world of Art. There are men who are devoid of the power of seeing it, as there are men who are born deaf and blind. But in the mass of mankind the Aesthetic faculty, like the reasoning power and the moral sense, needs to be roused, directed and cultivated; and I know not why the development of that side of his nature should be omitted from any scheme of education.[1]

An international education which, being really liberal and general, goes well beyond information and includes an appreciation of the art of other cultures and a discussion of the basis of morality in other cultures, is inevitably involved in the development of attitudes—embraces, if you prefer that terminology, the affective as well as the cognitive domain. Its intention is not simply to help the next generation to know better their enemies or their rivals, but to understand and collaborate better with their fellow human beings across frontiers. It was this kind of education which the United World Colleges were founded to provide and which the founders of the IB, together with the vast majority of teachers and students involved, have striven to develop.

'But', the reader may ask, 'is this not indoctrination, propaganda—and political propaganda at that?' At first sight it may seem so. A brief look at current national policies in education, for instance in the restored civics programme in France, the re-emphasis on national history in England, or the traditional courses of the Soviet Union, does show a strong emphasis on the teaching of patriotism and in educational terms it is sometimes assumed, wrongly in my opinion, that there is some kind of conflict between the teaching of patriotism and the teaching of internationalism. To demonstrate the falsity of this conflict requires an analysis over a rather longer time-scale of what we mean by 'patriotic' and 'international' education.

Theodore Zeldin has an illuminating story of a French *inspecteur* visiting a village school in the remote mountains of the Lozère in 1862.[2]

"In what country is the Lozère situated?" he asked. Not a single pupil knew the answer.

"Are you English or Russian?" he demanded. They could not say.

If, as he argues, it was the war of 1870 which finally unified the remoter parts of the French provinces into a nation state, it may well have been the same war which had an equally catalytic effect on Bavarians and Prussians. The political role of patriotic education at that period is clear enough, but the peasant children of the Lozère were expressing an element of truth which has a continuing value. Even during the first World War, W.B. Yeats wrote in 'An Irish Airman Foresees His Death':

> My country is Kiltartan Cross
> My countrymen Kiltartan's poor.
> No likely end could bring them loss
> Or leave them happier than before.[3]

The fluctuation in the nature of the unit to which patriotism is attached was vividly expressed to me by René Lejeune, Director of Ecolint in the early days of the IB. When I asked him why he was so committed to international education his reply was:

> My grandfather was conscripted into the French army in 1870; my father was conscripted into the German army in 1914; I was conscripted into the French army in 1939. We are tired of it—though I am devoted to my native land, Alsace.

If that was the experience of one family over three generations, what must now be the feelings of middle-aged individuals in East and West Germany educated in a common patriotism?

In patriotic education are there, then, two strands which need to be woven together? One might be described as the permanent, lasting, educational strand, the growing understanding of, sympathy with, and commitment to the person's own group and to his or her roots, the sense of *Gemeinschaft*, the obligation to Kiltartan's poor. The other is the fluctuating demand for political loyalty, the moral and legal obligation to accept a citizen's duties. Both, surely, should find a place in education, the first in the education of the emotions as a countervailing force to the atomistic threats of isolation inherent in so much of modern life, the second as part of civic education, where it appears in the French and Russian systems.

Two characteristics of the contemporary world seem particularly relevant to this discussion. The first is the large number of people who have, in this century, found themselves citizens of two different states at different periods of their lives, whether as a result of the two world wars or of the end of empires. The other is the revival of regionalism—Basque, Biafran, Breton, Corsican, Scottish, Sri Lankan, Tamil, Welsh, and many others—which is running concurrently with the formation of larger political groupings such as the EEC, and the replacement of the 'melting pot' concept in North America by the preservation of ethnic cultures and the cultivation of 'roots'. Both these factors seem to me to mean that the next generation needs a more subtle and sophisticated form of education for patriotism than has yet been achieved. The too frequent linkage of regional patriotism with terrorism points to dangers of romantic extremism which education should surely be striving to avert, while the rapid changes in the political state which lays claim to the civic patriotism of any one individual have produced a breeding ground of cynicism and moral emptiness. At one end of the scale one gets the English woman who, during the discussions of county boundary reform in England said: "I would rather that Yeovil was destroyed by an atom bomb than incorporated in Dorset"; at the other, spies on either side of the German border who seem to feel no real patriotic loyalty either to East or West Germany.

Would such a more sophisticated form of education for patriotism be in conflict with education for internationalism? Let us take the second, or civic, form of patriotism first. Statesmen in all countries, but particularly those with democratic constitutions, have always had to contend with the threats posed by populist jingoism—the "public men and cheering crowds" of Yeats's poem. Ever since Walpole said "They are ringing their bells now: they will be wringing their hands soon", and probably well before that, statesman have too often found themselves in the position of George Orwell in 'Shooting an Elephant':

> I did not in the least want to shoot him. I decided that I would watch him for a little while to make sure that he did not turn savage again, and them go home. But at that moment I glanced 'round at the crowd that had followed me. It was an immense crowd . . . I realised that I would have to shoot the elephant. The people expected it of me and I had got to do it; I could feel their two thousand wills pressing me forward, irresistibly.[4]

Such situations have forced statesmen over the last 150 years into tragic decisions: but they have not always seemed wholly tragic at the time and there have been elements of political compensation to hope for in the creation or preservation of nation states. Today every statesman in the Northern Hemisphere knows that to be forced into war by the pressure of popular patriotism would be the suicide of his own country. It must, therefore, be no more than expedient that in order to make the people governable in the national interest, the forces raised by patriotic education, whether local and emotional or national and civic, should be tempered by the 'countervailing force'[5] of international education.

All this may sound rather tame to the true internationalist, who is perhaps looking forward to the day when the interests of Spaceship Earth will transcend national interests in such forums as the UN or at least be allowed to count for something in the equation. These things take time, and meanwhile international co-operation has, in terms of Kiltartan's poor, scored in the latter half of this century one victory worth, in the long run, more than all the conquests of empires—the conquest of smallpox. All I hope to have shown is that here and now international education is as much in the interests of the governments of nation states as patriotic education in the second, or civic, sense.

On the first type of patriotic education, the understanding and emotional sympathy for the cultural and local community of which the child or growing youth is a member, the issues lie at a deeper psychological level. I can only hazard an occasional guess. Do the young need to be educated, as I was, as a patriotic Scot, and yet so educated they do not express this patriotism with bombs? And if so, how? Perhaps a closer analysis of the disease will help in the development of the right vaccine.

Why have members of local minorities turned recently so much more to terrorism and violence? Could it be for a reason perceived by T.S. Eliot, that human kind cannot bear much reality? Reality, in this context involves thinking, balancing one value against another, acceptance of ambivalence, ambiguity and uncertainty. People have escaped from it into passivity or moral paralysis, into romance (the romance of all for love in Europe or all for loyalty in Japan), into dogmatic religion, or into total commitment to a cause where the end justifies any kind of means, and where thought, balance, and moral uncertainties can be shed. In the past such a cause, such a 'zero-sum' game, such an escape from the unbearable stress of reality has often been a patriotic war. Is it possible that humankind, as this century draws to its close, recognises obscurely that war is no longer possible as an escape route from reality and that those who chose this route in the past are now choosing violent separatism? Is it possible that even in the world of sport, the cult of winning at all costs by fair means or foul, to which I referred in chapter one, is, at a lower level, part of the same human reaction? If it is possible, what antidote, what coutervailing face can education supply?

Football, to which a great deal of jingoistic patriotism has been transferred, may provide at least a pointer to some part of a reply. There does not seem to be any difficulty in stimulating passionately emotional loyalty both to Juventus and Italy, both to Tottenham Hotspurs and to England. Could it not be an aim of patriotic education to develop a patriotic commitment both to Catalonia and to Spain, both to Wales and to Britain? How this should be done is, perhaps, outside the theme of this book, but my own experience in trying to develop a patriotism directed to a Malayan nation as well as to the Chinese, Indian, or Malay community is that the key may be in a much more conscious attempt to develop sympathetic understanding of the other community. A word is relevant here, however, as to the theory of timing of these three phases on which the IB and UWC policy of international education is based. Without going here into all the arguments for and against teaching world history to ten-year-olds, I have been assuming that patriotic education in the sense of emotional commitment to Kiltartan Cross, together with its antidote, sympathy for another community, begins from the earliest stages of the primary school, that patriotic education in the sense of civic loyalty to the state is mainly the business of the middle school and that international education is best left mainly to late adolescence. Whether, as the French delegate at the Trieste Conference suggested, there should be an intermediate phase of bicultural education seems to me to depend on the specific environment.

One of the problems which from the start faced the IBO in developing an international curriculum was the tension between the academic requirements of university entrance procedures and these personal requirements of the whole human being growing up in an interdependent world. I have tried to show in chapter three how we set about trying to balance these requirements, but many of the outcomes to be hoped for from international education may increase the tension, since they are outcomes which are often regarded as irrelevant by those responsible for judging the competition for university places in the many countries where there is an effective *numerus clausus*. Consequently there have been a number of criticisms of the IB recently on the grounds that it is too dominated by the demands of university entrance, not genuinely international enough, too Western-oriented and too academic.

It would have seemed natural that such criticisms should have come mainly from the United World Colleges. They have, in the terms of their foundation, the more positive commitment to international action. One of the phrases in their *Guidelines*, quoted from Plato, is: "He who wishes to help his people must combine the power to think with the will to act."[6] In fact, however, it has been one of the aims of the colleges, ever since the founding of Atlantic College, to demonstrate that the successful completion of a rigorous academic course can be combined with, and even contribute to, an equally demanding commitment to a programme of social service, aesthetic activities, and international awareness.

How far they have succeeded in these aims is best left to the judgement of those who have visited the colleges and met the students. The criticisms seem to have not, in fact, come mainly from the United World Colleges but from a wide spectrum of IB schools. They deserve serious consideration.

It probably has to be accepted that the very structure of the IB, with its attempt to ensure the development of the general powers of the mind through a distribution requirement based on allocating familiar 'subjects' to one or other of the six groups, is a compromise. Because it is a compromise it needs a serious re-examination by IBO's newly established Curriculum Board. If that re-examination is to produce changes in the direction of more internationalism and less Western orientation, it seems to me that the Board will need a greater input from different nations and cultures. It is certainly right to involve the teachers in the international schools in any such process of curriculum revision, but I have explained in chapter three the reasons, linguistic and economic, for the high preponderance of teachers from the UK in international schools. We need for this part of the re-examination the help of more experts with a wider experience.

The criticism that the IB curriculum as a whole is too academic, too much oriented towards the values of scholarship rather than of action, too exclusively concerned with the development of the intellect rather than the will, too neglectful of the moral and aesthetic, is, I think, more profound—and much more difficult, if it is justified, to remedy. Here, the tension between the education of the whole person and the preparation of the candidate for university entry is more tense and, I believe, becoming tenser. It was well expressed by Sir Toby Weaver, introducing the first in a series of symposia on 'Education for Capability', organised by the Royal Society of Arts in London, in 1981:

> In the notion of capability we include, of course, the capacity to acquire and manipulate knowledge—preferably useful knowledge—and thereby to develop what the Robbins Committee called the general powers of the mind. We therefore, have no quarrel whatever with scholarly excellence, whether scientific or humane. Every civilised community depends on it.
>
> However, in tackling a problem, to comprehend aright what is the case—the proper end of science and scholarship—is necessary but not sufficient. Knowledge to be fruitful has to be applied in action. Yet our schools and higher education institutions are designed mainly to select, train and test the very small minority who are to become our future scholars and teachers, with the implication that academic

powers, the power to manipulate symbols and validate propositions, is the only true criterion of human excellence.[7]

It is in the word 'select' that the crux of the matter for the IBO is expressed. In the universities of Western Europe and those modelled on them—not in those of North America—the increasing degree of specialisation, the fragmentation of disciplines, the pressure on Arts and Humanities to develop techniques of scholarship approaching as nearly as possible to the conditions of the natural sciences, have all crept down to some extent into the selection process. Meanwhile many teachers of the classes preparing for this selection have themselves gone quite far along the road of academic scholarship and get their greatest satisfaction from starting off their ablest adolescent pupils upon it. It is between this tendency and the education of the whole person that I see an increasing tension developing.

There is a long Arnoldian tradition of using the teaching of literature and history as vehicles for the development of the moral and aesthetic judgement. Montaigne wrote of the good teacher that "he should not impress upon his pupil the date of the destruction of Carthage so much as the morals and behaviour of Hannibal and Scipio: nor where Marcellus died so much as why it was unworthy of his duty that he died there".[8] No doubt this element should fade out as the young man or woman strives to become a historical scholar at the university: but it has its place throughout life and above all in the secondary school. If it is too early eliminated by concentration on scholarship, what will take its place? Much the same is the case with the teaching of literature. The satirist, Auberon Waugh, in a recent article on the state of English, wrote:

> A vast English Lit. industry has sprung up since the war, providing harmless employment for large numbers of people who would otherwise be driven into local government or the 'caring' professions: Something had to be found for these people to do. They could not decently spend their time wallowing in the enjoyment of English Literature, without some quasi-academic justification. Some were sent to study the uncouth elements of our language in Anglo-Saxon and Middle English. While others invented new disciplines with their own vocabularies of pseudo-technical jargon to promote the illusion of activity: linguistics, semantics, structuralism, morphological functionalism—and now grammar.

One may not be wholly in sympathy with the satirist's tone, but it is surely true that for young people who are not going to become academic scholars in the field of English, it is better to acquire at school a taste for wallowing in the enjoyment of English Literature and a refinement of the moral judgement than an early introduction to the latest academic fashion in literary criticism. In so far as the university selection procedure encourages in the seventeen-year-old academic scholarship at a sub-university-specialist level, it often runs counter to the needs of educating the whole person. A.N. Wilson's professor of English and author of a massive tome on Swinburne, who remarked: "For pleasure? I guess it's a long time since I read a poet for pleasure", is no model for the ordinary student of English Literature.[9] Is there any way in which the total curriculum of the IB could be better adjusted to the educational needs of the whole person without sacrificing either the role of the rigorous academic disciplines in developing the general powers of the mind or the acceptability of the IB diploma for entry to universities in Europe? Perhaps the answer may lie in a review of the role of the three subjects taken at subsidiary level. There was initially a tendency to develop subsidiary-level programmes very much as half of the higher-level programme, differing in the range of content but not in intention. This was convenient to schools experimenting with the IB because it made it relatively easy to cover part one of the higher level in the same class with those taking the subsidiary level. It may still be convenient to offer such programmes as one type of subsidiary-level course, but I think we need to look for something better.

These three courses, chosen by the full diploma students at subsidiary level, fulfil a variety of roles in their total education. They do not normally lie in fields in which they intend to continue to work at the university, although some, notably Mathematics and the second language, may continue to be used as tools. In general the three higher-level subjects are those which are likely to be continued: the function of the subsidiary level is to provide the balancing element in the education of the whole person. For most students their experience of a subsidiary-level course will be their last involvement with the subject through formal education. It is for this reason that a subsidiary-level course which is simply half the higher level course is surely less than fully appropriate. It may be better than nothing, but a course designed as terminal rather than preparatory will be better still.

What then might be considered the special aims of a terminal course at this stage in a young person's education? In trying to assess what sort of subsidiary-level course the teachers would like to see introduced, it may be helpful to look at the following list of school-based, internally-assessed subjects approved in Group Six of the Diploma for 1985: "Drama, the Theatre, Theatre Arts, Marine Science, Nutritional Science, Natural Science, Applied Physics, Electronics, Experimental Psychology, Political Theory, Peace Studies, Social Studies, Chinese Studies, South Asian Studies, Classical Civilisation, Classical Greek and Roman Studies, Religious Experience of Man, Appreciation of fine Arts". Clearly a number of the courses are very similar and the different names probably represent no more than the particular interests of individual teachers. Moreover less than ten percent of diploma students were enrolled in such internally designed courses. But as an indication of the sort of courses which schools have wished to introduce at the subsidiary level they have certain features in common: they are more related to action, more related to the application of knowledge, more related to the environment of the school, less academic and more international. These are exactly the characteristics recommended in conclusions I and III of the Brussels Conference of 1981. Although there is no indication that these courses have become 'soft options' (their average grade in 1985 was 5.11 compared for instance with 5.11 for French A and 5.12 for French B), it would probably be unwise from the point of view of examination procedure to seek for an increase in their number. But could not the aims which they represent be incorporated in a new range of alternative subsidiary level courses within the general IB curriculum?

Let me go back to the aims of the IB as a whole—"to develop to their fullest potential the powers of each individual to understand, to modify and to enjoy..." If the primary aim of the higher-level subjects, continuing into higher education, is understanding, might there not be a substantial element of modification and enjoyment in the aims at subsidiary level? Of course these distinctions are not exclusive, but if a young person who has probably studied some form of history or science or literature for the previous five years is to take one final course in one of them before abandoning that field in formal education for ever, should we not lay more emphasis in that final course on the application of what he has learnt outside the world of schools and colleges and less on learning just a little bit more of the academic field? Unless the future scientist or mathematician who studies literature or history at school derives

from it a continuing pleasure and interest in literature or history—
even at the level of what the French call *vulgarisation*—it is difficult
to see what has been gained. Unless the student of these subjects
at the university has derived from his study of science at school
some interest in and understanding of the way in which science is
developed and how it affects the society in which he lives and
works, what has it profited him? At best, they will have totally
forgotten that on which they spent much of their school experience;
at worst they will have retained a muddle of confused ideas, bril-
liantly satirised in *1066 and All That*, and a distaste or distrust
for that whole area of human thought.[10] Jerome Bruner in the
passage already quoted (chapter three) refers to the "pitiably short
half-life in memory" of knowledge acquired without reference to
one's thinking beyond the situation in which the learning has occurred.

A first attempt at such a programme was a subsidiary level in
applied chemistry designed by Eric Antony, the chemistry teacher
at Ecolint. It consisted of a common core of basic principles and
eight optional fields of application (such as heavy industry, agriculture and food, or chemistry and health) of which the school
had to choose three. It was adopted as a regular programme by
the IBO and has been moderately popular—with 121 candidates
in 1985, compared with 748 for the standard subsidiary chemistry.
The next and more ambitious attempt at this kind of innovation
failed. The United World College of South East Asia had developed
an internally assessed 'sixth subject' in Nutritional Science. This
seemed to me to have two very attractive features. The first was
that through fieldwork on local diets it involved the students in
direct contact with their surrounding environment. It is only too
easy for international schools in developing countries to become
more or less affluent ghettoes, entirely cut off from the life of
surounding villages or poor city areas. It was one of the purposes
of CASS activities to help in crossing this frontier, but it seemed
to me that the inclusion of a programme of this kind within the
student's IB diploma course might do even more. The second was
that the nutritional science programme required that student to
apply insight from more than one area of academic study to the
consideration of human problems. This seemed to me a positive
advantage in those areas where she (girls tended to opt more than
boys for this programme) was not proposing to continue further
study of the subject in school or college. The concept interested

Unesco and I was able to get a small grant for an expert to discuss with teachers from other IB schools in the Far East the possibility of introducing the Singapore programme into the regular list of options in the same way that Ecolint's applied chemistry had been. The schools in Manila, Djakarta, and Hong Kong showed considerable interest but in the end none decided to adopt it. Today it continues as an internal sixth subject in Singapore and Mexico City, but that is all.

Readers may wonder why it matters so much that innovative programmes of this kind should be acceptable as satisfying the distribution requirements of the IB diploma in one, or better still, two of the first five groups rather than relegated to the sixth. The answer is a technical one. Almost all candidates for entry to the science faculties of European universities have to present at least two science subjects: with two languages, mathematics, and the Study of Man group absorbing four subjects, they are compelled to use their sixth subject slot for the second science. For them the sixth group, in which the internally designed programmes are included, is effectively barred off. The same is true generally for candidates for entry to modern language faculties who often need two foreign languages.

The experience of nutritional science convinced me of something I should have realised earlier—that, even in the experimental atmosphere of the IB schools, innovation in curriculum development could only succeed if it were accompanied by in-service teacher training. The main reason why none of the other Far Eastern schools adopted nutritional science was, I believe, that they had no one on their staffs qualified to teach it. And a $2,000 grant from Unesco was not going to finance the kind of in-service course and follow-up meetings that were necessary.

When, therefore, the next proposal for a subsidiary level course more geared to the application of knowledge to international human problems came forward in 1982 we got more substantial funds from the Rowntree Trust in the UK and the Sir Doragji Tata Trust in India. This enabled a programme entitled 'Science, Technology and Social Change' to be worked out at a series of meetings between the three sponsoring schools—Bahrain International School, Kodaikanal (South India), and the United World College of Southeast Asia—and advisers from such organisations as the Intermediate Technology Development Group, Volunteers in Technical Assistance, and the Universities of Sussex and Eindhoven. The three pilot schools were authorised by the IBO to introduce a common programme on an experimental basis, under the direction of Michael Brown, Director of the Science Studies Group at Sussex University and, after a preliminary meeting in Bahrain, a three-week in-service course was arranged at Kodaikanal. This was attended by teachers from three more schools, Hawaii Loa College, St Mary's college Nairobi, and the United World College of the Adriatic. If all goes well, which is by no means certain, it could soon be in operation in from six to ten IB schools round the world.

It seems unfortunate that this course, as well as some others which aim at a closer relation of academic learning to the solution of human problems, should have become involved in an educational controversy about 'interdisciplinarity'. It is not easy to determine in any historical or geographical context what is and what is not a 'discipline'. The classics, Latin and Greek, were always taught as a combination of language, literature, history, and culture. Is physics interdisciplinary because so much of it is mathematical? Is France guilty of interdisciplinarity because history and geography have been taught together in her schools throughout this century? Is geography itself not an interdisciplinary subject, combining earth science and social studies? Yet there are educationists who maintain that any course which involves more than one 'discipline' should be postponed until the separate disciplines themselves have been thoroughly mastered, which usually turns out to be at the post-graduate stage. This attitude seems to me to neglect two facts: the first is that the vast majority of students are never going to be post-graduates; the second is that it is much easier to motivate the vast majority of students for learning that seems relevant to human problems than for pure scholarship within a single discipline. At least I agree with the Brussels recommendation that IBO should provide the opportunity for those schools which want to give their students, all of whom are studying three disciplines at higher level, one such course as a subsidiary level option. Nor do I think that the inclusion of this small element of learning more directly related to international human problems, even if it is guilty of interdisciplinarity, will jeopardise these schools' chances in the competition for university entry. It is along such curricular lines that I would hope to see the International Baccalaureate and the United World Colleges developing further their joint experiment in international education. If, in the platonic phrase of the UWC Guidelines "he who wishes to help his people must combine the power to think with the will to act", and if his people are now both Kiltartan's poor and the the starving of Africa, then the UWCs and the like-minded IB schools should surely be seeking to integrate more closely the experiential learning of the social service activities with the intellectual learning of the academic programme. Such a course as Science, Technology and Social Change will be particularly important if the project for a UWC in India, for which a feasibility study was proposed in late 1985, comes to fruition.

For whom, then, should we be hoping to provide this kind of education for an interdependent world over the next decade? I ask the question not in terms of a possible Unesco resolution, but of the practical possibilities open to the two small voluntary organisations. Of course in the larger world one hopes that former UWC and IB students may, at some period of their lives, have some influence on their national systems of education; of course one hopes that the practice of introducing the IB into selected schools within national systems will spread, as it seems to be doing currently in Scandinavia and the Netherlands. But what should we be trying to do ourselves?

Let me illustrate this question of whom we should be serving by discussion of two issues, frequently recurring within our own ranks: 'balanced' expansion of IB and 'diversification' among UWCs. From the beginning there have been different opinions within the IBO about our policy on expansion, varying from Panchaud's original concept of an 'experiment' limited to a dozen schools, on the one hand, to a complete 'open door' policy on the other. The second intergovernmental conference (1978) recommended a 'carefully controlled expansion' but the principles on which control was to be exercised were not spelled out. There were still some who argued that if the IB or any part of it were a good programme, then there was no reason why it should be denied to any school that wanted it: control then simply meant not taking on more schools in any one year than our administrative resources could properly serve. The more schools the better, irrespective of their nature and the more schools, the more income. Hence the doubts expressed earlier about excluding proprietorial schools. At the other end of the spectrum were those who feared that if the number of schools or of candidates of any one type (such as schools in North America, UWC, or certificate candidates) expanded more rapidly than the rest, they would 'dominate' the IBO. Control, for them, meant restricting areas of excessive growth. In between were those who rejected fears of dominance, but who also favoured a more positive and deliberate plan for expansion rather than the completely open door. They rejected the restrictive dominance-based theory, not merely from agreement with the basic belief that if the IB were a good thing it should not be denied to those who wanted it, but because it was based on a misapprehension about the IB examinations and about the power structure within the IBO.

Fears that the very rapid expansion of the IB in North America would lead to 'North American dominance' of IBO would only have been justified if the composition of the IB Council had reflected the geographical distribution of IB schools. In fact only one element in it, the one-third representation elected by the conference of heads of schools, is in any way related to it; and this conference has never been influenced by such considerations in its elections. In 1984 roughly half the schools offering the IB were in North America but of the 24 Council members only four were North Americans, two of them heads of schools. The fear, sometimes expressed by other international schools, that the very large number of candidates from UWCs would distort the grading standards in the examinations, has already been dealt with. In a series of examinations where the grades are not established by reference to a statistical norm the performance of no sub-group of candidates can distort the standards expected from other groups. The same reasoning applies to a more recent complaint that the large number of candidates taking certificates in only one or two subjects distorts the standards expected from candidates taking the full diploma, because the certificate candidates can concentrate more on that particular subject.

The next intergovernmental conference (Brussels 1981) strongly reinforced the positive, as opposed to either the restrictive or the open-ended policy of controlled expansion by endorsing as part of the Ten Year Plan, the recommendation from the IBO that we should now seek to ensure that at least one school offering the IB was available in every city containing a large international community. Forty-seven of the cities identified then had at least one IB school and a further 30 had been added by the time of the 1985 conference in Trieste.

The policy of controlled expansion approved by the Trieste conference was one which maintained the objectives agreed in Brussels and added the concept of 'balance'—that is that rather than contemplate restriction of growth in any one area the IBO should seek, by a positive distribution of resources and effort, to balance it by growth in others. The principle of balance is not just a political device to avoid squabbles. Just as UWC has recognised that it is the movement as a whole rather than each individual college which must seek to be genuinely international, so the IBO is always seeking a balance of cultures and regions, not, as has been shown above, because that is required to ensure genuinely international control at the level of the Council, but for the value of the contribution which schools, teachers, and students in the different cultures and regions can make to the educational experience of the whole organization.

As far as the IBO is concerned therefore we seem to have arrived at an agreed policy that, while all manageable expansion in the use of the programme is to be welcomed, positive efforts should be concentrated on meeting the needs of the mobile international community and on maintaining within the organisation a cultural and geographical balance.

There has been a somewhat similar debate within the UWC movement centred round the word 'diversification'. Those who shared Mountbatten's belief that the movement should make a real contribution to world peace realised the implication that it must expand rapidly by the addition of more colleges. Those who knew from experience the huge cost of founding and then maintaining Atlantic College feared the drain on the potential sources of support for the first college or colleges which such expansion would involve. Sir George Schuster, with his usual foresight, was convinced that expansion on the scale Mountbatten envisaged would be possible only if governments adopted the movement and provided the major finance, and Mountbatten himself used to say that once we had established the first six colleges this was what we could reasonably hope for. There was, however, another path to expansion which, although it made some call on the movement's resources, did not involve capital or recurrent costs on the scale of Atlantic College. This was the association and then incorporation of existing international schools, such as Waterford KamHlaba and Singapore. It had never been the view of the original founders that all future colleges should follow the model of Atlantic College. Desmond Hoare had been a keen advocate of a much simpler, low-cost type of college in the Third World and a supporter of the proposal for a college in Thailand very different from Atlantic College, while Schuster, as we have seen in chapter five, warmly supported the Venezuelan project. Nevertheless there were some who viewed diversification suspiciously, and attempts by Moshi (Tanzania) and the British Schools Montevideo to enter into some form of association came to nothing.

The first move by a government, that of Canada, to give substantial and continuing support to the establishment of a college on its own territory, although it may prove in the long run to have been the breakthrough that Mountbatten hoped for, initially complicated the financial problems of the movement still further.

The original intention at Atlantic College was to provide a scholarship system so generous that no student selected for entry on merit would be unable to take up a place for lack of money. It was the hope expressed both by Desmond Hoare and by Mountbatten that a balance in the student body of 70% scholarship and 30% fee-paying students could be maintained. This pattern would have been difficult enough to establish on a continuing basis without substantial government support, but John Nicol's commitment in the Canadian Senate to '100% scholarships' substantially increased the difficulty by giving a lead which many people in the other colleges and the movement generally felt should be followed by all UWCs.

There was at first some doubt as to whether '100%' meant that all students should receive some degree of scholarship support or that all scholarships should cover the full cost of the student's two years at the college. When it became clear that it meant both, I argued for a division between tuition and boarding costs, with tuition free but families contributing to boarding costs in accordance with their means. I did so because this seemed to me to fit in with a primary long-term intention of the policy, which was to locate the colleges firmly in the public rather than the private sector of education. It could be argued, however, that since governments, national or local, commonly provide free education but not free maintenance, 100% UWC scholarships would be providing an additional subsidy to an élite, a subsidy which often went to families much richer than those whose donations or taxes were providing it. The commitment to the Canadian government, however, and the determination to avoid any possibility of wealth affecting selection were held to imply '100%' in both senses, and to be overriding. It was in this sense that the policy was also adopted by the United World Colleges of the Atlantic and Adriatic. The policy has proved extremely difficult, and in the case of Atlantic College, impossible, to implement.

The main reason for the difficulty has been that it runs counter to the policy of public authorities in many countries which provide scholarships, that is, financial aid for education. From the very earliest days, for instance, Atlantic College has relied on a regular intake of students from Federal Germany and Norway. Their Scholarships have been provided by public authorities—the *Studienstiftung* in Germany and the local authorities in Norway. For its British contingent it has relied on students sent on scholarship by the local education authorities. In all these cases the scholarships to a United World College have formed part of a public system of financial aid to poorer families for education and the amount of all such grants is calculated in accordance with the family's means. Hundred percent grants both for tuition and board to all families, irrespective of their means, would be unacceptable to such bodies. Yet it is on such governmental or semi-governmental bodies that in the long run UWCs must depend for support of many of their students.

When the Armand Hammer UWC of the American West was founded, enrolling for the first time a substantial proportion of US students, the 100% scholarship policy proved equally unacceptable within the private sector. The whole pattern of assessing the parental contribution to be expected from the recipient of a scholarship within the US system of education is so well established by custom and practice that any suggestion of a single college abandoning it seemed unthinkable. Would it not be bribing away the best students from other colleges by offering financial inducements that broke the accepted code?

The position today remains confused, perhaps because UWCs are moving in the direction that Mountbatten hoped, when a number of countries would establish a UWC as part of their national system, with an international agreement to fund the interchange of students, but have not fully reached that stage. For the moment, therefore, there seems no alternative to accepting diversification, in the sense that each college is responsible for its own scholarship policy and that even within colleges the policy with regard to funding of scholarships may differ as between those which are funded by the college itself or its home government and those which are funded by international agencies, semi-governmental bodies in other countries, or charitable sources. While such agencies or sources may accept a parental contribution based on assessment of means, the college itself has no such relations with parents or students and receives from the sponsors the full cost of the student's two years at college. All students then have the same status as scholars, though inevitably in the bedrooms or dormitories anecdotes are swapped. None of this, of course, applies to the incorporated international schools where UWC scholars are simply one part of a predominantly fee-paying student body and which, at present at least, certainly belong to the private rather than the public sector of education. It does not seem likely in the immediate future that nations or cities—even Geneva or New York—will assume responsibility for providing international schools within the public sector. If, therefore, the diversification accepted by UWCs in Singapore and Waterford is to be made really successful, one of the major tasks over the next few years must surely be to increase the proportion of UWC scholars in such schools to something nearer the target originally envisaged.

If the procedures of funding are, for the present, divergent, the process of selection is not. Selection for entry to the four residential colleges or for scholarships to the incorporated international schools is strictly 'on merit'. There may be some difficulty in identifying or weighting the factors which add up to 'merit' when national committees conduct their selection as far apart as Nairobi and Helsinki, but a wide degree of consensus has been achieved within the movement. The actual procedure of selection is best illustrated by that which was adopted for more than 20 years by the *Studienstiftung* in Federal Germany. First the selection committee circulates a sample of 300 schools. This differs each year and in 1984 produced more than 300 enquiries. Applicants then fill in a detailed form, scrutiny of which in 1984 reduced the numbers to 130. These were reduced by ballot to 70 who attended a two-day seminar with ten members of the selection committee, which included former UWC students as well as school principals and educationists, but has no possibility of contact with the candidates' families. On their assessment the award of places depends.

There is, therefore, a very considerable diversification already both in the age-range of the student body in the colleges and in the way in which the students have entered them. I have argued in chapter five that, from the point of view of the fundamental aims of the movement, students who have entered colleges at different ages and through different channels may develop similar commitments to the ideas of peace, justice, and international co-operation in the service of humanity. Yet if the movement expands—as those who believe in it are convinced it must—the role of the UWC 'scholar', the boy or girl seeking this kind of education because that is what they want, not because parental circumstances force it upon them, must expand with it. That seems to mean more United World boarding colleges, more United World scholars at Waterford and Singapore, and perhaps more associated or incorporated international schools. Where and how could such an expansion be attempted?

To ask where brings one up abruptly against the most manifest failure of the UWC movement. The one group of young people whom the students, whether Western or from the Third World, have little or no chance of meeting at a UWC is their contemporaries from the Socialist bloc of Eastern Europe. Yet students from East and West are the very ones whom the movement, in accordance with its fundamental aims, should be trying to bring together and perhaps the very ones who, at this stage in their youth, want to come together.

It has not been from want of trying. A handful of students from Czechoslovakia, Hungary, Poland, and Rumania have come, on scholarships raised by such donors as Mr. Maresi, to colleges in the West. Dr Hammer even succeeded in getting two students from the Soviet Union. But in spite of the success of individuals, long experience has shown that in the present political climate of confrontation, suspicion, and economic imbalance this kind of student interchange is impossible.

Everything depends upon the developing political situation, but I wonder whether, if a sufficient degree of *détente* were to be achieved, the best first step might not be either the establishment of a college in a 'non-aligned' country or the foundation of a United World College in Eastern Europe, bringing together students from all the socialist countries and from the non-aligned countries, but not from the West, committed to the promotion of international understanding. This would have to be a government-sponsored institution, and the degree of contact it would have with the UWC movement in the West would need a lot of negotiation. The curriculum would normally be Marxist-Leninist-oriented, but some sort of contacts with the IB might be possible though likely to prove as difficult as the reverse has been. All would depend on the degree of political *détente*, but it might be a more fruitful line of approach than continuing to try to attract the occasional Easterner to a Western college. If such a college were to be established the first contact with students from other colleges might be on short exchanges or co-operative participation in vacation work-camps.

The key to the 'how' problem is money. Does money come from the public or the private sector? The fund-raising capacity of the existing national committees is stretched already to the limit and in order to ensure their survival the existing colleges are struggling each to build up a scholarship endowment fund. The most promising project for a new college seems to me undoubtedly the Indian one and that is being pursued on the understanding that fundraising for it will not compete at all with, or 'fish in the same pool' as, the other colleges. It seems to me that there are only two possibilities. In 1982 Tony Besse put forward a proposal for a general UWC permanent scholarship endowment fund, designed to guarantee the needs in perpetuity of the first four boarding colleges with a target of fifty million dollars. It came at a bad time for fund-raising, the target was formidable, and although the principle met with support provided it did not cut across individual college efforts, no progress has yet been made. Could it possibly go beyond ensuring the future of four colleges? The other possibility is that to which Mountbatten looked forward, that governments would come to see the establishment of a UWC and the support of their own students at other UWCs as part of their national and international educational commitments. Here Canada and Italy have blazed a trail, but there is a long way to go yet.

An even greater degree of diversification is, of course, represented by the other government-sponsored initiative, the Venezuelan project. Sir George Schuster's argument that this was a legitimate diversification of UWC activity to a different field where our fundamental aims could be pursued by bringing young people of many nations together in a common course is still convincing. Over and above that, there is an educational problem which this college shares with the still embryonic plans for a college in India. In my own thinking the Indian College should be, like the Venezuelan, more specifically concerned with a great world problem, in this case the impoverishment of the rural areas and the deadly drift of destitute peasants to the great megalopolis—whether it be

Bombay, Lagos, or Mexico City. We in the West saw it a hundred years ago when Dickens wrote of the Great North Road:

> Day after day, such travellers crept past, but always, as she thought, in one direction—always towards the town. Swallowed up in one phase or other of its immensity, towards which they seemed impelled by a desperate fascination, they never returned. Food for the hospitals, the church yards, the prisons, the river, fever, madness, vice and death—they passed onto the monster, roaring in the distance, and were lost.[11]

What I would hope a college in India might do would be to combine an academic education, perhaps an IB including the new course in Science, Technology and Social Change, with direct experience of and participation in those schemes for rural revival through appropriate technological and economic development, in which India has played such a leading role. The problem for educationists in the Venezuelan College then seems to be how to integrate a greater understanding of other peoples and of international co-operation with the training of new farmers and the problem in an Indian College of how to integrate academic education with a greater understanding and experience of the problems of rural communities. In solving their problems, they might do worse than bear in mind some words of David Atterton, a former Chairman of the Atlantic College Governors: "I am advocating and supporting some dramatic changes in our educational system. We must concentrate more on developing the whole person and there should be no differentiation between education and training."[12]

But I am going too fast. Neither college yet exists, and fitting the education to the students will be something to be worked out gradually. If, then, this is the general type of international education that the IB and UWCs can give, and these are the sort of students to whom it can be given, what of the third question with which this chapter started: who should provide it?

Let us consider first three simple, or perhaps simplistic, possibilities: that it should be provided by private enterprise; that it should be provided by national governments; that it should be provided by an international agency, presumably an organ of the UN. The private enterprise of two groups of individuals undoubtedly launched these experiments in international education; but private enterprise alone could not maintain it or expand it as it should be expanded, unless it were to become available only to the children of the rich. National or local governments do not yet seem ready to accept in full such an objective. The nearest thing to an international school within a public system is probably the Lycée International de St Germain, but that as we have seen, is a mixture of public and private. In the present climate of politics and 'politicisation', no UN agency could possibly take responsibility for international education.

The only solution therefore seems to lie in an extension of the present system of, to use a term from the English educational system, 'voluntary aided' education. What will be important for the future will surely be that aid from individual governments should provide an increasing proportion of the costs. Together with that should surely go an increasing degree of influence over the policy of the voluntary bodies. This is always a delicate matter, but within both UWC and IBO such patterns as the governmental participation in the council of the IBO are already evolving which could be developed in this way.

Finally, has it all been worth it? And would it be worth it for governments to increase their support? Philip Ziegler, in his admirably balanced life of Mountbatten, reserves judgement, but is rather sceptical about the United World Colleges. I was returning in the car with two or three members of the 'old guard' from a Governors' meeting at Atlantic College, when this scepticism was discussed. "At any rate," said one, "we have created the most exciting school in the world: and it is open to all." Few, if any, who have actually spent any time with the students at a United World College would quarrel very much with that sentiment. Whether the colleges and international education generally have yet done much to prevent World War Three is another matter. Mountbatten, in movements of enthusiasm, used to talk of it, and he was a man whose enthusiasm for new ideas was unbounded, but he was also aware of practicalities and of the time-scale in which we are all working. Exaggerated claims may well produce scepticism, but it should surely be scepticism about the claims, not about the objectives.

It has been said that we have not inherited this world from our parents, but borrowed it from our children. Unless the next generation of the young are brought up in such a way as to stimulate, liberate, and educate their natural propensity to make friends across frontiers—national, racial, and cultural—we, the educators, are failing in our responsibility to our children. It is true that there are only just over 6,000 former UWC students alive today and only just over 10,000 IB diploma holders. As often happens in education, the first step in a new direction had to be taken by individuals. It is, no doubt, a very small step: but it is a small step for mankind.

Notes to Chapter Eight

[1] T.H. Huxley, Rectorial Address to the University of Aberdeen, 1874.

[2] Theodore Zeldin, *France 1848-1945: Intellect and Pride* (Oxford: Oxford University Press, 1980).

[3] William Butler Yeats, *The Wild Swans at Coole* (London: Macmillan, 1919).

[4] George Orwell, 'Shooting an Elephant', in *The Collected Essays, Journalism and Letters of George Orwell*, vol. I, *An Age Like This 1920-1940*, ed. Sonia Orwell and Ian Angus (London: Secker & Warburg, 1968). Originally in *New Writing*, no. 2 (Autumn 1936).

[5] For the concept of education as the 'countervailing force', see David Riesman et al, *The Lonely Crowd: A Study of the Changing American Character* (New Haven: Yale University Press, 1950).

[6] Plato. *Republic.* I have been unable to trace the exact quotation, which was a favourite of Kurt Hahn's, but the theme recurs again and again in the education of the Guardians.

[7] Sir Toby Weaver, 'Education for Capability', *Journal of the Royal Society of Arts* (1981).

[8] Michel de Montaigne, Essai XXV 'De l'institution des enfants', *Essais* (Bordeaux, 1595; later edition, Paris: Lefèvre, 1826).

[9] A.N. Wilson, *The Healing Art* (London: Secker & Warburg, 1980).

[10] W.C. Sellar and R.J. Yeatman, *1066 and All That* (London: Methuen, 1930).

[11] Charles Dickens, *Dombey and Son* (London: Chapman and Hall, 1848).

[12] David Atterton, 'Bridges to Industry', Address to the Headmasters' Conference, Oxford, 1985.

9
THE UNITED WORLD COLLEGES IN THE NEW MILLENNIUM
David Sutcliffe

Of course, the scorners often seemed wise. Yet you see the prophecy lay with him.[1]

"Finally, has it all been worth it?", Alec Peterson asked in his closing chapter in 1987.

In the late 1980s, two UWC headmasters travelled by invitation to China, on different occasions, to find out whether proposals to link a UWC college campus with a Chinese university were feasible. They were not, but 'QW' was typically unready to stand on the sidelines. QW—the Honourable Lee Quo Wei, GBM, JP, one of Hong Kong's most influential figures in banking and education, who had been raising scholarships since the 1970s to send young people from the territory to the United World Colleges— identified a foundation and other sources willing to provide funds, and negotiated with Hong Kong authorities and, through them, the Sino-British Land Commission, for a site for a College. Major decisions for Hong Kong had at that time to be agreed with Beijing, especially over the allocation of land.

The Chinese Ambassador in London spent a day at the Atlantic College in Wales. All went well, and the International President of the Council, HRH the Prince of Wales, performed the Opening Ceremonies of the Li Po Chun UWC of Hong Kong in November 1992. The essential facilities had been completed in a matter of months. Thus it became possible for United World College scholars to experience at first hand one of the great political transitions of the close of the Twentieth Century. A great step forward from the early 1970s, when National Committee Chairmen had protested to the Atlantic College Governing Body about the Headmaster's recruitment of Chinese students because they feared that their own students might be indoctrinated!

In Norway the dream of an Atlantic College graduate was about to be realised. For years, Tom Gresvig had resolutely—no, stubbornly—gone about persuading first Norwegians, then fellow Scandinavians, that the Nordic countries ought to be doing more than sending their students overseas to UWC, that they had a bigger role to play. Given Kurt Hahn's oft-expressed admiration for Nansen, it all seemed very appropriate. Once Norwegian governmental funding was assured, local councils all over Norway were invited to compete to host the College. The project took on an even stronger profile when agreement was reached with the Norwegian Red Cross for a joint enterprise.

Thus it was that the new President of the United World Colleges, Her Majesty Queen Noor of Jordan, was able to perform her first College Opening Ceremony in the autumn of 1995 in Flekke, north of Bergen. The site is spectacular. The College buildings have been created in timber on the lines of a small Norwegian fishing village. The students use the facilities of the adjoining Red Cross Centre and undertake part of their social service with the patients. There were some natural concerns about the climate and the long, dark Nordic winter. How would Africans and Latin Americans manage? The College has made some small calendar adjustments since opening, but has had no insurmountable problems in living the normal Northern Hemisphere academic year.

The campus is beautiful but remote, a matter of more potential concern to the teaching staff than to the students. Following Nordic traditions, the College has laid much emphasis on environmental matters and would like to see fellow Colleges and the International Baccalaureate attempting far more in this area. Distinctive, too, has been its priority in allocating scholarship funds to refugees, to students from the Baltic States and Eastern Europe in general, and to students with handicaps. The campus was designed for wheelchair access everywhere, but the degree of physical handicap which has proved manageable in the College has been an inspiring eye-opener to all observers including the other Colleges. The College is called The Red Cross Nordic United World College, and is supported by all the Nordic governments, with Norway in the lead.

Within two years of becoming President, Queen Noor was able to perform her second opening ceremony, an exotic, colourful affair some one and a half hours outside Puna in the Indian State of Maharashtra. No College has had a longer gestation. The first plans and the first sites were put forward in 1970. Successive Indian governments had resisted the concepts both of elitism and of foreign educational activity in India. Not even the former Viceroy and deliverer of their independence, Lord Mountbatten, could move them. Now, the generosity and determination of two of India's leading business figures, Harish and Keshub Mahindra, brought together money, agreement on the choice and purchase of a site, and governmental acceptance. By the time of the opening, Harish was seriously ill. Completion of the campus was forced through at extraordinary speed and achieved before his death. Once again, graduate influence had been vital though perhaps not quite as decisive as in Norway—his daughter-in-law had also attended Atlantic College and fascinated her father-in-law with recitals of her experiences there.

New Colleges, New Achievements

These three Colleges, all opened in the same decade, brought new vitality, strength, and confidence to the entire organisation. They were a confirmation of the original, the 'classical' concept of a United World College—the two-year pre-university course for students on scholarship, recruited by National Committees in their home countries and ready to leave home, school, and friends for the sake of the experience. They emphasised again one of the most important features which distinguish the Colleges from other international schools—the scholarship students arrive directly from their national schools and national traditions, and ensure that the Colleges are fired by the confrontation between the full-blooded and undiluted expressions of national cultures. They also carried forward the precedent established by all the earlier Colleges of having sites of extraordinary natural beauty. The Mahindra College is on a high plateau with long views over mountains and river countryside. Even the College in Hong Kong,

established a library and computer facilities for street children in New Delhi, funded twenty-six orphans in Ho Chi Minh City, Vietnam, raised the funds to build two schools in Nepal and Pakistan, and sponsored the education of another sixty pupils in Ladakh and twenty-eight in Bangkok. And this is only a partial list.

There has been a small and welcome increase in the number of UWC scholars sent by National Committees, and the College is itself offering an increasing number of scholarships to countries which cannot afford them. Members of the teaching staff have been consistently generous in sponsoring scholarships, often at other Colleges. The College has not however achieved its ambition of bringing other, similar all-age schools into membership of the United World Colleges.

Lester B. Pearson United World College of the Pacific

Pearson College has not faltered. The natural beauty of its woodland and seascape setting, and the warm informality of its elegant cedar wood buildings, continue to define its magical personality. Its early sea rescue services have evolved more and more towards care of the environment.

Race Rocks, the cluster of islands a little way off shore in the San Juan Channel and formerly the site of an important manned lighthouse, have now been entrusted to the College. The marine life—seals, sea lions, passing killer whales, a rich bird life—is closely monitored by the students. Not only that: Remote controlled cameras and microphones above and below water make the entire marine reserve available on the Internet [www.racerocks.com], and Race Rocks is fast becoming a model for discreet and fascinating observation of nature. Local generosity has provided the College with a magnificent observatory, equipped with computer controlled telescopes. Again, the observations are available on the Internet [www.astronomy/astromain.htm], and photographs reproduced in the national press in Canada and the United States of Halley's Comet were taken by College students.

From its opening onwards in 1974, the College has always been clear that all students must attend on scholarship. A recent major donation from the Canadian government has enabled the College to set aside more places for refugees and even to help with their post-College financial needs. The clarity and comprehensive nature of their graduate records is a model for the rest for the organisation, and it is a just reward that graduates have been so prominent in helping to create an endowment fund which is now coming close to covering the needs of the annual budget.

Waterford KamHlaba United World College of Southern Africa

Since its formal recognition as a 'full' United World College in 1982, the Waterford KamHlaba in Swaziland has had the kind of eventful life that one might have expected from developments in the region. After some initial hesitations and difficulties, UWC scholars nominated by a small group of National Committees developed a strong sense of loyalty to the school and pressed hard for a greater measure of genuine acceptance by fellow Colleges and by more National Committees. At the latest count, roughly one half of the senior IB students in the school have been nominated and sponsored by UWC National Committees.

Problems in the financial administration and an unhelpfully rapid succession of school Heads coincided with the period in which the College was having to redefine its role. Nelson Mandela, whose children and grandchildren had attended the College, was now the President of South Africa. In principle, the ideals for which the school had been founded back in 1963 were at last practicable in South Africa. Multi-racial schools were no longer illegal. In practice, life in South Africa has not been at all straightforward, and the College has no doubt that its task continues to be to stand in the front line of quality education for all races in Southern Africa. Meanwhile, its social services continues to be immensely impressive, as is the frank and courageous programme of Health Education it has formulated, compelled into action on account of the Aids crisis which is all about it. Many graduates are playing important roles in public life and administration in the new South Africa. They are distinguished witnesses to the accomplishments of the early years of this important school.

Armand Hammer United World College of the American West

The Armand Hammer United World College of the American West, as Alec Peterson noted, had set records in the speed with which it was set up in 1982. The name and wealth of its renowned founder, however, deterred other donors, and the College underwent several years of serious financial worry, continuing in the immediate period after Hammer's death in November 1990. More recently, the steady and thoughtful cultivation of old and new friends has brought a convincing measure of financial security. In particular, the dramatic generosity of nearby neighbours Mr and Mrs Shelby Davis in 1998 has endowed scholarships for one hundred American students at a time to attend the United World Colleges, fifty of them the American College, the other fifty overseas. With this gesture alone, the Shelby Davises have joined the small ranks of really major donors to the UWC, among them their fellow countrymen Sonny and Phebe Maresi, who played a similar role in the 1960s and 1970s for the Atlantic College.

The Shelby Davises have gone even further. They provided a 'challenge donation' for the restoration of the Montezuma Castle which overlooks the original College campus. Now the Castle has been magnificently renovated and offers major facilities for the College as well as serving as the Centre for the Bartos Institute for the Constructive Engagement of Conflict—the College has for many years made conflict resolution one of the strongest features of its educational program, extending its expertise to the other United World Colleges. The Bartos Institute is developing its activities nationally and internationally, the students the privileged beneficiaries of a remarkable College initiative. Since its earliest years, the College has also run summer workshops for several thousand teachers and prospective teachers of the International Baccalaureate. This has been a notable contribution to public education and to the dramatic growth of the IB in US state schools.

United World College of the Adriatic

The physical development of the Adriatic College in Trieste, founded in the same month as its American counterpart, has been slow. The challenge of creating a College in a small village, the need to anticipate and accommodate the anxieties of the local people who feared that the College might 'swallow them up', and the delay until December 2000 in the purchase of sufficient land on which to plan the final facilities, have been straightforward if frustrating facts of life for the College administration. The rich compensations have been the high quality of those facilities which have been completed, and the accelerating confidence of the regional and state authorities in the College's performance.

The Region of Friuli-Venezia Giulia has not hesitated in its self-imposed task of providing the College with its buildings and major equipment; and the Italian parliament has passed a law which covers one half of the annual financial needs from the budget of the Italian Ministry of Foreign Affairs. This remarkable support is certainly due to the relationship the College has developed with the countries of Central and Eastern Europe in years of rapid, sometimes tragic and bloodthirsty change. The College has been the Regional Office for the region on behalf of all the United World Colleges, and has helped to develop and administer a major scholarship programme involving hundreds of students in the past fifteen years.

Students from Formerly Communist Countries

With the addition of the new Colleges, it may be argued that the movement has come a little closer to achieving the national and cultural balance which was one of Alec Peterson's concerns. The most dramatic change, one that would have given him perhaps the greatest satisfaction, has been the setting up of committees and the recruitment of students from all the countries of Central and Eastern Europe and from many of the Republics of the former Soviet Union as well. With rare exceptions, these students have proved to be exceptionally able and well taught, especially

were to merit their claim to a global conscience and to peace-making.

Prince Charles was followed by two successors. In colourful and expressive ceremonies in November 1995 in Johannesburg and Swaziland, Her Majesty Queen Noor of Jordan was installed as President of the Organisation, and Nelson Mandela became President of the International Council for the five-year period before the Council was next due to meet. In the event he has stayed on as Honorary President in spite of giving up most other such positions on his retirement from the Presidency of South Africa, clearly an exceptional tribute to UWC. Her Majesty Queen Noor's readiness to visit Colleges and support profile-raising events has been very significant in helping Colleges to burnish their reputations and their fundraising. Her involvement in a host of other international causes, including that of the United Nations, has given added authority to the movement. She shares with her predecessors a remarkable talent for communicating with the College students.

Making Ends Meet

But governance matters do not begin and end with Presidents. It was one thing for a powerful personality like Mountbatten, ably seconded by Alec Peterson among others, to impose his will on a tiny international office and one or two colleges. The debate changes with ten financially autonomous institutions, all struggling to end the year with their heads above water, and some 120 committees. Central co-ordination is a must, but so is effective regional decentralisation and delegation. National and selection committees want a common line, but they also need and respond best to personal contact. The regional conferences run on modest budgets in different parts of the world in recent years have been among the most valuable and appreciated initiatives taken by the International Office. Colleges are vigorous institutions, led and staffed by vigorous personalities. Their success, even their survival, depends on their ability to relate effectively, often swiftly, to their own local and national circumstances, needs, opportunities, potential sponsors and official authorities.

The debate has gone backwards and forwards, as Alec made clear in the earlier chapters of this book, about a central scholarship fund and centralised fundraising. In the meantime, and perforce, the Colleges have got on with the job themselves and, broadly speaking, have little confidence in the prospect of successful fundraising from the centre. And yet co-ordination is necessary if donors are not to be angered and frustrated by multiple approaches. In principle, the case for support should be the more effective for being presented globally. The UWC needs as a single unit to cultivate its relationships with other major international organisations, including the United Nations and its various agencies. The fortunes too of Colleges wax and wane, and sometimes they do need help. The long-term solutions are not apparent, and the root cause is, quite simply, that the international organisation that would be needed to carry out all these functions cannot be afforded. Not many sponsors can be found for the costs of administration.

Meanwhile, Colleges continue to put a brave face on things when their contributions to London are due, and the National Committees, who are the most appreciative of the work done for them by the International Office, are too strapped for scholarship funds to envisage funding another office in addition to their own. The healthy aspect of this all-too-often hand to mouth management is the awareness shared by all active members of UWC—Trustees, Chairmen, and Heads of Colleges, administrators, teachers, students and graduates—that success really does depend on all of them individually. There is no big brother or big sister around to pull the irons out of the fire.

The UWC Relationship with the International Baccalaureate

The relationship between the UWC and the IBO has evolved. The most evident change has been at the governance level. No longer does one find the same people on the two senior governing councils, or College Heads (2001) on the IB Heads Representative Committee, the single exception being the President of the IB Council of Foundation, who was also, in 2001, a member of the

UWC International Board. Older UWC and IB hands will find this 'unimaginable' and regret it. However, the reliable performance of UWC students in the annual examinations, the consistent contributions of many UWC teachers as IB workshop and subject group leaders and the high number of IB assistant examiners to be found within the Colleges, combined with the continuing disproportionate number of school-based syllabuses innovated by the Colleges, all suggest that the IB role of the United World Colleges remains an essential feature of IB life. With the advantages of residential life, and of students selected for scholarships on grounds of idealism and personality, the Colleges continue to play a strong hand in setting standards for the IB concerns with the development of human attitudes—activities, community service, the study of global issues.

New Tasks and Challenges

And the challenges of the future? Some of these are inherent in the movement as it exists today. Others lie waiting to be recognised and seized—or to be judged as irrelevant or beyond our grasp.

Alec Peterson describes how his last act as Chairman of the UWC Board was to sign the agreement aimed at the acceptance of the proposed Simon Bolivar Vocational College of Agricultural Management in Venezuela into the movement, and how this attempt at a practical response to the problems of the third world had come about at the insistence of the Prince of Wales. Even so, some years passed before the College opened. It has had far more than its fair share of problems. Official support in Venezuela, a key consideration, has come and gone with changes of government and President and with the volatile economic fortunes of the country. Knowledge about the College and its *raison d'être* across the movement has been patchy. The College is Spanish-speaking and this has been a natural but additional hurdle. The older age (19 upwards) of the students, and their wholly different backgrounds and intentions in life, have not encouraged a common sense of purpose with the students in other Colleges.

For a while, it looked as if there might be a second, very similar member of the organisation. The South African delegation which attended the 1990 International Council Meeting in Duino had been inspired by the Prince of Wales's observations to commission a series of highly professional feasibility studies for a College of Agricultural and Rural Skills in their own country. Again, governmental support was critical. Ultimately, after lengthy negotiations, it was not forthcoming, and the project was very quietly, almost surreptitiously shelved. Yet the Venezuelan College has achieved World Bank recognition for its programs, which may be widely adopted in Venezuela and elsewhere in the Caribbean region. Its rural aid programs have helped scores of families to set up small businesses and have taught hundreds of women skills which are helping them to achieve education and independence.

Another College financial crisis in 2000 persuaded the International Board to institute both a short-term and a long-term study for financial viability. Will this gesture simply be a loyal helping hand to a member of the organisation in trouble, or will it signify a deeper acceptance of the role of vocational education in the developing world within the UWC mission? It is too early to tell.

Controversy over Scholarships and Fees

Debate has continued to flourish over UWC scholarship policies. Is a private, fee-paying entry permissible? Clearly, it has to be in the all-age Colleges in Singapore and Swaziland, although both are seeking vigorously to increase the annual number of students on scholarship from National Committees. The debate concerns the two-year Colleges. With their entries in 2000, the Pearson and Adriatic Colleges insisted that their full scholarship policies meant exactly that—not only must all students have a scholarship, but also their scholarship must cover all the costs without recourse to family contributions. Their reasoning? First, this is what their sponsors, whether governmental or private, had understood when they pledged their support; second, awareness before applying that family contributions will be required deters many from applying in the first place, especially where the public system of education is free and/or there are several children in the family to be provided for.

As a general principle, these two Colleges wish to distance themselves clearly from private schooling. Alec Peterson is ambivalent, empirically noting that when the Pearson College policy was announced back in 1974 by the Founder Chairman John Nichol, it immediately added to the financial problems and prospects of the entire organisation. It is quite clear that, for the foreseeable future, a full scholarship policy in this extreme sense is beyond the means of most Colleges. But the concept is also not acceptable as a matter of principle to a number of the longer established National Committees, all of them in Western Europe. They believe that, as long as the integrity of the selection is assured and is explicitly not influenced by the families' economic and social circumstances, the available monies should be shared as widely as possible. Alec, perhaps inadvertently, hands a card to the Pearson and Adriatic Colleges when he comments: "Yet if the movement is to expand, . . . the role of the UWC 'scholar', the boy or girl seeking this kind of education because that is what they want, not because parental circumstances force it upon them, must expand with it." Fifteen years on, one might feel inclined to add 'and not because parental circumstances make it possible', the more so if one sees a moral duty for international education to penetrate increasingly those countries, communities, and parts of the world which are in such desperate need of its message but simply do not have the means to afford it. It has been interesting to note the change of emphasis at the US College with the arrival of the Shelby Davis endowment which, against traditional national thinking, has placed all American UWC students on complete scholarship support. Can it be long, one is tempted to ask, before students from all parts of the world at this College are funded with similar generosity?

Equally interesting, albeit looking a long way into the future, was the declaration of the Chairman of the Mahindra College in India to the International Board that his ultimate aim was scholarship support without parental involvement. The Indian National Committee is expecting within the near future to be receiving up to 20,000 applications a year for a total of some sixty places. They will be grading their criteria in a deliberate awareness of the degree of sophistication of background of their applicants. Thousands will be from small rural schools. Financial considerations must, in their most carefully considered view, be excluded totally, explicitly and beyond any attempt at manipulation or further debate. The scholarship debate will without doubt continue to exercise many committed minds within the UWC, but there is absolute consensus on the importance of the maximum scholarship support possible in every College, and the distribution of the funds, whether of Colleges or National Committees, on the basis of merit as best it can be perceived. In the mean time, many of the Colleges, in agreement with their host National Committees, are exchanging scholars without exchanging money.

More Recognition, Less Risk

In one important respect, the Colleges have been the direct victims of their own success. In selecting students, committees have always been concerned to seek a sense of adventure, of the readiness to take risks in pursuit of a 'higher' goal. Nothing easier if the reputation of the Colleges is insecure! Italian students entering the Duino College in 1982 had no guarantee that their final examinations (the IB) would be recognised for their university entry. In fact, this was not achieved until the November after they had left. Under such circumstances, the weak-hearted do not come to the starting line. But now the Colleges, all of them, represent a proven route to impressive examination grades and ready access to the enthusiastic university admissions officers who now commute around the Colleges in the early part of the academic year, scholarship funds in their hip pockets. This trend has been further reinforced by the quite remarkable new generosity of Shelby Davis and his family in providing sponsorship at several American university campuses for UWC graduates, irrespective of which College they come from.

The more the Colleges seek to enter the poorer parts of the world—Eastern Europe, developing countries, refugee and immigrant communities, the stateless—the more the Colleges may be valued for their material benefits and their avenues into yet further scholarship support. At a one-week 'retreat' in June 2001, the College Heads spent much time wondering how to secure the right kind of personal commitment 'up front' to the ideals of the movement. It was a measure of the seriousness with which they were looking at the issue that many left, excited by the potential of initiating a three-year program, the second year of which would be given over to community service in a new cultural setting. No IB Diploma without a year of completed community service! One College has already decided to offer four three-year scholarships for 2001 to students from countries currently in conflict with one another in the Balkans to test the concept. Not far away from all these considerations is of course the classical problem of the brain drain. Although the 1960s policy of insisting that students return home for their university education has substantially gone by the board, the return rate on completion of higher education has been encouraging and has hovered around the seventy-percent mark. This is however another area in which a more detailed follow-up of graduates' lives is becoming increasingly critical to a serious evaluation of the movement's accomplishments.

Opportunities and Resources

Can the funds be found to strengthen the international organisation, and if so, what form should the organisation take for the longer term? One Head recently expressed the strong personal conviction that it should be moved to a third-world country for economic reasons and to make an appropriate statement about future priorities. Will concerns for the developing world lead to a consolidation and development of vocational training and rural skills? Can Short Courses grow into a secure and soundly administered feature of the movement, switching flexibly between regions and countries but maintaining reliability of performance and quality of leadership?

For a few years now, following a regional conference in Petra in 1996, it has been hoped to found a United World College of the Middle East in Jordan. The aim is noble, the difficulties immense, and it remains a commitment. France and the francophone culture continue to be untouched and uninvolved to any serious degree. Is it not time for a College in the Hispanic world—in Spain or Latin America, or in both as a twin undertaking? Massive investment in residential schools in China, especially in and around Shanghai, tempts one to think of a second College in that country. Japan has been strongly resistant, citing linguistic, economic, academic, and administrative problems, but the longer-term view suggests that the UWC will not wish to remain permanently absent from that important nation (and very able Japanese students have been attending the UWC since 1971).

Does the movement tend to overlook grave problems which exist within national borders and which merit a response from international education—European cities with large immigrant populations and racial tensions, for example? Another College Head recently commented that one needed to find out where today's most idealistic young teachers were seeking to work—if not in international education (and in the United World Colleges), then we are not doing our jobs properly. And what about the Internet? One National Committee Chairman sees the future of the UWC above all in that medium, although some discussions held within Colleges have so far judged the absence of personal contact, thought to be key to the UWC experience, to be an important deterrent.

The debate about globalisation is vigorous and often violent. The issues are as complex for educators as they are for the politicians, the businessmen and the international civil servants. In the final chapter of his *The Far East: A Social Geography*, published in 1949, Alec Peterson wrote: "What the people of the Far East require are food, order, justice, and peace." Not the Far East alone! Can international education make a difference? Are these four requirements not, in the last resort, the thoughts that must motivate international schools above all others?

The present Director General of the International Baccalaureate has used the words "The schools that need not have been" when talking about the United World Colleges, an eloquent tribute to the idealism of their founders and sponsors, with whom, despite the scorners, the prophecy lay. Within the Colleges, there is the conviction that, yes, 'they need not have been', but in truth they are needed more than ever.

One of the reviewers of *Schools across Frontiers* when it first appeared, commenting on Alec Peterson's inspiring leadership, could not escape "the nagging doubt" as to whether the International Baccalaureate and the United World Colleges had "enough energy to sustain themselves without equally charismatic successors."

On that score, all is well.

Note to Chapter Nine

[1] A remark about Mazzini, from George Eliot's *Daniel Deronda*.

10
PHENOMENAL
GROWTH OF THE IB
Ian Hill

The IBO has expanded rapidly in size, diversity, quality, and credibility. It has more schools authorised to offer its programs (including many more state schools), more office space, more staff, and a greater number of programs, and it commands increasing recognition and respect. Educators and parents see that the IB diploma prepares students for a future in a global society— it provides an international, intercultural perspective in an academically rigorous framework with an emphasis on critical thinking skills, whilst promoting personal development.

The IB diploma is not about other parts of the world; it *is* other parts of the world. This is an international organisation whose programs belong to no particular country. The phenomenal growth of the IB has led to more extensive consultation with teachers, with ministries of education, with intergovernmental organisations such as UNESCO, OECD, and the Council of Europe, as well as universities and independent experts.

The IBO continually questions the profile, the content, and the approach of its programs, and the appropriateness of its student evaluation procedures. It also questions growth itself: should it be contained to a certain level to preserve quality? Is the organisation growing in ways other than a rise in the number of schools teaching its programs? In which other ways should it grow? One of the major challenges to growth is how to balance increased efficiency and automation with the need to retain a personal and caring service to schools.

The IBO in 1986 and Today

The first generation of IB diploma graduates has given rise to families where one or both of the parents and one or two children have all 'done the IB'. At the end of 1986 there were 313 authorized IB diploma schools in fifty-one countries; by the end of June 2002 there were 1,043 of them in 110 countries. There were 8,600 students who presented themselves for IB diploma examinations in 1986 compared with 51,986 students in November 2001 and May 2002 combined.

The percentage and number of students being examined for the full diploma has steadily increased and continues to do so as the IBO implements its policy of not authorising schools that intend to offer only certificate subjects—that is, not offering the six subjects, the extended essay, the Theory of Knowledge, and CAS (creativity, action, service; a change from the original CASS terminology)—to any student. In 1986 there were 2,852 students (or 32 percent of all those doing examinations in May and November) who attempted the full diploma. In May and November 2002 the corresponding figures were 22,616 (19,677 and 2,939 students respectively) or 43 percent being examined for the full diploma.

The total full-time staff of the IBO was 45 in 1986; in 2002 it had risen to 262 around the world. The examinations office from 1984 occupied a top floor corridor in the northwest building of Bath University, England. In 1986 there were 21 people in that corridor (three of whom had computers) and two more in the computer department which was housed in the basement of a separate building. The five computers were linked to the mainframe computer of Bath University. In 1988 the IBO bought its first mainframe computer while still in Bath; it was huge and underpowered by today's standards. The data preparation of examination entries (received on paper from schools) was done off site in the south of England and the computer tape was sent by courier to Bath.

Today the examinations office and the computer department are part of IBO's new three-storey building of 5,000 square meters in the Cardiff Gate Business Park situated in a suburb of Cardiff, Wales, occupied by 167 staff. It also houses academic affairs (curriculum development and student assessment for all three programs), business and finance, human resources, and publications. IB diploma schools now, of course, register examination candidates electronically.

During its time at Bath, the IB Examinations Office made a number of important innovations, capitalizing on its location within a university environment. These included the creation of the Assessment Research and Development Advisory Committee (ARDAC) consisting of the Director of Examinations, the chair of the Examining Board and a research officer. This committee oversaw assessment research, later broadened to include a wider curriculum dimension. The committee ceased to exist in 1990.

Readers will have noticed a change in terminology. Prior to 1994 'the IB' meant the two-year program at the end of secondary education which leads to higher education studies. When the IBO was invited to take on the Middle Years Program (MYP) in 1994 and the Primary Years Program (PYP) in 1997, the terminology had to differentiate between three IBO programs. So from 1994 the long-standing IB program covering the last two years of secondary education came to be officially called the IB Diploma Program. Many people still refer to 'the IB', which usually means the Diploma Program.

How did this diversification of programs come about and how has the IBO expanded from where it was in 1986 to where it is today?

The Middle Years Program (MYP)

As recounted by Alec Peterson in Chapters 2 and 3 above, the International Schools Association (ISA) had given birth to the IBO and the diploma program. In 1980 at a meeting of ISA at the International School Moshi, Tanzania (the first IB school in Africa in 1971), a decision was made to develop an international program for children from 11 to 16 years which would cover the five years of secondary education prior to the last two years of the IB Diploma Program. The relevant section of the report of the 1980 meeting reads:

> It was agreed that there was a great need for a curriculum in the junior secondary group that would lead to an International Certificate of General Education to be taken at about 16 or 16+. . . . The ISA Governing Board agreed to make this whole subject a substantial focus of interest in the coming year; co-ordination and impetus would be provided by the ISA Curriculum Committee. *(ISA Bulletin 93,* April 1981)

The same meeting discussed the importance of environmental education and community service, which were both later included in the 'areas of interaction' of which 'approaches to learning' was to become a core element (see the IBO website for a description of the program).

Proponents of this new secondary education program who were present at the meeting included Nansi Poirel (former teacher of English at Ecolint who had worked on the first IB diploma English syllabus and was secretary of ISA at the time of the Moshi meeting); Ruth Bonner (who later concentrated on the 'health and social education' component); Lister Hannah (director of Moshi International School at the time and now headmaster of a school in Thailand); and Elizabeth Fox (then at UNIS—she retired in 1999 as director of Santiago College, Chile, and sadly died in 2001 after a struggle with cancer); these were all fervent supporters of the Diploma Program. This project became the ISA Curriculum (ISAC). From the start it sought to incorporate key elements of the IB diploma philosophy and was conceived as a 'pre-IB' course although it was not a prerequisite for doing the diploma.

Development of the ISAC was slow until Robert Belle-Isle, director of UNIS in New York and later president of ISA, organised a series of workshops in conjunction with the annual July ISA conferences in Eerde 1984, Wellesley 1985, Cévénol 1986, Svendborg 1987, and Singapore 1988. Other workshops took place throughout this period to advance the ISAC and these were attended by a large number of teachers including Fred de Haas of the International School the Rijnlands Lyceum Oegstgeest, Netherlands; he later worked for the IBO as an MYP curriculum officer and consultant. Gérard Renaud, who had retired as Director General of the IBO in 1983, was involved in the organisation of these meetings and was a major contributor to the educational concept. Malcolm Davis (secondary school principal at

Vienna Inter-national School) was also a firm believer who made an important impact. The discussions led to the idea of an octagon with the intellectual and personal development of the child at the centre. Next came the transdisciplinary components—the areas of interaction—which were to be addressed through the subject areas.

Thanks to Robert Belle-Isle's links with Quebec, the education ministry there showed great interest in the pedagogical ideas of the program and implemented it in some 27 state secondary schools in French by the beginning of the 1990s. When Robert died in November 1988, three major pilot schools had been operating: l'Ecole d'Education Internationale de Chambly (Quebec); the International School the Rijnlands Lyceum Oegstgeest (Netherlands); and St. Catherine's–Moorlands School (Buenos Aires). The first two are state schools and the other a private school and they represented the three languages of the IBO: French, English, and Spanish. Other pilot schools emerged through the enthusiasm of heads who were ISA members. Robert Belle-Isle is generally recognised as the driving force who enabled the ideas of the 1980 Moshi conference to be translated into action.

History was to repeat itself. ISA depended on the goodwill of its voluntary members and its elected board; there was no permanent infrastructure—in short, plenty of idealism but no machinery. As with the Diploma Program some 20 years before, the development of ISAC became too demanding for ISA which turned towards the IBO (its own creation) in 1992 to take over the program and its future development. It was thus that the ISA Curriculum was officially adopted by the IBO in 1994 and became the Middle Years Program (MYP). In 1994 the IBO authorized the first fifteen MYP pilot schools in Argentina, Austria, Canada (Quebec), Chile, Netherlands, Slovenia, Sweden, and the United States. There was, however, in spite of efforts to recruit suitable people, insufficient staff support for the program at the IB Curriculum and Assessment (IBCA) office until the first MYP manager was appointed in January 1997. By June 2002 there were 221 authorized MYP schools in 51 countries.

Until 1997, the MYP developments were slow and not well co-ordinated in the absence of sufficient staff and an MYP committee to recommend policies about authorisation criteria, publications, workshops, and so on. The moderation of student results and the establishment of assessment criteria for all subjects and the personal project hardly progressed at all. The result was that schools became skeptical of the program, particularly when they heard inconsistent policy statements made at workshops, and some developed their own assessment criteria in the absence of direction from the IBO. The IB North American office placed a moratorium on authorizing MYP schools in that region until policies, publications, and criteria for authorisation and student assessment were more firmly established. Impressive developments have taken place since 1997; the criteria for student assessment, program evaluation and authorization would now stand up to rigorous scrutiny from anyone genuinely interested in an international educational program of quality.

A description of the program can be viewed on the IBO's website. An octagon represents eight major disciplines or groups of subjects which must be studied during the five years: a first language, a second language, social sciences, experimental sciences, mathematics, the arts, technology, and physical education. Traversing these subjects are five areas of interaction: approaches to learning, community service, health and social education, *Homo faber*, and environment. These areas of interaction should be woven into the content and skills of the subjects, thus giving rise to an interdisciplinary approach. In essence, the IBO prescribes the skills to be learned, the open-minded approach, and the assessment criteria. The content of each subject area is left up to the schools, but sample curricula and sample lesson plans incorporating the areas of interaction into subjects are provided. An important distinction with the Diploma Program is that the MYP is for students of all abilities and does not have an external examination at the end although students can obtain an MYP Certificate of Results based on an international, external moderation process.

The Primary Years Program (PYP)

The impetus for an international program for pre-secondary school children (from three to twelve years) came from a discussion in Rome in 1990 during a European Council of International Schools (ECIS) conference for administrators. Kevin Bartlett, then primary principal at the Vienna International School, raised the issue of a lack of coherence and inconsistency in the educational programs of international schools and urged the meeting to work towards the identification of common elements of an international education. There followed a somewhat heated discussion, where some participants spoke of the threat to their schools' national identities and autonomy while others were supportive. As a result of his intervention, Kevin was approached informally by a group of fellow primary/elementary administrators mainly from Europe who were interested in meeting to discuss the possibility of schools collaborating on curriculum development.

The November 1990 ECIS conference was held in Vienna, where a meeting of those interested in the primary program was convened. It was decided to start with the social studies curriculum which was considered to be dependent on national textbooks with little, if any, international perspective or openness to other interpretations. If it fell into place the rest would follow. This is reminiscent of Bob Leach starting with history in 1963 at the International School of Geneva for the Diploma Program; it was thought that developing an international history program that could suit all cultural perceptions would be difficult to achieve. Once established, the IB diploma history course emphasised the sources of history and the legitimacy of various cultural perceptions. The ISCP placed a similar emphasis on process: it prescribed a pedagogical approach without imposing subject content. It was agreed to hold meetings in schools to which other schools would be invited to send representatives. At these meetings the curriculum would be written. This proved not to be as simple as it sounded.

The first meeting was hosted by the International School of Amsterdam in March 1991. Some twenty-five schools were represented. This was followed by a meeting at the Vienna International School in October 1991. At the following meeting in 1992 at Frankfurt International School a structure with a steering committee led by Kevin Bartlett was established. It produced a mission statement for the idea which was named the International Schools' Curriculum Project 3–12, or ISCP.

The need for external support was clear from the start. This came initially from the European Council of International Schools

(ECIS) which recognised the significance of the project and provided both moral and practical support. This was replicated by the IBO's Director General at the time, Roger Peel. Kevin Bartlett was seconded for the school year 1993–94 to work on this project and ECIS accreditation; the IBO and ECIS each paid 50 percent of his salary. Kevin Bartlett was invited to address the 25th IBO Council of Foundation meeting in Geneva in 1992 where he explained the project and said: "I look forward to the day when the IB begins at three." The IBO continued to contribute to meeting the costs of the ISCP curriculum development teams until 1997.

As with the Diploma Program and ISA Curriculum in their first stages, much was achieved by many willing, enthusiastic, unpaid teachers and administrators in committed schools around the world, meeting in various locations as and when they could. Unlike the MYP, the ISCP developed in English-speaking schools only. By 1995 the Social Studies Curriculum document was already in its second pilot year, science in its first pilot year. Mathematics and language pilots were being finalised and the area of personal social and physical education was in the first year of its development with plans to begin working on the arts. Some one hundred schools actually became ISCP members. They contributed to the content of two volumes which appeared in 1996 and which described the program and how to implement it. ECIS shepherded the process, and some thirty primary schools in different continents tried out the ISCP across all, or almost all, of their classes. The task then started to become too large for the ISCP group, a loose structure without any permanent office or staff, and the ISCP committee began discussions with the IBO in 1996 with a view to the IBO taking over the program and its development. So in 1997 the IBO inherited the incomplete ISCP which was renamed the Primary Years Program (PYP), and the first PYP manager was appointed in the Cardiff office in August of the same year.

The International School of Amsterdam became the first authorised PYP school in July 1997 and, at the same time, the first authorised school to offer all three IBO programs. By June 2002 there were eighty-seven authorised PYP schools in forty-three countries. With the inclusion of the PYP the IBO became the only education system in the world to offer a comprehensive, international program covering kindergarten to pre-university level.

A description of the PYP and its emphasis on learning through enquiry can be viewed on the IBO's public website. It builds on the natural curiosity of young children and provides simple, fundamental questions to guide the pedagogical and curriculum process in which teachers' unit planners play an important role. Unlike the Diploma Program the PYP is for all abilities and has no external examination at the end.

The Geneva Headquarters

The gracious Palais Wilson housed the League of Nations from 1920 and was named after its initiator, Woodrow Wilson. The IB Office (as it was then called) occupied space in this prestigious building until it moved in December 1983 to 15 Route des Morillons, Grand-Saconnex, in close proximity to the World Health Organisation and the International Labour Office. The Director General, Deputy Director General, Corporate Relations, and the Geneva departments of Finance and Personnel and Administration work from this site, which also provides accommodation for the Africa/Europe/Middle East regional office.

In 1993 when I began work in the regional office there was a total of 10.5 staff in Geneva: 7 in headquarters and 3.5 in the regional office. By June 2002 the total was 35. Since 1998 there had been a need for larger facilities but extra office space in the same or neighbouring buildings was impossible to find. All organisations in Geneva seemed to be looking to expand and the waiting lists for accommodation became longer. Gradually we relinquished our meeting room, reduced the corridor space (to fill it with filing cabinets and cupboards) and shared more offices as we searched for alternatives.

Just as we were despairing of ever finding appropriate additional accommodation an organisation on the same floor as IB headquarters approached us to exchange their large space for a small part of ours, thus providing an extra 125 square metres. We took up that option in early 2001.

Academic Affairs in Cardiff, Wales

The IBO Examinations Office in Bath moved to St Mellons Technology Park near Cardiff in 1989. "We took over a cavernous warehouse and in the space of 10 weeks converted it into an elegant office" *(IB Bulletin 1989,* p. 5) said Colin Jenkins, the director of examinations at the time.

A new Director of Examinations was appointed beginning in 1990 at the new rented premises in St Mellons, called IBEX (IB Examinations). IBEX was in fact a misnomer as the Cardiff office was vitally involved in curriculum development for the Diploma Program and then for the MYP and PYP, and not just examinations for the diploma. In 1991 the annual report mentioned that more emphasis was to be given to systematic curriculum development (for the diploma) and a curriculum support team was established, starting in January 1992.

The "cavernous warehouse" soon became too small and in 1993 the IBO rented a sister building across the street in St Mellons. At that point the two companion spaces became known as the Green Building and the Red Building.

By 1994 there were 545 diploma schools (up from 313 in 1986) and the rented premises at St Mellons were no longer adequate to house the increasing staff and the examination scripts, so a search for new premises was under way. In January 1996 a new, much larger building, still in St Mellons and just a short distance from the rented premises, was purchased and occupied in April. This was the first piece of real estate to be owned by the IBO. It was a two-storey building of 2,232 square meters in a technology park at St Mellons, Cardiff, and 124 staff occupied it when the IBO moved in. HRH Princess Sarvath El Hassan of Jordan officially opened the building in October 1996 and named it 'Peterson House' after Alec Peterson.

During 1994 the Cardiff office ceased to be called the Examinations Office and adopted a title much more in keeping with the work it had been doing for many years and which was soon to be enhanced by the MYP and PYP, where no external examinations apply. It became the IB Curriculum and Assessment office or IBCA for short. The Cardiff operation had always been the base for curriculum development, student assessment techniques, examinations, financial management, computing, information technology, and publications, just like its predecessor in Bath. Two major divisions—Academic Affairs, and Business and Finance—were established in the Cardiff office in 1997. A new Director of Academic Affairs was appointed in the same year and a new title of Director of Business and Finance with increased responsibilities was given to an existing senior staff member. In 1999, when Peterson House was no longer adequate, further space was rented in an adjacent building, and acquiring more space became a priority in early 2000. By the end of that year, the IBO had arranged to rent new premises under construction in Cardiff Bay. So the Cardiff office moved again in April 2001. The new building was also named Peterson House, and was opened in November 2001 by the Assistant Director General of Education for UNESCO, Sir John Daniel (formerly Vice Chancellor of the Open University in the UK and vice-president of the IBO Council of Foundation 1996–99).

A Translation Unit was created in 1997 to oversee all translation work. Six people who are native speakers of either French or Spanish were employed full time starting in 2001. They oversee the translation of subject guides in all programs, of examination papers, promotional literature, other IBO publications, and some of the IBO website material; they check for consistency in the use of IBO terminology. This unit has added a considerable degree of professionalism to the translation work of the IBO. By October 2002 it comprised eleven people, including one Chinese translator.

New Initiatives

During 1992–93 the office in Cardiff had a variety of educational exchanges and visits with the University of Cambridge Local Examinations Syndicate (UCLES) in the UK and with ministries of education in Chile, Germany, New Zealand, Finland, Canada (Quebec), and Slovenia; this signalled a growing awareness that the IBO had curricular and assessment procedures of interest to governments.

An innovation, in the interests of increased transparency, was made in June 1993: twelve teacher observers were invited at IBO expense to attend grade-award meetings in particular subject areas in Cardiff. This proved extremely successful and the practice continues each year. It showed the care with which the IBO assesses student performance and the humane handling of borderline results and cases of hardship such as bereavement in the immediate family, war breaking out during the examination period, and so on. For example, the May 1998 examinations were seriously disrupted in Jakarta due to civil unrest; the IBO was able to award grades and therefore give personal attention to students in adverse circumstances.

Another initiative which was very well received by the schools was the establishment of a help desk at IBCA in 1995, allowing schools to phone or email their questions for a quick response. In May and November of the same year the number of full diploma candidates (9,515) rose to 39 percent of the total number of examination candidates, in line with a trend which has continued. This is a response to a deliberate policy of not accepting any schools wishing to do only certificates (that is, one or more single subjects) and to emphasize the importance of the full diploma and its educational philosophy.

The following new diploma subjects were in place between 1994 and 1997: Design Technology, Theatre Arts, History of the Islamic World (HIW), and Information Technology in a Global Society (ITGS). Design Technology responded to the need for innovative ideas to assist everyday living. The IB Theatre Arts curriculum requires students to research theatre from multicultural perspectives. HIW was created particularly for schools in non-muslim countries so that students would appreciate the importance and origins of Islam, in the hope of redressing the sometimes inaccurate view that Western people have of muslim culture. ITGS emphasises the ethical dimension associated with advances in computer technology and its uses in society.

A number of schools have developed interesting school-based courses approved by IBO, examined at Standard Level only, and replacing other subjects of the Diploma Program. This allows schools to propose subjects which might have a particular attraction to their students. A rigorous approval procedure is followed before a course can be accepted; the subject and content must be intellectually challenging and able to be assessed in the same way as regular diploma subjects. Some school-based courses became mainstream subjects—Environmental Systems and Dance are examples. Amongst some twenty school-based courses being offered in 2002 are: European Studies, Peace and Conflict Studies, World Cultures, Political Thought, World Religions, Agricultural Science. Any school may offer a school-based syllabus which has been approved by IBO.

Eleven languages A2 and ten languages *ab initio* were first examined in 1995 for very advanced or bilingual students and for beginners respectively. This created a very wide offering of language levels for IB diploma candidates.

Markschemes (grading schemes) were published as a source of information and guidance to schools. Internal assessment is not done through markschemes as such, but through assessment criteria which are much more generic. Assessment criteria were published to enable teachers to apply a common standard within each subject.

An attempt to introduce some cross-curriculum work among the sciences and further afield appeared in 1997 with the 'Group 4 Project' of ten hours of practical work spanning two subjects (one or both of them an experimental science) and done collaboratively by students.

The MYP and PYP sections of IBCA have gradually increased their staffing quotas to handle curriculum development, student evaluation techniques (in the MYP), and the production of publications to support these activities. As with the diploma, practising teachers are in the majority on committees which are convened to undertake these tasks. While there is no external examination for the MYP, there is moderation of students' results in accordance with established IBO assessment criteria at the end of the fifth year. The IBO then issues records of achievement and certificates to students whose schools have registered them for the moderation process by the IBO examiners. Details of certification procedures are to be found in the *MYP Co-ordinator's Handbook* and in the subject guides. IBO student evaluation procedures are criterion based. In the PYP no moderation of student results exists. There is, however, discussion about eventually providing guidelines of expected achievement at each grade level in terms of the student skills which are being developed. The emphasis in the MYP and PYP is on process: the promotion of attitudes and skills associated with education for life.

In 1993 the idea of providing innovative, interdisciplinary courses at SL alongside the more traditional subjects of the Diploma Program was raised. This was the same year as Georges Laforest's Peterson Lecture entitled 'Transdisciplinarity'.[1] In 2000 the development of three such courses began for the first time: Text and Performance SL (Groups 1 and 6), Ecosystems and Societies SL (Groups 3 and 4) and World Cultures (Groups 3 and 6). These transdisciplinary subjects provide new ways of exploring internationalism, and give students access to the six groups in alternative ways, which allows, for instance, more access to the arts subjects in Group 6. Pilots of these subjects began in a small number of schools in 2002.

The Curriculum Review Process

In 1993 a new model of diploma curriculum review emerged with the following five tenets: it should be "consultative, participative, internationally informed, fully resourced, and managed" *(Report of the Director of Examinations, 1993)*. The regular five-year curriculum review cycle, whereby each syllabus would have a shelf life of five years before changes would be made, was established. This meant that a five-year cycle was adopted for each subject group on a rotating basis. During the last three years of that five-year cycle, a committee would be formed to *review* (not necessarily change) the syllabus and assessment procedures; this is known as the '3 + 5 Curriculum Review'.

The subject committees comprise a majority of practising teachers from different continents together with the appropriate subject-area manager and the chief examiner or an outside expert. New draft syllabus documents are circulated to all IBO member schools seeking comments as the revised syllabus takes shape. Some subjects might change noticeably and others hardly at all, depending on educational and curriculum trends, and on advances in technology. The impact of the curriculum review and development model for all diploma subjects has been very significant since the last half of the 1990s.

Committee Structures

With the 'new look' Cardiff office came a new committee structure to cater for the diversification of programs and to bolster the much expanded work of the IBO. The expansion was twofold: there were an increasing number of schools seeking authorisation for the Diploma Program and there were now two new programs to manage. The inaugural meeting of an academic affairs board took place in November 1997 and this became the Academic Advisory Committee in 2000. This is a body which makes recommendations about future academic developments for all programs. It comprises the Director General, the Director of Academic Affairs, the Chair of the Examining Board of the IBO, and an IBO Council of Foundation representative together with two heads of schools and four external consultants.

Curriculum and assessment committees to oversee the development of each of the three programs were established at the same time. Each program committee also has at least one representative from the other committees to ensure that articulation between the programs is not ignored. Membership of the PYP and MYP committees (which were launched in September 1997) comprises teachers or school administrators, regional office representatives, and other IBO personnel as appropriate. The Diploma Program Committee has in addition chief examiners, subject area managers, and the Assessment Director; it oversees the quality, consistency, structure, and financial impact of changes in relation to the Diploma Program. A Diploma Review Committee was also established which concentrates on curriculum review, assessment, and recommendations concerning the appointment of senior examiners.

A research committee was established in November 1998. In addition to a number of IBO personnel, there were six external consultants on this committee which included, at the time of writing, educational researchers from China, the United States, and Australia. It is worth noting that the research unit established through Bill Halls of Oxford University's department of education lasted from 1968 to 1974 and the Assessment Research and Development Advisory Committee (ARDAC) started at Bath University in about 1985 and finished in 1990 at St Mellons,

Cardiff. The establishment of this latest committee, the appointment of a Director for International Education and the simultaneous appointment of a research officer marks a return to the importance of research. The IBO research committee initiates educational research concerning all three IBO programs and establishes explicit links with leading research bodies which may propose, sponsor, supervise or evaluate such research. A resource facility at the Cardiff office houses research concerning IBO programs, particularly masters and doctoral theses. In 2000 an IBO research unit was established at the University of Bath under the direction of Professor Jeff Thompson, IBO Director for International Education, thus re-establishing a link which was discontinued in 1989.

A Special Educational Needs Sub-committee reports to the Final Award Committee on matters that affect students sitting the diploma examinations. Through this committee the IBO wishes to include students who may have physical or other disabilities and facilitate their access to its programs and examinations. Each year a variety of arrangements take place such as examinations in braille, enlarged examination papers, an amanuensis, a person to read, rest periods during examinations, and additional time. The IBO continues to address, quickly and humanely, difficult adverse circumstances with which candidates and schools may be confronted.

New Technology

Information communication technology (ITC) has taken great strides in the IBO since the days of the examinations office in Bath. There are three major needs: data processing for examination administration, internal communication, and external links to member schools.

It is a measure of the advance of technology in the IBO that in 1986 there were five personal computers and no messages by email. In 1991 a Local Area Network (LAN) was installed in Cardiff where networked computers were provided for almost every member of staff and applications such as email were regularly used internally. During the next few years electronic mail links were extended to Geneva and New York. Today there are more than 200 personal computers and one email every eight seconds throughout the organisation. When the IBO bought its first mainframe computer in Bath in 1988 the backing up of data was done to single megabyte disks about the size of a large frying pan. Today eight thousand times as much data is backed onto a device slightly bigger than a matchbox.

From 1989 the main data-processing system for examinations was done by the Data Processing Unit (DPU) in Cardiff using an in-house IBM minicomputer. Many improvements to the system have been made. November 1993 saw the first electronic transfer of diploma results to the Victoria Tertiary Admissions Centre in Australia for distribution to universities. The DPU expanded into the Computing and Business Services (CBS) department which handled all the data related to the administration of examinations. From January 2002 the functions of CBS were redistributed and this entity no longer exists. A Head of Management Information was appointed to oversee the migration of data to a new database system, the production of official IBO statistics and implementation of a worldwide protection strategy for the IBO.

Having improved the internal ICT system, the next step was to improve communication with schools. With hindsight, the IBO was ahead of its time and certainly two or three years ahead of reliable technology. Nevertheless work began on the development of a PC-based global network called IBNET. Co-ordinators were able to register diploma examination candidates, receive results and send simple email messages. In the early days it just about worked! There were times when the team almost abandoned the project, then something would happen which persuaded them to carry on. One morning in 1994, staff arrived in the office to find 250 candidate registrations which had appeared overnight from Jakarta International School and had been automatically processed without error—this probably saved the project.

An ICT department started operating as a separate unit in 1996 with two main functions. The first was to support the needs of the IBO offices (PCs, application software, data networks, and so on). The second was to develop applications such as IBNET and the Online Curriculum Centre, discussed below.

In 1997 the ICT unit developed a Windows version of IBNET. People were only just beginning to talk about the Internet. The

ICT team then took a big chance: they dropped the Windows version and put all their efforts into developing a web-based version of IBNET. It was launched in January 1998; more than 80 percent of schools were using it by 1999. IBNET was, and remains, ahead of just about any other examination administration system.

In 1998 examination results were made available to students for the first time via the web using a confidential personal identification number (PIN). To the best of our knowledge, the IBO is the first organisation to have done this for examination results.

The interactive Online Curriculum Centre (OCC) was launched in September 1999 giving direct support through the web to IB teachers in the form of curriculum resources, discussion forums, curriculum developments, news and information, and online training for users of the OCC through a user name and password. A team of sixty-one faculty members consisting of specialist IB teachers and consultants monitor and contribute to the site. The development of the OCC was a collaborative project between staff in the curriculum support unit (the academic input), publications (the content) and ICT (the programming). Towards the end of 2001 the IBO secured a one-million-dollar grant from Goldman Sachs to further develop the OCC.

Other ICT improvements have put IB diploma recognition information on the public website for all regions and provided subject guides in all three programs and other publications on the OCC. By the end of 2003 schools will be able to register teachers for workshops via an online system which will then automatically generate billing, hotel reservations, lists of participants by various categories, and so on. Since 2001 the organisation has been operating five websites under the responsibility of a Websites Management Committee with support from the ICT and corporate relations departments: the public site (with special sections for higher education institutions and governments, prospective schools, publications, research, document library, regional office pages), IBNET for IB co-ordinators, the OCC for teachers in IB schools, INTRANET for IBO staff, and EXAMNET for facilitating the work of diploma examiners whereby some script marking can be done electronically and sent through the system to the examinations section.

In early 2000 video conferencing equipment was installed in the headquarters in Geneva, in Cardiff and in New York as one of the measures to reduce travel costs and time for IBO staff. This has proved very effective.

Human Resources Management

Prior to the appointment in Cardiff of a Personnel and Administration Manager in October 1996, the main personnel activity had been recruitment. Since the establishment of a Joint Consultative Committee (JCC) of Cardiff staff in 1997 a number of matters received attention: health and safety, induction and assessment of staff, best practices in managing staff, reviews of personnel policies and procedures, recommendations on space utilisation, and the introduction of a staff appraisal system.

The Human Resources Department finalised a computerised flexitime system for all Cardiff staff. A small number of people in the Cardiff and Geneva offices have availed themselves of working at home on occasions via computer equipment linked to the IBO email and telephone systems.

The main task of the Human Resources Department is to establish and then extend corporate principles, policies, and procedures to all IBO offices, allowing for regional differences within the over-arching policies.

Printing

Prior to 1995, all examination papers and curriculum material were printed off site and this had led to various problems. On one occasion the management of the printing firm had locked out the employees due to an industrial dispute. This was at a time when examination papers were being produced and the action generated a considerable amount of concern at IBCA, or IBEX as it was then known.

The installation of a Docutech machine in 1995 meant that the IBO had complete operational control of the printing staff and machines and did not have to make large investments in equipment or recruit staff—this was done by the Xerox Corporation.

The IBO's responsibility was to pay only for copies printed. What is printed, when it is printed and in what quantities is entirely under the control of the IBO; we had to guarantee a minimum number of 550,000 copies each month which was easily met. With the introduction of new equipment this has now been increased to 800,000. The normal amount of monthly copies averaged just over one million in 2002.

In terms of operational efficiency and control, the introduction of the Docutech facility has probably had the most significant impact on printing within IBCA. About 55 percent of exam papers are produced in house with areas such as geography and chemistry still going outside. The vast majority of curriculum and other material is produced by Docutech under the control of IBCA staff.

Regional Offices

In September 1991 the Regional Representatives in Buenos Aires, Geneva, New York, and Singapore were renamed Regional Directors to oversee four geographical areas. The Singapore office serves the Asia-Pacific region; the Buenos Aires office serves Latin America, and the New York office serves the US, Canada, and the Carribean. The Buenos Aires and New York offices held a joint conference in 1997 in addition to their regional conferences for North America and Latin America. Another joint conference took place in Costa Rica in 2001. The Geneva office serves the region of Europe, Africa, and the Middle East. Part-time Regional Representatives to assist the Regional Directors were established in Australasia, India, Japan, Jordan, Kenya, Mexico, Russia, and Vancouver.

The main tasks of the regional offices are:

•to disseminate information about the IBO programs to interested schools and to counsel schools;
•to conduct the authorisation process for schools wishing to offer an IBO program and sending a subsequent report to the Director General;
•to monitor the quality of the three programs after authorisation;

•to administer a comprehensive, annual teacher training program of workshops and conferences to support all three IBO programs;

•to attend to issues of recognition for the diploma and to a lesser extent the MYP *vis-à-vis* universities, ministries of education or other awarding bodies; and

•to promote the IBO programs with ministries of education, universities, private enterprise, and the general public.

The following annual quality assurance procedures for the Diploma Program had been operating for some time through the regional offices:

•unscheduled visits to schools to check on examination administration;

•random sampling of student CAS records;

•perusal of examination results and contacting schools with particularly poor results; and

•identification of schools not regularly sending teachers to IBO workshops and conferences.

An important additional measure was introduced in 1996 by the North American regional office, a questionnaire to be sent to 20 percent of diploma schools each year which had had the program for at least five years and was called 'The Five Year Program Review'. It enquired into program implementation, maintenance, and future prospects. The North American questionnaire has since been used in an adapted form in other regions; the responses are analyzed by the IBO regional offices and feedback is given to the school with commendations and recommendations. This is repeated every five years for each school.

Now the MYP and PYP have an ongoing quality assurance mechanism which is the compulsory program evaluation visit three or four years after authorization and every five years thereafter. This is the responsibility of the regional offices. Some joint program evaluation visits for the MYP and the PYP are undertaken with ECIS accreditation visits in order to avoid duplication of effort for MYP and PYP schools which are also ECIS members.

In 2002 regional offices became involved in the curriculum development of the MYP and PYP to allow for regional accommodations of the central principles of these programs. This was the first time that curriculum development, a task previously confined to IBCA, was devolved in part to the regions; the co-ordination of this work remains with the head of each program in Cardiff.

IB North America (IBNA)

A 1986 IBNA Board of Directors study revealed that a significant number of authorised schools had withdrawn from participating in the diploma program, and that the principal cause seemed to be inadequate preparation. By 1988 the New York office undertook an improved procedure for counselling and evaluating schools seeking authorisation by the IBO. Schools were now expected to undergo training, complete a comprehensive self-study, submit a formal application, and schedule a two-day visit to the school by a team of IB delegates—a total process that could take as long as two years. This intensive preparation for offering the diploma program produced dramatic long-term results. Some ten years into this new authorisation process the attrition rate had declined from forty-five percent to four percent.

In 1987, for the first time, IBNA produced a document compiling about eighty recognition policies of North American universities. This document met with such success and approval by member schools, that it became an ongoing project for the office. By the end of 1999 the number of published policy statements had grown to some 800 and it is now published exclusively on the IBO website.

During the 1990s, sub-regional associations of IB schools continued to expand as more and more schools received IB authorisation. By 2001, there were twenty-one such associations: Alabama, Alberta, Arizona, Atlantic Canada (New Brunswick, Nova Scotia, Prince Edward Island, Newfoundland) British Columbia, California, Colorado, Florida, Georgia, Great Lakes (Wisconsin, Illinois, Indiana, Ohio, Michigan, Kentucky), Manitoba, Mid-Atlantic (Maryland, Washington DC, and Virginia), Midwest (Kansas, Missouri, Oklahoma, Arkansas), Minnesota, North Carolina, Northeast (New England, New York, and New Jersey), Northwest (Oregon, Washington, Alaska), Ontario, Quebec, South Carolina, and Texas. The work of the New York office has been greatly enhanced by this active partnership with schools.

In September 1994 the first Middle Years Program (MYP) manager for a regional office was appointed, and the first MYP workshops were held in March and June of 1995 in Denver and at the United World College of the American West in Montezuma, New Mexico. When the IB Organisation accepted responsibility for developing and delivering the Middle Years Program, some twenty-seven schools in Quebec had already been offering the program, then known as the International Schools Association's Curriculum Project. Sanctioned by the provincial Ministry of Education in Quebec, the ISA's program was locally organised and supported by the Société des Ecoles d'Education Internationale. Since then, the Société has worked closely with the IBNA office to ensure a smooth authorisation of these schools by the IBO.

During the 1994–95 school year, Minnesota and Texas joined Florida in providing state money to public schools participating in IB programs. Subsidies, administered through state departments of education, for teacher training and for student examination fees have created powerful incentives for schools throughout these jurisdictions to encourage their students to participate in a rigorous international education program that prepares them for university work. By the end of 1999, legislation was in effect in several states that provided over $15 million annually to support IB programs. IBNA has played an important role in the development and ongoing support of this legislation.

By the end of 1997, the growth of authorised schools throughout North America had placed tremendous demands for support services on the strained resources of the New York office. Plans were developed to redesign the management structure of the IBNA office, to add staff, and to relocate IBNA to a larger suite of offices. Throughout 1998, the office moved from the 20th floor of 200 Madison Avenue to the 23rd floor, the staff was increased to 20 full-time employees, and the management was restructured to include associate directors who assumed daily responsibilities for school services, recognition and outreach, and finances. The office outgrew the space and another move took place in September 2000 to much larger premises across town at 475 Riverside Drive.

By June 2002 there were 464 diploma schools, 103 MYP schools, and 16 PYP schools authorised in the North American region. The regional office had an annual workshop calendar that provided training to over 6,500 teachers and administrators. In 2002 IBNA authorised sixty new IB programs; this does not mean sixty new schools since some schools offer more than one of the IB programs. Many schools in the United States are now adopting IB programs as an international benchmark to improve academic standards.

IB Latin America (IBLA)

In 1986 the Latin American regional office was located in one small room of about six square meters in the Regional Director's house at St George's College in Quilmes, Buenos Aires. There was just enough room for two desks and a couple of filing cabinets, but the photocopier had to keep company with household utilities and interviews took place in the living room. When a third filing cabinet became necessary it had to be placed in one of the bedrooms. Office facilities consisted mainly of an IBM typewriter, an old portable typewriter, and a telephone which could only dial direct within the country and to neighbouring Uruguay. International communication was mainly through telexes relayed over the telephone to an agency in the city centre.

Despite these limitations the number of schools had doubled in the four years since the office opened in 1982, and stood at 30. By June 2002 there were 147 authorised diploma schools in all major Latin American countries, plus twenty-four schools authorised to teach the Middle Years Program and nine authorized to teach the Primary Years' Program. There are international schools, state schools, and pre-university schools run by centres of higher education, as well as the more commonly found array of private and bilingual schools. In 2001 IBLA authorized thirteen new IB programs.

Growth was very diverse: explosive in Argentina, from three to forty-three diploma schools, plus nine MYP and three PYP schools, making Buenos Aires the city with more IB schools than any other in the world. The 2002 economic crisis in Argentina is a solemn reminder that IBO revenue is vulnerable to national financial problems where there is a high concentration of IB schools in any one country.

The increasing number of teacher-training workshops are organised in circuits in which the workshop leaders fly to different national venues, mainly in IB schools, so that teachers do not have to travel long distances to these events. Originally these were rather leisurely in character, as there were few participants, but between October 1998 and February 1999, for example, there were more than 1,100 teachers who attended workshops.

Latin America is not without its local colour. The workshops on the Pacific coast of Ecuador in February 1997 coincided unexpectedly with a day's national strike in protest against the government's economic policies. The workshops were due to take place in the naval base at Salinas, a secure location some ten miles away from the hotel. Early departure was essential, and two of the leaders missed the buses. They found a lift through the suburbs of Salinas where demonstrators were already burning barricades of tyres to prevent traffic moving round the town.

Diploma recognition agreements signed with universities tend to be elaborate signing ceremonies such as the one at the Universidad San Martín de Porres in Lima in June 1999. It was held in the impressive auditorium of the new medical faculty, with speeches to an audience of about 100 people comprising the faculty deans and representatives from IB schools in Lima. The ceremony included a video presentation of the university, an orchestral performance by IB students, and a Peruvian folklore show by students from the university.

It is not every day that the IBO has a head of state to open an event, but President Menem did just that in 1993 in Buenos Aires for the World Conference of Heads of IB schools.

To celebrate twenty-five years of the IB in the region, the IB conference returned to its Montevideo origins in 1996 where mature IB graduates from the early years reflected on their experiences. The first Americas Conference occurred in Puerto Rico in 1997, with an excellent attendance from the IBNA and IBLA regions.

One of the features of IB in this region is the interest it has aroused among governments seeking to modernise their education systems which have been traditionally modelled on encyclopedic patterns. The IB has served as a 'pedagogical laboratory' for the successful application of ideas. Here the small number of Latin-

American state schools using the IB have been of special importance. For example, the IBO was asked to contribute to the educational reform in Argentina, first by a global appraisal of the government's plans, and subsequently by indicating how IB thinking could specifically be incorporated. In Chile the government organised a special meeting to invite more state schools to adopt the IB. In Peru the admiralty supported the introduction of the Diploma Program in their school for the children of naval employees. This has led to the prospect of recognition in state universities and increased credibility for the IB as the country creates its own national baccalaureate system. However, despite all this interest, the fact remains that only five percent of IB schools in the region are state-run, and located only in Argentina, Chile, Mexico, and Peru. If the IBO is to reach beyond the privileged socio-economic group it currently serves in Latin America, it will need to develop new strategies for greater implementation outside the private sector.

Local associations of schools have sprung up over the last ten years or so in Colombia, Venezuela, Argentina, Chile, Ecuador, and Mexico, as they have done in the other IBO regions. In conjunction with the regional office, they organise a series of complementary activities such as teacher meetings, sub-regional conferences and inter-school student events—intensive TOK weekends, extended essay orientation, debates on international themes, and inter-CAS meetings.

Two MYP pilot schools, St Catherine's Moorlands in Buenos Aires and Santiago College in Chile, have been generous in assisting the regional office in authorisation visits and providing leaders for MYP seminars and workshops. The first MYP workshops occurred in 1995. The number of MYP schools continues to grow in the region and a committee oversees MYP workshop organisation and content.

1998 saw the establishment of a team of five PYP consultants for the region. This group has been able to respond to requests for information seminars, and on-site workshops for schools due to enter their initial trial year.

The generous suite of offices at St Andrew's Scots School in the northern suburbs of the city of Buenos Aires is a far cry from the IBLA offices of 1986; it has a computer network with state-of-the-art technology, rapid international communication through fax and email, and eight full-time staff in 2002.

IB Asia Pacific (IBAP)

During 1986 the IB diploma was increasingly discussed in Southern Asia (India, Pakistan, Sri Lanka), Australia, and New Zealand. Beyond the two schools which had been members of the IBO since 1981, interest was sparked in Australia when David Sutcliffe, head of the UWC of the Adriatic in Italy, and then Vice-President of the IB Council of Foundation, visited New South Wales, Victoria, and Tasmania in 1986 to promote the UWCs and the IB. Fortuitously he met with the Minister for Education in Tasmania, Hon. Peter Rae who took a great interest in both concepts and, as Chair of the Australian Education Council (AEC of Ministers of Education) at the time, placed them on the agenda of the next meeting. As a result, the AEC authorised me (then Senior Private Secretary to the Hon. Peter Rae) to represent the Council of Ministers at the next and subsequent IBO Standing Conference of Government Meetings held in Geneva. Robert Blackburn, deputy Director General of the IBO, undertook a three-week tour of Australian states in 1988 to meet with officials in ministries of education, private schools, and private school associations. He was joined by Roger Peel, Director General, and John Goodban, Regional Director IBAP, for the final few days of that marathon tour. When Roger Peel addressed the AEC in Darwin as part of that visit, it was the first time that the AEC had allowed an outside speaker to do so.

As a result of the address to the AEC and the contacts made, much interest developed in Australasia in the Diploma, and subsequently in the MYP and the PYP. The Australasian IB Schools Association was formed in 1988. The Hon. Greg Crafter was then Minister for Education in South Australia, and he supported the IB diploma being taught at Glenunga High School. This was only the second state school in the country at the time to offer the IB diploma, Narrabundah College in the ACT being the first. By June 2002 there were fifty-one authorised IB programs in Australia, the largest number in any one country in the region.

A part-time IBO representative was appointed in India in 1988, located at Kodaikanal International School in Tamil Naidu. In September 1991 the regional office was upgraded to a full-time operation with two staff, a director, and a secretary. A part-time representative for Australasia was appointed. The UWC of South East Asia, Singapore generously allowed the office to remain on its campus where it still is today. In September 1994 the office acquired a full-time regional representative for South East Asia, based in Singapore, and the Australasian representative was upgraded to full time.

The plan in 1991 was to develop a network of sub-regional representative offices that would span the entire Asia-Pacific. This objective was realized in January 2000 with the opening of a part-time office in Beijing to serve the rapid growth of IB interest and schools in China. There are now five sub-regional representative offices, for Australasia, China, Japan (since 1996), South East Asia, and South Asia (since 1994). This network of offices has encouraged a generally balanced growth pattern across the region, promoted a greater understanding of the region's cultural complexity, and has acted as a catalyst to give this diverse region a strong intercultural sense of coherence and unity for schools focused on the IB.

The growth in attendance at regional workshops is testimony to this regional coherence. There were eleven participants at the first conference in Manila in 1984. Over 180 met in Cairns, Queensland, in 1999 to celebrate the fifteenth annual gathering. Memorable conference locations come easily to mind: a performance of the Ramayama in a Balinese garden on a starlit evening against the backdrop of the Indian Ocean; delegates desperately struggling to keep their balance on a bitterly cold Tianaman Square—that day the world's largest skating rink; the panoramic view of the massive Annapurna range from Nagokot; snorkelling on the Great Barrier Reef. Since 1999 the total workshop attendance each year has exceeded a thousand.

The number of schools continues to grow with the largest interest in South East Asia. By June 2002 there was a total of 164 authorised IB programs in the Asia-Pacific region, approximately double that of three years earlier. The majority of schools are international or private national schools, with very few state schools. In 2001 IBAP authorised seventeen new IB programs.

November 1994 saw the tenth Annual Regional Conference

taking place in Beijing as a result of marked interest by Chinese educational authorities; this has led to a small number of state schools now doing the diploma and MYP. The Chinese Education Association for International Exchange translated all of the MYP documents into Chinese (Mandarin) so that teachers could implement it in some state schools in that language. In 1997 Chinese (putong hua) was added as an MYP working language for curriculum materials, moderation of sample student work and teacher training. This improved the accessibility of one of the IBO programs in the world's largest nation. Including a non-European language in the IBO was an important step. During 1994–95 interest in teaching the MYP in some state schools bilingually in English and Bahasa Indonesia, Japanese, or Pilipino was expressed by the ministries of education of those countries.

IB Africa/Europe/Middle East (IBAEM)

The regional office for Europe, Africa, and the Middle East had been at the Institute of Education at London University with Robert Blackburn, Deputy Director General of the IBO, until July 1986 when responsibility for Europe (but not the UK) moved to Geneva with a newly established regional office. In 1988 there were seven IB diploma schools in Africa: Ethiopia (1), Kenya (2) Lesotho (1), Morocco (1), Nigeria (3), Swaziland (1), and Tanzania (2). Unfortunately all three schools in Nigeria dropped out of the program within the next five to six years for financial reasons, but the others are still member schools. By June 2002 there were thirty- one IB programs in Africa and twenty-three in the Middle East. In 2001 IBAEM authorized thirty-nine new IB programs and by June 2002 there were 327 diploma schools, sixty MYP schools, and thirty-seven PYP schools.

Robert Blackburn died unexpectedly of a heart attack in 1990. The 'Blackburn Room' was named after him in the new Cardiff offices and the 'Blackburn Award' for CAS was created in 1991 through donations. The London office then moved to the IBO's Cardiff premises to create the regional office for the UK, Africa and the Middle East from 1990 until 1993. Responsibility for the UK moved to the European regional office in Geneva the following year. The regional office for Africa and the Middle East in Cardiff then closed in July 1994 and moved to Geneva as part of the expanded Africa/Europe/Middle East region with a new Regional Director.

In 1987 the Geneva regional office had no member schools in Central/Eastern Europe. One third of IB member schools in Western Europe were state schools. Visits were made to Yugoslavia, Slovenia (one of six Yugoslavian republics at the time), and Hungary as the first interest in the IB diploma started to emerge from that part of the world. Plans were also considered for an IB diploma school in Bulgaria. The first visit to Moscow to discuss the IB diploma with Ministry of Education officials occurred in 1989. This interest coincided with the overthrow of Communism and the need to reform the education systems; the IB diploma was seen as an alternative worth exploring. The first schools in Eastern Europe to implement the Diploma Program emerged when two Slovenian state schools, Druga Gimnazija Maribor and Gimnazija Bezigrad, were authorised on the same date in 1990. In 1994 an IB information centre was established in Moscow by the State Pedagogical University of Moscow and the Ministry of Education.

In October 1993 the Geneva regional office had a total staff of three and a half plus one and a half in Stockholm. In 2002 there were eighteen staff in Geneva and three in Stockholm. From July 1994 the Geneva office became the regional office for Africa/Europe/Middle East, with the sub-regional office in Stockholm servicing the Nordic countries and Central/Eastern Europe.

The first workshop for librarians in IB schools took place in 1994 at Sevenoaks School in the UK and the first part-time regional representatives for the Middle East (based in Amman, Jordan) and Central/Eastern Africa (based in Nairobi) were appointed. Another first occurred in 1996 when the IB diploma Recognition Handbook for Africa/Europe/Middle East was published and contained statements by hundreds of universities. This information now appears on the IBO's public website and is updated as soon as amendments come to hand.

The first university scholarships to be available exclusively to IB Diploma-holders were granted by the American College London (now the American Intercontinental University London),

University of Bath, and Richmond College London in 1995. The University of Reading offered three scholarships covering full tuition fees for undergraduate study from 1997—one for a student from Africa, one from Asia, and one from anywhere in the world.

The first PYP regional manager was appointed in September 1999 and the first MYP regional manager in January 2000, both located in Geneva. This provided the expertise which was needed to respond to the growing demand for these two programs.

The number of workshops and conferences each year has increased along with attendance at each event as more schools joined the IBO. Teacher training is an obligatory part of preparation for authorisation to teach IBO programs. The arrival of the MYP and then the PYP necessitated workshops for these programs in addition to those already organised for the diploma.

The first French-speaking workshops in Europe for Theory of Knowledge and Philosophy were held with assistance from the French Ministry of Education in 1987. Subject workshops in Biology, Maths Studies, and Maths Methods have been offered regularly in French (in addition to French language itself). There were only eight schools in Europe and two in Africa teaching IB diploma subjects in French by June 2002. (The province of Quebec hosts the largest number of French-speaking schools.)

The first five-day annual (northern hemisphere) 'summer workshops' for teachers new to the IB diploma began in Szeged, Hungary, in July 1992. Some 280 participants from 65 schools in 32 countries attended. These events have grown each year and have been held in Gdynia, Poland (1993), Prague (1994), Bratislava (1995), Warsaw (1996), Ljubljana (1997), Budapest (1998), Vienna (1999), Zagreb (2000), and Vienna (in 2001, with a record 600 participants). For the first time these workshops were split over two weeks in Riga, Latvia (2002) because the number of participants had grown to more than 700 which was too many at one time.

In an effort to provide teacher training in Africa, the first of what was to become an annual January diploma workshop was held in Nairobi in 1995, and Malta was the venue for the first MYP workshop in the region in the first half of the same year. The first PYP workshop organised by the regional office took place in Rome in April 1998. In 2001 some 3,000 people attended workshops.

The first regional IB Diploma Co-ordinators' Conference to be held outside Europe took place in West Africa in October 1997 and some ninety participants took part. We began the conference in Togo at the British School of Lomé and finished it in Tema (Ghana) at the SOS—Hermann Gmeiner International College (SOS-HGIC). It was a resounding success and those who had not attended, mainly through feelings of insecurity about becoming ill or civil unrest occurring, regretted it when they heard from participants that it had been an unforgettable experience. We were treated to African hospitality at its best and to fascinating insights into African culture via students and staff in both schools. All agreed that this had advanced an understanding of Africa on the part of those Europeans who had never been there, and it led to some European schools supporting needy schools in Africa: provision of laboratory equipment and books, paying for teachers and students to visit Europe, and sending teachers and students to Africa.

For the conference, participants crossed from Togo into Ghana by bus. Border crossings were reminiscent of the American wild west: dusty roads, dilapidated buildings for the customs and police officials, bustling lines of people passing in both directions carrying merchandise and animals, large wooden gates that let you pass from one section to the next once the paper work has been completed, long lines of vehicles of all types (most would not pass a roadworthy test in Europe), and all within a wonderfully nonchalant, multilinguistic context of English, French, and a number of African languages.

On the return journey we were late departing from Tema and one of the smaller buses had two flat tyres (the roads were worn away in a number of places). Our group flight was leaving that evening around 8:00 p.m. We arrived on the Ghana side of the border just after 5:30 p.m., not long before the border closed for the evening at 6:00 p.m., after which time people must wait until the next morning. Our passage was relatively swift through the Ghanaian paperwork. As we approached the last barrier on the English-speaking side, the director of the British School of Lomé appeared out of nowhere, boarded our bus and explained how he had had to negotiate with the Togolese border authorities to remain open until our bus arrived, otherwise we would have had to stay in Ghana and would have missed our flight. What we had not realized was that the Togo side closed at 5:30 p.m. each day, half an hour before the Ghana side—one of those wonderful idiosyncrasies of Africa! We moved into French-speaking Togo in time for our flight.

In October 1999 the second regional IB Diploma Co-ordinators Conference to be held outside Europe took place in Muscat, Oman with 165 participants. This was the first time the regional conference had been held in the Middle East. In 2002 the second regional IB Diploma Co-ordinators Conference ever to be held in Africa took place in Nairobi with 240 participants.

A number of sub-regional associations of IB diploma schools have grown in different places. They are to be found in Germany, the Netherlands, the UK (the IB Schools and Colleges Association—IBSCA), the Nordic countries, the Middle East and a looser structure in Spain. These groups assist the IBO in recognition issues and serve other interests of their students and teachers in a similar way to those in North America.

The IB Diploma is now well recognised and even appreciated by most universities and ministries of education in the Africa/Europe/Middle East region. With few exceptions, the holder of an IB diploma has the same rights as a holder of the national school-leaving diploma: some countries such as Spain, Greece, and Turkey require additional university entrance examinations while in others the IB diploma (like the national diploma) gives direct access to university, as in the UK, France, Italy, the Nordic countries, and elsewhere. A breakthrough occurred in German-speaking Switzerland in 1999 when the diploma was fully recognised on a trial basis for the first time. Another breakthrough also occurred in Germany early in 2000. A new law was passed to allow students of German nationality taking the IB diploma within Germany to be accepted at the national universties.

CAS (Creativity Action Service)/Community Service

CAS in the Diploma Program became a regional office responsibility in 1991. A CAS Committee was appointed and met for the first time in 1993. It was chaired by a Regional Director and produced a CAS Guide. Regional offices then monitored CAS programs in schools each year and implemented standardized criteria to ensure the integrity of the program. This was a response to some inequities and confusion which had prevailed amongst schools as to what constitutes CAS.

As part of CAS, and as Community Service in the MYP, all students are required to commit themselves for some period of time to service towards an individual or group in the community or in other countries (as a number of the IBO schools do) who are disadvantaged in some way—socially, economically, physically, or mentally.

A Blackburn Award was established in honour of Robert Blackburn, through donations from schools and friends of the IBO. The money was invested and each year a prize of £500 is given to support the best CAS project from schools in Africa. (An exception was made one year to award the prize in the Middle East.)

Recipients of the award thus far have been:

•1993: International School Moshi Ltd, Tanzania, for constructing a house to assist needy local children;

•1994: International School of Tanganyika Ltd, Dar-es-Salam, Tanzania, for improvements to the residential facilities in the Kindwitwi Leprosy Village, including the construction of a rainwater collection system;

•1995: Amman Baccalaureate School, Jordan, for its first Carnival Care Fun Fair to raise funds in support of the disabled people that the students visit regularly;

•1996: SOS-Hermann Gmeiner International College, Ghana, for bringing fresh water by pipe to the Kakasunaka village;

•1997: No competition;

•1998: Lincoln International School, Uganda, for its project to give weekly moral support to families with an HIV-positive parent;

•1999: International School of Lusaka, Zambia, for asking street children what were their greatest needs and then setting up an ongoing survival and recreational skills program at the school to address those needs;

•2000: Machabeng College, Maseru, Lesotho, for the production of fuel bricks from recycled paper as a meaningful activity with street children;

•2001: Saint Mary's School, Nairobi, for providing financial and moral support (through weekly visits) for the Kibagare Primary and Secondary School, a boarding school for children from an impoverished district, and the New Life Home, for abandoned and orphaned babies born HIV-positive;

•2002: International School of Tanganyika Ltd, Dar-es-Salaam, Tanzania, for its project "Eyesight for All"; students organise and publicise regular camps in poorer regions of the country to provide eye treatment for those who cannot afford it; this has saved the eyesight of hundreds of people.

A fundamental premise of community service is that the IB students must have a continuing, regular interaction with other people and they must reflect on their experiences; this is true of each of the above projects.

Intergovernmental Organisations

The IBO Executive Committee recognised the importance of contact with intergovernmental organisations and NGOs (Non-Government Organisations). This has enhanced the image of the IBO and often corrected false impressions, particularly related to the so-called 'elitist' nature of the Diploma Program, discussed later. The IBO has had consultative NGO status with UNESCO since 1967 and with the Council of Europe since 1987. It became a member of ECOSOC (the Economic and Social Council) of the UN and therefore of the CONGO (Conference of NGOs to the UN) in 1997.

As explained by Alec Peterson earlier in this book, UNESCO financially supported the development of the diploma courses and student evaluation techniques through a series of contracts for some ten years during the initial stages of the program. High-ranking UNESCO officials such as Leo Fernig also gave moral support in gaining credibility for this educational venture with national ministries of education and university authorities. Gérard Renaud as Director General from 1977 until his retirement in 1983 paid much attention to the UNESCO link and was for a few years the Chair of the UNESCO NGO Liaison Committee.

Due to other pressing priorities concerning the expansion of the IBO, this contact waned until Gérard Renaud's successor, Roger Peel, included exchanges with UNESCO and other UN organisations in the job description of the Regional Director for the newly formed Africa/Europe/Middle East region from September 1994. The IBO again became a regular participant in UNESCO NGO consultations in Paris. This led to exchanges of ideas and invitations to meetings such as the Mediteranean Convention for the Mutual Recognition of Higher Education Qualifications, which included qualifications giving access to higher education. The inroads that IBO had made in gaining acceptance of the diploma for university entry in so many countries was of interest to UNESCO and our university recognition handbooks were used at meetings as examples of what could be achieved. During the International Year of Tolerance (1995) the IBO was asked to give a presentation to other UNESCO NGOs about its philosophy and how intercultural understanding is promoted through IB schools.

Dr Ibtissam Al-Bassam, formerly Director, Section for Teacher Education, Division of Higher Education and currently Professional Assistant to the Assistant Director General of Education UNESCO (Paris), has always been a strong supporter of the IBO and its programs. This has led to a number of joint UNESCO/IBO activities under the UNESCO project SOUL (Schools of Universal Language) which Dr Al-Bassam created in 1998. SOUL seeks to promote intercultural understanding through IBO schools working with local schools, particularly in the developing world. The IBO is appreciative of her support and that of Dr Colin Power, Deputy Director General for Education (UNESCO, Paris). Dr Power retired in 2000 and was succeeded in April 2001 by Sir John Daniel, formerly Vice-Chancellor of the Open University (UK) and Vice-President of the IBO Council of Foundation, 1996–99. We are indeed fortunate to have as the educational leader of UNESCO a person who has been so closely involved with our organisation.

The International Bureau of Education (IBE) was created in Geneva in 1925 by Piaget. It later became an important educational arm of UNESCO. Located as it is on three floors in the same building as the IBO at 15 Route des Morillons, between the World Health Organisation and the International Labour Office, numerous exchanges have occurred and continue to occur. The director of the IBE until 1998, Juan Carlos Tedesco, was a member of the IBO Council of Foundation. Dr Toshio Ohsako, Program Specialist with the IBE until 1997 (when he moved to the UNESCO office in Hamburg), saw the IBO network of schools as a fertile educational laboratory for ideas concerned with international education. The current Director, Dr Cecilia Braslavsky from Argentina, gave a paper at the conference 'Interpreting International Education' in September 2002 in Geneva. The conference brought together educators who were interested in the nature of international education and was jointly organised by the IBO and the Centre for the Study of Education in an International Context (CEIC), University of Bath whose Director, Professor Jeff Thompson, is also Director for International Education for the IBO.

A number of joint UNESCO/IBO initiatives developed during the late 1990s. These included projects related to art as a reflection of culture, promoting inter-generational learning, global issues, promoting intercultural understanding in South Africa, and secondary education reform.

The Delors Report addressed the issue of how to develop citizens of the world—in line with the mission statement of the IBO. This was a most significant report of recommendations for education in Europe and beyond.[2] Colin Power, a former Director General of Education in Queensland, Australia, then commissioned Professor Phillip Hughes to do several in-house papers with tangible ideas as to how the recommendations of the Delors Report might be implemented in Europe and internationally. As it happened, Phil Hughes was an Australian, in fact a Tasmanian, who had been Deputy Director General of the state education department when I was a young teacher, and I came to know him well when, after some distinguished education posts outside Tasmania, he returned as Professor of Education to the University of Tasmania in the 1980s and retired from that post in 1991. He supervised my PhD thesis on the International Baccalaureate which I commenced before leaving Tasmania in 1990. He contacted me to say that he would be in Paris from June to August 1998 at UNESCO and would welcome an IBO contribution to his work. He was particularly attracted to the community service aspect of the diploma in forming good citizenship habits and fostering humanitarian values.

A joint UNESCO/Council of Europe Convention for the

Recognition of Qualifications for Higher Education (and access to higher education) was signed in April 1997 in Lisbon by all EU members, plus the USA, Canada, and Australia. It then became known as the 'Lisbon Convention', which still remains to be ratified by all parties. In 1994 the IBO had endeavoured to have the diploma included since it promoted student mobility, the main objective of the agreement. In 1996 I addressed a meeting of the UNESCO/Council of Europe committee drawing up the convention in Strasbourg. The decision was, however, not to include the diploma because there was no provision for qualifications other than national qualifications. Dr Paul Heywood from Malta, a member of the IBO Standing Conference of Governments (SCG) and of the UNESCO/Council of Europe group, later urged the inclusion of international qualifications in the Lisbon Convention. Subsequently UNESCO set up a working party to explore this question. It met twice in 1998 to make recommendations which were accepted. In July 1999 a subsidiary text urging parties to the convention to consider international qualifications giving access to higher education was included. This was a major achievement. The wording of the text was based on detailed discussion of what constitutes an international qualification, using the IB diploma as a model.

In June 1999 the IBO was invited to submit a paper to a meeting on secondary education reform convened at UNESCO in Paris. Various agencies and a small number of NGOs were invited including the World Bank, USAID, Association for the Development of Education in Africa (ADEA), Education International (representing teacher associations world wide), UNICEF, International Labour Office, OECD, Agence Internationale de la Francophonie, and the Swedish International Development Co-operation Agency (SIDA). Colin Power and Phil Hughes (who organised the meeting) were helpful in ensuring that the IBO was present. A working partnership on citizenship education was established with the UNESCO Department of Education for a Culture of Peace and Department for the Renovation of Secondary and Vocational Education.

Malcolm Skilbeck, a distinguished Australian educator, was director of the Centre for Education, Research and Innovation (CERI) of the OECD in Paris until his retirement in 1997. I went to see him during the early part of 1994 to explain the IB diploma and the MYP with a view to having an educational exchange of ideas between the IBO and the CERI which, the year before, had completed a very useful and interesting comparison of secondary school curricula trends in the OECD member countries. It was one of those extraordinary coincidences. As I proceeded to explain what the IBO was about, he stopped me to say that he knew all about it since he had just examined my PhD thesis entitled *The International Baccalaureate: Policy Process in Education.* (I was awaiting the results from three examiners whose identities were unknown to me at that time). He took an interest in the IBO programs. As a result, three IBO staff presented the IBO to CERI staff in the latter part of 1994. Another distinguished Australian educator, Barry McGaw, succeeded Malcolm Skilbeck at the OECD and was a member of the IBO Academic Affairs Board. An official letter from Skilbeck to me as he was about to retire finished with the following phrase: " I wish the IBO continuing success. It's a very fine educational organisation with much to offer."[3]

During 1997–99 much progress was made in establishing links with the World Health Organisation (WHO) particularly in relation to the Health and Social Education area of interaction of the MYP. WHO had traditionally interacted with very few NGOs. Thanks to the persistence of Ruth Bonner (who was involved in the creation of the IB diploma in the 1960s), WHO came to include the IBO in discussions about school health.

By 1999 collaboration between WHO and the IBO had moved ahead in several ways: making the IBO schools aware of WHO's Global School-Health Initiative, including WHO expertise for the Health and Social Education (HSE) area of interaction of the MYP in the Online Curriculum Centre, having a WHO representative on the HSE curriculum guide writing committee, and documents on health education in the classroom being reviewed by practising teachers in IBO schools.

The Myth of IB Elitism

Two of the most common misunderstandings of the IB are that IB schools are only for rich kids and that only unusually gifted students can succeed at an IB diploma. Initially there *were* more private, international schools than state schools (where students pay no tuition fees) doing the diploma, but there has been an increase of interest from some national ministries of education to the extent that forty-three percent of all diploma schools are now state-funded. The largest numbers of state schools are to be found in the US, Canada, the Nordic countries, the UK, Spain, the Netherlands, and Central/Eastern Europe. As for the MYP, Quebec has forty state schools doing this program (thirty-six in French and four in English), and there were three state schools in the Netherlands offering it by June 2002. In addition, the IBO has made conscious efforts, again supported by the Executive Committee, to bring the IBO programs to national schools (both state and private) in the developing world by seeking funding from donors to enable implementation and maintenance over an initial period of some years. For instance, Preca College, Korçe, Albania was sponsored by the Maltese government and SOS Albania (an NGO). Sadly, the school was looted during the civil unrest in 1997, and all the equipment was either stolen or destroyed just a few months after the diploma program had begun. The school was forced to suspend the IB diploma program.

A striking example is the SOS-Hermann Gmeiner International College (HGIC) in Tema, Ghana. It was established by the SOS Kinderdorf Organisation in Innsbruck, Austria as the only SOS secondary school in the world leading to the IB diploma. Plans for a similar Spanish-speaking school in Costa Ricca are underway. The funding from Austria enables the school to take in refugee and orphaned children from SOS villages around Africa supplemented with some revenue from Ghanaian students who can afford to pay school tuition fees.

The IB diploma is within the reach of solid, average students who are prepared to work consistently throughout the two-year program; it is not restricted to the academically gifted. On the other hand, the IBO has never pretended that students of any ability could successfully complete an IB diploma; it has been, and remains, a course giving access to higher education and is therefore no more or less elitist in this sense than most national systems where students must reach a minimum academic standard before proceeding to university. However, the MYP and PYP are designed to be available to all intellectual abilities.

Most students studying the IBO programs—from those in private schools with very high tuition fees (and therefore accessible mainly to the wealthy) to those in schools of much more modest means, including the many state schools without tuition fees—are giving something to the less privileged and are receiving something in return through CAS activities in the diploma or Community Service in the other programs. This surely mitigates the charge of 'elitism'.

A small part of the Goldman Sachs grant was designated to assist local schools in Africa. It was later agreed to concentrate on Nairobi where there were by June 2002 five IB schools—the largest number in any one African city or country. In 2002 each of the IB schools became mentors to two local schools and are providing materials, pedagogical training, and access to the IBO's OCC (by paying for computers and Internet access in the local schools) for further on-line professional development. It is hoped that this experience can be improved upon and transferred to other parts of the developing world.

The Moshi International School (Tanzania), as an example, had already adopted a local, state primary school several years ago as a CAS project. I was privileged to visit the local school with staff and IB students. The IB school had provided three new buildings: a toilet block, a library/teacher study, and a small dining facility with kitchen. It had also provided books and other teaching materials. Class sizes were surprisingly low for Africa: about thirty students per teacher. The day of my visit, one of the teachers had not yet arrived for her class. I volunteered to teach the children. It was an English lesson with the most senior group who were about 10–13 years of age. The head of the school showed me the page of the English class text they had reached and left me with the class. We revised some grammatical structures in a practical way focusing on sentences I wrote on the blackboard. Then I wanted to refer to a story in the textbook. I asked them to turn to a specific page. The students jumped from their desks and made three groups of about ten in different parts of the room looking up at me in silent anticipation. There were only three class texts and they had placed themselves in an optimum position to be able to look on. Through questioning I discovered that the government supplied free of charge all class textbooks (for this reason the school had not asked for these texts to be bought by Moshi International School) but that these often arrived late or not at all, and almost always in grossly insufficient numbers when they did appear. The parents of three students in this class had worked and saved to purchase the English textbook which cost about fifty US cents. As soon as I told Moshi International School of the problem they took steps to supply a textbook to each student. Even the tiniest assistance goes a very long way to improving education in the developing world.

Notes to Chapter Ten

[1] Georges Laforest, doyen (person in charge) of the Inspection Générale, Ministry of Education, France, was for many years examiner for the IB Diploma Program subjects of Philosophy and Theory of Knowledge.

[2] Jacques Delors, *Learning: The Treasure Within. Report to UNESCO of the International Commission on Education for the Twenty-First Century* (Paris: UNESCO, 1996).

[3] Malcolm Skilbeck, letter to Ian Hill, 20th March, 1997.

11
THE PEOPLE WHO MADE THE IBO
Ian Hill

A number of individuals have contributed in significant ways to the IBO. Some of those who made their mark during the early developmental stages of the IB diploma are no longer alive and others are still involved today. Some have been staff members of the organisation for a long time and other staff have had particular senior responsibilities in the IBO since 1986.

Alec Peterson

Peterson was born in Edinburgh in 1908. While director of the Department of Educational Studies at Oxford, he became part-time director of ISES in July 1966. The involvement of Peterson and Oxford extended the international prestige of the IB project beyond the group of visionaries clustered around the International School of Geneva. From the late 1950s, the school in Geneva had been engaged in a project with Oxford Department of Education whereby selected teachers in training were sent to Geneva for a term of teaching practice in an international school. Alec Peterson was director of the Oxford Department of Education from 1958 to 1973 where, in the early 1960s, the two main research interests were the structure of the sixth form curriculum and a comparative study of upper secondary curricula and examinations in conjunction with the Council of Europe by Dr W. Halls, a member of Peterson's staff. Hence the teacher training and research projects brought first Halls then Peterson into contact with ISA and later ISES in the 1960s. Peterson attended his first ISES Council meeting in November

1965. In connection with his research, Halls had already visited Geneva and had had contact with ISES prior to Peterson's involvement.

During World War Two, having entered the teaching profession in 1932, Peterson was Deputy Director of Psychological Warfare for South-East Asia Command, serving on Lord Mountbatten's staff; from 1952 to 1954 he was Director General of Information Services during the Malaysian emergency. This military background was to provide him with contacts at the highest levels—contacts which greatly assisted the acceptance of the IB by ministries of education and governments. Lord Mountbatten was very influential in this regard.

Alec Peterson was headmaster of government and independent schools in England, the last of which was Dover College, where he had started an international sixth form, before he took up his post at Oxford in 1958. As long-time chair until 1977 of the editorial board of the prestigious journal *Comparative Education* he was a recognised expert in that field and a leading pioneer in international education in Britain and beyond. He met Kurt Hahn at a conference on international education in Belgium in 1957 (see page 1 of this book). Through this acquaintance with Hahn's educational philosophy and his military connections he visited Atlantic College at St Donat's, Wales, for the first time in 1961 (before any students had been enrolled). Kurt Hahn had helped to establish the school with Rear-Admiral Desmond Hoare as founding headmaster and Robert Blackburn as deputy-headmaster. During the summer of 1962 Peterson worked with Blackburn to provide a broad academic curriculum to the students who were to enter this first of the United World Colleges in September of the same year.

Peterson was a staunch campaigner against what he regarded as the over-specialisation of British education at pre-university level. In 1960 he published a report *Arts and Science Sides in the Sixth Form* based on research funded by the Gulbenkian Foundation. It is noteworthy how closely the content of the report resembles not only the philosophy but also the structure of the IB diploma program which had only begun to be elaborated a few years later.

Peterson's enthusiasm for the IB project is therefore not surprising. Here was the embodiment of an educational ideal he had long been unsuccessfully promoting in the UK. His particular interest in the Theory of Knowledge course was the fulfillment of something he had already foreshadowed in the Gulbenkian-funded report of 1960. Peterson had also shown interest in a range of assessment techniques which would gauge "the whole endowment and personality of the student" and which complemented his curriculum development ideas. His concept of student evaluation, developed over a number of years, later formed part of a study he did for the Council of Europe in 1970. He did not want good teaching to be distorted by intensive examination preparation. He thought highly of oral examinations with a visiting examiner (a hallmark of IB language A, now A1, examinations for many years), of mixing a small amount of multiple-choice testing with essays, of assessing analytical skills and cultural sensitivity rather than factual recall, of qualitative measures of affective development (identified particularly via CAS in the IB diploma programme).

Peterson was a person of high leverage in educational and diplomatic circles. Said Monsieur Scherer, the *proviseur* of the Lycée of St Germain-en-Laye, Paris, the first French school to offer the IB: "He was a great man of vision." Ritchie, the Director of ISA, characterised Peterson as "A visionary with charisma. He had the necessary academic standing to make the IB credible. He was very competent and convincing in public." David Sutcliffe, who retired in 2001 as head of the United World College of the Adriatic in Trieste and was a teacher at Atlantic College (where he later was headmaster) when it opened in 1962, described Peterson as "rational, imaginative, with fantastic persistence. He was a good speaker and writer who made an enormous contribution. He wanted to broaden the A-levels through the IB."

"Peterson had a great reputation. The Ford Foundation accepted him; he had the contacts and the academic standing" (Leach). "He was admired by his students. He was concerned about the *whole* person. He was *un sage*" (Renaud). "Peterson was very impressive. He had a major role in developing the philosophical underpinnings of the IB. He was an outstanding international education figure" (Gellar, head of the International School of Copenhagen when the IB project began). Hanson (of the American College Board) describes Peterson as a "bright, caring, civilised" person who "disliked the A-levels and was educationally attracted to the IB." Gathier (a former president of the IBO

Council of Foundation) said "Peterson was the backbone, the mental father of the IB. He was devoted and zealous—a continuing source of inspiration. He knew everybody and had good ideas and international contacts." Blouke Carus (long connected with the IB in North America) said he had "incredible energy and enthusiasm, and was a phenomenal chairman." The IB project became firmly established when Peterson was made part-time director of ISES from 1966. When the ISES officially became the IB Office in 1968 he continued as director until July 1977.

When Peterson was appointed director of the International Schools Examination Syndicate (ISES) in July 1966 he visited Geneva frequently but worked from his office at Oxford University. From January 1967 he lived in Geneva for a little more than six months while on sabbatical leave from Oxford in a villa about 100 metres from the IB offices in Cologny. He then resumed his full-time duties as head of the department of educational studies at Oxford with "the IB as my major research interest" (page 91 above). So Peterson was a peripatetic, but extremely effective, part-time director general of the IBO. He was based in the UK while Gérard Renaud looked after the Geneva office as deputy director general. Until his retirement in 1973 from Oxford, Peterson used his office there for IB work.

It is a mark of his devotion to education that, after his retirement from Oxford, he moved to London and became a part-time teacher of Theory of Knowledge at Hammersmith and West London College of Further Education from September 1973 where he was provided, at no cost, with "a largish cupboard which served IB as the office of the director general." In 1976 Peterson negotiated an agreement with London University's Institute of Education for office space and he spent his last year, 1976–77, there as director general of the IBO.

Alec Peterson maintained a fervent interest in the IB until the end. At the Council of Foundation meeting in November 1988, the year in which Alec died, Robert Blackburn said:

> Alec always looked forward. Until the morning of his death (when I had from him two manuscript letters and the copy of a draft speech) he was interested in the introduction of new subjects and new ideas in the IB. . . . He was . . . particularly interested in the current debate on the role of internationalism in the IB. Those of us involved might well refer to his brilliant last chapter [Chapter 8 above] on the nature of internationalism in *Schools Across Frontiers*.

Peterson shaped the educational philosophy of the IB, based on his own deeply humanist and liberal beliefs. This is discernable particularly in the following features: the choice of courses to stimulate the imagination rather than filling the mind with facts, the obligation to do independent research, the balance of academic work and community service, the development of critical thinking skills and the central role of Theory of Knowledge.

A glance through the volumes of Peterson correspondence in the IBO Geneva archives shows just how prodigious he was. Peterson read and wrote French with ease; during the many times when secretarial assistance was at a minimum or nonexistent, there are to be found dozens and dozens of long, very neat, handwritten letters in English and French seeking funding, putting forward educational ideas to curriculum committees and examiners, discussing administrative and political matters concerning the ISES and IBO Council of Foundation, answering queries from schools, alerting an ambassador or a minister for education to the IB project, detailing long-term plans for the future, questioning the budget figures, following up with individuals met at conferences, providing background notes for Council agenda items, and so on. In a 1968 message to Goormaghtigh (chair of the IBO Council at the time) Peterson remarks as an aside: "I think I am doing about twenty letters a day." He provided the energy, the pedagogical vision, the educational stature and the administrative competence which gave credibility to the IB project. His contribution was inestimable and his legacy will long be remembered.

John Goormaghtigh

The 1998 Montreux meeting of IBO to celebrate the first thirty years saw the return of a number of stalwarts who had been missing from the Council of Foundation meetings since they had been held outside Switzerland from 1994: Piet Gathier (IBO President, 1984–1990), Tony Besse (a former Vice-President of the IBO and of UWC), Jacqueline Roubinet (a former Executive member of the IBO and former head of the Ecole Active Bilingue Jeannine Manuel, Paris), Gérard Renaud (former Director General of the IBO), and Ruth Bonner (former Executive secretary of the IBO).

John Goormaghtigh was unable to come due to ill health; he died a few months later at the age of seventy-nine. The IBO would not be what it is today without his great determination and unselfish commitment over a long period. An international lawyer by profession, he was the first President of the Council of Foundation from 1968 to 1981 while he was Director of the European Office of the Carnegie Endowment for International Peace in Geneva, and continued to attend all Council meetings until 1993. He was also treasurer of the International Schools Association (ISA) from 1957 to 1962 and Chairman of the Board of the International School of Geneva from 1960 until 1966.

John has been described by other important IBO protagonists as "resourceful, articulate, an excellent chairman, realistically idealistic, provocative, well-connected in UN circles." He had *le calibre international* to successfully promote the IB diploma and its ideals.[1]

Of Belgian descent, John Goormaghtigh was completely bilingual in English and French. In his retirement he lived at his family home near Strasbourg, from where he contacted me one day in 1996 to suggest that I visit the state Lycée-Collège International in Strasbourg; the new Proviseur had shown interest in the IB diploma. We met in a restaurant near the main railway station one cold day in December, and after lunch he suggested we walk to the lycée, about a kilometre away. I can still see his tall, erect figure, despite his age and his cane, moving briskly through the streets of bustling Christmas shoppers. He talked enthusiastically about the IB, the crises through which it had passed, and the success of the diploma, and expressed faith in it for the future. This was the last time I was to see him. He still emanated that imposing assurance and fearless devotion to the cause which had impressed the many people fortunate enough to have known him.

Desmond Cole-Baker

Desmond Cole-Baker, one of the driving forces behind the Diploma Program was head of the English Section of the International School of Geneva (Ecolint) during 1962–64 and head of the whole school during 1964–67. He prepared the submission which led to the successful Ford Foundation grant and went to New York to meet with officials of that organisation in 1964.

Desmond came from his New Zealand home to visit Geneva in April 1999. It was then that I met him for the first time at a lunch in his honour given at the International School of Geneva. I had corresponded with him some years before about his involvement in the launching of the IB diploma. In a letter to me in 1989 he had indicated that he wanted the ISA to undertake international education in grades K–12:

> I set about tackling three matters: an international Primary School Curriculum, an international Leaving Certificate . . . and giving assistance in forming or reorganising schools in mainly developing countries. You will notice that the middle school was left out for the moment but I had to set priorities.[2]

The international leaving certificate became the IB Diploma Program. As for the primary project, teachers from international schools met in their spare time in different schools and, as the project developed, certain schools were given the task of preparing a specific part of the program. *An International Primary School Curriculum ISA,* compiled and edited by Cole-Baker, was first published in 1966 and revised in 1970. It was not widely distributed and few copies remain today. The International Schools Curriculum Project group was not aware of its existence when they launched the international primary program which was to become the IBO's PYP in 1997.

The Cole-Baker document represents guidelines for "internationally standardised curricula" rather than placing emphasis on an international perspective. This may have been deliberate, given that governments at the time might not have supported an international perspective but would have been attracted to setting standards across the world for education. Seven subject areas are identified: the language of instruction, mathematics, environmental studies, science, language teaching, creative activities (art and music), and physical education. Social studies (history and geography) are integrated to some extent into the science and environmental studies subjects and do not stand alone. Much stress is placed on using new teaching methods of the time, and on teaching *how* to learn. Working co-operatively, adaptability and relating to the real world are stated aims of the program.

The content of the 192-page book is uneven: 100 pages are devoted to the science course, twenty pages to mathematics, and a few pages to the rest. An emphasis on inquiry learning in the science, mathematics, and environmental studies programs provides a link with the current PYP: "Children's questions are extremely important: the child's own question is the most significant for him and has the most motivating power."[3] A hint of the PYP holistic and transdisciplinary approach appears as part of scientific inquiry which should lead back into mathematics, language, and other areas: ". . . and this is truly the world of the child who sees the world as a whole and not in terms of subjects."[4]

Cole-Baker was gratified to see that his vision became a reality some thirty years later. The PYP (and the MYP) have benefitted from the respect that the IBO has gained through the Diploma Program, which would not have been possible had ISA or the fledgling IBO attempted all three at once in the 1960s.

Desmond Cole-Baker is a forceful character who ruled at Ecolint with an iron hand and enthused with his missionary zeal to develop international education and then spread it around the globe, thus leading, as he hoped, "quarrelling humanity into the path of peace."[5] Desmond was given the ISA Distinguished Service Award for International Education in February 2000.

Robert Blackburn

I met Robert at my first Council of Foundation meeting in Geneva in 1987 and spent time with him when he undertook the three-week tour of Australian states a year later. He was indefatigable and articulate, always alert for opportunities to disseminate the philosophy of the IB and to bring another worthy school into the fold. He was able to chair difficult meetings with authority and encourage those around him.

Robert was the first Deputy Head of the new Atlantic College in Wales in 1962 and Chief Staff Officer of the London UWC office under Lord Mountbatten in 1968. He joined the IBO's London office in 1978 as Deputy Director General with responsibility for the UK, Africa, and the Middle East, until he died suddenly of a heart attack in 1990. The Blackburn Award was established in his honour: Each year a prize of £500 is given to support the best CAS project from schools in Africa. As another fitting tribute, one of the meeting rooms in Cardiff bears the name 'The Blackburn Room'.

We owe much to Robert for his work in the development of the Diploma Program, for bringing it to the notice of British universities, for his promotion of the program in Africa, and for his work as secretary to the Standing Conference of Governments.

Roger Peel

Born in England, Roger spent a large part of his working life in the US, where he was professor of Spanish and of Modern Languages at Middlebury College from 1969 until 1982. He was Director General of the IBO from 1983 to 1998. Until his retirement in December 1999 he was Senior Development Consultant for the IBO.

As the IBO's third and longest-serving Director General, he influenced the organisation at a difficult time. It was no longer a fledgling. Roger steered it through the troublesome teenage years and into adulthood. Bridging the transition between a homespun, quite intimate group of people and the installation of more management structures to correspond to a corporation-in-the-making was not an easy task. Inevitable tensions were created, many of them healthy with positive outcomes. Roger encouraged the purchase of Peterson House, the arrival of the MYP and PYP, the development of new diploma subjects, the regular review of curricula and student assessment techniques, the appointment of more staff in all areas, the creation of academic committees, the streamlining of the business and finance side, and improving services to schools. He supported the investment of time and money to acquire state-of-the-art information technology which would assist communication between IBO personnel, provide good databases, and support contact with schools. Two of Roger's main concerns were the concept of international education and providing access to IBO programs for children in the developing world—these he raised year after year in his annual reports and at meetings.

Roger was never flustered but always in good humour despite the many calls upon his time. He was often able to pour oil on troubled waters and this assisted many a staff member. In the most aggressive of public meetings he remained calm and found the right form of words to improve the situation. This was his *forte*. Colin Jenkins said of him: "At the end of the day he could laugh about himself and the rest of us. Seeing the funny side and laughing uproariously was surely one of his trademarks."[6] He treasured his short summer vacations sailing in the Caribbean and came back even more refreshed than he usually looked. Roger maintained a gruelling travel schedule but he had the stamina to do it. His enthusiasm for the IBO and its programs came across infectiously as he addressed people across the world in English, French, or Spanish. He made himself readily available to staff and others who wished to see him in Geneva, in Cardiff, in the regional offices or during his travels. Whenever his counsel was sought on an issue he would put the interests of the students first.

Roger Peel was adventurous and energetic. He bonded the organisation together at a time when it needed it most and prepared it to become a corporate adult.

Some ISA Award Winners

Apart from Desmond Cole-Baker, three other people who have had an important involvement with the IBO and its programs have been recipients of ISA awards.

Gérard Renaud was the first to receive the ISA Distinguished Service Award in 1995 "for the highest ideals in international education, excellent teaching, and leadership in curriculum development and research." He was the second Director General of the IBO (1977–83) and played a major part in the development of the MYP as he had done with the diploma some twenty years before. He is a visionary, a pedagogue, a philosopher. His powerful intellect and curriculum development skills have had a large impact on the diploma and on the early developments of the MYP. He lectures and writes on international education and maintains strong links with the International School of Geneva where he was amongst the first to develop IB diploma courses. Gérard visits the Geneva IBO office and maintains a lively interest in IBO developments through his many translations into French which, in turn, lead to many stimulating discussions on international education. We trust that his innovative, inspiring presence will be with us for many years to come.

Ruth Bonner and Nansi Poirel were the first to receive the ISA International Humanism Award and they did so simultaneously in 1995. Nansi was head of English at Ecolint in the 1960s and was very involved in the creation of the English A1 course; she was for many years an examiner for this subject and a regular attender at the annual IBO Council of Foundation meetings. She died in 1998.

Thanks to the persistence of Ruth Bonner, former Executive Secretary of the ISES (International Schools Examination Syndicate) then IBO from 1965 until 1980, the World Health Organisation (WHO) came to include the IBO in discussions about school health in 1997. Ruth was involved in the early development of the Health and Social Education part of the MYP as well as in the IB diploma in the 1960s at Ecolint. Since her retirement she devotes her time to representing the IBO at UN agencies and gatherings in Geneva. I witnessed how effectively she operated on many occasions at UN, WHO, or IBE meetings. She would approach ministers and other high-ranking officials and ask them: 'Have you heard of the IB?' Because of her petite stature, her determination, and being *une dame d'un certain âge* no one resisted and we gained quite a number of converts through this method. Ruth is a regular visitor to the IBO offices in Geneva and remains very committed to the ideals of the organisation. She is the official IBO representative to the UN organisations in Geneva.

The Hon. Greg Crafter received the ISA Distinguished Service Award in 1999. As Minister for Education and Children's Services in South Australia during 1985–92 he established the first government school to offer the IB diploma in that state— Glenunga High School, Adelaide. Greg was appointed to the IBO Council of Foundation in 1992 and became president of the IBO Executive Committee at the 1996 Council meeting in Amman, Jordan. The following year he was also elected president of the Council of Foundation. He is a solicitor by profession, and the

IBO benefits greatly from his wise chairmanship, his congenial manner, his sharp mind, and his enthusiasm for the promotion of the IBO and its programs. He is particularly concerned to improve access to IBO programs for children in the developing world and to raise the profile of the organisation amongst governments, inter-governmental organisations and international corporations.

Other Key Individuals

Professor Jeff Thompson, Director of the Centre for the Study of Education in an International Context (CEIC), University of Bath, was one of the first to produce questions for the trial examinations in chemistry in 1968 and was, successively, Chief Examiner in Chemistry and in Physical Sciences for the IBO, Co-ordinator for Group 4 subjects (the Sciences), and Chair of the Bureau and Examining Board from 1984 until 1989. He also presided over curriculum committees for the introduction of environmental systems and design technology. Jeff was a member of the original Curriculum Board, the Executive Committee, and the Council of Foundation. He chaired the research committee which was established in November 1998. In January 2000 Jeff became an IBO staff member as Director of International Education, based in Bath, where he is responsible for the IBO Research Unit. In September 2002 he was appointed Academic Director at the Cardiff office.

Dianne Williamson was the longest-serving employee when she retired in 2000 after 25 years of service with the IBO in the UK. She was the link with the chief examiners, Editor of Curriculum Publications, Assistant to the Director of Examinations, and Information Technology Project Evaluator.

Thuy Gaudin was in her twenty-third year with the IBO in Geneva in 2002. She commenced as Data Processing Officer at the Palais Wilson in 1979. From 1992 she was Office and Finance Manager (at 15 route des Morillons) and in 2000 became Personnel and Administration Manager for the Headquarters and Regional Office in Geneva.

Peter Stoyle obtained a languages degree from Oxford and then did his diploma in Education under Alec Peterson at the Department of Educational Studies in the late 1950s. He spent four years teaching in Zimbabwe. Ten years later, as head of the British Schools, Montevideo, Uruguay, he was visited by Alec and this led to the school being the first to offer the IB diploma course in Latin America. He voluntarily represented the IBO from 1978 in Buenos Aires and became regional representative in 1980. The regional office opened officially under his leadership in 1982 in Buenos Aires, with Elizabeth Dwerryhouse, who was still working in the office in 2001. Peter retired as Regional Director for Latin America in December 2000 having worked twenty-two years for the IBO.

John Goodban commenced with the IBO in 1980 as Regional Representative for South East Asia in Singapore where he was later Deputy Headmaster of the UWC of South East Asia and fifty-percent IBO Regional Representative. He was also UWC representative for the area from 1980 until 1991. In 1991 he became full-time IBO Regional Director for Asia-Pacific, still based in Singapore. John retired in 2002 after twenty-two years with the IBO.

In 1992, Nancy Weller, Regional Director for IBNA, became involved in developing a communication portfolio for the IBO which would project a corporate image to the world. The first issue of *IB World* was produced under her editorship that year. The magazine appeared three times annually until 2001 when a new-look *IB World* began to appear four times per year. It presents not only the news on the developing IB curriculum and assessment, but also includes news articles, CAS projects, opinions, updates, and a worldwide teacher-training workshop calendar. In September 1994 Nancy Weller became Director of Communication in Geneva, and Bradley Richardson, who had been the deputy Regional Director in North America was appointed Regional Director. Nancy left the organisation in 1998 after fourteen years. She had elevated IBO publications to a greater professional level and enhanced the corporate image of the IBO with the creation of tasteful IBO ties, scarves, pins, pens, and T-shirts. Her major legacy remains the *IB World* magazine (with assistance from Ellen Wallace who became editor in 1996 and also external relations and media attaché in 1999). Ellen Wallace is currently Head of Corporate Relations.

Tony Martell was with the IBO for a short period due to his untimely death. He was Finance and Administration Manager, commencing in 1987 at the office in Bath. He played a key role in securing the new properties at Cardiff and oversaw the considerable logistics involved in the move in 1989, including that of a huge mainframe computer. Tony died in February 1993 following a six-month struggle with cancer. He introduced the computer-generated payment of examiners and at the time of his death was working on an integrated accounting system for all IB offices worldwide. His sociable nature and good sense of humour made him a congenial colleague who is sadly missed.

Bradley Richardson joined the New York office in 1985 as an administrative assistant, having taught English at college level in the US. He became Regional Director for North America in 1994, a position he still holds. In the same year, Nélida Antuña Baragaño, from Spain, was appointed Associate Regional Director in the Africa/Europe/Middle East office in Geneva and in 2000 Nélida became Regional Director there. She studied at the University of Liège, Belgium (in French) and taught Spanish at the first IB diploma school in the Middle East—Iranzamin in Teheran—from 1971 to 1980. She then became head of Spanish and Directora Técnica at the International College Spain, Madrid, until she joined the IBO.

Stuart Chapman worked in senior accounting and finance posts in Zambia from 1972 to 1975 with National Freight Corporation and later Union Carbide, and continued with the latter company in Ghana from 1976 to 1978. On return to the UK he worked for thirteen years with Gould Inc., a large multinational US electronics company, rising to International Financial Controller. Stuart was appointed Director of Business and Finance in the Cardiff office in 1994. He is responsible for all financial, administrative and information technology matters—in fact for those essential non-academic aspects without which the IBO could not function.

In 1986 Derek Goulden was Director of Examinations at the office at Bath University. He was followed by Colin Jenkins, who held this post from 1987 to 1990. The office moved to rented premises in a technology park at St Mellons, Cardiff, in 1989. Colin was a member of the Executive Committee from 1997 until 2001 (Vice President from 1999) and has contributed greatly to the development of the IBO. He is a gifted speaker who thinks deeply about international education and does not toe any party line; you can be sure that it will not be dull when Colin is around and that we will all have benefitted from reflecting on his provocative and thoughtful comments. He was followed by Clive Carthew from 1990 until 1996. Clive had an interesting sense of humour and a fine pedagogical mind; he brought about a number of important educational and administrative innovations.

In 1997 Helen Drennen became Director of Academic Affairs, which included curriculum development and student assessment for all IBO programs. Helen has very competently overseen a rapidly expanding Academic Affairs Division in Cardiff and has earned much respect and appreciation for her work. Later in 2002 she moved to Singapore to become Regional Director of the IB Asia-Pacific office.

From 1974 to 1980 Monica Flodman was Director of the Swedish Section at the Lycée International de St Germain-en-Laye, Paris, one of the first IB diploma schools. She then became Director of the International Section of the Sigtunaskolan, Sweden, from 1980 until 1985, where she introduced the diploma program. In 1985 she started to work for the IBO in Geneva, assisting the Director General, and then became Regional Director for Europe from 1986 until 1993. In 1993 Monica became Associate Regional Director at a new office in Stockholm responsible for the Nordic countries and Central/Eastern Europe. She took the initiative to introduce the highly successful, annual (northern hemisphere) 'summer workshops' for teachers new to the IB diploma, the first of which took place in Hungary in July 1992.

From July 1998 until September 1999 Professor Derek Blackman was Director General. He had been Chief Examiner for IB Psychology from 1989 to 1994 and Chair of the Examining Board from 1993 to 1998. An internationally-renowned scholar, Derek was appointed Professor of Psychology at the University of Cardiff in 1976. He was a member of the Executive Committee from 1993 until 2001.

Key Figures on the Council of Foundation

The IBO now has its sixth President of the Council. They have all represented different cultures, have had an important role to play in shaping the IBO, and have left their mark in different ways. The six presidents are:

•John Goormaghtigh (1968–1981), Belgium;
•Seydou Madani Sy (1981–1984), Senegal: former Rector of the University of Dakar, Minister for Justice, Ambassador to London, Special Advisor to the President, currently the Ombudsman for Senegal;
•Piet Gathier (1984–1990), Netherlands: former Director of Secondary Education in the Netherlands, retired;
•Thomas Hagoort (1990–1996), USA: an international lawyer, involved in the founding of the Washington International School and in the relocation of the United Nations International School in New York; long-time member and treasurer of the Executive Committee;
•Bengt Thelin (1996–1997), Sweden: former Director of Education at the Board of Education, Sweden and former chair of the IBO Standing Conference of Governments;
•Greg Crafter (1997–2003), Australia.

The Standing Conference of Governments (SCG) elected nine people to sit on the IBO Council of Foundation and two of these, usually the Chair and Vice-chair, sat on the Executive Committee. The following people have been elected chairs of the SCG since its foundation in 1978:

•Piet Gathier (1978–84), Netherlands;
•Jean Dumortier (1984–88), Belgium: Secretary General in the Ministry of Education for French-speaking Belgium;
•Bengt Thelin (1988–93), Sweden;
•Mrs Zoe Pohjanvirta (1993–96), Finland: Government Counsellor;
•Raymond Jourdan (1996–2000), Switzerland: head of the Collège Claparède in Geneva, and Swiss representative to the Council of Europe;
•Mrs Haifa Dia Al-Attia (2000–01), Jordan: Education Advisor to HRH Princess Sarvath.

The Standing Conference of Heads (HSC) comprises all the heads of IBO schools. A Heads Representative Committee (HRC) of nine is elected with power to co-opt a further six members for a three-year period, renewable once. The HRC represents the IBO schools in the governance of the organisation and four of its members sit on the Executive Committee. The following heads have been chairs of the HRC since it was founded in 1977:

- René-François Lejeune (1977–78), International School of Geneva;
- Phil Thomas (1978–1984), International School of Geneva;
- Jacqueline Roubinet (1984–1986), Ecole Active Bilingue Jeanine Manuel, Paris;
- Michael Maybury (1986–1989), Vienna International School;
- Bob Pearmain (1989–1992), Winston Churchill High School, Alberta;
- Leif Berntsen (1992–1996), Copenhagen International School;
- Robert Snee (1996–1999), George Mason High School, Virginia, USA;
- Margaret Nkrumah (1999–2001), SOS-Hermann Gmeiner International College, Ghana.

In 2001 the HRC changed its name to the International Heads Representative Committee (IHRC) to distinguish it from the four Regional Heads Representative Committees (RHRCs). The Chair of the IHRC from 2001 is Malcolm Lamb, of Pembroke School, South Australia.

Phil Thomas arrived at the International School of Geneva just as the school was embarkiing on the creation of the IB in 1963. He co-taught the first IB history class and later was very involved in establishing the first geography and economics IB programs. Phil retired from the school in 1998 having served in several positions from teacher to Assistant Director General. In 1978 Phil was elected head of the HSC; this led him to serve for twenty years on the Council of Foundation, fifteen as its Secretary and six on the Executive Committee. He has also undertaken the IB Diploma Holders Research Project since 1986; this is a database of the university destinations of IB diplomates and, in certain cases, it tracks their performance. From 1996 to 1999, Phil acted as co-ordinator of ISA's International Education System Pilot

Project, which is testing the feasibilty of creating a world system of schools. Phil renewed his association with IBO by acting as an interim staff member in the IBAEM office, responsible for diploma affairs during 2000.

Director General George Walker

I first met George Walker in the summer of 1991 just after his arrival as Director General of the International School of Geneva (Ecolint). He gave me accesss to the minutes of the Ecolint Board meetings which I needed to complete my research on the origins of the International Schools Association (ISA) and the IB Diploma Program. At the time I was Director of the International School of Sophia Antipolis, a bilingual English/French IB diploma school in the South of France. Ecolint is a complex organisation to manage and few have succeeded in doing it successfully. George Walker is one of those few.

George studied chemistry at Oxford and music at the University of Capetown in South Africa. After teaching science in Britain and then lecturing at the University of York he became Head of Heathcote School and then of Cavendish Comprenhensive School before going to Geneva. He assisted the founding of the Centre for the Study of Comprehensive Schools and was a member of several British government educational committees. This led to the award of an OBE in 1992 by the Queen for his services to education. In 1990 he returned to South Africa to write articles for *The Times* and taught in a school in a large township near Capetown. During his time as Director General of the International School of Geneva he has also been Visiting Professor of Education at the University of Bath from 1997, in the Centre for the Study of Education in an International Context.

George took up the position of Director General of the IBO in October 1999 in Geneva. He did not have to travel far—just across town to the other side of the lake from his previous location at the Grand Boissière School campus. This was a rather fitting transfer: from the birthplace of the Diploma Program to its present headquarters at 15 Route des Morillons.

George has written extensively on international education and school leadership. He is thoughtful, enthusiastic, inspiring, congenial, and a lateral thinker. He is an extremely accomplished classical pianist to the delight of those who have had the pleasure of hearing him play. The IBO is fortunate indeed to have as its Chief Executive Officer a person of his calibre.

Achievements of IB Students

There has been little research on the effect of the IB diploma on its thousands of graduates, but such research is slowly increasing. There is now ample evidence to show that IB students go on to lead interesting lives and to excel in different pursuits. Over the years, students have participated in many conferences and workshops to give feedback about how the IBO affected them and their careers. A few examples out of thousands follow.

One of the many highlights at the Montreux conference of 1999 was the presence of Julie Payette from Montreal, the first astronaut-in-training with an IB diploma (from Atlantic College in Wales). She went into space later in 1999.

Camilla Bredholt was Danish Woman of the Year in 1994 for her work in establishing Médecins Sans Frontières in Denmark, an organisation which gave assistance in Rwanda.

Eluned Morgan from Wales was the youngest member of the European Parliament in the last half of the 1990s and was appointed to the IBO's Council of Foundation in 2001.

Felicity Leach (daughter of Bob Leach who created the first diploma history program) from Geneva has been several times World Champion of the Lightweight Division of the single sculls for women.

The Crown Prince of the Netherlands, Prince Willem Alexander, is an IB diploma graduate.

Among IB diploma graduates active in various fields in 2000, Marcelo Calliari was Commissioner for CADE, the Brazilian equivalent of the US Trade Commission, appointed by the president; Andres Franco was Colombian Deputy Ambassador to the UN; Gaurav Kumar (from India) was working in the Navajo Nation on a research project sponsored by Johns Hopkins

University, involving the development of a new vaccine for children; Kristine Hauge Storholt (from Norway) was working for the World Bank on early childhood development in conflict and post-conflict countries in sub-Saharan Africa; Maria Dokmanovic (from Serbia) was doing genetic research related to obesity and was involved in a project to prevent child malnutrition in Serbia.

As a result of the war with Iraq in 1991, the Amman Baccalaureate School took the initiative to organise the first IB Student World Conference in July 1993, so that students could discuss the issues of conflict resolution, intercultural understanding, and how to aim for world peace. Other student conferences ensued in Osaka (1994), Dar-es-Salaam (1995), and Brisbane (1996), each with an attendance of about 150. The International School of Geneva organised a Students' Conference in October 1999 at the Palais Wilson (Headquarters of the UN High Commission for Human Rights) on 'Schools as Agents for Change'. The outcome was a Charter on Global Citizenship. The conference was attended by more than 200 students from fourteen IB schools across the world. The next IB World Student Conference was hosted by Upper Canada College, Toronto, in August 2002.

Notes to Chapter Eleven

[1] Ian Hill, *The International Baccalaureate: Policy Process in Education* (Unversity of Tasmania: PhD thesis), 115.

[2] Desmond Cole-Baker, letter to Ian Hill, 16th April, 1989.

[3] Desmond Cole-Baker, *An International Primary School Curriculum ISA* (Geneva: International Schools Association, 1970), 51.

[4] Cole-Baker, *International Primary School Curriculum ISA*, 161.

[5] *Ecole Internationale de Genève: 50e Anniversaire 1924–1974* (Geneva: Sprint, 1974), 225.

[6] *IB World* (December 1999), 49.

12
LOOKING AHEAD
Ian Hill

Where should the IBO be going? A number of controversial issues have arisen since 1986. The Director General in his Annual Report of 1985–86 argued that the IBO should address global issues such as pollution, nuclear proliferation, poverty, and the impact of new technologies.

This concern raised the more narrow question of whether there has been sufficient international balance in the IB diploma curriculum—a theme that has recurred almost every year. What does it mean to be international? Roger Peel offered the following thoughtful response:

> Is the IB just another variant of the proliferation of national systems around the world, or do we in fact provide a service that transcends such boundaries in ways that are unique? The answers to such questions depend to a large degree on our interpretation of 'international' and how we choose to infuse it into our curriculum. From my own perspective, the honesty of the IB stems from the fact that we require all students to relate first to their own national identity—their own language, literature, history, and cultural heritage, no matter where in the world this may be. Beyond that we ask that they identify with the corresponding traditions of others. It is not expected that they adopt alien points of view, merely that they are exposed to them and encouraged to respond intelligently. The end result, we hope, is a more compassionate population, a welcome manifestation of national diversity within an international framework of tolerant respect. Ideally, at the end of the IB experience, students should know themselves better than when they started while acknowledging that others can be right in being different. (*1988 Report of the Director General to the Council of Foundation*)

In 1989 the Director General recommended a new academic policy board to replace the Curriculum Board and take over some functions of the Bureau of Chief Examiners. The new body was to have the responsibility of overseeing all major issues of policy concerning the IB diploma curriculum and examinations (*Annual Report 1989*, 10). One of the academic policy board's first tasks was to have defined more precisely IBO's *international* aims and objectives across the curriculum. This body was not actually created until 1997, as the Academic Affairs Board.

Making the IB diploma more international continued to preoccupy the IBO during a four-day retreat in the US in 1993, where the future relevancy of the IB Diploma Program, particularly the Theory of Knowledge (TOK), was discussed. The retreat addressed the need to concentrate more on international issues and debated how to include them in TOK: the causes of conflict, environmental decay, consequences of intolerance, dangers of mob psychology, and acid rain. Content alone is not enough; the way content is discussed and delivered by remaining open to other cultural points of view is inherent in the development of an international perspective.

For the next three years the need to establish a research agenda dominated the discussion and in the Director of Examinations' Report for 1995–96, the development of a research unit at IBCA was mooted to analyse diploma examination results and seek answers to questions such as:

•How does the performance of girls compare with that of boys, by subject and level, within a session and between sessions, from one culture to another?

•What is the relationship between teachers' predicted grades and grades achieved?

•Does the accuracy of predicted grades increase the longer schools are in the programme?

•Is there a relationship between the size of the Diploma program in a given school and the quality of the predicted grades?

•Can parity of standards between subjects be ascertained and continuity of standards guaranteed year on year?

•Would greater use of archived scripts help answer some of these questions?

This is in-house statistical research related to diploma examinations (and to MYP moderated results) and is not to be confused with the Research Committee, which has a much wider agenda.

1996–97 saw the Director General encouraging a more imaginative design of the curriculum and asking again whether it was as international as it should be. There was also concern about overload of work for students and whether the IBO was over-assessing. Were the same skills being tested several times across different subject areas?

During 1998–99 a significant recommendation for the diploma was to develop Group 6 as an arts-only group to give more recognition to this area. This came into effect in September 2002 but students could still substitute a second subject from another group for an arts subject in Group 6. Dance and film as diploma subjects were first piloted in a small number of schools commencing in 2001 and this has further strengthened the presence of the arts in the IB diploma program.

Competition in the Educational Marketplace

Some research exists concerning the performance of IB students in higher education. Hayden and Wong reported that a small sample of admissions tutors in the UK "were all of the opinion that IB students are broadly knowledgeable, are equipped with research skills, are independent and able to work in teams. They are also recognised to be open-minded with respect to other cultural identities and modes of thought (354)."[1] As Hayden and Wong point out, it is difficult to demonstrate that these characteristics are due to the IB curriculum alone. Nevertheless, these comments echo those that have been made frequently over many years.

Phil Thomas of the International School of Geneva began a research project for the IBO in 1986 to track IB diploma holders through their university studies. One of the objectives was to solicit from a random sample of students and university lecturers in the US, Canada, and the UK whether the IB was an adequate preparation for tertiary studies.[2] Thomas's report concludes that the IB is a good preparation for university and that IB grades are reliable predictors of success in higher education.

Student responses to an IBO survey which each school completes every five years have consistently mentioned that the IB provides good preparation for higher education, teaches time management, allows students to acquire an *overall* understanding not restricted to single subjects, teaches students to 'think, not memorise', and prevents students from specialising too early. On the negative side, some students have said that the IB program is too stressful, the content of some subjects is excessive, deadlines for completion of assignments should be better spaced, and the obligation to do language A1 penalises those without literary appreciation skills.

Flodman, Malmström, and Thelin obtained data on the university destinations of 362 Swedish diploma holders from forty-four schools in different countries, the majority of them state schools in Sweden, during 1971–93.[3] Amongst the twenty-one questions in the survey instrument was the following: "How valuable do you think your diploma studies have been for university studies, other studies, career, life in general?" Responses were selected from a five-point scale: excellent, good, useful, little value, no value. Sixty-three per cent of the students attended universities in Sweden, 12 percent in the UK, 10 percent in the US, and the remainder in other countries. In relation to this question, 84 percent of the respondents said that the IB Diploma Program was an excellent (54 percent) or good (30 percent) preparation for university. Eighty-one per cent said that it was an excellent or good preparation for a career and for life. Only three percent indicated that the IB Diploma Program was of little or no value for university study, career, and life. The study shows a very high level of satisfaction with the IB Diploma Program.

In 1999 Duevel surveyed the registrars and (former and current) IB students of twelve US universities (including Columbia, Cornell, Harvard, and Stanford) to determine whether earning an IB diploma was a predictor of success at university and beyond.[4] The students had come from IB schools both in the US and overseas. Academic results showed that the successful completion of an IB Diploma Program was an effective predictor of completion of a first degree at university. IB diploma holders, reflecting as adults on their high school experiences, university performance, and career choice indicated that a combination of the following factors of the IB program contributed to their success:

> challenging integration of topics offering both breadth and depth; necessity to be highly productive throughout the two-year course; requirement to develop strong study skills; emphasis on developing

strong writing, research, and analytical thinking skills; adopting a global view and considering one's role within the wider world. (Duevel, 94)

Some concern about possible competition from Cambridge University with its AICE (Advanced International Certificate of Education) and the USA AP International Certificate was expressed in the mid-1990s. The IBO policy has been to grow slowly and steadily without deliberately seeking out markets which would result in a large number of schools applying for IBO authorisation. Quality has always been more important than quantity.

The IBO maintains very cordial relationships with both UCLES (University of Cambridge Local Examinations Syndicate) and the United States College Board. Representatives from UCLES have been invited to IBCA for discussions about examination procedures and other educational exchanges, and from the early 1960s Harlan 'Harpo' Hanson, Director of the College Board's Advanced Placement Program, was involved in the development of the IB diploma, and regularly attended Council of Foundation meetings until just before his death in 1996.

The IBO realises that it is in an ever-increasing market place for international education; at the same time the IBO is unique in that its programs belong to *no* country and its mission is unashamedly global but respectful of people's cultural origins.

The real test is whether schools continue with the IB and whether interest grows. The evidence published in the annual statistical bulletins of the IB Organisation and on its public website, is that few schools leave the organisation, while the average world growth rate in the number of schools was around fifteen percent in 2001. It would appear to be fulfilling the expectations of the vast majority of its students, their parents, and teachers in providing quality preparation for higher education.

Access to IB Programs in the Developing World

During the last ten years or more the IBO Executive Committee and Council of Foundation have been grappling with the vexed question of equity of access to the Diploma Program (and more lately to the MYP and PYP) for schools in the developing world. The reality is that there are 'first-world schools' (usually international schools for expatriates) in third-world countries where the budget of the school is not largely dependent on local economic conditions. Although these schools suffer from having to send teachers on long-distance flights to attend IBO workshops and from the increased communication costs that distance imposes (the advent of email has assisted here) they generally do not have major problems in meeting the IBO annual fees. Then there are the 'national' schools—private or state—where the school budget is linked to the economy of the country and the cost of IBO's annual fees, sending teachers to workshops in other countries, postage costs, and so on, represent a very large part of their income. The IBO programs are therefore overpriced for them and they are under-represented in the lists of IBO schools.

Implementing a sliding scale of IBO annual fees is not the answer. It has been discussed on several occasions and it would create more problems than it would solve. Soft currencies are notoriously fluctuating and unpredictable, so arriving at any equitable comparison of buying power in developing countries is extremely difficult, particularly if one adds the factor of potential political instability and the individual nature of schools themselves. The solution which has been agreed to is that the IBO should seek financial support for projects involving local schools. Possible donors might be USAID, the World Bank, the European Union, the African Development Bank, private companies, and individual benefactors. Regional offices can identify the schools which genuinely need assistance and funds raised would then be targeted at specific projects so that the donors know exactly where the money is going. A few projects in this vein are being undertaken or developed.

A development plan for the next five years of the IBO was produced in 1985 by the Executive Committee. One of its main objectives was "to increase the number of international schools in the developing world, to introduce the IB diploma into a number of selected national institutions in developing countries, and to seek financial assistance from government and international aid programs."[5] Each subsequent annual report until the present refers to the need to assist schools in the developing world to offer the IBO programs. The Executive Committee in 1988 reiterated that the IBO has an important role to play in the developing world where the main obstacle is financial. "Grants should be sought from international aid agencies and intergovernmental organisations to fund special projects and scholarship programs which have been investigated and approved by the IBO" (*IBO Annual Report 1987–88*, 24). In relation to these objectives how much was achieved by 2002?

The number of *international* schools in the developing world *did* increase over the years in parts of Asia and Africa, while in Latin America, Eastern Europe, and the Balkans the increase has occurred in *national* schools, both state and private. This is because there are not many international schools in those regions; for example, in Latin America there were only seventeen international schools out of a total of 142 by June 2002. There were, for example, 22 state schools in Eastern Europe by June 2002, one of these had been financed from European Commission funding to the government, and 22 private schools, including six national schools (no state schools) in Africa. There was European Commission funding from 1986 until 1996 for eighteen Basotho students to cover their IB Diploma Program fees at Machabeng High School, Lesotho (in Southern Africa) and a similar number of Swaziland students benefited from these scholarships to study the IB diploma course at the UWC of Southern Africa— Waterford Kamhlaba in Mbabane. After 1996 the scholarships were maintained by private and semi-government bodies.

From 1994 a number of approaches were made to the European Commission and to the respective governments for the funding of a state school in Dakar, Senegal and Soweto, South Africa. The government in Senegal agreed to put the IB diploma in to the Maison d'Education Mariama Bâ on the island of Gorée and to make this an IB lycée of excellence also open to some students from other countries in West Africa; however the funding from the European Commission became problematic and in 2000 it became necessary to renegotiate with a new government and new minister for education—this was accomplished but funding has not yet been found. The government of South Africa was warming to the idea of the IB diploma being established in a state school, the Reasoma High School, Soweto in 1999 after several years of negotiations. The Linden International School in

Johannesburg (an IB diploma school until 2002) found funding through an organisation in the Netherlands to send ten teachers from the school to an IBO training workshop in Budapest in 1998. The Reasoma High School is one of the best-performing state schools for black children in South Africa. The enthusiastic head, Mrs Smileth Ntutela, told me that at the beginning of each year there is a line of over 100 parents with children who wait for days to obtain a place; some remain in her office all day—sitting, hoping, weeping quietly when she tells them that the school is full. Those who have suffered through lack of education place an extremely high value on such opportunities for their children; it is a lesson to any of us who take good education for granted.

Government permission to allow a foreign program in state schools is not always easy to obtain, and this is no less true of Africa; it can take considerable time to build up credibility and establish the IBO's good intentions. Having an IB program in one or two state schools would provide an educational laboratory for pedagogical exchanges between the IBO and the governments (as has occurred very well in Eastern Europe, parts of Latin America, China, and Vietnam, for example), and this mutual benefit needs to be emphasised. The Ford Foundation was revisited and the World Bank, but more remains to be done. A major problem is to gain continuity of funding, especially following the worldwide donor fatigue of the 1990s and with the knowledge that it is educationally unwise—and perhaps morally reprehensible—if schools enter an IBO program only to drop out because of a lack of ongoing support.

Alec Peterson's Three Questions

Alec Peterson finished the first edition of this book in 1986 with a chapter then entitled 'Some Issues for the Future' (Chapter 8 above) in which he attempted to answer three questions:

1. What do we mean by international education and is it desirable?
2. If desirable, how should it be taught and to whom?
3. Who should provide it?

All these years later, how relevant are these questions and to what extent has the IBO responded to them?

The concept of international education is elusive, like the concept of an international school. Alec's analysis emphasises the role of international education in promoting intercultural understanding with a view to eradicating terrorism and ethnic conflicts. He sees a need to educate for national pride at the same time as for respect of other cultures. The rationale for an international education includes the protection of the environment, the global nature of communication and economics, and the need for global ethics in science and technology—because of the fact that the world is increasingly interdependent. The IBO has been constantly asking how international its programs are and has tried to identify some content and objectives pertaining to an international education. So the question is indeed still relevant and the IBO continues to exist because an international education (whatever that means exactly) *is* desirable. It is only through education which teaches respect for others and mutual understanding that there is a possibility of moving towards the 'culture of peace' which UNESCO attempts to promote.

After some years of discussion, the IBO Council of Foundation adopted in 1996 a mission statement which expounds the principles of international education on which its three programs are based:

> Through comprehensive and balanced curricula coupled with challenging assessments, the International Baccalaureate Organisation aims to assist schools in their endeavours to develop the individual talents of young people and teach them to relate the experience of the classroom to the realities of the world outside. Beyond intellectual rigour and high academic standards, strong emphasis is placed on the ideals of international understanding and responsible citizenship, to the end that IB students may become critical and compassionate thinkers, lifelong learners, and informed participants in local and world affairs, conscious of the shared humanity that binds all people together while respecting the variety of cultures and attitudes that makes for the richness of life. (IBO Mission Statement, 1996)

Alec suggests a further manifestation of international education in the IB diploma: the development of a different type of Standard Level (SL) subject which would be interdisciplinary, more related to international human problems and a terminating course (rather than as preparation for a corresponding university discipline). Is it by accident or design that the IBO has been piloting three interdisciplinary subjects at standard level along these lines since 2001?

•Text and Performance SL (Groups 1 and 6: literature and the arts);
•Ecosystems and Societies SL (Groups 3 and 4: humanities and experimental sciences);
•World Cultures SL (Groups 3 and 6: humanities and the arts).

The second question—how should an international education be taught and to whom?—is very pertinent to the discussion of growth and equity of access for the IBO. Alec cites an IBO Ten Year Plan recommending that the IB diploma should be available in "every city containing a large international community." This aim has been achieved but the IBO needs to move further. What commenced essentially as a program for international schools (which are usually taken to mean private schools with internationally mobile students of many nationalities) has increasingly attracted the interest of state and private 'national' schools. So both national and international students are receiving an IB education. The IBO's target for some years now has been to extend its influence to 'national' students in the developing world.

In his discussion about who should provide the IB diploma, Alec dismisses the idea of a UN agency or national governments taking on the role because of the need to maintain educational independence from politics. He proposes that individual governments furnish an increasing proportion of the costs to allow the IBO to continue. The reverse has taken place: almost all revenue, since the late 1980s, has been coming from annual school registration fees. Aside from government payments of fees to cover the registration of state schools in their countries, only Canada, Germany, Hong Kong, Japan, Norway, and Switzerland now contribute any annual sum to the IBO. Governments do assist in different ways; they are partners with whom the IBO can exchange ideas and who can integrate educational practices from IBO programs into national systems as an investment for a peaceful future. For example, recent secondary education reforms in Malta and Switzerland have incorporated compulsory versions of

Theory of Knowledge and an Extended Essay respectively. A number of government representatives have also promoted IBO programs in intergovernmental organisations, particularly those associated with the UN, the Council of Europe, and the European Union. The IBO is looking elsewhere to raise money for certain projects from a range of donor agencies and individuals.

At the school level, it is no longer international schools which are the major providers of international education; national schools, both state and private, are now almost equal partners.

The IBO and the Future

Will the IBO one day move into higher education with accredited international programs? Will the IBO open up the Diploma Program in the future to include vocationally-oriented courses and thus make it available to a wider ability range than at present? Neither of these suggestions has been considered a priority in the short term; there are other preoccupations.[6]

The December 1993 Council of Foundation meeting "was marked by the unhappiness expressed by a minority of long standing members . . . that the organisation had abandoned its past and was losing its way" (*Annual Report 1993–94*, 2). Director General Roger Peel, with customary diplomacy, pointed to a possible lack of communication to the Council members about what was actually being achieved. Nevertheless, this incident sparked a somewhat turbulent episode in the IBO's history and perhaps gave the first warning that some reform would be necessary in the future.

During the latter half of 1998 and 1999 the IBO Executive Committee employed outside consultants to review the governance and management of the IBO and to make recommendations for the future. The major agenda for reform sought to streamline the governance structure, to strengthen the role and representation of the regions, and to make the distinction between management and governance.

The IBO was governed by a Council of Foundation with a tripartite structure of nine representatives from each of the following areas: governments, heads of IBO schools, and *ad personam* members. This structure was changed at the Council of Foundation meeting in May 2000 and came into full effect from May 2001 when the Council was reduced to sixteen members drawn from the following:

•one from each of the four newly-created Regional Advisory Committees (RACs);
•one from each of the four newly-created Regional Heads Representative Committees (RHRCs);
•the Chair of the International Heads Representative Committee (IHRC);
•three *ad personam* members: the President, Treasurer and Chair of the Board of Examiners, and the Director General (the only non-voting member).

Regional committees correspond to the four administrative regions of the IBO: Africa/Europe/Middle East, Asia-Pacific, Latin America, North America and the Carribean. The Executive Committee was subsumed by the Council of Foundation and ceased to exist separately.

The Standing Conference of Governments (SCG) was created in 1977 and membership of the SCG required an annual financial contribution to the IBO. By 1987 there had been a decline in the financial support from governments; this led to a new form of collaboration whereby membership of the SCG meant either contributing financially or undertaking activities that would promote IB programs in the country. The SCG met annually at the same time as the Council of Foundation and nine of its members were elected to the Council for a three year term. From May 2001 a new Government Advisory Committee (GAC) was formed by the Director General and the SCG ceased to function; the reader will have noted that government representation is not guaranteed on the new council although any one or more of the RAC nominations may be a government representative. The GAC consists of ten senior civil servants or advisors on education in diverse government systems appointed by the Director General for an initial two-year term. The purpose of the group is to further promote IBO-government co-operation in a number of ways which include: official recognition of IBO programs, exchanges of pedagogical ideas, research of mutual interest, setting up pilot projects in state schools in developing countries, teacher training, and IBO input into national education reforms seeking to internationalise the curriculum.

The Conference of Heads of IB Schools (HSC), founded in 1978, comprises all IBO schools who elected a Heads Representative Committee (HRC) worldwide. The HRC met two or three times a year and nine of its members were elected to the Council of Foundation; this gave a third of the voting rights under the old system. As one of its tasks it organised world conferences of heads of IB schools; these have been held, at first annually, and then every two years since 1994. From 1986 the following conferences have taken place: Paris 1986, Washington DC, 1987; Geneva, 1988; Singapore, 1989; Anaheim, California, 1990; Barcelona, 1992; Buenos Aires, 1993; Ottawa, 1994; Jakarta, 1996; Montreux, 1998; Ghana, 2000; and Cancún, 2003.

Attendance at the conferences has increased over the years from about 100 in Paris in 1986 to 400 in Montreux in 1998, except for the workshop in Ghana in 2000; this was the first in Africa for the HSC and it attracted a lesser number of participants (110) due to the longer distances, increased cost, increased time away from schools and—regrettably—apprehension on the part of some that Africa presented dangers from malaria and civil unrest. These conferences provide an important opportunity for heads of IB schools to meet, for exchanges of information and ideas with IBO staff, and for getting to know how IBO programs function in schools in different parts of the world.

Under the new structure the HRC's name changed to the IHRC (International Heads Representative Committee) in 2001, and this body was no longer directly elected by the heads of IBO schools. Instead heads elected their own Regional Heads Representative Committees (RHRCs) of eight members towards the end of 2000, voting only for candidates in their own region. Each RHRC then nominated four of its members to form the IHRC. Once formed, the IHRC elected its chair, vice-chair and secretary, and recommended four of its members—one from each of the RHRCs represented on the international committee—plus the chair of the IHRC to be members of the Council of Foundation. This is the new procedure; it ensures more equitable geographical representation on the IHRC and provides for more informed voting since heads of schools are no longer asked to consider candidates worldwide.

The Council of Foundation had usually been held in November at the Palais des Nations, Geneva. A change occurred in November 1994 when it was held outside Geneva for the first time—in Copenhagen. There was no meeting in 1995 as the annual timing changed to May, so the next Council of Foundation meeting occurred in May 1996 in Amman, Jordan, at the invitation of HRH Princess Sarvath El Hassan. In the following years the annual Council of Foundation meeting was held in Boston (1997), Montreux, Switzerland (1998), and Budapest (1999). The Montreux conference celebrated the 30th Anniversary of the IBO. In May 2000 and subsequent years the Council of Foundation May meeting returned to its 'home' at the Palais des Nations, Geneva.

The new governance structure which came into effect in 2001 provided for Regional Advisory Committees in each of the four IBO regions—Africa/Europe/Middle East, Asia Pacific, Latin America, and North America (where a Board already existed). Membership includes heads of IBO schools, government and university representatives, with provision for other members drawn from one or more of the following: intergovernmental organisations (UNESCO, for example), former IB students, donor agencies, international corporations, and non-government organisations. These committees are to support and advise the Regional Directors on matters which include the recognition and promotion of IB programs, coping with growth, targetting particular countries or sub-regions which are under-represented with IB schools, assisting with any difficult authorization recommendations, service to prospective and existing IB schools. One member from each of the four Regional Advisory Committees is nominated to the council, thus strengthening the input from the regions.

A number of management issues were signalled, including the implementation of a corporate human resources policy, checking for legal consistency in all IBO public documents, using technology to improve internal and external communication (the installation of video-conferencing facilities to reduce staff travel and the establishment of the On-line Curriculum Centre for schools, for example), and setting standards for a corporate image in publications, web pages, and media presence.

An external relations and media attaché was appointed to the IB headquarters in Geneva in late 1999. This position was renamed Head of Corporate Relations in 2000 and the Corporate Relations Department came into existence in 2001 with the appointment of an assistant. The academic committee structure also underwent some changes to improve its responsiveness to educational issues surrounding the IBO programs. Regional Directors had not been part of the senior management team. In line with the increased involvement of the regions in the governance structure, all Regional Directors became fully integrated into the senior management team of the IBO in early 2000 and the heads of information communication technology and human resources were added to that team a few months later.

The Challenge of Expansion

The increasing number of schools applying for authorisation to do one or more of the IBO programs caused the IBO to ask: 'Do we want to continue to increase the number of schools in this way or do we want to look at using our accumulated reputation in developing new partnerships and influencing the education system of others; that is, to grow in different ways?'

The organisation took a decision to grow in different ways as a number of ideas were discussed. Consideration was given to establishing criteria to target certain types of schools and thus limit the number of schools accepted in a given year (if this should become necessary); this would also free up more time for other activities. Preference for authorisation might be given to certain categories—for example, schools offering only IBO programs, schools with at least fifty percent of the corresponding total school population involved in an IBO program, schools which have something particular to bring to the organisation (for example, links in a country where there was previously no IBO program, a school which can influence practices in local state schools, a school teaching in French, Spanish, or Chinese), schools offering more than one IBO program, schools in clusters which provide a critical mass to attract funding. Offering an IBO program should be seen as more than a competitive marketing device.

Another way to create time for existing personnel, to keep abreast of growth without having a commensurate increase in staff, and to involve the member schools was to out-source certain activities to teachers, administrators, schools, or clusters of schools on short-term contract. This might include certain teacher-training workshops for a region, authorisation and program evaluation visits, and exam inspection visits for the diploma. This was already occurring to some extent around the world, but again not in a systematic way.

The strategic plan identified "horizontal growth" as the expansion of authorised schools which takes place naturally. This horizontal growth had been achieved at the expense of "vertical growth"—the development of activities beyond accumulating member schools. The plan was to redress the imbalance and to ensure that the IBO had structures and time to undertake the important dimension of "vertical growth." A number of areas were identified and procedures were put in place to move this forward.

Future Developments

Activities beyond sustaining the membership included research in international education, consultancies, new approaches to learning, and partnerships with a range of institutions or individuals: intergovernmental organisations (UN agencies, European Union, Council of Europe), higher education institutions, governments, assessment authorities, non-government organisations (for example, ISS, ECIS), private companies, and donor organisations. Some of these activities had been taking place, but on an *ad hoc* basis. The plan for the future was to strengthen these aspects, to provide time for them, and to make them officially part of the organisation's agenda.

An IBO research unit was established at the beginning of 2000 at the University of Bath in the Centre for the Study of Education in an International Context. To strengthen the intellectual underpinning of the organisation, a Director of International Education was appointed at the beginning of 2000 who was responsible for the research unit and for stimulating discussion on international education issues. The quality and international dimension of the IBO programs must be maintained and developed in line with research in international education. The IBO has increasingly become a major player in undertaking such research, in discussing international education issues through publications and conferences, and in implementing practices in its own programs. An IBO electronic and printed *Journal of Research in International Education* was launched in September 2002 in conjunction with the joint IBO/CEIC conference on international education in Geneva.

The IBO commenced work on enunciating a common set of values and pedagogical principles for the PYP, MYP, and Diploma Program, with appropriate continuity and progression. Monographs on each of the programs and one on the articulation between them were published in 2002. The status of the arts was enhanced in the Diploma Program together with more flexibility in the hexagon. Beginning in 2002 the PYP and MYP became more regionally responsive in the way they are put into practice within a centrally determined framework. Therefore a balance between central and regional responsibilities was established for the future development, management, quality control and dissemination of these two programs. Policies and procedures to allow schools to teach the PYP and MYP in languages other than the official IBO languages of English, French, and Spanish (and Chinese for the MYP) were introduced. The PYP and MYP offer frameworks with the potential to fundamentally transform the educational thinking and practice of a school.

A committee to review current linguistic practice and recommend a language policy for the future was established in 2002. The cost of translation of documents and simultaneous interpretation at conferences is significant and the number of schools offering IBO programs in French is regrettably low and decreases each year in proportion to the number of new IB schools, the majority of which teach in English. The IBO needs a policy which is culturally sensitive and financially acceptable. At the same time, the IBO has signed a contract with the German government to provide three diploma subjects in German beginning in 2003: History, Biology, and Theory of Knowledge. This is a pilot project for five years which is being funded by Germany so that the IB diploma can be offered initially in fourteen German overseas schools. Jordan and Dubai have shown interest in funding a project to offer some subjects in Arabic in the diploma.

A new Deputy Director General position was created and filled at the commencement of 2000, and part of that role was to develop existing relationships and to seek out new relationships with intergovernmental organisations, governments, and other institutions. Mrs Sylvia Gordon, a former teacher at the United Nations International School (UNIS), was appointed the IBO's representative to the UN in New York in 2000, in the same way that Mrs Ruth Bonner was for the UN and its agencies in Geneva.

Equity of Access

The IBO's claim to offer an international education from age three to the end of secondary school was somewhat at odds with the fact that it was still too expensive for state and many national private schools in the developing world. Raising money to implement IBO programs in those countries was part of the solution, but only a part. There was much work to do in the training of teachers in a pedagogical approach which depends on an understanding of the principles of international education on which IBO programs are based. This takes time. Then there was the political problem for a government in the developing world being seen to offer education privileges to one or two state schools, even if someone else was paying.

The IBO explored how its programs could be enjoyed more widely and be more acceptable to governments in the developing world. Modest attempts had already been made, with some success in Eastern Europe, to set up a state school as an 'educational laboratory' with one or more IBO programs, thus promoting a pedagogical exchange between the government and IBO education experts. This is particularly useful where a government is undertaking a reform of its education system. Because they are for all ability ranges and there are no external examinations, the PYP and MYP offer even more possibilities than the Diploma Program for 'exploitation' by governments.

Already a number of local state schools in the developing world were benefitting from some of the community service activities of IB schools. Students provided books, writing utensils, school buildings, furniture, and so on. They taught literacy and numeracy skills to younger children and adults; they devised survival skills programs for street children and invited them regularly into their schools. At this level, IBO schools were supporting the Education for All initiative co-ordinated by UNESCO after the famous meeting in Dakar, Senegal, in April 2000, and were assisting the governments of some countries to provide education to their people. These examples of collaboration needed to be expanded.

In 2001 and 2002 a project was developed with the Nigerian government to set up four model schools in the country offering the PYP and to use these schools as laboratories for research into teacher professional development in collaboration with teacher training institutions in the country and abroad. The idea was not to introduce the PYP *en masse* into schools in Nigeria but to find out which PYP pedagogical approaches would be transferable to local Nigerian schools to improve the quality of education. A similar project was being developed in 2002 with a state school in a disadvantaged neighbourhood of Casablanca in partnership with he Ministry of Education and a private bank.

In September 2002 primary school teacher-training workshops took place in two cities in Cambodia, run by PYP teachers in partnership with UNESCO, the Cambodian government and the IB regional office in Singapore. Again, the idea was to apply some PYP pedagogical approaches to state schools, not to have more schools adopting the PYP *per se*.

The IBO established a development office within the New York regional office in 2001, to assist new and existing projects which would enable the organisation to extend its influence beyond its immediate family of schools. The office seeks appropriate funding from donor agencies and individuals. In addition to enhancing the IBO presence in the developing world, funding is sought to support research projects and initiatives such as the Online Curriculum Centre.

Success and Recognition

By its very existence, the IBO defines international education: principles of international education underpin its three programs. It is the major provider in the world of this type of education for school-age children. It is the only provider of international education in three languages: English, French, and Spanish. (The MYP is also available in Chinese). The Diploma Program is setting an international benchmark for other national awarding bodies in many countries. More national systems are showing interest in applying IBO ideas or in implementing one or more of its programs. The ten thousandth diploma was awarded in 1985; the hundred thousandth diploma in the May 2000 exam session. By June 2002 there was a total of 1,368 IBO member schools in 113 countries; 161 schools were teaching two of the programs, and 31 were offering all three. Of this total, 150 schools were teaching in Spanish and 82 in French.

The following comments are an indication of the increasing impact that the IB diploma has in the world today. There is no reason why the younger MYP and PYP cannot have a similar impact.

Hywel Jones, Director, Task force Human Resources, Education, Training and Youth, Commission of the European Community (Brussels, 1990):

> The IB is one of the most innovative contributions to international education this century. It is a bold experiment that has been remarkably successful, and it has made an invaluable contribution both to the promotion of international understanding and as an educational service for a professionally mobile population.

Annick Goulet, former IB diploma student at the Collège de Jean-de-Brébeuf, Montréal (1991):

> After the IB diploma, I began to evaluate the program in terms of contributions to new life experiences. It was then that I came to consider the IB as a real heritage because it bequeaths to its former students more than well-articulated knowledge and skills in the traditional disciplines. It really inculcates a critical approach, an efficient work method, a way of synthesising, a discipline and, more than anything else, an openness to the world.

Lord Mountbatten went to Geneva in 1971 to present the first official IB diplomas for the International School of Geneva. Georges-Henri Martin, member of the board of the school and editor of the *Tribune de Genève,* received him on behalf of the city and the international school and exclaimed: "Le jour viendra où Genève sera fière d'avoir été le berceau de deux grandes idées généreuses—la Croix-Rouge et le Baccalauréat International" ['The day will come when the city of Geneva will be proud to have been the birthplace of two great and noble ideas—the Red Cross and the International Baccalaureate.']⁷

The IB is not yet as well known as the Red Cross and Red Crescent but its reputation continues to grow. The founding fathers have much to be proud of. The IBO remains alert to the needs of those it serves and to the currents of education around the globe, and is engaging in more partnerships (beyond those schools which offer its programs) which will be mutually rewarding as the IBO pursues its grand mission: the shaping of world citizens.

Notes to Chapter Eleven

¹ M. Hayden and C. Wong, 'The International Baccalaureate: International Education and Cultural Preservation', *Educational Studies*, vol. 23, no. 3 (1997): 349–361.

² Phil Thomas, *IB Diploma Holders Research Project: Progress Report Prepared for the Director General* (Geneva: IBO, 1991).

³ M. Flodman, H. Malmström, and A. Thelin, 'Swedish IB Diploma Holders Research Study, 1971–1993', *IB Research Notes*, vol. 2, issue 2 (April 2002). See the IBO research pages at http://www.ibo.org.

⁴ L. Duevel, *The International Baccalaureate Experience: University Perseverance, Attainment, and Perspectives on the Process* (Purdue University: PhD thesis, 1999).

⁵ *Annual Report 1985–86: Prepared for the Council of Foundation* (IBO, November 1986), 25.

⁶ The following discussion draws heavily on the new Director General's strategic plan for the five years beginning 2000 and this plan's subsequent revisions. See George Walker, *A Draft Strategic Plan* (Geneva: IBO, February 2000).

⁷ G. Renaud, 'Genèse d'une Révolution Pédagogique', in M. Manzitti and J. McLellan, eds., *International Schools Association: 50 Years of International Education, 1951–2001* (Humboldt, Argentina: Lotrec Artes Graficas, 2001).

APPENDIX A

SCHOOLS OFFERING THE IB
DIPLOMA PROGRAM
OCTOBER 2002 (1,050 SCHOOLS)

For more information about IB programs and schools, go to www.ibo.org.

Antilles

Curaçao International School

Argentina

Asociación Escuelas Lincoln
Colegio Bluebell
Colegio De La Salle
Colegio Lincoln
Colegio Mark Twain
Colegio Martín y Omar
Colegio Padre Luis María
Colegio Palermo Chico
Colegio Puerto Madryn
Colegio San Ignacio
Colegio San Marcos
Colegio San Martín de Tours
Colegio San Pablo
Colegio San Patricio
Colegio San Pedro Apóstol
Colegio Suizo

Colegio Tarbut
Colegio Todos Los Santos
Escuela de Educación
Escuela Goethe Rosario-8222
Escuela J.F. Kennedy
Holy Trinity College
Instituto San Jorge
Instituto San Patricio
Instituto Santa Brígida
Islands International School
New Model International School
Northern International School
Northlands School
Quilmes High School
Riverside School
Southern International School
St Andrew's Scots School
St Catherine's School
St George's College
St George's College North
St John's, Argentina
St Mary of the Hills School
St Mary's International College
St Xavier's College
Sunrise School
Villa Devoto School
Washington School

Australia

Bega Valley Christian College
Carey Baptist Grammar School
Central Coast Grammar School
Friends' School
Geelong Grammar School
German School J. Gutenberg
Glenunga International High School
Ivanhoe Grammar School
Kilmore International School

King Khalid Islamic College of Victoria
Kooralbyn International School
Kormilda College
Launceston College
Lauriston Girls' School
Macedon Grammar School
Mercedes College
Methodist Ladies' College
Methodist Ladies' College School
Montessori School Kingsley Inc.
Narrabundah College
New England School
Pembroke School
Presbyterian Ladies' College
Prince Alfred College
Queenwood School for Girls
Somerset College
St Leonard's College
St Paul's School, Penrith
St Peter's College
Sydney Church of England Co-educational Grammar School,
    Redlands
Sydney Institute of Technology
Tintern Grammar School
Trinity Grammar School
Wesley College, Melbourne
Woodcroft College

Austria

American International School, Vienna
Danube International School
Linz International School Auhof
Vienna International School

Azerbaijan

International School of Azerbaijan

Bahrain

Bahrain Bayan School
Bahrain School
Ibn Khuldoon School
Modern Knowledge Schools
Naseem International School

Belgium

Antwerp International School
Brussels International School
Scandinavian School, Brussels
St John's International School Waterloo

Bermuda

Bermuda High School for Girls

Bolivia

Bolivia American International School

Bosnia-Herzegovina

Druga Gimnazija Sarajevo

Botswana

Westwood International School

Brazil

Associação Escola Graduada de São Paulo

British School Rio de Janeiro
Colégio Suíço-Brasileiro
Curitiba International School
Escola Americana de Rio de Janeiro
Escola Maria Imaculada
Escola Suíço-Brasileira
St Nicholas School
St Paul's School, São Paulo

Brunei

International School Brunei

Cambodia

International School of Phnom Penh

Canada

Abbotsford Senior Secondary School
Academie St Cecile International School
Archbishop MacDonald High School
Ashbury College
Bellerose Composite High School
Britannia Secondary School
Burnaby South Secondary School
Cameron Heights Collegiate Institute
Campbell Collegiate
Catholic Central High School
CEGEP de Saint-Jérôme
CEGEP Régional de Lanaudière à l'Assomption
Central Elgin Collegiate Institute
Champlain Regional College
Collège André-Laurendeau
Collège Catholique Franco-Ouest
Collège Français
Collège François-Xavier-Garneau

Collège Jean-de-Brébeuf
Collège Laflèche
Colonel By Secondary School
E.L. Crossley Secondary School
Ecole Mathieu-Martin
Elmwood School
Father Lacombe High School
Glenlyon-Norfolk School
Halifax Grammar School
Harry Ainlay High School
Henry Wise Wood High School
Holy Heart of Mary High School
Holy Trinity Academy
Jasper Place High School
John G. Diefenbaker High School
Kelvin High School
King's-Edgehill School
Kingston Collegiate and VI
L'École S.P. Deslauriers
Le Petit Séminaire (Hull)
Lindsay Thurber High School
Lo-Ellen Park Secondary School
Lord Elgin High School
Luther College
M.E. La Zerte High School
McNally School
Michael Power-St Joseph High School
Miles Macdonell Collegiate
Moira Secondary School
Mountain Secondary School
New Westminster Secondary School
Nicholson Catholic College
North Battleford High School
Notre Dame Secondary School
Old Scona High School
Park View Centre
Pope John Paul II Catholic Secondary School
Port Moody Secondary School
Regiopolis-Notre Dame Catholic High School
Richmond Secondary School

Ross Sheppard High School
Salisbury High School
Semiahmoo Secondary School
Séminaire de Sherbrooke
Silver Heights Collegiate
Sir Winston Churchill CVI
Sir Winston Churchill High School, Calgary
Sir Winston Churchill Secondary School, Vancouver
St Francis Xavier Secondary School
St John High School
St Mary's High School, Calgary
St Robert Catholic High School
Strathcona-Tweedsmuir School
Sydney Academy
Thom Collegiate
Toronto French School
Turner Fenton Campus
United World College of the Pacific/Lester B. Pearson
Upper Canada College
Vanier College
Vaughan Road Academy
Victoria Park Secondary School
Victoria School
West Vancouver Secondary School
Western Canada High School
Weston Collegiate Institute
Westwood Collegiate
Winston Churchill High School
York School

Chile

Colegio La Maisonnette
Colegio SEK-Chile
Craighouse
Grange School
Liceo Siete
Mackay School
Mayflower School

Nido de Aguilas International School
Redland School
Santiago College
St Gabriel's School
St John's School Chile
St Margaret's School
St Paul's School
Wenlock School

China

Beijing BISS International School
Beijing Huijia Private School
Beijing International School
Beijing World Youth Academy
Chinese International School
French International School, Hong Kong
Guangdong Country Garden School
Li Po Chun United World College of Hong Kong
Nanjing International School
Sha Tin College
Shanghai American School
Shanghai High School
Taipei American School
TEDA International School, Tianjin
Yew Chung Secondary International School

Colombia

Aspaen Iragua
Colegio Anglo-Colombiano
Colegio Bogotá
Colegio Británico
Colegio Colombo Británico
English School Bogotá
Gimnasio del Norte
Gimnasio Los Alcázares
Gimnasio Los Cerros

Costa Rica

British School of Costa Rica
European School, Costa Rica
Lincoln School

Croatia

XV Gimnazija

Cyprus

American International School, Cyprus

Czech Republic

British International School, Prague
English College in Prague
Prague International School

Denmark

Birkeröd Gymnasium
Copenhagen International School
Herlufsholm Skole
Nörre Gymnasium
Nyborg Gymnasium

Dominican Republic

St George School

Ecuador

Academia Cotopaxi American International School

British School, Quito
Colegio Americano de Guayaquil
Colegio Americano, Quito
Colegio Experimental Alberto Einstein
Colegio Intisana
Colegio Los Pinos
Colegio Politécnico (COPOL)
Colegio SEK-Ecuador, Guayaquil
SEK-Ecuador, Quito

Egypt

Cairo British International School
Cairo College
Egypt American International School

El Salvador

Academia Británica Cuscatleca

Ethiopia

International Community School of Addis Ababa
Sandford English Community School

Fiji

Suva International School

Finland

Helsingin Suomalainen Yhteisko
Helsinki International School
Joensuun Lyseon Lukio
Jyväskylän Lyseon Lukio

Kuopion Lyseon Lukio
Mattlidens Gymnasium
Oulun Lyseon
Tampereen Lyseon
Tikkurilan Lukio
Turun normaalikoulu
Vasa övningsskola

France

American School of Paris
Centre International de Valbonne-Sophia Antipolis International
    School
Ecole Active Bilingue Jeannine Manuel (Lille)
Ecole Active Bilingue Jeannine Manuel (Paris)
International Bilingual School of Provence
International School of Nice
International School of Paris
International School of Toulouse

Germany

Bavarian International School
Berlin Brandenburg International School
Berlin British School
Berlin International School
Bonn International School e.V.
Dresden International School e.V.
Düsseldorf International School
Frankfurt International School
Friedrich-Ebert-Gymnasium
Goethe-Gymnasium
Hamburg International School
International School of the Hannover Region
Leipzig International School e.V.
Munich International School
Schule Schloss Salem
Stuttgart International School

Ghana

Lincoln Community School
SOS-Hermann Gmeiner International College

Greece

American Community Schools of Athens
Anatolia College
Athens College (HAEF)
Campion School
Costeas-Gitonas School
Doukas School
Geitona School
I.M. Panayotopoulos School
Moraitis School
Pinewood School of Thessaloniki
St Catherine's British Embassy School
TASIS Hellenic International School

Guam

St John's School

Gautemala

Centro Escolar 'El Roble'

Honduras

American School of Tegucigalpa

Hungary

American International School of Budapest
British International School Budapest
Karinthy Gimnázium

Iceland

Menntaskóliin vid Hamrahlíd

India

American Embassy School, Delhi
American School of Bombay
Canadian School of India
Chinmaya International Residential School
Good Shepherd International School
International School of Bangalore
Kodaikanal International School
Mahindra United World College of India

Indonesia

British International School
Gandhi Memorial International School
Jakarta International School
Sekolah Pelita Harapan
Sekolah Pelita Harapan-Sentul

Iran

Tehran International School

Ireland

St Andrew's College

Israel

Anglican International School

Italy

American International School in Genoa
American Overseas School
Deledda International School
Florence American International School
Marymount International School Rome
Milan American School
Milan International School
St George's British International School
St Stephen's School
Turin International School
United World College of the Adriatic
Vicenza International School

Japan

Canadian Academy
Katoh Gakuen Gyoshu Senior High School
Osaka International School
Seisen International School
St Mary's International School, Tokyo
St Maur International School
Yokohama International School

Jordan

Ahliyyah School for Girls
Amman Baccalaureate School
Modern Montessori School

Kazakhstan

Miras International School

Kenya

Aga Khan Academy
Braeburn High School
International School of Kenya
Makini School Limited
St Mary's School

Kuwait

American International School, Kuwait

Latvia

Riga State Gymnasium No. 1

Lebanon

American Community School at Beirut
International College
Sagesse High School

Lesotho

Machabeng College, International School of Lesotho

Lithuania

Vilnius Lyceum

Luxembourg

International School of Luxembourg

Macedonia

Josip Broz Tito High School

Malawi

Bishop Mackenzie International School

Malaysia

International School of Kuala Lumpur
International School of Penang (Uplands)
MARA College Banting
Mont'Kiara International School

Malta

Verdala International School

Mauritius

Le Bocage International School

Mexico

American School Foundation
Bachillerato Alexander Bain
Centro de Enseñanza Media
Centro de Enseñanza Técnica y Superior
Colegio Americano de Puebla
Colegio Arjí
Colegio Británico, The Edron
Colegio Hebreo Maguen David AC
Colegio Vista
Escuela Bancaria

Escuela John F. Kennedy
Escuela Lazaro Cardenas
ETON Santa Fe
Greengates School
Instituto Cervantes AC
Instituto Educativo Olinca
Instituto Tecnológico y de Estudios Superiores de Monterrey
(Campus Eugenio Garza Sada)
Instituto Tecnológico y de Estudios Superiores de Monterrey
(Campus Toluca)
Instituto Tecnológico y de Estudios Superiores de Monterrey
(Campus Ciudad de México)
Liceo de Monterrey
Liceo de Monterrey Centro Educativo
Mexico City School

Monaco

International School of Monaco

Morocco

Casablanca American School
Rabat American School

Namibia

Windhoek International School

Netherlands

American International School of Rotterdam
American School of the Hague
Amsterdam International School
Arnhem International School
International School Eerde

International School Hilversum 'Alberdingk Thijm'
International School Maastricht
International School of Rotterdam
International School of the Hague
International School The Rijnlands Lyceum Oegstgeest
International Secondary School Eindhoven
Maartenscollege

New Zealand

John McGlashan College
Kristin School
Mt Anglem College
St Margaret's College
Wellington Diocesan School for Girls-Nga Tawa

Nicaragua

Notre Dame School

Norway

Ås videregående skole
Berg Videregående skole
Bergen Katedralskole
Lillestrom videregående skole
Nesbru videregående
Oslo International School
Sandefjord videregående skole
Skagerak International School
St Olav skole
Stavanger International School
Trondheim Katedralskole
United World College/Red Cross Nordic

Palestine

Friends Boys School

Oman

American-British Academy

Pakistan

Aljamea-tus-Saifiyah, Arabic Academy, Karachi
International School

Panama

International School of Panama

Papua-New Guinea

Port Moresby International School

Paraguay

Colegio SEK-Paraguay
St Anne's School

Peru

Asociación Educacional: Williamson Newton College
Colegio Las Casuarinas
Colegio Magister
Colegio Peruano Británico
Colegio Pestalozzi (Colegio Suizo del Peru)
Colegio Roosevelt-The American School of Lima

Colegio Sagrados Corazones 'Recoleta'
Colegio San Silvestre
Davy College
Hiram Bingham School
Liceo Naval 'Almirante Guise'
Markham College

Philippines

Brent International School-Baguio
Brent School-Manila
Cebu International School
Manila International School

Poland

I Prywatne Liceum: Ogólnoksztalcace
II L.O. im. Gen. Zamoyskiej i. H. Modrzejewski
III Ogólnoksztalcace, Gdynia
V Liceum Ogólnoksztalcace im Gen. Jakuba Jasinskiego
33 Liceum im. M. Kopernika
American School of Warsaw
British School, Warsaw
High School No. 111 in Gdansk
Paderewski Private Grammar School

Portugal

American International School of Lisbon
Colegio Cedros
Colégio Planalto
Oporto School
St Dominic's International School
St Julian's School

Qatar

Qatar Academy

Romania

Bucharest American International School

Russian Federation

Anglo-American School, Moscow
British International School, Moscow
Medical Technical Lyceum
Moscow Economic School
Moscow School 45
School Premier

Saudi Arabia

American International School-Riyadh
British International School of Jeddah

Senegal

West African College of the Atlantic/Lycée International Bilingue

Singapore

Canadian International School
International School of Singapore
Overseas Family School
United World College of South East Asia/Singapore

Slovakia

Gymnazium Jura Hronca

Slovenia

Druga Gimnazija Maribor
Gimnazija Bezigrad

South Africa

Johannesburg American International School

South Korea

Seoul Foreign School

Spain

Aloha College
Bell-lloc del Pla
Colegio Gaztelueta
Colegio Heidelberg
Colegio Marcote
Colegio Meres
Colegio Obradoiro
Colegio Retamar
Colegio SEK Castillo
Colegio SEK Ciudalcampo
El Plantío International Schoolof Valencia
IES
IES 'Bachiller Sabuco'
IES 'Carlos III' de Toledo
IES 'Lucas Mallada'
IES 'Miguel'
IES Jaume Vicens Vives

IES Santa Clara
Instituto Cardenal Lopez
Instituto José M. Usandizaga
Instituto Martinez Montañes
Instituto Praxedes Mateo
Instituto Ramiro de Maetzu
Instituto Rosalia de Castro
International School at Sotogrande
Liceo Europa
Madrid American School
Newton College
Real Instituto Jovellanos
Santa Clara Schools
Spain International College

Sri Lanka

Overseas School of Colombo

Swaziland

United World College (Southern Africa/Waterford)

Sweden

Björknässkolan
Ehrensvärdska gymnasiet
Filbornaskolan
Grennaskolan Riksinternat
Hvitfeldtska Gymnasiet
International School of Helsingborg
International School of Nacka
International School of Stockholm
Katedralskolan in Linköping
Katedralskolan in Lund
Katedralskolan in Uppsala
Kungsholmen's Gymnasium

Lundsbergs Skola
Malmö Borgarskola
Östra Gymnasieskolan
Per Brahegymnasiet
Saltsjöbadens Samskola
Sannarpsgymnasiet
Sigtunaskolan Humanistiska
Skärholmens Gymnasium
Söderportskolan
St Eskils Gymnasium
Sven Eriksonsgymnasiet
Täby Gymnasium
Tingvallagymnasiet
Torsbergsgymnasiet
Västergårdsgymnasiet
Växjö Katedralskola

Switzerland

Basel International School
Berne International School
Ecole Nouvelle (Chailly)
Geneva International School (Châtaigneraie)
Geneva International School (English)
Institut Le Rosey
Institut Montana
Inter-Community School Zürich
International School Lausanne
Leysin American School
Lyceum Alpinum Zuoz
Mutuelle d'Etudes Secondaires
TASIS Switzerland American School
Zürich International School

Syria

International School of Aleppo

Taiwan

Taipei European School

Tanzania

Moshi International School
Tanganyika International School

Thailand

Bangkok International School
Bangkok Patana School
Dulwich International College
Garden International School
Prem Tinsulanonda International School
Regent's School
Ruamrudee International School
Thailand International School

Togo

British School of Lomé
École Internationale Arc-en-Ciel

Tunisia

American Co-operative School of Tunis

Turkey

Bilkent University Prep School
British International School
Dogus Schools
Eyüboglu High School

Istanbul International Community School
Koç School
Kultur High School
MEF Schools of Turkey
TED AnKara High School
Ugur College
Yuzyil International Schoolil High School

Uganda

Lincoln International School

Ukraine

Pechersk School International

United Arab Emirates

Abu Dhabi American International School
Dubai American Academy
Emirates International School

United Kingdom

Aberdeen International School
American Community School, Cobham
American Community School, Egham
American Community School, Hillingdon
Anglo-European School
Ardingly College
Bedford High School
Bolitho School, Penzance
Broadgreen High School
Brockenhurst College
City College, Kingshurst
Dartford Grammar School for Girls

Dartford Grammar School
Exeter College
George Dixon International School
Goffs School
Haileybury
Hastings College
Henley College
Hockerill Anglo-European College
Impington College
King William's College
King's College School
Kings College for the Arts and Technology
Kings International College
Llandrillo College
London International School
Maidstone Grammar School
Malvern College
Marymount International School
Oakham School
Price William School
Rossall School
Sevenoaks School
Southbank International School
St Clare's
Swansea College
Truro College
United World College (Atlantic College)
Whitchurch High School
Woodside Park School
Worth School

United States of America

A.C. Davis Senior High School
A.C. Flora High School
Aiken High School
Allen D. Nease High School
Allen High School
Amarillo High School

Anderson High School
Annandale High School
Armijo High School
Aspen High School
Atherton High School
Atlanta International School
Atlantic Community High School
Atlee High School
Auburn High School
Aurora High School
Austin Community Academy High School
Awty International School
Aynor High School
Baltimore City College
Barry Goldwater High School
Bartow High School
Battery Creek High School
Beaufort High School
Beaverton High School
Beddingfield High School
Bellaire High School
Benjamin A. Banneker Academic High School
Benjamin H. Hardaway High School
Bernards High School
Bethesda-Chevy Chase High School
Binghamton High School
Bonita Vista High School
Booker T. Washington High School
Boyd Anderson High School
C. Leon King High School
Cajon High School
Calhoun High School
Campbell High School
Canandaigua Academy
Canyon High School
Cape Henry Collegiate School
Capital High School
Carlisle School
Castle Park High School
Centennial High School

Central High School, Capitol Heights
Central High School, Macon
Central High School, Springfield
Central High School, St Paul
Central High School, Tuscaloosa
Chandler High School
Charlotte Day School
Charter Oak High School
Cherry Hill High School West
Cheyenne East High School
Choctawhatchee High School
Christ Church Episcopal School
City Honors School
Clarke County High School
Classen School of Advanced Studies
Cleveland High School
Cocoa Beach High School
Columbia River High School
Commack High School
Coral Gables Senior High School
Coral Reef High School
Coronado High School (California)
Coronado High School (Texas)
Curie Metropolitan High School
Cypress Creek High School
Dalton High School
David Starr Jordan School
Deerfield Beach High School
Deland High School
Desert Mountain High School
Detroit School
Diamond Bar High School
Dobbs Ferry High School
Douglas County High School
Dwight School
Earl Wooster High School
East Hartford High School
East Mecklenburg High School
Eastside High School
Edmonds-Woodway High School

El Toro High School
Eugene International High School
Fairmont High School
Fairmont Prep Academy
Fairport High School
Fairview High School
Firestone High School
Fleming-Ruffner Magnet Center
Foothill High School
Foothill High School
Fort Dorchester High School
Fort Myers High School
Franklin High School
Franklin High School
French American International School
Fullerton Union High School
Garfield Senior High School
Garland High School
Gateway High School
George C. Marshall High School
George Mason High School
George School
George Washington High School (Colorado)
George Washington High School (Illinois)
Glen A. Wilson High School
Granby High School
Grand Rapids Senior High School
Granite Hills High School
Greece Odyssey High School
Greeley West High School
Green Valley High School
Gresham High School
Grimsley High School
Groves High School
Guajome Park Academy
Gulliver Preparatory School
Hampton High School
Harding High School
Harding University High School
Harriton High School

Henrico High School
Henry Foss High School
High Point Central High School
High School of Commerce
Highland High School
Highland Park Senior High School
Hillcrest High School
Hillsboro High School
Hillsborough High School
Hillside High School
Hilton Head High School
Hilton High School
Hinkley High School
Hirschi Math-Science Magnet School
Hoboken High School
Holmes High School
Hoover High School
Hubbard High School
Hunt High School
Hunters Lane Comprehensive High School
Hyde Park Academy
Independence High School
Inglemoor High School
Ingraham High School
Interlake High School
International Academy
International School of Indiana
J.E.B. Stuart High School
J.P. McCaskey High School
James International Schoolland High School
James S. Rickards High School
James W. Robinson, Jr. Secondary School
Jefferson County IB School
Jerome I. Case High School
Jim Hill School
John F. Kennedy High School
John Marshall High School
John Tyler High School
John Wesley North High School
Judson High School

Kennewick High School
Kent-Meridian High School
Kenwood High School
Killeen High School
Kinston High School
La Quinta High School
Laguna Hills High School
Lakewood High School
Lamar Academy
Land O'Lakes High School
Laurel High School
Lawrence D. Bell High School
Leander High School
Lee's Summit High School
Lee's Summit North High School
Lee-Davis High School
Lincoln High School
Lincoln College Academy
Lincoln Park Academy
Lincoln Park High School
Lindbergh High School
Linden High School
Littleton High School
Loara High School
Louisiana State University Laboratory School
Lubbock High School
Luther Burbank High School
Lycée International de Los Angeles
Madison University High School
Marietta High School
Martinsville High School
Massena Central High School
Meadowbrook High School
Meadowdale High School
Mercyhurst School
Metro Academic and Classical High School
Midlothian High School
Mid-Pacific Institute
Milford Mill Academy High School
Millard North High School

Mira Loma High School
Mirabeau B. Lamar Senior High School
Miramar High School
Mission Viejo High School
Modesto High School
Montgomery High School
Morgan Park High School
Mount Saint Mary Academy
Mount Vernon High School
Mt. Rainier High School
Murphy High School
Myers Park High School
Natrona County High School
Needham B. Broughton High School
Newark Academy
Newark Memorial High School
Newbury Park High School
Niceville High School
Nicholas Senn High School
Niwot High School
Nogales High School
Nogales High School
Norcross High School
North Atlanta High School
North Augusta High School
North Canyon High School
North Central High School
North High School
North Kansas City High School
North Little Rock High School West Camp
North Mecklenburg High School
North Miami Senior High School
Northern Nash Senior High School
Northport High School
Northwest Whitfield High School
Northwestern High School
Ocean View High School
Oceanside High School
Orangeburg-Wilkinson High School
Our Lady of Good Counsel High School

Owatonna High School
Palm Harbor University High School
Palmer High School
Palmer High School
Palmyra-Macedon High School
Parkdale High School
Patrick Henry High School
Patrick Henry Senior High School
Paxon School
Pensacola High School
Pine Bush High School
Pinecrest High School
Plano East Senior High School
Pleasant Valley High School
Portage Central High School
Portage Northern High School
Poudre High School
Princess Anne High School
Princeton High School
Prosser Career Academy
Prout School
Pueblo East High School
Quartz Hill High School
Ralph L. Fike High School
Rampart High School
Rancho Buena Vista High School
Rancho Cotate High School
Red Hook Central High School
Reidsville High School
Richard Montgomery High School
Richwoods High School
Ridgeview High School
Riverview High School
Riverwood High School
Roald Amundsen High School
Robbinsdale Cooper High School
Robert E. Fitch Senior High School
Robert E. Lee High School
Rock Hill High School
Rocky Mount Senior High School

Rowland High School
Rufus King High School
Rutherford High School
S.P. Waltrip High School
Sacred Heart Academy
Salem High
San Angelo Central High School
San Clemente High School
San Diego High School
San Jose High Academy
Santa Margarita Catholic High School
Schenectady High School
Schenley High School
Scotts Valley High School
Sebastian River High School
Seminole High School
Sequoia High School
Shawnee Mission East High School
Skyline High School
Smoky Hill High School
Socastee High School
Sol C. Johnson High School
Sonora High School
South Charleston High School
South Fork High School
South Forsyth High School
South Lakes High School
South Salem High School
South Side High School, Fort Wayne
South Side High School, New York
South St Paul High School
South View High School
Southeast High School
Southeast Whitfield High School
Southridge High School
Southside High School
Southwest High School
Springbrook High School
Spruce Creek High School
St Louis Park Senior High School

St Petersburg High School
St Scholastica Academy
Stanton College School
Steinmetz Academic Center
Stonewall Jackson High School
Suitland High School
Sumner Academy
Sumter High School
Suncoast High School
Sunny Hills High School
Sunset High School
Temple High School
Thomas Alva Edison High School
Thomas Jefferson High School
Thomas Kelly High School
Thornton High School
Tigard High School
Trabuco Hills High School
Tracy Joint Union High School
Trinity College Preparatory High School
Trinity Episcopal School
Trinity High School
Troy High School
Tualatin High School
United Nations International School
United World College (Montezuma/Armand Hammer)
University High School
Upper St Clair High School
Valley High School
Valparaiso High School
Vanguard High School
Vestal Senior High School
Victor Central High School
Vincentian Academy, Duquesne University
Virginia High School
Vista High School
W.G. Enloe High School
Walnut High School
Warren G. Harding High School
Warwick High School

Washington International School
Washington Irving High School
Washington-Lee High School
Wausau East High School
West High School Salt Lake City
West Morris Central High School
West Morris Mendham High School
Westwood High School, Austin
Wichita High School (East)
William Howard Taft High School
Wilmington Friends School
Wilson High School
Wilson Magnet High School
Winter Park High School
Withrow High School
Woodburn High School
Woodland School
Xaverian High School
Yonkers Middle/High School
York High School
Yosemite High School

Uruguay

British Schools, Montevideo
Colegio Stella Maris
Escuela Integral
St Catherine's School

Venezuela

Colegio Bellas Artes
Colegio de Caracas
Colegio Los Campitos
Escuela Campo Alegre
Instituto de Educación Activa
Instituto Juan XXIII
Liceo Camoruco

Liceo Los Robles
UE Academia Washington

Vietnam

Hanoi International School
Ho Chi Minh City International School
United Nations International School-Hanoi

Zambia

American International School Lusaka
Lusaka International School

Zimbabwe

St John's College

APPENDIX B

SCHOOLS OFFERING THE MIDDLE YEARS PROGRAM OCTOBER 2002 (222 SCHOOLS)

For more information about IB programs and schools, go to www.ibo.org.

Argentina

Colegio San Ignacio
Colegio Suizo Jacques-Dalcroze
Escuela Agropecuaria
St George's College
St George's College North
St Mary's International College
St Xavier's College
St.Catherine's School
Washington School

Australia

Concordia College
Glenunga International High School
Immanuel College
King Khalid Islamic College
Mercedes College
Norwood Morialta High School
Pacific Hills Christian School
Prince Alfred College

St Hilda's School
Walford Anglican School
Woodcroft College

Austria

Vienna International School

Azerbaijan

International School of Azerbaijan

Belgium

St John's International School Waterloo

Brazil

Escola Suíço-Brasileira

Cambodia

International School of Phnom Penh

Canada

Académie Lafontaine
Baie-Saint-François
Chambly Academy
Collège Charlemagne
Collège de l'Assomption
Collège de Lévis
Collège Esther-Blondin
Collège Jésus-Marie de Sillery

Collège Mont Notre-Dame
Collège Notre-Dame
Collège Notre-Dame-de-Lourdes
Collège Saint-Louis
Collège Saint-Maurice
Collège Saint-Paul
Collège Ville-Marie
Curé-Antoine-Labelle
École d'éducation internationale
École d'éducation internationale, Laval
École internationale de Montréal
École Marie-Clarac
École Mont Saint-Sacrement
École Paul-Hubert
École Polyvalenta Le Carrefour
École Polyvalente Le Boisé
École secondaire André-Laurendeau
École secondaire Armand-Corbeil
École secondaire de l'Île
École secondaire de Neufchâtel
École secondaire de Rivière-du-Loup
École secondaire de Rochebelle
École secondaire De-La-Salle
École secondaire des Chutes
École secondaire des Patriotes-de-Beauharnois
École Secondaire des Sources
École secondaire du Phare
École secondaire Georges-Vanier
École secondaire Grande-Rivière
École secondaire Henri-Bourassa
École secondaire Jean XXIII
École secondaire Jean-Baptiste-Meilleur
École secondaire Jean-Jacques-Bertrand
École secondaire Kénogami
École secondaire La Courvilloise
École secondaire Ozias-Leduc
École secondaire Roger-Comtois
École secondaire Saint-Joseph
École secondaire Serge-Bouchard
École secondaire Soulanges

École St-Edmond
Grey Gables School
John Paul/Laurier Macdonald High School
L'Externat Saint-Jean-Eudes
Lakeside Academy
Le Collège Saint-Bernard
Macdonald-Cartier High School
Marymount Academy
Pavillon Les Sentiers
Pensionnat Saint-Nom de Marie
Petit Séminaire de Québec
Pierrefonds Comprehensive High School
Polyvalente Deux-Montagnes
Polyvalente Hyacinthe-Delorme
Polyvalente Le Carrefour
Polyvalente Marie-Rivier
Polyvalente Saint-François
Polyvalente Saint-Jérôme
Rive-Nord/St Gab/Hubert Maisonneuve
Séminaire Ste-Marie Shawinigan
St Thomas High School
Vaudreuil/Lionel-Groulx
Vaughan Road Academy
Victoria School of Performing and Visual Arts

Chile

Redland School
Santiago College

China

American International School of Guangzhou
Beijing No. 55 Middle School
Beijing Shuren Private School
Guang Ya School
Guangdong Country Garden School
Nanjing International School

Suzhou Singapore International School
TEDA International School, Tianjin
Tianjin Experiment High School
Utahloy International School
Zhengzhou Middle School

Croatia

XV Gimnazija

Denmark

Copenhagen International School
Herlufsholms Skole
Hørsholm International School

Ecuador

American School of Quito
Centro Educativo Integral

Egypt

École Oasis de Maadi

Estonia

International School of Estonia

Fiji

Suva International School

Finland

Turun normaalikoulu

Germany

Bonn International School e.V.
International School of Hannover Region
Munich International School

Greece

American Community School of Athens

India

American School of Bombay
Mercedes-Benz International School

Indonesia

Bali International School
Medan International School
Sekolah Pelita Harapan

Japan

Katoh Gakuen Gyoshu Junior High School

Jordan

Amman Baccalaureate School

Kazakhstan

Interntional School of Almaty of Nazarbaev EF

Latvia

International School of Latvia

Mexico

Colegio Ciudad de Mexico
Colegio Vista Hermosa
Grupo Alexander Bain
Instituto Educativo Olinca

Monaco

International School of Monaco

Mongolia

International School of Ulaanbaatar

Morocco

Casablanca American School
Les écoles Al Madina

Netherlands

Amsterdam International School
International School Hilversum Alberdingk Thijm
Maartenscollege
Rijnlands Lyceum

Norway

Bergen International School

Pakistan

International School, Karachi

Paraguay

St Anne's School

Peru

Colegio Hiram Bingham
Davy College

Portugal

St Dominic's International School

Romania

American International School of Bucharest

Russian Federation

Educational Centre
Educational Centre Schkola
European Gymnasium
Linguistic School 1531
Moscow Economic School
Moscow School 45
School Premier

Singapore

Overseas Family School

Slovenia

Gimnazija Bezigrad

Spain

Colegio Inter. SEK-Catalunya
Colegio San Francisco de Paula
Colegio SEK Castillo
Colegio SEK Ciudalcampo
Colegio SEK-Atlantico
Newton College
Spain International College

Sri Lanka

Overseas School of Colombo

Sweden

Bladin's International School
International School in Nacka
International School of Helsingborg
International School of the Gothenburg Region
Sigtunaskolan Humanistiska
Stockholm International School

Switzerland

Basel International School
Haut-Lac International Bilingual School

Inter-Community School Zurich
Riverside School

Tanzania

International School of Tanganyika

Thailand

Thailand International School

Turkey

Eyüboglu School
Istanbul International Community School

Ukraine

Pechersk School International

United Kingdom

American Community School, Egham
Marymount International School UK
Southbank International School

United States of America

Anderson/Murchison
Atlantic High School/Carver Community Middle School
Booker T. Washington High School
Burnett Academy
Centennial High School
Cherry Hill High School West

Christ Church Episcopal School
Davidson Middle School
Dobbs Ferry Middle/High School
Dwight School
Fleming-Ruffner Magnet Center
George H. Moody Middle School
Godwin/Gar-Field
Guajome Park Academy
Hillside/Shepard
Hirschi/Zundy
Kennedy/Suncoast School
Mira Loma High School
Morgan Park High School
Mountain Ridge Middle School
North/Palmer
Northwest/Siwell/Jim Hill
Poudre High School
Quaker Valley High School
Ruckel/Niceville School
Scotts Valley High School/Middle School
Southside High School/Beck Academy
Thornton High School
Upper St Clair High School
Washington International School
Wilson High School/Williams
Wilson Middle School/Blair High School

Uruguay

Saint Catherine's School
St Patrick's College

Vietnam

United Nations International School, Hanoi

Zambia

American International School of Lusaka

APPENDIX C

SCHOOLS OFFERING THE PRIMARY YEARS PROGRAM OCTOBER 2002 (93 SCHOOLS)

For more information about IB programs and schools, go to www.ibo.org.

Angola

Luanda International School

Argentina

St Catherine's Moorlands
St Catherine's Tortuguitas
St George's College North

Australia

Geelong Grammar School
Mercedes College
Prince Alfred College
Ruthven Primary School
St Andrew's School
St Michael's College
Wallan Primary School

Austria

Vienna International School

Azerbaijan

International School of Azerbaijan

Bahamas

St Andrew's School

Belgium

St John's International School

Canada

École Chabot et du Châtelet
École des Ursulines
École Internationale de Montréal
École Internationale Primaire de Greenfield Park
Sunnybrook School

Chile

Santiago College

China

Beijing BISS International School
Nanjing International School

Denmark

Copenhagen International School

Egypt

Oasis School of Maadi

Fiji

International School Suva

Germany

Bavarian International School
Berlin Brandenburg International School
Bonn International School
Frankfurt International School
Munich International School

Greece

TASIS Hellenic International School
American Community Schools of Athens

India

American School of Bombay
Mercedes-Benz International School

Indonesia

Bogor Expatriate School
Sekolah Tiara Bangsa

Italy

American International School in Genoa

Japan

K. International School, Tokyo
Yokahama International School

Latvia

International School of Latvia

Mexico

Colegio Ciudad de Mexico-Plantel Contadero
Colegio Ciudad de Mexico-Plantel Polanco
Instituto Educativo Olinca
Winston Spencer Churchill School

Mongolia

International School of Ulaanbaatar

Namibia

Windhoek International School

Netherlands

Amsterdam International School
Violenschool International Department

New Zealand

Kristin School

Oman

American-British Academy

Portugal

St Dominic's International School, Portugal

Romania

American International School of Bucharest

Russian Federation

Moscow Economic School
School Premier

Singapore

ISS International School Singapore
Overseas Family School

Slovenia

Danila Kumar Primary School

Spain

International College Spain

Sri Lanka

Overseas School of Colombo

Sweden

Bladin's International School
International School of Helsingborg
International School of Nacka

Switzerland

Inter-Community School Zürich
International School of Geneva
International School of Zug
Zurich International School

Tanzania

International School of Tanganyika

Thailand

Kesinee International School
New International School of Thailand

Turkey

Istanbul International Community School

Ukraine

Pechersk School International

United Kingdom

American Community School, Egham
Southbank International School

United States of America

Academy International Elementary School
Broad River Elementary School
Christ Church Elementary School
Dunn Elementary School
Dwight School
Frank C. Martin Elementary School
Hilton Head Elementary School
McGraw Elementary
Morikami Park Elementary School
Paul D. Burbank Elementary School
Port Royal Elementary School
Rockrimmon Elementary School
Santa Rosa Charter School
Washington International School
Westward Elementary

Uruguay

St Catherine's School

Vietnam

United Nations International School, Hanoi
International School, Ho Chi Minh City

Zambia

American International School of Lusaka

INDEX

scholarship policy?

65p

75p.